TESI GREGORIANA

Serie Teologia

14

T0163270

1ª Edizione 1996
1ª Ristampa 2004

SCOTT BRODEUR

THE HOLY SPIRIT'S AGENCY IN THE RESURRECTION OF THE DEAD

An Exegetico-Theological Study of
1 Corinthians 15,44b-49 and Romans 8,9-13

EDITRICE PONTIFICIA UNIVERSITÀ GREGORIANA
Roma 2004

Vidimus et approbamus ad normam Statutorum Universitatis

Romae, ex Pontificia Universitate Gregoriana
die 11 mensis iunii anni 1994

R.P. Prof. JEAN-NOËL ALETTI, S.J.
R.P. Prof. UGO VANNI, S.J.

ISBN 88-7652-720-6
© Iura editionis et versionis reservantur
PRINTED IN ITALY

GREGORIAN UNIVERSITY PRESS
Piazza della Pilotta, 35 – 00187 Rome, Italy

ACKNOWLEDGMENTS

The successful completion of a doctoral dissertation heralds the termination of a long, arduous and solitary endeavor. As an intellectual enterprise, a thesis requires from the graduate student great discipline and perseverance as well as much creativity and imagination: without the former qualities the project would never get done, and without the latter the young scholar would have nothing original to offer his colleagues. Except for a few minor revisions in content and some major revisions in style, this present work represents the published version of my dissertation defended at the Gregorian University in June, 1994.

With much gratitude and appreciation, therefore, I wish to express my heartfelt thanks to all my family and friends who have supported me over these years. I extend a special word of thanks to those close spiritual companions whose faith, hope and love have profoundly enriched me. In addition, much of the credit for this work belongs to the students of my Romans seminar. Over the past few years, these young men and women have challenged me to keep fresh in mind an overview of Paul's major themes and topics, thus preventing me from getting too lost in the details and minutia of the brief passages that have captivated me. Their hard work, enthusiasm and dedication have taught me that with sufficient direction and encouragement, second year theology students can indeed make fine beginning exegetes. May God continue to bless and keep them well and may he greatly enrich the Church through their zealous and well-informed preaching of the gospel.

In particular, I would like to acknowledge by name those individuals who were especially helpful to me during the period of my research and writing. Henry Bertels, S.J., the gracious and friendly librarian of the Biblical Institute, was always available to order the latest work on Paul or track down a rare book in the *deposito* for me. I am especially grateful for his willingness to purchase new books for the library in the field of ancient Greek science. Future

Biblicum and Gregorian students will profit greatly from his wise planning and foresight. Fred Brenk, S.J. facilitated my research into Hellenistic medicine by pointing out the most recent translations of Galen's works as well as other articles related to this fascinating topic. Éduard des Places, S.J. helped me to come to a deeper understanding of the Greek suffix -ικός in light of the work of Chantraine, the great French Hellenist. I am thankful for his support in my interpretation of Aristotle's teaching on reproduction with respect to 1Cor 15,36. Silvano Votto, S.J. proved to be a ready interlocutor in many discussions on Greek grammar and syntax and I thank him for his helpful insights. Ron Wozniak, S.J., graciously programmed my computer and I am most indebted to him as well.

I would also like to thank my religious superiors in a special way. My former formation director in the United States, James Lafontaine, S.J., has been a great support to me and I appreciate his personal interest in this project. I also want to thank Ed Babinski, S.J., a trusted member of the provincial staff, for taking care of so many practical details for me during my absence from Boston. I am also most grateful to my provincials: first Robert Manning, S.J., who sent me to the Pontifical Biblical Institute as a student and then William Barry, S.J., who has recently missioned me to the Pontifical Gregorian University as a professor. In fact it was Bill who, as vice provincial for formation of the New England province, first urged me to consider exegesis as my chief apostolate in the Society of Jesus. In 1982 he assigned me to philosophy studies in Paris and I have felt at home in Europe ever since.

An earnest word of thanks is also in order for Ugo Vanni, S.J., the second reader of my dissertation. Many of his insightful observations have found their way into the present text. I am indeed very indebted to him for his close reading of my dissertation, and I thank him from my heart for his kind words of praise and encouragement.

Lastly, to Jean-Noël Aletti, S.J., my dissertation director, I extend my sincerest thanks, fraternal esteem and genuine appreciation. I am especially grateful to him for his close reading of my text as well as for his valuable insights and suggestions. Although I remain responsible for my own errors and oversights, it is chiefly thanks to his friendly and supportive direction that this thesis has improved over time. He has truly been a trusted guide and reliable mentor to me and for that I am most grateful.

Rome, September 1996

GENERAL INTRODUCTION

The following work seeks to provide a clear and intelligible presentation of Pauline pneumatology as articulated by the Apostle in 1 Corinthians 15,44b-49 and Romans 8,9-13. More specifically, it puts forward and defends the thesis that according to Saint Paul, the Holy Spirit is indeed the divine agent in the resurrection of the dead. The reader will discover in these pages an exegetico-theological study which treats these two significant passages on God's life-giving Spirit. In short, this work intends to highlight in a special way the Apostle's profound and authoritative teaching on the resurrection of the dead: God the Father raised Christ Jesus and likewise will raise all who believe in him, through the agency of the Holy Spirit.

For too long Catholic scholars have neglected serious study of the Holy Spirit and the significant role he plays in the divine plan of salvation, especially with regard to his agency in the resurrection of the dead. In the spirit of the Second Vatican Council and in response to its authoritative call for further scientific investigation into the Sacred Scriptures, this dissertation strives to fill a regrettable lacuna in Roman Catholic theology[1]. Theologians who are investigating crucial topics such as the resurrection of the dead, Spirit christology, or the Spirit's procession from the Father and the Son will find in this work some helpful and relevant information for their reading and research. In particular, dogmatic and fundamental theologians may discover the following insights into the person and action of the Holy Spirit to be especially helpful for their study. For that matter, any well-educated Christian who is interested in learning more about Paul's doctrine of the resurrection of the dead and the nature of the spiritual body could also appreciate these exegetical insights and theological reflections, finding in them plenty of data to enrich and

---

[1] See Vatican II, *Dei Verbum*, § 23.

focus his own meditation on some of the most important dogmas of the Christian faith.

This innovative study of the Apostle's pneumatology is limited to two very brief passages, namely 1 Corinthians 15,44b-49 and Romans 8,9-13. It examines both of these texts in light of the specific composition of the letter in question, striving all the while to do justice to Paul's theology as articulated elsewhere in his other genuine letters. By purposely restricting the analysis in this way, we shall be able to scrutinize these important and influential texts in great detail and thereby arrive at some solid and reliable conclusions. The novelty of my exegesis can be found primarlily in my new understanding of Paul's overall argumentation in 1Corinthians 15 and in my interpretation of the range of possibilities with regard to the past, present and future in Rom 8,10.

This book is divided into three distinct sections. Part One is dedicated to a study of 1 Corinthians 15,44b-49, Part Two treats Romans 8,9-13, while Part Three puts forward the dissertation's conclusion. Since they present a detailed study of the given text in question, the first and second parts could easily be read and appreciated on their own. This of course represents the synchronic aspect of the Book. Part Three, the conclusion, seeks to compare and contrast the two previous sections by pointing out the continuity in Paul's theology, all the while underscoring that which is new and ground breaking in the Apostle's thought. This obviously represents the diachronic aspect of the present work.

The method adopted in this dissertation is an exegetico-theological one. The principal parts of this book, the ones on 1 Corinthians and Romans, have been each subdivided into three distinct chapters. Chapter I considers 1Cor 15,44b-49 as a literary and semantic subunit; Chapter II proposes a close reading of the text; and Chapter III offers three distinct theological reflections on related themes that flow from the exegesis. Similarly, Chapter IV studies Rom 8,9-13 as a literary and semantic subunit; Chapter V presents a close reading of the text; and Chapter VI offers three more brief theological essays based on the exegesis of this passage from Romans. By proceeding in this way, we shall manage to remain grounded in the biblical text and also arrive at some relevant findings which should prove helpful and enlightening for people today. The concluding section, Chapter VII, sums up much of the information that has come before and serves to buttress my thesis: in these two pericopes the Apostle clearly characterizes the Holy Spirit as the divine agent of the resurrection of the dead.

I believe that this book can make an original contribution to Pauline studies for several reasons. It underscores the anthropological and pneumatological importance of 1 Corinthians 15,44b-49, a difficult text that has been traditionally interpreted primarily in christological terms; it emphasizes the trinitarian dimension of Paul's doctrine on the resurrection of the dead in Romans 8,9-13; in addition, it highlights the continuity of the Apostle's eschatological thought as developed in both of these letters, all the while pointing out the novelty of his doctrine in the letter to the Romans. In short, the work that follows offers a fresh approach to Paul's understanding of the life-giving Spirit since it focuses in a special way on the Spirit's role as the divine agent of the resurrection of the dead.

Lastly, a word of explanation concerning the title of this book is in order. Although in the pages that follow we shall examine in great detail many ramifications of the Spirit's activity on our behalf, Paul never restricts his pneumatology to such a consideration, as significant as it is. The Apostle is not only concerned with what the Spirit does, but also with who the Spirit is. Thus it would be unjust to restrict this thesis on Paul's pneumatology solely to a study of the Holy Spirit's action. My close reading of the pericopes will highlight the particular terms and expressions Paul uses so as to describe both the Spirit's relationship to God and to Christ as well as his life-giving relationship to all those who believe in the Lord Jesus.

The exegesis of these two principal texts will reveal the Apostle's astute and penetrating concern with the Spirit's identity as well as with his activity. Given this fact, one which of course will be proved in the pages that follow, we would be far more faithful to the Pauline text if we spoke of the Holy Spirit's agency in the resurrection of the dead. An agent is after all someone who acts with the full authority of the one who sends him; he stands in the place of another as his official emissary or representative. Thus it seems best to use the terms «agent» and «agency» so as to reflect in the best way possible the Apostle's teaching on the Spirit's role in the resurrection of the dead.

In short, the thesis to be proved is best summed up in the full title of this dissertation: *The Holy Spirit's Agency in the Resurrection of the Dead*. An Exegetico-Theological Study of 1 Corinthians 15,44b-49 and Romans 8,9-13. With these brief introductory remarks in mind, we are now ready to focus our attention on the essential task of exegesis. Since Paul wrote to the saints in Corinth before he addressed his fellow Christians in Rome, we shall respect the chronological order of his correspondence and begin the present study with the passage from 1 Corinthians.

PART ONE

1 CORINTHIANS 15,44b-49
THE LIFE-GIVING SPIRIT
AND THE TWO ADAMS

INTRODUCTION

Part One of this book sets forth my detailed study of 1 Corinthians 15,44b-49. In order to prove the existence of the spiritual body, St. Paul proposes a very convincing anthropological argument based on Scripture to his addressees in Corinth. In this particular subunit he contrasts the earthly human being, the first Adam, to the heavenly human being, the last Adam and then presents each one as a representative of his own type of humanity. In the course of this insightful and very profound teaching on Christian anthropology, the Apostle also makes mention of «a life-giving Spirit» (15,45b). But who precisely is this Spirit? Are we correct in stating that Paul is in fact referring to the Holy Spirit? And if so, what role, if any, does the Apostle ascribe to him in the resurrection of the dead? In the hope of providing some answers to these important questions, this first part of the dissertation seeks to investigate the Spirit's agency in the creation of the spiritual body. In this exegetico-theological study of the passage, our way of proceeding is as follows.

Chapter I examines 1 Corinthians 15,44b-49 as a literary and semantic subunit. Since we must first understand this subunit's place in chapter fifteen as a whole, section 1 presents 1 Corinthians 15,44b-49 in its context. This brief overview then invites us to address one of the essential topics of the chapter, namely Paul's presentation of the various kinds of earthly and heavenly bodies. This crucial question is dealt with in section 2, 1 Corinthians 15,35-44a and the different kinds of bodies. Next, given Paul's complex cultural background as a diaspora Jew, we must consider those factors which most affected the development of his ideas and convictions. Hence section 3 treats the cultural background of the Apostle's early formation; it examines in some detail the current scholarly debate which locates either Tarsus or Jerusalem as the locus of Paul's formative years. Then, in section 4, we turn to a very important excursus on ancient Greek science. Thanks to the findings of contemporary scientists and historians of science, this fascinating data can help us arrive at a better understanding of Paul's and the Corinthians' scientific worldview. The excursus in turn is subdivided into four distinct parts: 4.1, introduction; 4.2, biology: botany, zoology and medicine; 4.3, on creation and perishability; and lastly 4.4, astronomy. Since the findings of this research must then be applied to the Pauline text, in section 5 we return to 1 Corinthians 15,35-44a so as to read the subunit attentively in light of the important data learned from the excursus. Lastly, in section 6, we consider 1 Corinthians 15,44b-49 as a distinct subunit. This in turn is subdivided into three different parts: 6.1, human body language; 6.2, antithetical parallelism; and 6.3, Paul's argumentation within the subunit.

Chapter II is devoted exclusively to a close reading of 1 Corinthians 15,44b-49. We shall analyze every major word in the subunit in order to grasp its exact meaning and function. By comparing and contrasting references from 1 Corinthians as well as from Paul's other genuine letters, we shall arrive at a better understanding of the particular term under discussion. This method of exegesis, painstaking though it may be, in fact provides the diligent scholar with many significant insights. Most of all, it allows us to focus on the subunit in question without losing sight of the Pauline corpus and the Apostle's many broader concerns.

Lastly, Part One concludes with Chapter III, a brief collection of some theological reflections which sprang from my exegesis of the subunit. The first is devoted to the human body, and it considers some ramifications for us today in light of Paul's teaching on the natural and spiritual body. It represents in effect a brief discussion on Christian anthropology. The second reflection offers a considered meditation on the life-giving Spirit; it seeks to put forward a lucid presentation of Paul's pneumatology. The third essay was inspired by the Apostle's exhortation to bear the image of the last Adam (1Cor 15,49b). It provides some insights into Paul's parenesis to the Corinthian Church and seeks to explain why it is essential for Christians of every age to imitate Christ, their Lord. As such this final essay attempts to explore the very foundations of the Apostle's ethics.

With this overview of our way of proceeding in mind, we are ready to begin our detailed study of the passage. We now turn to Chapter I, an analysis of 1 Corinthians 15,44b-49 as a literary and semantic subunit.

1Cor 15,44b-49 as a
Literary and Semantic Subunit

1 Corinthians 15 forms a truly distinct section in the letter. The larger unit that comes before, chapters twelve through fourteen, is principally devoted to a study of the spiritual gifts given to believers in Christ. «Now concerning spiritual gifts, brothers, I do not want you to be uninformed» (1Cor 12,1). For the good of the whole Church, each believer has received the manifestation of the Spirit by whom he exclaims, «Jesus is Lord!» (1Cor 12,3). Chapter thirteen is devoted to Paul's magnificent praise of love, while chapter fourteen addresses the situation at Corinth with regard to the spiritual gifts of prophecy and speaking in tongues. The Apostle ends this section in his usual hortatory manner. «So, my brothers, earnestly desire to prophesy and do not forbid speaking in tongues; but all things should be done decently and in order» (1Cor 14,39-40).

Although chapter fifteen puts forward a new topic, namely the resurrection of the dead, it is not at all out of place in the larger context of the letter. Paul positioned it after these chapters which deal with the spiritual gifts because the resurrection of the dead also concerns the Holy Spirit. Since «by one Spirit we were all baptized into one body» (1Cor 12,13) and thus incorporated into the community of earthly believers, so too is it with the resurrection of the dead. It is by the same Spirit that the dead will be changed, their natural bodies being transformed into spiritual bodies at the parousia and thus incorporated into the community of heavenly believers.

Thus 1 Corinthians 15 is a logical outgrowth of what has come before, even though it constitutes a self-contained unit within the letter. The broader discussion of the spiritual gifts has given way to a more specific consideration of spiritual bodies of human beings. In these very profound and significant verses, the Apostle affirms with great conviction that God will indeed raise the dead bodily and transform the natural bodies of believers into spiritual ones[1]. The Holy Spirit is the common thread that weaves these chapters together and binds them to the letter's purpose as expressed by Paul in the beginning. «And I was with you in weakness and in much fear and trembling; and my speech and my message were not in plausible words of wisdom, but in demonstration of the Spirit and of power, that your faith might not rest in the wisdom of human beings but in the power of God» (1Cor 2,3-5). God demonstrates his saving power most magnificently by raising the dead to eternal life through the agency of the Holy Spirit. Hence 1 Corinthians 15 serves as a fitting climax to the unit on the spiritual gifts as well as to the entire letter considered as a whole[2].

---

[1] In 1Cor 15 Paul refutes those in the Corinthian Church who hold «that there is no resurrection of the dead» (v. 12). Scholars continue to debate over both the identity and position of these deniers of the resurrection. What precisely were these Corinthians denying and conversely, what were they affirming? For a very fine presentation of the current *status questionis*, see M.C. de BOER, *The Defeat of Death*, 96-105. He groups the many positions and their proponents into four basic headings: 1) The Corinthian deniers did not believe in life after death (K. BARTH), or Paul at least thought that they did not (R. BULTMANN, W. SCHMITHALS); 2) The Corinthian deniers believed that only the living at the time of the parousia would enter into the new age (A. SCHWEIZER, E. GÜTTGEMANNS, B. SPÖRLEIN, H. CONZELMANN); 3) The Corinthian deniers denied the notion of the bodily resurrection, not that of life after death. They affirmed the immortality of the soul (P. BACHMANN, H. LIETZMANN, R.J. SIDER, J. MURPHY-O'CONNOR, P. HOFFMANN) or of the spirit (F.W. GROSHEIDE, B.A. PEARSON, R A. HORSLEY, A.J.M. WEDDERBURN); and 4) The Corinthian deniers claimed that the resurrection has already taken place. As a result, they were already living in the world of the Spirit and looked forward to at last becoming free of the contemptible outer husk of the body. Hence 1) and 2) affirm that the Corinthian deniers believed life ended with death and 3) and 4) assert that the deniers rejected bodily resurrection and not the possibility of an afterlife.

[2] Beker maintains that the basic theme of 1Cor is in fact the interrelation between the Spirit and the human body. «I conclude, then, that chapter 15, with its apocalyptic focus on the resurrection and its emphasis on the ultimate significance of the resurrection-body, is indeed the climax of that interpretation of the gospel that the Corinthians had to hear according to Paul. The coherent center of the gospel is in 1 Corinthians unfolded as the correlation of Spirit and body, in the light of the apocalyptic resurrection-body. To Paul, the rejection of this theme by the Corinthians means that they have rejected the gospel» (J.C. BEKER, *Paul the Apostle*, 176).

1. 1Cor 15,44b-49 in its Context

Chapter fifteen displays a very elaborate rhetorical structure composed primarily of two different concentric arguments. It can be divided into an introductory subunit followed by two principal parts. In addition, each of these larger sections can be subdivided into three smaller ones.

In the introduction (vv. 1-11), the Apostle presents the tradition of the Church which he received and preached with regard to Christ's death and resurrection from the dead. This section serves a double purpose in the chapter: it focuses the argument that follows on Christ and it establishes Paul's own authority as an Apostle who saw the risen Lord. In his brief opening remarks Paul reminds his addressees that they have indeed believed the tradition passed on to them (vv. 1-2). Next the Apostle goes on to confess the tradition of faith which he shares in common with them and with all who believe that Jesus is the Christ, the Son of God (vv. 3-10). Lastly, he concludes this short introduction by returning to his first point about his preaching of and their common belief in the apostolic tradition they all share (v. 11).

In Part I (vv.12-34) Paul is concerned with the resurrection per se. He challenges the Corinthians to face their illogical contradictory beliefs (namely, that Christ was indeed raised, yet they will not be) and correct them. This part is subdivided into three subunits. First, Paul provides a concise summary of the Corinthians' incorrect belief concerning the resurrection and demonstrates their absurd conclusion (vv. 12-19). If Christ has not been raised, then they are among human beings the most to be pitied. Second, he puts forward his own christological thesis with regards to the resurrection (vv. 20-28). He insists that since Christ has been raised, then Christians will also be raised. Jesus represents the firstfruits of a great eschatological harvest. And third, Paul returns to the position of his addressees, but this time he focuses on their absurd behavior (vv.29-34). Through the use of Greek rhetoric, he makes *ad hominem* appeals to their experience for an accurate and consistent belief in the resurrection, thus making a connection between Christian belief about the future and Christian behavior in the present.

If Part I deals with the «that» of the resurrection («How can some of you say *that* there is no resurrection of the dead?» v. 12), Part II develops the «how» («*How* are the dead raised? With what body do they come?» v. 35). Here Paul insists on the bodily resurrection of the dead: if Christ was raised bodily, then believers will also be changed so that they too can be raised bodily on the last day. The Apostle's insistence on change and discontinuity makes it very clear that this, God's great saving deed on behalf of humanity, has nothing to do with the resuscitation of corpses. At stake is the complete transformation of the human body so that believers can inherit the Kingdom of God. Although there is still not yet any real consensus among exegetes on the most accurate division of 1 Corinthians 15,35-58 (many divide this pericope into two parts)[3], it is better to divide the second half of chapter fifteen into three subunits[4]. First, Paul begins with an argument from reason. He refers to plants, animals and heavenly beings in order to compare the different types of bodies visible to the

---

[3] Here is a list of those exegetes who acknowledge two distinct subunits. They in turn can be subdivided into three smaller groups:
a. vv. 35-44a and vv. 44b-58. See E. WALTER, Der erste Brief an die Korinther, 302-17.
b. vv. 35-49 and vv. 50-58. Cf. C.K. BARRETT, The First Epistle to the Corinthians, 368-385; H. CONZELMANN, 1 Corinthians, 279-293; F.W. GROSHEIDE, Commentary on the First Epistle to the Corinthians, 379-395; M.M. MITCHELL, Paul and the Rhetoric of Reconciliation, 286-291; L. MORRIS, The First Epistle of Paul to the Corinthians, 217-231; J. RUEF, Paul's First Letter to Corinth, 170-179; K. USAMI, «How "are the dead raised?" (1 Cor 15,35-58)», 473-478; and N. WATSON, The First Epistle to the Corinthians, 174-181. Agreeing with this basic division, two commentaries emphasize the important role of the concluding verse. Hence they divide the unit into vv. 35-49, vv. 50-57 and v. 58. Cf. A. ROBERTSON and A. PLUMMER, The First Epistle of St. Paul to the Corinthians, 365-380 and W.F. ORR and J. A. WALTHER, 1 Corinthians, 340-354.
c. vv. 35-50 and vv. 51-57 (with v. 58 serving as a conclusion). See D. PRIOR, The Message of First Corinthians, 271-277.
[4] Many recognize a division into three distinct subunits. These scholars may be subdivided into three major groups:
a. vv. 35-44, vv. 45-49 and vv. 50-58. See G.D. FEE, The First Epistle to the Corinthians, 778-809.
b. (intro. question, v. 35), vv. 36-45, vv. 46-49, vv. 50-58. See C H. TALBERT, Reading Corinthians, 96-104.
c. Other scholars in their three part division recognize a major break in the text after v. 44a.
1. vv. 35-44a, vv. 44b-49 and vv. 50-58.
Cf. E. BRANDENBURGER, «Alter und neuer Mensch, erster und letzter Adam-Anthropos», 205-212; J. GILLMAN, «Transformation in 1 Cor 15,50-53», 309-310; J. MURPHY-O'CONNOR, «The First Letter to the Corinthians», 813-814. Similarly, after the initial questions in v. 35, WEISS also recognizes the subunits as vv. 36-44a, vv. 44b-49 and vv. 50-58. See J. WEISS, Der erste Korintherbrief, 367-380. Lastly, Bonneau explicitly asserts that vv. 35-44a and 44b-49 are subunits. Although he does not refer at all to vv. 50-58, its existence as the final subunit of ch. 15 could easily be deduced from his article. See N. BONNEAU, «The Logic of Paul's Argument on the Resurrection Body in 1 Cor 15,35-44a», 90-91.
2. (intro. question in v. 35), vv. 36-44a, vv. 44b-50, vv. 51-58.
See G. SELLIN, Der Streit um die Auferstehung der Toten, 210.

human eye (vv. 35-44a). He stresses the discontinuity between the natural body that is sown and the spiritual body that is raised. Second, he develops an argument from Scripture by proposing his own anthropological thesis for the resurrection of the dead. He develops an elaborate midrash pesher of Genesis 2,7, thereby firmly grounding his teaching in the Word of God (vv. 44b-49). Given its reference to «the life-giving Spirit» in the context of a comparison between the first Adam and last Adam, this subunit provides the subject matter for the close reading of the text which follows later in this chapter. And third, the Apostle concludes the chapter by revealing «a mystery» to the Corinthians: the previous comparison of bodies is now applied to the living and the dead who will be changed and made imperishable at the Lord's return (vv. 50-58). Here again Paul returns to the relation between Christian belief about the future and Christian behavior in the present. In fact his teaching on the last things never strays too far from his deeply ethical and pastoral concerns.

After having considered the common themes and topics of the chapter as a whole[5], we now have to take a closer look at the development of Paul's argument in the second half, namely vv. 35-58. We have already seen how this passage exhibits an A B A' concentric structure; this pattern must now be explained in greater detail. In the presentation of the Greek text that follows, note how each individual subunit is also divided into three parts, I, II and III. In addition, notice how an A B B' A' structure is used almost exclusively in the first (vv. 35-44a) and third (vv. 50-58) subunits, while an A B structure characterizes the second subunit (vv. 44b-49). The concentric structure of the text appears as follows.

The Concentric Structure of 1Cor 15,35-58

A. First Subunit, vv. 35-44a — An Argument from Reason about the Resurrection Body: a Tale of Two Analogies
   1. Two Introductory Questions

---

[5] Many exegetes have recognized a concentric structure in 1 Corinthians 15. A valuable contribution to our understanding of the chapter's organization can be found in the results presented by the French language group, as reported by J.-N. ALETTI, at a Biblical conference held in 1985. First, he lists the data from vv. 12-34 and vv. 35-58 and highlights their common themes. Second, he presents the concentric structure of 15,35-55 as A = 35-44a, B = 44b-49, A' = 50-55. The group believes that Paul is insisting primarily on the transformation of the human body, as opposed to its corporeity, in vv. 35ff. See J.-N. ALETTI – al., *Résurrection du Christ et des chrétiens (1 Co 15)*, 258-259.

v. 35   Ἀλλὰ ἐρεῖ τις, Πῶς ἐγείρονται οἱ νεκροί; ποίῳ δὲ σώματι
          ἔρχονται;
2. Two Analogies Drawn from Creation
First Analogy: the Sowing of Seed
v. 36 A   ἄφρων, σὺ ὃ σπείρεις οὐ ζῳοποιεῖται ἐὰν μὴ ἀποθάνῃ·
v. 37 A' καὶ ὃ σπείρεις, οὐ τὸ σῶμα τὸ γενησόμενον σπείρεις
          ἀλλὰ γυμνὸν κόκκον εἰ τύχοι σίτου ἤ τινος τῶν λοιπῶν·
v. 38a B ὁ δὲ θεὸς δίδωσιν αὐτῷ σῶμα καθὼς ἠθέλησεν,
v. 38b B' καὶ ἑκάστῳ τῶν σπερμάτων ἴδιον σῶμα.
Second Analogy: the Differences between Earthly and Heavenly Bodies
v. 39 A   οὐ πᾶσα σὰρξ ἡ αὐτὴ σάρξ, ἀλλὰ ἄλλη μὲν ἀνθρώπων,
          ἄλλη δὲ σὰρξ κτηνῶν, ἄλλη δὲ σὰρξ πτηνῶν, ἄλλη δὲ
          ἰχθύων.
v. 40a B καὶ σώματα ἐπουράνια, καὶ σώματα ἐπίγεια·
v. 40b B' ἀλλὰ ἑτέρα μὲν ἡ τῶν ἐπουρανίων δόξα, ἑτέρα δὲ ἡ τῶν
          ἐπιγείων.
v. 41 A' ἄλλη δόξα ἡλίου, καὶ ἄλλη δόξα σελήνης, καὶ ἄλλη δόξα
          ἀστέρων· ἀστὴρ γὰρ ἀστέρος διαφέρει ἐν δόξῃ.
3. Examples Applied to the Resurrection of the Dead
v. 42a Οὕτως καὶ ἡ ἀνάστασις τῶν νεκρῶν.
v. 42b A σπείρεται ἐν φθορᾷ,   B ἐγείρεται ἐν ἀφθαρσίᾳ·
v. 43a A σπείρεται ἐν ἀτιμίᾳ,   B ἐγείρεται ἐν δόξῃ·
v. 43b A σπείρεται ἐν ἀσθενείᾳ,   B ἐγείρεται ἐν δυνάμει·
v. 44a A σπείρεται σῶμα ψυχικόν,   B ἐγείρεται σῶμα
                                          πνευματικόν.
B. Second Subunit, vv. 44b-49 — An Argument from Scripture about the
Resurrection Body: the First and the Last Adam
1. Thesis Statement: There is a Spiritual Body
v. 44b A εἰ ἔστιν σῶμα ψυχικόν, B ἔστιν καὶ πνευματικόν.
2. Midrash on Gen 2,7
v. 45a οὕτως καὶ γέγραπται,
          A Ἐγένετο ὁ πρῶτος ἄνθρωπος Ἀδὰμ εἰς ψυχὴν ζῶσαν·
v. 45b B ὁ ἔσχατος Ἀδὰμ εἰς πνεῦμα ζῳοποιοῦν.
v. 46a A ἀλλ' οὐ πρῶτον τὸ πνευματικὸν
v. 46b B ἀλλὰ τὸ ψυχικόν, ἔπειτα τὸ πνευματικόν.
v. 47a A ὁ πρῶτος ἄνθρωπος ἐκ γῆς χοϊκός,
v. 47b B ὁ δεύτερος ἄνθρωπος ἐξ οὐρανοῦ.
3. Application to Believers

v. 48a A οἷος ὁ χοϊκός, τοιοῦτοι καὶ οἱ χοϊκοί,
v. 48b B καὶ οἷος ὁ ἐπουράνιος, τοιοῦτοι καὶ οἱ ἐπουράνιοι·
v. 49a A καὶ καθὼς ἐφορέσαμεν τὴν εἰκόνα τοῦ χοϊκοῦ,
v. 49b B φορέσωμεν καὶ τὴν εἰκόνα τοῦ ἐπουρανίου.

A'. Third Subunit, vv. 50-58 — the Necessity of Transforming the Natural Body into the Spiritual Body: Necessary Change and the Victory Over Death[6]

1. The Necessary Change into Eschatological Life

v. 50   A Τοῦτο δέ φημι, ἀδελφοί,
           ὅτι σὰρξ καὶ αἷμα βασιλείαν θεοῦ κληρονομῆσαι οὐ δύναται, οὐδὲ ἡ φθορὰ τὴν ἀφθαρσίαν κληρονομεῖ.

v. 51-52a B ἰδοὺ μυστήριον ὑμῖν λέγω· πάντες οὐ κοιμηθησόμεθα, πάντες δὲ ἀλλαγησόμεθα, ἐν ἀτόμῳ, ἐν ῥιπῇ ὀφθαλμοῦ, ἐν τῇ ἐσχάτῃ σάλπιγγι·

v. 52b   B' σαλπίσει γάρ, καὶ οἱ νεκροὶ ἐγερθήσονται ἄφθαρτοι, καὶ ἡμεῖς ἀλλαγησόμεθα.

v. 53   A' δεῖ γὰρ τὸ φθαρτὸν τοῦτο ἐνδύσασθαι ἀφθαρσίαν καὶ τὸ θνητὸν τοῦτο ἐνδύσασθαι ἀθανασίαν.

2. Divine Victory Over Death

v. 54   A ὅταν δὲ τὸ φθαρτὸν τοῦτο ἐνδύσηται ἀφθαρσίαν καὶ τὸ θνητὸν τοῦτο ἐνδύσηται ἀθανασίαν, τότε γενήσεται ὁ λόγος ὁ γεγραμμένος, Κατεπόθη ὁ θάνατος εἰς νῖκος.

v. 55   B ποῦ σου, θάνατε, τὸ νῖκος; ποῦ σου, θάνατε, τὸ κέντρον;

v. 56   B' τὸ δὲ κέντρον τοῦ θανάτου ἡ ἁμαρτία, ἡ δὲ δύναμις τῆς ἁμαρτίας ὁ νόμος·

v. 57   A' τῷ δὲ θεῷ χάρις τῷ διδόντι ἡμῖν τὸ νῖκος διὰ τοῦ κυρίου ἡμῶν Ἰησοῦ Χριστοῦ.

3. Conclusion: Closing Exhortation to Believers

v. 58 Ὥστε, ἀδελφοί μου ἀγαπητοί, ἑδραῖοι γίνεσθε, ἀμετακίνητοι, περισσεύοντες ἐν τῷ ἔργῳ τοῦ κυρίου πάντοτε, εἰδότες ὅτι ὁ κόπος ὑμῶν οὐκ ἔστιν κενὸς ἐν κυρίῳ.

---

[6] Gillman has proposed a two part division similar to this, with vv. 50-53 as division I, vv. 54-57 as division II and v. 58 as the conclusion. However he proposes an A B A' pattern in the first two divisions. See J. GILLMAN, «Transformation in 1 Cor 15,50-53», 320-322.

This concentric structure must now be explained and developed. In order to do so, we shall pay close attention to the rhetorical markers, syntax and structures which identify the individual subunits. A study of the thematic content of particular verses will also help demonstrate how Paul has organized his argument in the passage as a whole.

We begin with the first subunit, vv. 35-44a, Paul's presentation of the argument from reason concerning the resurrection body. After the two introductory questions, the Apostle offers his addressees two analogies drawn from the visible world[7]. Since both of these examples are taken from common, every day realities, they would have been simple for the Corinthians to grasp and comprehend. We shall now examine each example in greater detail.

The first analogy in vv. 36-38 has to do with the sowing of seed and it forms a distinct literary and theological subunit[8]. It is marked by the presence of personal subjects (σύ, θεός) and action verbs (σπείρεις, ζωοποιεῖται, ἀποθάνῃ, δίδωσιν, ἠθέλησεν). The conjunction καί links v. 37 to v. 36, while the particle δέ joins v. 38 to v. 37. Note how v. 36, A and v. 37, A', share a parallel grammatical structure and are expressed negatively: ὁ σπείρεις οὐ...ἐὰν μὴ in A and ὁ σπείρεις, οὐ... ἀλλὰ in A'. The activity

---

[7] «In vv. 36-41, Paul employs two related yet distinct examples, the first contained in vv. 36-38, the second in vv. 39-41» (N. BONNEAU, «The Logic of Paul's Argument», 83). For other authors that also recognize the presence of two examples, cf. R. MORISSETTE, «La condition de ressuscité», 208-228; C.K. BARRETT, *The First Epistle to the Corinthians*, 370-371; and H. CONZELMANN, *1 Corinthians*, 280-282. For other exegetes who argue for three examples, cf. W.L. CRAIG, *Assessing the New Testament Evidence*, 126-131 and G.W. DAWES, «"But if you can gain your freedom" (1 Corinthians 7,17-24)», 687-689. As regards this last article, DAWES prefers to speak of Paul's use of illustrations as he employs the rhetorical technique of *digressio*. He shows how Paul uses two illustrations in 1Cor 3,5-7, i.e., the image of a field and a building; two illustrations in 1Cor 7,17-24, i.e., circumcision and slavery; and three illustrations in 1Cor 15,35-44a, i.e., the metaphor of sowing in vv. 36-38, the different types of body and flesh in v. 39 and the analogy of heavenly and earthly bodies in vv. 40-41. DAWES' argument proves that there are in fact two distinct illustrations in both 1Cor 3,5-7 and 1Cor 7,17-24 and this information provides us with further evidence with regard to 1Cor 15,35-41. When using the technique of *digressio* in 1Cor, it seems that Paul tends to offer his addressees two examples in order to prove his point. Hence we conclude that this is also the case here.

[8] «In vv. 36-38 Paul's skillful use of language oscillates among three levels: agricultural, anthropological and theological. He relates the agrarian image of a buried seed and new plant to the human experience of life, death and new life. For Paul the emergence of new life is not attributed to a law of biology, operative within nature (as if corpses would sprout like seeds), but rather to the creative activity of God» (J. GILLMAN, «Transformation», 325).

of dying ἀποθάνῃ in A and the state of weakness and vulnerability γυμνὸν κόκκον in A' are contrasted to the denial of a future activity ζῳοποιεῖται in A and a future state τὸ σῶμα τὸ γενησόμενον in A'. In addition to their structural similarity, both verses also convey the same basic idea, namely, that life comes after death: A expresses a general principle of reproduction while A' states a more specific principle with regard to the reproduction of grains. The conjunction at the beginning of v. 37 is best understood as a καί *consecutivum*[9]: it serves to coordinate both statements by using one so as to demonstrate the other. If this is the case here, then Paul's point is best rendered in English as «Just as A, so A'».

In contrast to the somewhat negative tone that marks the beginning of the analogy, B and B' both strike a positive theological note by expressing the creative activity of God who gives a body as he chooses. The αὐτῷ of v. 38a refers back to the γυμνὸν κόκκον of v. 37, thus connecting B to A'. B' is associated with A in a similar, yet more general way. The phrase ἑκάστῳ τῶν σπερμάτων in B' represents a more scientific description of the more general ὃ σπείρεις of A, since the noun σπέρμα denotes both seed and semen in

---

[9] For an explanation of the καί *consecutivum*, cf. BDR § 442.2.a and HS § 252,29.a)2. Note that BDR, HS and Bauer offer Mt 5,15 as an example: «ἀλλ᾽ ἐπὶ τὴν λυχνίαν, καὶ λάμπει» Although he does not give 1Cor 15,37 as an example under this heading, nevertheless Bauer explains the consecutive use of καί under 2-f in this way: «zur Einführung d. Folge, die sich aus dem Vorhergehenden ergibt: *und so, und dann*». For his part Zerwick provides a longer clarification of this use of the particle and explains it by presenting 1Cor 12,3 as an example. «This Semitic habit of paratactic thought and expression sometimes accounts for texts which, to those accustomed to more accurate subordination, must seem obscure, or at least strange. Thus e.g. we read in 1 Cor 13,3 "none that speaks in the Spirit of God says 'Jesus is anathema' and none can say 'Jesus is Lord' but in the Holy Spirit". At first sight this seems perfectly clear and straightforward: with the Spirit none can reject Christ and without the Spirit none can accept him. Some have however seen in the first of the two statements a reference to pseudo-charismatics who "in the Spirit" said "Jesus is anathema" and there has been much discussion as to who they might be; and thanks to the attention thus drawn to the passage, it has been noticed that the seemingly obvious sense is not so good as the one which is obtained by understanding a subordination of comparison: not simply "none can say in the Spirit 'Jesus is anathema' (sic) and none can say without the Spirit 'Jesus is Lord'", but *"just as* none can say..."* (which is obvious), *"so* none can say..."* (which is what Paul wishes to show). This type of construction (the coordination of two assertions, of which one is merely a comparison for the demonstration of the other) is not foreign to the OT, indeed is very frequent in Prov, e.g. "the heaven above and the earth below and the heart of the king (are) inscrutable" 25,3; so too 25,3.23.25.27; 26,7.9.14 etc» (ZERWICK, § 451).

Greek[10]. All living things on earth, whether plants, animals, or human beings, propagate themselves thanks to their σπέρματα. Lastly, while both A and A' refer to human activity, σὺ ὃ σπείρεις and ὃ σπείρεις...σπείρεις, B refers to God's activity in the giving of the new body, ὁ δὲ θεὸς δίδωσιν αὐτῷ...ἠθέλησεν. This divine action clearly carries over into B' since the subject and verb of this clause are both taken from B.

In short, the subunit reveals a perfectly balanced structure. A and A' assert negatively what B and B' affirm positively: what a man cannot do, God can. Moreover, ζῳοποιεῖται, the passive form of the verb in v. 36, is contrasted to δίδωσιν and ἠθέλησεν, the active forms in v. 38. All of this serves to underscore the positive and active nature of God's role in the giving of new life[11].

What point then is Paul making by means of this example? The example of the sowing of seed underscores the reality of discontinuity: one kind of seed is sown, it dies and then God gives it a particular body. In other words, God causes a transformation to happen over a given period of time. Before the change occurs, there is a seed; after the death of the seed and thanks to divine intervention, there is now a new body. Therefore this first example shows that God is able to achieve a profound and genuine transformation in his creatures by calling them through death to life.

The second analogy in vv. 39-41 has to do with the differences between earthly and heavenly bodies. In fact, v. 39 begins a new subunit. Since there are no particles connecting it to what has come before, we may conclude that this is an example of rhetorical asyndeton[12]. In contrast to vv. 36-38, this subunit is marked by the striking absence of personal subjects and action verbs. With the exception of διαφέρει, there are no verbs at all. Since the verb «to be» is implied, we are left to express the existence of these diverse creatures by adding «there is» or «there are» to the English translation.

In the chiastic structure outlined above, v. 39 represents A in its subunit; it emphasizes the differences between the kinds of flesh of four different earthly

---

[10] Cf. W. BAUER, «σπέρμα», and S. SCHULZ, «σπέρμα, σπείρω», in *ThWNT*; and W. HACKENBERG, «σπείρω», in *EWNT*.

[11] «In v. 38 Paul sets over against the activity of the one who sows the creative activity of God (cf. the adversative δέ). The life-giving power comes neither from the sower nor the seed but from God» (J. GILLMAN, «Transformation», 326).

[12] For more information on asyndeton, the occurrence of unconnected words, sentences, or units in a given text, see BDR § 462.

creatures. v. 40a, B, begins with the particle καί, a conjunction which now introduces a new idea to the argument: there are in fact two radically different kinds of bodies, some celestial and some terrestrial. Next follows B', introduced by ἀλλά at the start of v. 40b. This particle interjects a slight nuance into the argument, all the while building on the assertion just made: there is a difference between the glories of celestial and terrestrial bodies. Lastly, v. 41, A', like v. 39 before it, also begins without a rhetorical marker. This second example of asyndeton invites us to look back at the start of the subunit in v. 39, thus connecting A' (v. 41) to A (v. 39). In A' Paul gives some examples of the varying glories of the different celestial bodies.

In short, this second subunit also reveals a perfectly balanced structure; unlike the first, it is truly chiastic in form. A and A' illustrate the differences among bodies within a group (A highlights the differences according to the category of flesh, while A' highlights the differences according to the category of glory), while B and B' emphasize the difference between the groups themselves. Hence A and A' list examples of creatures within a given genus, the first earthly, the second celestial; B underscores the contrast between the two distinct genera; and B' accentuates this contrast still further by introducing the notion of glory and by insisting on the differing glory of each genus. Moreover, it seems that Paul is also alluding to the creation account of Genesis 1 in both A and A', yet it is interesting to note that he does not list the creatures according to biblical order as one might expect. Instead, he lists the progression of their creation in reverse order. In A we first find those earthly creatures formed on the sixth day: human beings (Gen 1,26) and animals (Gen 1,24-25) and then those created on the fifth day: birds (Gen 1,20b) and fish (Gen 1,20a). In A' Paul lists the heavenly bodies created on the fourth day, yet this time he reverses the sequence and proceeds in biblical order: first the sun, the moon and then the stars (Gen 1,16). Hence the movement from A to A' conveys something of a countdown effect. Paul starts with human beings, the summit of God's creation and then moves backwards, as if heading back to the origin of created things. In this way the unfolding of the text reveals Paul's concern with the genesis of the human body. This is a matter which he has already alluded to in vv. 36, 38b. He will return to it again in the application that follows, vv. 42-44a, as well as in the argument from Scripture, vv. 44b-49.

In addition, the four members which compose the A B B' A' structure of the subunit find an echo in the fourfold repetition of the word σάρξ in A and δόξα in A'. Thanks to this highly effective technique of contrast and repetition, Paul provides this subunit with a brilliantly balanced rhetorical structure. In this way he succeeds quite well in conveying the point he desires to make.

What then does Paul intend to illustrate by means of this second example? We saw above how the analogy of the sowing of seed makes a chronological point: it serves to underscore the distinction between the before and after state of the body. Rather than chronological, however, the second example makes a spatial point: it emphasizes the qualitative difference between earthly and heavenly bodies due to their location in the universe. And more than that, it also implies that the material constitution of any given body reflects its particular environment. Bodies of flesh are found only on earth and never in the heavens, while celestial bodies, the sun, moon and stars, are seen only in the heavens and never on earth. God has created every unique body and placed it in its appropriate place in the universe, either on earth or in heaven. Moreover, Paul asserts that a body possesses its own unique degree of glory, depending on whether it dwells on earth or in heaven. In short, God has created his universe in such a way that there is a clearly marked division which separates the earthly from the heavenly realm.

Paul next moves on to the third and final section of the subunit, his application of both examples in vv. 42a-44. By relating the two points of these analogies to the resurrection of the dead, the Apostle manages to combine the before and after motif of the first point to the earthly and heavenly motif of the second. His addresses may have asked themselves, But how could someone who has died ever come to experience new life? And how is it possible for anyone to make the seemingly insuperable passage from the earthly to the heavenly realm[13]? In this conclusion of the subunit, the Apostle now takes the before/after point of the first example and combines it with the earthly/heavenly point of the second. Hence it is clear that both examples were carefully chosen and developed so as to highlight the transformation and discontinuity that results through the act of resurrection, the fundamental point he has wanted to make all along. In short, Paul insists with great assurance that

---

[13] «The full import of vv. 36-41 lies in the merging of the main points of the two examples — the time axis of the first example and the space axis of the second example — to form a new implied question: Can God transform (before/after) an earthly body into a heavenly body (below/above)? Only this question can adequately lead to discovering the particular configuration of the resurrection body» (N. BONNEAU, «The Resurrection Body», 86).

God can change a dead, earthly body into a living, heavenly one through the resurrection of the dead.

Returning to a study of the concentric structure of the text, we note that the application of the examples begins in v. 42a with a simple declarative sentence introduced with the words οὕτως καί. The conjunction καί links the verse to what has come before, while the adverb οὕτως announces that which is to follow. Four pairs of balanced antitheses, A and B, now appear in vv. 42b-44a. In each of the four sentences, A is introduced by the verb σπείρεται followed by a substantival phrase, while B begins with the verb ἐγείρεται which is also followed by a substantival phrase. Both verbs are best understood as impersonal passives and they serve to connect the application to what has come before (σπείρεται calls the reader back to σπείρεις in vv. 36-37 and ἐγείρεται to Πῶς ἐγείρονται οἱ νεκροί; in v. 35). The contrast of these two verbs serves to underscore the notion of discontinuity: if from the first example we learn that man sows but God alone gives a body, in vv. 42b-44a Paul insists that man sows but God alone raises. The substantival phrases, for their part, emphasize the differences illustrated in the second example: those of A characterize the earthly realm and those of B describe the heavenly one. The application reaches its crescendo when the three phrases give way to the noun σῶμα, modified first by the adjective ψυχικόν in A and then by πνευματικόν in B. In this way, Paul marshals his images and brings them together so as to advance his final point. He begins with an apocalyptic description of the world (depicted by the abstract qualities φθορᾷ, ἀτιμίᾳ, ἀσθενείᾳ on the one hand and ἀφθαρσίᾳ, δόξῃ, δυνάμει on the other) and proceeds to the more concrete description of the noun σῶμα, the most significant word in vv. 35-44a[14]. At this point, the end of the application of the two examples, Paul has successfully answered the two questions posed in v. 35. With the help of two analogies drawn from the visible world, he has proven from reason that God can indeed change a dead natural body into a living spiritual one through the resurrection of the dead.

The second subunit, B, vv. 44b-49, represents Paul's argument from Scripture. It begins with the conditional sentence of v. 44b, continues with a

---

[14] «The only body, moreover, which can be the object of such a dual transformation is the human body. This explains why the essentially anthropological word *sōma* is the only word which appears in all three parts of the argument from analogy — in the question, in each of the two examples and in the application» (N. BONNEAU, «The Resurrection Body», 89).

lengthy midrash of Genesis 2,7 in vv. 45-47 and ends with an application to believers in vv. 48-49. Since these verses represent the central part of our study in the present work, we shall return to them in greater detail in section 6 below, «1Cor 15,44b-49 as a Distinct Subunit», as well as in Chapter II, «A Close Reading of 1Cor 15,44b-49». At this point it is enough to make mention of their most salient feature: antithetical parallelism. In fact, the A B antitheses begun in vv. 42b-44a continue throughout vv. 44b-49. These antitheses make up the rhetorical backbone which supports Paul's contrast between the first and the last Adam in his argument from Scripture.

Finally, we turn next to the final subunit of the passage, A', vv. 50-58. These verses insist on the necessity of transforming the natural body into the spiritual one. By asserting that that which is human cannot enter heaven unless it is changed, Paul is returning to the principal theme of the first subunit, A, vv. 35-44a which focused on the otherness of bodies. Both subunits share certain words or cognates. For example, the adjective ἄλλος, «another, other», occurs seven times in vv. 39-41, while the verb ἀλλάσσομαι, «to be changed or altered» occurs twice in vv. 51-52. The contrast between the perishable and the imperishable, first made in v. 42a, σπείρεται ἐν φθορᾷ, ἐγείρεται ἐν ἀφθαρσίᾳ, is repeated four times in the chapter's final subunit: in v. 50, ἡ φθορὰ τὴν ἀφθαρσίαν κληρονομεῖ, in v. 52b, οἱ νεκροὶ ἐγερθήσονται ἄφθαρτοι in v. 53, δεῖ γὰρ τὸ φθαρτὸν τοῦτο ἐνδύσασθαι ἀφθαρσίαν and lastly in v. 54, ὅταν δὲ τὸ φθαρτὸν τοῦτο ἐνδύσηται ἀφθαρσίαν καὶ τὸ θνητὸν τοῦτο ἐνδύσηται ἀθανασίαν. Nevertheless, in vv. 50-58 Paul proposes something new. With the help of apocalyptic imagery, he reveals his mystery (v. 51) to the Corinthians by describing in broad strokes what the anticipated eschatological change will be like both for the living and the dead.

As with the two previous cases, this subunit is also composed of three parts. In part one, vv. 50-53, Paul emphasizes the fact that change is needed for both the living and the dead. In part two, vv. 54-57, he shows that God will indeed be victorious over death. And lastly in part three, v. 58, he concludes the subunit (and the entire chapter) on a forceful exhortatory note. As far as the chiastic structure of the passage is concerned, Paul now returns to the A B B' A' pattern he last used in vv. 39-41. In addition to the presence of common themes, this rhetorical structure provides even further proof that allows us to see a connection between the first and final subunit.

In part one, vv. 50-53, Paul proposes an anthropological argument. In this section, there is a clear parallel between A, v. 50 and A', v. 53, A is a *subpropositio* which presents a negative formulation with regard to the theme of transformation, while A' presents a positive conclusion to his argument. Also note the presence of two significant verbs: οὐ δύναται in v. 50 and δεῖ· in v. 53 express a compelling sense of necessity. As proof for the argument, B, v. 51a-52a and B', v. 52b, express the reality of transformation; both contain verbs in the first person plural as well as the apocalyptic image of the trumpet blast. However, B and B' differ from one another in that the first deals with the living while the second concerns the dead. The essential point to be grasped of course is that both the living and the dead must be changed; both groups will come to experience a completely new life when Christ returns in glory. In as much as A' does not merely repeat A, Paul has made his message more specific by claiming that all who share this mortal nature (both the living and the dead) must put on the imperishable.

Next Paul leaves aside his discussion of human beings and turns his focus on the works of God. In part two, vv. 54-57, he presents his theological argument. Although it is true that the repetition of the words «death» (four times) and «victory» (three times) provides a clear concatenation of themes in these four verses, nevertheless on the thematic level a case can still be made for the presence of a chiastic structure. There is a distinct contrast made between A, v. 54 and A', v. 57, while A announces God's victory over humanity's chief enemy, death (thereby highlighting the evil that is van-quished), A' claims victory «through our Lord Jesus Christ», (thereby emphasizing the divine hero who gloriously conquers his foe). In the center of the argument, B, v. 55 and B', v. 56, present a brief rhetorical dialogue: B asks a question of death and B' answers it with regard to death's sting, sin and its power, the law. In short, part two ends beautifully on both a theological and christological note. Lastly, Paul sums up his teaching on the resurrection by concluding with a final exhortation to his addressees in part three, v. 58. In this way he brings this extraordinary chapter to a resounding and triumphant close.

2. 1Cor 15,35-44a and the Different Kinds of Bodies

We saw above in the overview of chapter fifteen how Paul deals with the various kinds of earthly and heavenly bodies in 1 Corinthians 15,35-44a. If we are to grasp his argument from Scripture concerning natural and spiritual bodies in vv. 44b-49, then it is essential for us first to take a closer look at Paul's understanding of the different kinds of bodies in the universe as developed in vv. 35-44a. In order to do this, we must bring to our exegesis a better understanding of the cultural context in which Paul lived and wrote. The two examples presented in 1 Corinthians 15,36-41 are foreign to us precisely because the scientific theories which underpin them, although prevalent and widespread in the Hellenistic age, are now radically different from our own. How then did Greeks in the first century of our era explain the germination and growth of seeds and semen? How did they understand the nature and composition of earthly and heavenly bodies? In order to answer these questions, it would be profitable for us to collect and consider some relevant information gathered from a concise study of ancient Greek science. Only in this way can we come to a better understanding of Paul's world view, as well as that of his addressees in Corinth.

In 1 Corinthians 15,35-44a, the Apostle insists on the dissimilar material nature of earthly and heavenly bodies[15]. He wants to emphasize a common

---

[15] Over the years, a few exegetes have recognized this crucial insight. In these vv., Paul is insisting on the different kinds of matter of which earthly and heavenly bodies are made. «Vers. 39. Σάρξ est malheureusement un terme polyvalent chez l'apôtre [...] Ici nous rencontrons un 5ᵉ sens, que nous pourrions appeler (cum grano salis) le sens chimique: le genre de matière dont un corps est composé. Celle-ci, d'après les conceptions de l'antiquité diffère selon les classes des animaux. Naturellement les "corps célestes", c'est-à-dire les corps vivants de certains anges qui nous apparaissent sous forme d'étoiles, sont d'une autre matière que les corps terrestres. De plus, ceux-là diffèrent autant entre eux que ceux-ci (vers. 41-41)» (J. HÉRING, La première épître de saint Paul aux Corinthiens, 146); «The word body here means rather what we would call nature, as, for instance, the nature of wheat, that is different for each species but common to all of the same species. The same appears in his use here of the word flesh, whether that of men, animals, birds, or fish (v. 39) [...] In the argument here body and flesh come to the same thing insofar as neither specifies so much the individual as rather the nature of a thing: wheat nature, human nature, animal nature, bird nature, fish nature, sun nature, moon nature, star natures» (B. SCHNEIDER, «The Corporate Meaning and Background of 1 Cor 15,45b», 146-147); «In verses 39-41, certainly, the issue is the substance or stuff of things, not their mere form. Héring has pointed out that the ancients thought that different classes of animals had different kinds of matter. Galen for instance thought the flesh of lions differed from that of lambs. The heavenly bodies differ, in respect to their substance, from earthly things. Verse 38 then probably reflects Paul's assumption that different kinds of plants have different kinds of bodies just as, according to Galen, the bodies of lions and lambs are qualitatively different. Such botanical and zoological views of course jar modern ears. Hence Bultmann assumed that Paul must mean in v. 38 (each seed has its own body) that different plants have different forms. Paul on the other hand probably thought that just as the flesh of birds is qualitatively different from the flesh of man and fish, so the substance of one type of plant is different from that of another kind of plant» (R.J. SIDER, «The Pauline Conception of the Resurrection Body», 430); and «In antiquity it was believed the different classes of animals were composed of different kinds of matter [...] Likewise, it was believed that the character

assumption that was completely taken for granted by him and his contemporaries: plants, animals and human beings, as well as the sun, moon and stars, all these in fact have bodies made up of different kinds of matter. Paul compares them in order to make an important point about the embodied condition of those who are raised from the dead, and more specifically still, to insist on the existence of a new kind of body, namely the spiritual one. Most of all, however, he wants to underscore in the clearest possible terms the necessary discontinuity between the natural body that is sown in human weakness and the spiritual body that is raised in divine glory. For the Apostle, therefore, the magnificant change that occurs in the very act of rising from the dead transfers the human being from the earthly realm to the heavenly one. In other words, the transformation of the material composition of the body also represents a very significant change in its status and honor: those who are to be raised from the dead will enjoy a greater share in God's glory, grandeur and splendor.

3. Paul's Early Formation: Tarsus or Jerusalem?

At this point in our study, we next have to address the rather complicated question of the makeup of Paul's early education and formation. Was the young Paul trained primarily in Tarsus or Jerusalem? During his studies, was he more influenced by Hellenistic culture or by Palestinian Judaism? Other than the Bible (which obviously represents the dominant influence on his thought and worldview), what were the great works of literature and philosophy that formed his mind? Who were the writers and thinkers who left their mark on him and influenced his way of reasoning? Unfortunately, there is still as yet no agreement among scholars on these rather difficult questions. Nevertheless, it seems clear that Paul managed to profess his faith in Jesus' resurrection, all the while integrating a respectable knowledge of Greek literature and philosophy into his Jewish beliefs, training and background. In 1 Corinthians 15, the Apostle certainly remained true to the traditional pharisaic doctrine on the resurrection with regard to the embodied nature of the risen life[16]. But most of all, as a Greek-speaking Jew from Tarsus[17], Paul the

---

of the heavenly bodies (sun, stars, moon) differed from that of earthly forms and it was recognized that each of the heavenly bodies had its own distinctive radiance» (C.H. TALBERT, *Reading Corinthians*, 100-101).

[16] For example, Paul's pharisaic background comes through in his insistence on the need for a new body, one which would be suitable for heavenly existence. «We have previously insisted that for Paul the Christian dispensation was a new creation which could be com-

Apostle also managed to convey his teaching to others in a very effective and compelling way. He made good sense both to Hellenized Diaspora Jews as well as to his Gentile converts and so he was able to convince them to believe in and accept his gospel of Christ crucified (cf 1Cor 1,17)[18]. Although many

---

pared and contrasted with the old creation [...] Just as the first Adam had introduced an order of life on the physical plane or the earthly plane, so Christ, the Second Adam, had introduced a new order of life in the spirit. Hence it followed that even as the first Adam had needed a body suitable for existence on the earthly plane, so Jesus had need of a body suited for existence in the spiritual plane. Paul assumes that the latter plane will need a 'body' and that therefore the resurrection of believers would have to be a resurrection into 'bodies', similar to that which Jesus had assumed in the world of 'spirit'. Paul thus remains true to his pharisaic background in that he insists on the embodied nature of the resurrection life. Further, the analogies which he uses in order to express this truth reveal the essentially Rabbinic cast of his thought» (W.D. DAVIES, *Paul and Rabbinic Judaism*, 304-305).

[17]At the height of its prosperity in the time of Augustus, Tarsus enjoyed special imperial privileges which helped to make it a great hub of intellectual life as well as the proud home of many significant cultural and educational institutions. «According to Strabo (14.5.131), the people of Tarsus in the 1st century C.E. were keen students of philosophy, the liberal arts and the entire encyclopaedia of learning; this was true to such a degree that it surpassed both Athens and Alexandria as a center of culture and learning, even though people did not, as a rule, come from other regions to study in its schools. Native Tarsians, however, went on to study elsewhere and frequently held educational and civil posts of importance throughout the empire» (W.W. GASQUE, «Tarsus», in *AncBD*).

[18] The social and educational level of the Corinthian Christians is now recognized as being much higher than was first thought at the beginning of the century. Many scholars today recognize that the church was made up of individuals from various classes and social strata. We may conclude then that at least some members of the Corinthian church came from the educated classes. These are undoubtedly the «wise» mentioned in 1Cor 1,26ff. Although we cannot be certain as to the precise character of their intellectual formation, we can presume that they would have been somewhat familiar with the basic philosophical and scientific notions of the time. For further information on the social background of the Corinthians, cf. H.D. BETZ, «The Problem of Rhetoric and Theology», 24-25; W.A. MEEKS, «The Social Level of Pauline Christians», 51-73; J. MURPHY-O'CONNOR, «Corinth», in *AncBD*; and G. THEISSEN, «Social Stratification in the Corinthian Community», 69-119.

The Corinthians were very open to new notions and beliefs and they had the necessary intellectual formation to debate, refute and in general, argue with, the Apostle who founded their church. 1Cor gives ample evidence of Paul's response to these quarrelsome yet fervent believers who lived in one of the major Roman colonies of the Empire. For a recent article that also insists on the important influence of Hellenistic popular philosophy on the Corinthians, see H.W. HOLLANDER – J. HOLLEMAN, «The Relationship of Death, Sin and Law in 1 Cor 15,56», 290.

scholars today still downplay it[19], this kind of success in the Greco-Roman world would only have been possible for someone who, like Paul, had received a good Hellenistic education and was quite familiar with Greek culture and civilization[20]. In short, it seems highly probable that Paul did in fact receive some kind of formal intellectual training during his youth in Tarsus. We may deduce from this, therefore, that he would have been somewhat familiar with the major ideas of popular Greek philosophy, history and science[21].

---

[19] Although the precise nature of Paul's education remains an open question, scholars today are pretty much divided into two opposing positions: those who emphasize a Palestinian formation based in Jerusalem and those who stress a Hellenistic one based in the Diaspora, namely, at Tarsus.

As for the first group, W.W. Gasque (in agreement with W.C. van Unnik, F.F. Bruce, C.J. Hemer and J. Finegan) has recently asserted that Paul was sent to Jerusalem as a youth to receive a proper Jewish education there. For a presentation of this argument and for more bibliographical entries in favor of his thesis, see GASQUE, «Tarsus», 334. In a recent book, Hengel also agrees with this group of scholars; he too associates Paul with Jerusalem from his early youth. See M. HENGEL, «Upbringing and Education: Tarsus or Jerusalem?», 18-39.

[20] The second group of scholars maintains that Paul received a solid Hellenistic formation, most probably in Tarsus. At the beginning of the century, Ramsay stressed the fundamental influence of Tarsus on its famous son. «But the crowning glory of Tarsus, the reason for its undying interest to the whole world, is that it produced the Apostle Paul; that it was the one city which was suited by its equipoise between the Asiatic and the Western spirit to mould the character of the great Hellenist Jew; and that it nourished in him a strong sense of loyalty and patriotism as the "citizen of no mean city"» (W. M. RAMSAY, «The University of Tarsus», 228-235). This thesis has passed the test of time and other scholars still share it today. Cf. J. BECKER, *Paul: Apostle to the Gentiles*, 55; H.D. BETZ, «Paul», in *AncBD*; J.D.G. DUNN, *Romans*, xl; J.A. FITZMYER, «Paul», 1332; ID., *According to Paul*, 6; N. PERRIN, *The New Testament*, 89; and E. P. SANDERS, *Paul*, 8.

[21] Even if we do not adopt Ramsay's more extreme position, it is clear nonetheless that the Apostle would have been acquainted with popular Hellenistic philosophy. This of course would have included some notion of the basic scientific explanation of plant, animal and human reproduction, as well as the nature of the makeup of the planets and the stars. For a rather conservative appraisal of the philosophical foundation of Paul's Hellenistic education, consider Conzelmann's position. «Despite all the associations, there are no indications that Paul studied philosophy. The points of agreement do not go beyond the terms and ideas of popular philosophy with which it was possible for any and everyone to be acquainted. Moreover, it has to be borne in mind that Hellenistic Judaism had taken over philosophic ideas and in the course of its thinking had transformed them in terms of the Jewish understanding of God and the world» (H. CONZELMANN, *1 Corinthians*, 10). Lastly, Vanni emphasizes Paul's contact with some literary and philosophical elements originating in the Hellenistic world. «Paolo appartiene a tutto diritto alla letteratura greca:

4. Excursus: Ancient Greek Science

Before examining in greater detail the two principal examples given by Paul concerning both that which is sown (vv. 36-38) and the celestial and terrestrial bodies (vv. 39-41) — as well as his important teaching on the resurrection of the dead (vv. 42-44a) — it would be worthwhile for us to get a better grasp of how people in the first century understood the growth, development and reproduction of living things. In recent years, much has been written about the history of science both in ancient Greece as well as in the Hellenistic age. Since even the most rudimentary principles of their science are foreign to us today, all too often we fail to grasp simple observations and conclusions which must have seemed quite obvious to them. With this in mind, we next turn to an excursus on ancient Greek science. This investigation consists of 4.1, a concise introduction; 4.2, a presentation of ancient biology; 4.3, their contemporary notions of creation and perishability; and lastly 4.4, some basic concepts about their astronomy. Then, thanks to the insights gained through this research, we shall be in a much better position to return to the text and apply them to our exegesis of the second half of 1 Corinthians 15.

4.1 *Introduction*

From the earliest days of ancient Greece, philosophers struggled to identify and comprehend the basic stuff, matter, or nature (φύσις) which makes up the universe. In our day, of course, this field of scientific inquiry is called physics. In antiquity, however, the distinction between philosophy, on the one hand and science, on the other, was not nearly so clear and distinct: Greek philosophers observed, examined and scrutinized the material world and also sought to understand the basic ontological principles which govern it. By the time of Aristotle (384-322 B.C.), three distinct ways of approaching the problem of matter had in fact emerged. The first is called the mechanistic theory; the

---

un contenuto caratteristico che comporta anche un modo particolare di esprimersi e di gestire gli elementi linguistici. È in questo contenuto che abbiamo riscontrato punti di contatto interessanti e significativi con il mondo culturale greco: Paolo cita i poeti, Paolo conosce e riprende elementi di filosofi; conosce, riprende e rielabora concetti — come quello di "corpo" — diffusi nell'ambiente sia filosofico sia popolare, ma sempre tipici dell'ambiente greco. Indubbiamente l'ambiente greco ha esercitato su di lui, sulla sua cultura, sulla sua mentalità una forte pressione, lasciandovi una impronta indelebile che difficilmente può essere negata» (U. VANNI, «Due città nella formazione di Paolo», 28-29).

second, the mathematical; and the third, the qualitative. Since each of these theories exercised an enormous influence on Western science over the succeeding centuries and indeed, well into the modern era, it would be worthwhile for us to consider them in greater detail[22].

The first solution to the problem of the composition of nature is represented by the mechanistic theory (also sometimes called the physical or material theory). In the Hellenistic Period, its most famous representatives were Epicurus (300 B.C.) and Lucretius (first century B.C.). This of course is the model that underpins modern science, the paradigm that proved the test of time and research. This way of looking at nature stresses the permanence of movement and matter and it was originated by the Ionian philosophers of Miletus, chiefly Thales, Anaximander and Anaximenes. In the atomic theory of the pre-Socratics philosophers Leucippus and Democritus, both of whom lived in the fifth century B.C., this view attained its highest expression. Over the centuries, certain philosophers and scientists have espoused this theory of the material, atomic nature of the universe and it has become the one accepted by the scientists of our day.

The second solution to the problem of matter can be called the mathematical view (also known as the geometrical or formal theory). It held that the world which we perceive with our senses is passing, while the permanent, real world is the one of ideas, concepts and forms. Some would trace the origin of this view back to Pythagoras and his followers, who would seem to make out of numbers the basic stuff of the universe. Of course this formal view of the cosmos was most systematically expressed by Plato, its most famous and influential champion. Although eclipsed for over seven hundred years, this theory made an important comeback with the rise of Neo-Platonism in the fifth and sixth centuries of our era.

Lastly, the third doctrine, known as the qualitative theory, was promoted by Aristotle and his followers. This theory could be considered as a kind of compromise between the first two. Aristotle had rejected the exclusive stress which the materialists placed on matter and the Platonists put on form and instead postulated that matter and form are inextricably bound up together. He maintained that if one is to understand nature, one must stress the equal

---

[22] For an intelligible and easy-to-follow presentation of the three theories of matter (of which the following presentation is but a brief and cursory summary), cf. M. CLAGETT, *Greek Science in Antiquity*, 49-53 and S. SAMBURSKY, *The Physical World of Late Antiquity*, 21-61.

importance of both matter and form. Aristotle emphasized the becoming of things that exist in potentiality: for him, nature is motion understood as any sort of change. Hence he was concerned with the generation and corruption of living things, especially their organization and their causes. Aristotle's view made a profound impact on his disciple, Theophrastus, the Father of Greek botany. This was to become the principal doctrine of the Hellenistic Period[23]. Accepted and promoted first by the Stoics, its principles were later fostered by and circulated in the works of Plutarch, Galen and Alexander of Aphrodisias. Medieval philosophy and science could be considered to be heirs of the qualitative theory. Only in the sixteenth century would scientists begin to chisel away at this theory of nature and then gradually yet relentlessly begin to replace it with our modern view.

4.2 Biology: Botany, Zoology and Medicine

From the time of Homer onward, the ancient Greeks observed and studied the anatomy, physiology and reproduction of living things. This fascination with life, most especially with human life, found expression primarily in their philosophical and scientific investigation (what today we would call biology) as well as in their art, literature and passion for sport and war. Athletes needed to be trained properly, the wounded had to be attended to correctly and the sick in general needed to be cared for with the appropriate prescription of herbs, spices and other medicines. Science grew both as the result of human curiosity and ingenuity as well as out of the pressing necessity to respond to specific needs in society at large. In short, by Aristotle's time, some scientists had begun to specialize either in the study of plant life (botany), animal life (zoology), or the health and welfare of human beings (medicine). Aristotle himself, for example, was neither a botanist nor a physician. His own writings reveal a particular interest in the philosophy of science and zoology; unable to devote himself to everything, he left for others the professional investigation of botany and medicine.

Although the specialized study of living things finds expression in separate sciences by the fourth century and this thanks chiefly to Aristotle, it is only fair to state that many of his theories on life and natural history can be traced back to the pre-Socratics. Chief among these is Empedocles (c.493-c.433 B.C.), the

---

[23] For a fine discussion of the development of the qualitative theory in the natural sciences after Aristotle, see G.E.R. LLOYD, *Greek Science after Aristotle*, 75-90.

first Greek philosopher to speak of the existence of the four elements and to speculate on the results of their combinations. For him, the All is a spherical *plenum* in which the four ultimate «roots» — fire, air, water and earth — join and separate to cause the generation and perishing of living things[24].

We come next to Hippocrates (469-399 B.C.), the father of Greek medicine and one of the most influential figures of the ancient world[25]. In his work *Nature of Man*, he claims that the four humors (blood, phlegm, yellow bile and black bile) are elemental in human beings and as such are unchangeable. These four humors are in fact analogous to the four elements (earth, water, air and fire) proposed by Empedocles and a few other philosophers of that age. What is important for Hippocrates, however, is not so much the humors in themselves, but rather their mixture, or in Greek, their κρᾶσις. It is in fact the proper combination of the four constituents which insures the patient's good health. Disease is caused when the humors become out of proportion. The physician therefore has the task of helping the body restore itself by helping to return it to its original mixture. The patient is restored to good health when the perfect mingling of the elements which make him up has been regained.

II. [...] I for my part will prove that what I declare to be the constituents of a man are, according to both convention and nature, always alike and the same; it makes no difference whether the man be young or old, or whether the season be cold or hot. I will also bring evidence and set forth the necessary causes why each constituent grows or decreases in the body.
III. Now in the first place generation cannot take place from a unity. How could a unity generate, without copulating? Again, there is no generation unless the copulating partners be of the same kind and possess the same qualities; nor would there be any offspring. Moreover, generation will not take place if the combination of hot with cold and of dry with moist be not tempered and equal — should the one constituent be much in excess of the other and the stronger be much stronger than the weaker. Wherefore how is it likely for a thing to be generated from one, when generation does not take place from more than one unless they chance to be mutually well-tempered? Therefore, since such is the nature both of all other things and of man, man of necessity is not one, but each of the components contributing to generation has in the body the power it contributed. Again, each component must return to its own nature when the body

---

[24] A.J.D. PORTEOUS, «Empedocles», in *OCD*.
[25] For more information on the extraordinary life, work and influence of this great man, see G. SARTON, *Ancient Science Through the Golden Age of Greece*, 331-391.

of a man dies, moist to moist, dry to dry, hot to hot and cold to cold. Such too is the nature of animals and of all other things. All things are born in a like way and all things die in a like way. For the nature of them is composed of all those things I have mentioned above and each thing, according to what has been said, ends in that from which it was composed. So that too is whither it departs[26].

In the study of medicine, moreover, the ancients associated the four elements with human physiology in this way:
1. Fire. Associated with hot, rough, red blood; spring; choleric temperament.
2. Water. Associated with cold, smooth, white phlegm; winter; phlegmatic temperament.
3. Air. Associated with dry, salt, sweet, black bile; autumn; melancholic temperament.
4. Earth. Associated with moist, acid, yellow bile; summer; sanguineous temperament.
Not only did the Greeks practice their medicine with this theoretical schema in mind, but so too did the Romans. In fact, by the time of the Empire, Greek medicine had made such a significant impact on its Roman counterpart that the two had become virtually inseparable[27]. This philosophical explanation of the four elements, as first articulated by the great precursors like Hippocrates and Empedocles, underpinned the practice of medicine throughout the Greco-Roman period and well beyond[28].

Plato (c.429-347 B.C.) also wrote about the four elements, as we see in this excerpt from the *Timaeus*.

---

[26] HIPPOCRATES, *De natura hominis*, II. 31–III. 29.

[27] «As Pliny saw, the history of Roman medicine, however defined, is inseparable from that of Greek medicine. But, as this paper has tried to show, that is no reason for adopting Pliny's perspective of moral decline and the decay of *Romanitas* and for thereby equating the medicine of the Roman Empire with the corrupt and the ineffective. Such parallels as have been used to demonstrate its inferiority are frequently fallacious, especially as they omit to notice the great social and economic differences between *urbs Roma* and the towns in which the healers of the Hippocratic Corpus practised» (V. NUTTON, «Roman Medicine», 74).

[28] For further study of the indispensable influence which Greek medicine exerted over the Romans, see J. SCARBOROUGH, «Roman Medicine to Galen», especially section IV, «Greek Medicine and the Romans», 22-29, section VI, «Medicine in Everyday Life of the Roman Empire», 33-40 and section VII, «Learned Medicine and the Philosopher-Physicians», 40-48.

Now that which has come into existence must needs be of bodily form, visible and tangible; yet without fire nothing could ever become visible, nor tangible without some solidity, nor solid without earth. Hence, in beginning to construct the body of the All, God was making it of fire and earth. But it is not possible that two things alone should be conjoined without a third; for there must needs be some intermediary body to connect the two. And the fairest of bonds is that which most perfectly unites into one both itself and the things which it binds together; and to effect this in the fairest manner is the natural property of proportion. For whenever the middle term of any three numbers, cubic or square, is such that as the first term is to it, so is it to the last term, — and again, conversely, as the last term is to the middle, so is the middle to the first, — then the middle term becomes in turn the first and the last, while the first and last become in turn middle terms and the necessary consequence will be that all the terms are interchangeable and being interchangeable, they all form a unity. Now if the body of the All had to come into existence as a plane surface, having no depth, one middle term would have sufficed to bind together both itself and its fellow-terms; but now it is otherwise: for it behoved it to be solid of shape and what brings solids into unison is never one middle term alone but always two. Thus it was that in the midst between fires and earth God set water and air and having bestowed upon them so far as possible a like ratio one towards another — air being to water as fire to air and water being to earth as air to water, — he joined together and constructed a Heaven visible and tangible. For these reasons and out of these materials, such in kind and four in number, the body of the Cosmos was harmonized by proportion and brought into existence. These conditions secured for it Amity, so that being united in identity with itself it became indissoluble by any agent other than Him who had bound it together[29].

Plato was to make a profound impact on a young impressionable student who had come to Athens at the age of seventeen in order to study under him. That brilliant and inquisitive student, of course, was none other than Aristotle. The latter went on to found the Lyceum, humanity's first great center for the collection and organization of scientific data. It was there that Aristotle and Theophrastus, his associate and successor, produced their greatest works on the natural sciences[30].

---

[29] PLATO, *Timaeus*, 31 B–32 C.

[30] For more information on the contribution of Aristotle and Theophrastus to the study of botany, cf. M. CLAGETT, *Greek Science*, 63-70 and G. SARTON, *Ancient Science*, 546-558. For an excellent presentation of Aristotle's many works devoted to zoology, see

With this as a background, we are now in a position to examine the physical view which underpins Aristotle's natural science. First of all, it is essential to note that Aristotle distinguished between the terrestrial and celestial realms. In the terrestrial region, the four qualities, hot, cold, dry and moist, combine to form the four elements, fire, air, water and earth. In the celestial region, there is only one element, ether, of which all the heavenly bodies are composed[31].

We begin by surveying Aristotle's explanation of the primary manifestations of matter in form in the terrestrial realm.

3. Now since the elementary qualities are four in number and of these four six couples can be formed, but contraries are not of a nature which permits of their being coupled — for the same thing cannot be hot and cold, or again, moist and dry — it is clear that the pairs of elementary qualities will be four in number, hot and dry, hot and moist and, again, cold and moist and cold and dry. And, according to theory, they have attached themselves to the apparently simple bodies, Fire, Air, Water and Earth; for Fire is hot and dry, Air is hot and moist (Air, for example, is vapour), Water is cold and moist and Earth is cold and dry. Thus the variations are reasonably distributed among the primary bodies and the number of these is according to theory[32].

The four elements are arranged concentrically around the center of the universe. Earth, water, air and fire make up the successive spheres which precede outward from the center of the earth. Change happens when the elements are transformed into one another in an ongoing process of variation and metamorphosis. This process is called κρᾶσις, which is best translated by the English word blend[33]. Since each element seeks to return to its rightful

---

G. SARTON, *Ancient Science*, 529-545.

[31] See M. CLAGETT, *Greek Science*, 84-89.

[32] ARISTOTLE, *De generatione et corruptione*, 330 a 30–330 b 10.

[33] «(34) The notion of κρᾶσις (blend) was not invented by Aristotle, nor was he the last to make use of it. It is found in earlier philosophic writing and in the Hippocratic corpus and the term has given rise to such modern terms as temper, temperature and temperament. In the Hippocratic treatise π. διαίτης the theory is expounded that the human organism, body and "soul" alike, is compounded of Fire and Water (which means, ultimately, out of the hot, the cold, the solid and the fluid substances) and in ch. 35 of the first Book we find a list of the different varieties of the blend (κρῆσις, σύγκρησις) of Fire and Water which may be found in the "soul" of different individuals; upon this blend its health and sensitivity depend. A similar belief is found in Aristotle. At *P.A.* 650 b 28 we read that in an animal whose heart has a watery blend the way is already prepared for a timorous disposition. Man is the most intelligent animal: this proves his εὐκρασία — the excellence of his blend: the

place in the cosmos, nature remains in a constant state of movement, thanks primarily to the continuous movement of the heavenly spheres.

Hence Aristotle and indeed all those who shared his qualitative view on the nature of matter, believed that all material things change and develop. He was convinced that all elementary matter, whether animal, vegetable or mineral, developed in a physiological way. This in fact is precisely the opposite view of modern science, which of course holds that matter will tend to stay static and inert unless it is acted upon. For example, an elementary chemical substance like iron is inanimate and it will never develop like a living organism. Iron will stay iron unless it is oxidized and turned into rust. This basic distinction between biological development and physico-chemical change was firmly established only after 1780[34]! Given these completely different ways of looking at the phenomenon of change in the universe, it is no wonder why people today are often bewildered by the scientific treatises of the ancients.

What follows is a collection of brief excerpts from the works of Aristotle, Theophrastus and Galen. Each of them serves as an example of the expansive sweep of the qualitative theory of matter from the fifth century B.C. through the early centuries of our era.

– Aristotle on the generation of plants and animals:

---

heat in the heart is purest in man (G.A. 744 a 29)... (35) On the purely physical level, health depends upon κρᾶσις. Melancholics (i.e., those who have too much black bile) are always in need of medical attention, because their body is in a state of irritation owing to its blend (Eth. Nic. 1154 b 13). Health and well-being, says Aristotle, we consider to lie in the κρᾶσις and συμμετρία of hot things and cold, either with regard to each other or with regard to the surrounding environment (Phys. 246 b 4ff). The definition of health as the συμμετρία of hot things and cold is twice mentioned in the Topics (139 b 21, 145 b 8). Indeed, the nature of many things can ultimately be traced back to these two ἀρχαί (see § 12), the hot and the cold P.A. 648 a 24). In generation, says Aristotle, male and female need συμμετρία towards each other, because all that is produced by art or by nature exists in virtue of some due proportion (λόγῳ τινί ἐστιν): in this case, the heat must be σύμμετρος (G.A. 767 a 17ff.) and at 777 b 28 we read that heatings and coolings μέχρι συμμετρίας τινὸς ποιοῦσι τὰς γενέσεις, after that they produce dissolutions [...]» (A.L. PECK, «Notes on Terminology» in vol. I of his translation of Aristotle's Historia animalium, lxxv-lxxvi).

[34] For an excellent presentation of these perceptive insights into the whole question of matter theory, see S. TOULMIN and J. GOODFIELD, The Architecture of Matter, 21-22 and 124.

We find a feature which is common to animals as well as plants. Some plants come into being from seed produced by other plants, whereas some are spontaneously generated — i.e., when some seed-like «principle» has taken shape;   and of these spontaneously-generated plants, some derive their nourishment from the earth, while some come into being in other plants: this has been dealt with in my treatise on *Plants*. So also with animals: some come into being from animals whose natural form is of the same kind as their own; others spontaneously and not from animals of the same kind as themselves: and the latter are subdivided into (a) those which arise out of putrefying earth and plants, which is the case with many of the insects; and (b) those which arise inside animals themselves out of the residues in their parts[35].

– Aristotle on the generation of plants. The case of spontaneous generation when certain parts of the plant undergo decomposition:

The same sort of thing is found in plants too: some are formed our of seed, others as it might be by some spontaneous activity of Nature — they are formed when either the soil or certain parts in plants become putrescent, since some of them do not take shape independently on their own, but grow upon other trees, as for instance the mistletoe does[36].

– Aristotle on the three methods of generation for plants:

We must here apprehend the ways in which plants are generated. Some plants are formed from seed, some from slips planted out, others by sideshoots (*e.g.*, the onion tribe)[37].

– Aristotle on the spontaneous generation of plants:

Now as for plants, the manner in which those plants take shape which are generated spontaneously is uniform: they are formed from a part of something and some of it forms into the «principle», some into the first nourishment of the germinating plants[38].

---

[35] ARISTOTLE, *Historia animalium*, 539 a 16-25.
[36] ARISTOTLE, *De generatione animalium*, 715 b 26-30.
[37] ARISTOTLE, *De generatione animalium*, 761 b 27-30.
[38] ARISTOTLE, *De generatione animalium*, 762 b 18-21.

– The treatise *De plantis*[39] explains the natural and artificial transformation of various plants:

> VII. Some plants, we are told, are transformed into a different type when they grow old, like nuts. They say too that the catmint changes into the sweet-smelling variety and the hypericum if cut and planted by the sea will become thyme. They also say that corn and flax change into other species. The deadly nightshade which grows in Persia becomes fit to eat if transplanted to Egypt or Palestine. Similarly almonds and pomegranates change from their natural poorness to a better condition under cultivation. Pomegranates improve when pig manure is put on their roots and by drinking sweet cold water; almonds when nails are fastened into them and when gum exudes from the holes for a long space of time. By such treatment many wild plants become cultivated. Situation and cultivation contribute a great deal to these and particularly the season of the year which the planters most often choose. Most of the planting is done in the spring, a little in winter and autumn and least of all in the summer after the rising of the dog-star. Such planting is employed in few places and is only done very rarely, as in Rome, at this season. In Egypt planting is only done once a year[40].

– Aristotle on the elements. A body's material constitution corresponds to its environment:

> XIV. [...] As for the explanation which Empedocles gives, in a sense what he tries to establish is reasonable, but his account is not correct. For while those who suffer from excess of any condition find relief in places or seasons of a contrary nature, their constitution is best preserved in the region corresponding to it; for the matter of each individual animal is not the same thing as its states and dispositions. What I mean is this: if nature were to form anything out of wax, she would not preserve it by placing it in a hot atmosphere, nor if she had made a thing out of ice; for it would be rapidly destroyed by its contrary; for heat melts that which is constituted by its contrary. Nor if she made a thing out of salt or nitre would she have taken it and placed it in water; for water destroys that which is constituted by heat and dryness. If, then, the matter of which all bodies are composed is the wet and the dry, naturally that which is constituted of wet

---

[39]Although attributed to Aristotle, most scholars today recognize that he did not write this work, at least in its present form. Bekker's text, which has come down to us, represents a poor translation of a medieval Latin copy which was itself poorly translated from the Arabic. Hence the Greek text is often simply impossible to understand. Nevertheless this work was indeed known in Antiquity and for this reason an excerpt from it is included here.

[40] ARISTOTLE, *Scripta minora*. De plantis, 821 a 27–821 b 8.

are composed is the wet and the dry, naturally that which is constituted of wet and cold lives in water [and if it is cold, will live in the cold], but what is constituted of the dry will live in the dry. For this reason trees do not grow in water, but in the earth. Yet on the same theory he would assign them to the water because they are too dry, just as he says of the too fiery. On this theory they would enter water not because it is cold, but because it is wet.

Thus the material constitution of anything corresponds in fact to its environment; in water live wet things, in earth dry and in air hot. But the physical states which are excessively hot find greater relief in the cold and those that are excessively cold in the warm; for their environment neutralizes the excess of their state. The means to this end must be sought in the regions appropriate to each kind of matter and in the changes of the common seasons; for bodily states can be contrary to their environment, but matter cannot. Let this, then, suffice to show that it is not because of their natural heat, as Empedocles says, that some animals are aquatic and others terrestrial and to explain why some have lungs and some have not[41].

– Aristotle on the teaching that a particular creature comes from a particular seed:

Further, no abstraction can be studied by Natural science, because whatever Nature makes she makes to serve some purpose; for it is evident that, even as art is present in the objects produced by art, so in things themselves there is some principle or cause of a like sort, which came to us from the universe around us, just as our material constituents (the hot, the cold, etc.) did. Wherefore there is better reason for holding that the Heaven was brought into being by some such cause — if we may assume that it came into being at all — and that through that cause it continues to be, than for holding the same about the mortal things it contains — the animals; at any rate, there is much clearer evidence of definite ordering in the heavenly bodies than there is in us; for what is mortal bears the marks of change and chance. Nevertheless, there are those who affirm that, while every living creature has been brought into being by Nature and remains in being thereby, the heaven in all its glory was constructed by mere chance and came to be spontaneously, although there is no evidence of chance or disorder in it. And whenever there is evidently an End towards which a motion goes forward unless something stands in the way, then we always assert that the motion has the End for its purpose. From this it is evident that something of the kind really exists — that, in fact, which we call «Nature», **because in fact we do not find any chance**

---

[41] ARISTOTLE, *Parva naturalia*. De respiratione, 477 a 13–478 a 11.

creature being formed from a particular seed, but A comes from a and B from b; nor does any chance seed come from any individual. Therefore the individual from which the seed comes is the source and the efficient agent of that which comes out of the seed. The reason is, that these things are so arranged by Nature; at any rate, the offspring *grows* out of the seed. Nevertheless, logically prior to the seed stands that of which it is the seed, because the End is an actual thing and the seed is but a formative process. But further, prior to both of them stands the creature out of which the seed comes. (Note that a seed is the seed «of» something in two senses — as well as «of» that which it came — e.g. a horse — as well as «of» that which will arise out of itself — e.g. a mule). Again, the seed is something *by potentiality* and we know what is the relation of potentiality to actuality[42]. [italics added by Peck, bold by this author]

It is important to pay careful attention to Aristotle's teaching on the connection of a particular seed to a particular body. Unfortunately, Peck translated σῶμα as «individual», and not «body», so the force of the original Greek has been lost in his translation. Here is the original text of the passage which is found above in bold type: οὐ γὰρ δὴ ὅ τι ἔτυχεν ἐξ ἑκάστου γίνεται σπέρματος, ἀλλὰ τόδε ἐκ τοῦδε, οὐδὲ σπέρμα τὸ τυχὸν ἐκ τοῦ τυχόντος σώματος.

– Aristotle on the generation of human beings:

Hence, too, with the generation of human beings and quadrupeds, if once upon a time they were «earthborn» as some allege, one might assume them to be formed in one of these two ways — either it would be by a larva taking shape to begin with, or else they were formed out of eggs, since of necessity they must either contain the nourishment for their growth within themselves (and a fetation of this sort is a larva) or they must get it from elsewhere and that means either from the female parent or from part of the fetation [...][43]

In a note on this curious text, Peck, the translator, points out that the belief that human beings were born of earth is old and traditional.

– Aristotle's Understanding of the Reproduction of Animals:

For Aristotle, the various kinds of soul, ψυχή, have to do with some kind of physical substance which is found in the semen of all animals. In fact, animal semen contains a hot substance, the so-called θερμόν which makes it

---

[42] ARISTOTLE, *De partibus animalium*, 641 b 11–642 a 1.
[43] ARISTOTLE, *De generatione animalium*, 762 b 28-35.

other earthly elements, since it does not contain the principle of life, the ζωτικὴ ἀρχή. Rather, semen contains a physical substance called πνεῦμα which is analogous to ether, the celestial element that makes up the stars.

Now so far as we can see, the faculty of Soul of every kind has to do with some physical substance which is different from the so-called «elements» and more divine than they are; and as the varieties of soul differ from one another in the scale of value, so do the various substances concerned with them differ in their nature. In all cases the semen contains within itself that which causes it to be fertile — what is known as «hot» substance, which is not fire nor any similar substance, but the *pneuma* which is enclosed within the semen or foam-like stuff and the natural substance which is in the *pneuma*; and this substance is analogous to the element which belongs to the stars. That is why fire does not generate any animal and we find no animal taking shape either in fluid or solid substances while they are under the influence of fire; whereas the heat of the sun does effect generation and so does the heat of animals and not only the heat of animals which operates through the semen, but also any other natural residue which there may be has within it a principle of life. Considerations of this sort show us that the heat which is in animals is not fire and does not get its origin or principle from fire.

Consider now the physical part of the semen. (This it is which, when it is emitted by the male, is accompanied by the portion of soul-principle and acts as its vehicle. Partly this soul-principle is separable from physical matter — this applies to those animals where some divine element is included and what we call Reason is of this character — partly it is inseparable.) This physical part of the semen, being fluid and watery, dissolves and evaporates; and on that account we should not always be trying to detect it leaving the female externally, or to find it as an ingredient of the fetation when that has set and taken shape, any more than we should expect to trace the fig-juice which sets and curdles milk. The fig-juice undergoes a change; it does not remain as a part of the bulk which is set and curdled; and the same applies to the semen.

We have now determined in what sense fetations and semen have Soul and in what sense they have not. They have soul *potentially*, but not *in actuality*[44].

Hence semen is a kind of foam-like substance which contains both water and πνεῦμα, that latter being a substance similar in nature to ether. There is a kind of heat in all πνεῦμα which Aristotle calls «soul-heat».

---

[44] ARISTOTLE, *De generatione animalium*, 736 b 30–737 a 18.

Animals and plants are formed in the earth and in the water because in earth water is present and in water *pneuma* is present and in all *pneuma* soul-heat is present, so that in a way all things are full of soul; and that is why they quickly take shape once it has been enclosed[45].

In short, the πνεῦμα acts as an instrument of the ψυχή in the generation of new life.

– Theophrastus, *De causis plantarum*, on the several modes of generation of plants:

That plants have several modes of generation has been said earlier in the *History*, where we have also enumerated and described them. Since not all occur in all plants, it is proper to distinguish the modes that occur in the different groups and give the reasons why, resting the explanations on the special character of the plant, for the explanations must first of all accord with the account given there.

(1) From Seed

Generation from seed is common to all plants that have seed, since all seeds are able to generate. That they do so is not only evident to sense, but in theory too it is perhaps a necessary conclusion: nature not only does nothing in vain but does so least of all in what immediately serves her aims and is decisive for their achievement; now the seed has this immediacy and decisiveness; hence the seed, if unable to generate, would be in vain, since it is always aimed at generation and produced by nature to achieve it.

That all seed are able to generate we can set down as a point of general agreement by all but a few persons. But because with some plants farmers do not use the seed (since the plant matures more rapidly from spontaneous growths and again because in some it is difficult to secure the seed, seeds of trees as well as of herbaceous plants), some growers for these reasons are not quite convinced that it is possible for plants to come from seed. And yet, in the case of the willow (as was said in the *History*) production from seed is in fact quite evident.

(2) From «Spontaneous» Growth

Seed-bearing plants come up in still another way when some spontaneous growth arises somewhere from the collecting of a pool and from decomposition (or rather when a natural alteration occurs).

Now it is evident that generation through the seed is common to all; and if some are generated in both ways, spontaneously as well as by seed, there is no

---

[45] ARISTOTLE, *De generatione animalium*, 762 a 19-22.

absurdity: so some animals similarly come from two sources, both from other animals and from the earth[46].

Note that in the first paragraph, «the special character of the plant» ταῖς κατὰ τὰς ἰδίας οὖσις could also be translated as «the distinctive essences or natures of the plant». For Theophrastus, as for Aristotle, every plant enjoys its own unique nature since it is formed from a singular mixture of the elements that make up bodies in the terrestrial realm.

– Theophrastus repeats this point again at the end of Book II of *De causis plantarum*:

> In dealing with all other occurrences in trees or plants we must endeavor to start with the study of the trees, taking as our bases the distinctive nature of each and the nature of the country, since from these bases the common affections and the differences between kinds and what comports with and is appropriate to each kind become evident. We must also be able to discern what is merely similar and what is identical, since many occurrences that differ are considered not to do so, as in other matters[47].

The most important figure in ancient medicine after Hippocrates was Galen (129-200 A.D.)[48]. One of the greatest medical authorities in antiquity, he produced an enormous corpus of medical and scientific treatises which would come to make a profound impact on medicine in the Middle Ages. It is important to note that Galen came to the practice of medicine thanks to his study of philosophy[49]. This background allowed him to excel in what he did best, namely, the articulation of his medical theory. He, too, finds a place in this long line of adherents to the qualitative theory of matter, thereby showing the continuation of this view of matter in the second century after Christ.

– Galen on the four interacting qualities and his statement on the complete alteration of substances:

---

[46] THEOPHRASTUS, *De causis plantarum*, I 1.1–1.2.

[47] THEOPHRASTUS, *De causis plantarum*, II 19.6.

[48] For an excellent summary of Galen's life and work, see G.E.R. LLOYD, *Greek Science after Aristotle*, 136-153.

[49] For more information on Galen's formative years as a student of philosophy and more specifically, his later contributions to the study of drugs and drug therapy as a means of balancing the four humors of the human body (earth, air, water and fire), see J.M. RIDDLE, «High Medicine and Low Medicine in the Roman Empire», 113-117.

[...] In fact, of all those known to us who have been both physicians and philosophers Hippocrates was the first who took in hand to demonstrate that there are, in all, four mutually interacting *qualities* and that to the operation of these is due the genesis and destruction of all things that come into and pass out of being. Nay, more; Hippocrates was also the first to recognise that all these qualities undergo an intimate mingling with one another; and at least the beginnings of the proofs to which Aristotle later set his hand are to be found first in the writings of Hippocrates.

As to whether we are to suppose that the *substances* as well as their *qualities* undergo this intimate mingling, as Zeno of Citium afterwards declared, I do not think it necessary to go further into this question in the present treatise; for immediate purposes we only need to recognize the *complete alteration of substance*. In this way, nobody will suppose that bread represents a kind of meeting-place for bone, flesh, nerve and all the other parts and that each of these subsequently becomes separated in the body and goes to join its own kind; before any separation takes place, the whole of the bread obviously becomes blood; (at any rate, if a man takes no other food for a prolonged period, he will have blood enclosed in his veins all the same). And clearly this disproves the view of those who consider the elements unchangeable, as also, for that matter, does the oil which is entirely used up in the flame of the lamp, or the faggots which, in a somewhat longer time, turn into fire[50].

Galen also wrote extensively on the anatomy and physiology of animal reproduction. If it is true that his views about the reproductive organs and the development of the fetus can be found in many of his works (e.g., De uteri dissectione and De foetuum formatione), his scientific theories on procreation are nevertheless most clearly and forcefully put forth in his book *De Semine*. In this important treatise Galen does not intend to give a systematic account of the scientific theories of those who preceded him; rather, he develops his own understanding of how both the male and female make essential contributions to the formulation of the fetus and the surrounding membranes. Although he refutes many of Aristotle's positions, Galen nevertheless owes much to his master and quotes him with great respect and admiration. What follows are three brief excerpts from this important work.

– Galen on the use and power of semen:

---

[50] GALEN, *De naturalibus facultatibus,* I.II.5-6.

1. What is the use and what is the power of semen? Is it to reckoned as two principles, the material and the active, as Hippocrates supposed, or only one of them, the efficient, as in the opinion of Aristotle, who holds that it provides a beginning of motion for the menstrual blood but does not grant that any part of the animal is formed from it? The matter deserves to be investigated and the disagreement of such great men adjudicated, not by recourse to plausible arguments, which the majority of physicians and philosophers delight in, but by a demonstration that begins from and proceeds through what is clearly evident. And since Aristotle too believes that the premises for demonstrations should be taken from experience pertinent to each matter under investigation, let us first examine closely the following point: whether the semen remains within the one who is about to become pregnant or whether it too is voided[51].

– Galen's attack on those who misrepresent Aristotle's views:

3. I have mentioned these matters on account of certain present-day philosophers who give themselves the name of Aristotelians and Peripatetics. For my part, I would not call them by those names; they are so ignorant of Aristotle's view that they think he held that the male semen which is injected into the uterus of the female imparts a beginning motion to the menstrual blood but is thereupon excreted, becoming no part of the bodily substance of the fetus. They have been misled by the first book (of the treatise) On the Generation of Animals, which alone of the five they appear to me to have read. It contains the following passage: «For as we said, one might posit as not the least principles of generation the female and the male, the male as having the principle of motion and generation, the female (the principle) of matter». This passage is not far from the beginning. Further on in the work he also writes as follows: «But it happens as is reasonable, since the male provides the form and the principle of motion and the female the body and the matter, just as in the curdling of milk the milk is the body and the fig-juice or rennet is that which possesses the coagulation principle». Taking their start from these passages, some think that after the semen has provided to the menstrual blood the principle of motion it is in turn ejected again; but some (of them) assert that he does not say what all of us who take his words in the natural way thought he was saying, but rather that the female contributes only matter to the fetus-to-be, whereas the male contributes matter and also form. So one of them thought us utterly ridiculous if we should suppose that (on Aristotle's view) the semen is discharged back again to the outside by the female, or that while remaining within it is dissolved into nothing. For this,

---

[51] GALEN, De semine, I 1,1-3.

they say, is what follows if we think that its bodily substance is not mixed and blended with the matter of the fetus[52].

– Galen's refutation of Aristotle's position that the body of the semen is dispersed and evaporates:

4. Let us now leave those who are Aristotelians in name but in reality fall so short that they do not even understand what he wrote in the first or the second book On the Generation of Animals; let us return to Aristotle himself and his claim that the semen «is dispersed and evaporates» in the uterus. If we assume that it somehow evaporates in the way in which we know that moisture changes to air in new wine, then a very large amount of air will be formed from a very small amount of liquid substance. This is seen also in the case of the winds that blow from rivers or lakes or from the sea, for example the so-called gulf breezes and sea breezes. Sometimes they blow in very great volume, as if their substance became most plentiful from the smallest amount of moisture. And indeed even land breezes, as they are called, point to this same thing; winds of this kind blow when the moisture in the earth has been quite suddenly dissolved into air. Why then, if at the beginning of conception the semen evaporates, is the uterus observed at that time to be smaller and less windy, wrapped tightly about the fetus on all sides? For surely, just as we observe the flatulent stomach to be swollen and distended to the greatest degree, we ought to see the uterus, too, increased in size and feeling pain because of the distention. But clearly that does not happen here; the uterus is contracted and without pain. And if a person is willing to dissect an animal that has recently conceived, he will see the uterus closely surrounding the semen. Furthermore, no expelled air appears at the female pudendum, as happens in the case of a flatulent stomach, when eructations and the passing of wind downward empty it of air and reduce the swelling. Therefore we have nothing even slightly persuasive to say as proof of the view that the semen evaporates, no (emissions of) wind outward through the neck of the uterus, no evident mass remaining within, no distention or pain perceptible to the one that has begun the pregnancy[53].

Galen next goes on to give his position on the question: for him, the semen forms out of itself a membrane which is joined to the uterus at the mouth of the uterine blood vessels. Hence Galen's formulation represents an important step forward in the Greek understanding of the reproductive process. By refuting

---

[52] GALEN, De semine, I 3,1-8.
[53] GALEN, De semine, I 4,1-11.

Aristotle, he correctly advanced the theory in his treatise *De Semine* that the male does in fact contribute indispensable material in the formation of the fetus.

4.3 *On Creation and Perishability*

From the very dawn of Greek thought, philosophers had reflected on the antithesis between γίγνεσθαι, «to come to be», and its antithesis φθείρεσθαι, «to perish», «to be destroyed». In their attempt to understand the visible world, these outstanding thinkers came to believe that matter underwent an ongoing process of creation and dissolution. As we saw above in the presentation on ancient Greek biology, Aristotle had posited the ongoing transformation of the four terrestrial elements.

> We maintain that fire, air, water and earth are transformable one into another and that each is potentially latent in the others, as is true of all other things that have a single common substratum underlying them into which they can in the last resort be resolved[54].

This is in fact a brief summary of his position as presented earlier in *De generatione et corruptione* ii. 1,4 and *De caelo* iii. 6,7[55].

Yet even before Aristotle, the pre-Socratics had struggled with this fundamental question in their attempt to understand their own lives and indeed, the very existence of the universe[56]. What endures in this life and what changes? What stays the same and what undergoes alteration? What lasts and what passes away? Every philosopher approached the question in his own way. Theagenes claimed that what abides is the all as such, while the parts are perishable. Xenophanes, as quoted by Diogenes, claimed that all that has come to be is perishable. Parmenides, as reported by Plutarch, held that what can be perceived only with the intellect is eternal and incorruptible. Empedocles, for his part, believed that the elements are that which endures. Epiphanius in his treatise *De Fide* claimed that Melissus was concerned with proving the phenomenon of corruptibility in nature. For Heraclitus, what endures is movement. And for Anaximander, the infinite is the cause of creation and

---

[54] ARISTOTLE, *Meteorologica*, 339 a 37–339 b 2.

[55] For a fine explanation of Aristotle's teaching on change in the physical world, see G.E.R. LLOYD, *Magic, Reason and Experience*, 207-210.

[56] For an excellent summary of the philosophical usage of the Greek words which express perishability, see G. HARDER, «φθείρω, φθορά, φθαρτός», in *ThWNT*.

perishability. What all these philosophers share in common is the desire to know what endures in the midst of the continuous changes going on in nature.

If one truly seeks to understand the apex of Greek thinking on the question of the corruptible and the incorruptible, then one must turn to Aristotle. This is in fact the task he sets for himself in one of his earlier works, *De generatione et corruptione*. The book begins in this way.

> 1. In discussing coming-to-be and passing away of things which by nature come-to-be and pass-away, as exhibited uniformly wherever they occur, we must distinguish their causes and definitions; further, we must deal with «growth» and «alteration», and inquire what each of these means and whether we are to suppose that the nature of «alteration» and coming-to-be is the same, or whether each is of a separate nature corresponding to the names by which they are distinguished[57].

Forster's translation of γένεσις and φθορά as «coming-to-be» and «passing-away» is excellent. He captures the true meaning of the Greek terms in this way, thus showing a fine appreciation for Aristotle's philosophical insights into the nature of change in the universe. These English terms express the movement which Aristotle wants to convey in his description of the act of becoming and ceasing to be.

While it is not our purpose in this brief section to attempt a complete summary of this philosopher's understanding of coming-to-be and passing-away, nevertheless it is crucial that we examine the essential distinction made by Aristotle between coming-to-be and alteration. To this end, it is worth our while to refer to the philosopher's own words on the matter. Here is Book I, Chapter 4 of *De generatione et corruptione*.

> 4. Let us now deal with coming-to-be and «alteration» and discuss the difference between them; for we say these forms of change differ from one another. Since then, the substratum is one thing and the property which is of such a nature as to be predicated of the substratum is another thing and since change takes place in each of these, «alteration» occurs when the substratum, which is perceptible, persists, but there is change in its properties, which are either directly or intermediately contrary to one another; for example, the body is healthy and then again sick, though it persists in being the same body and the bronze is spherical and then again angular, remaining the same bronze. But when

---

[57] ARISTOTLE, *De generatione et corruptione*, 314 a 1-6.

the thing as a whole changes, nothing perceptible persisting as identical substratum (for example, when the seed as a whole is converted into blood, or water into air, or air as a whole into water), such a process is a coming-to-be — and a passing-away of the other substance — particularly if the change proceeds from something imperceptible to something perceptible (either to touch or to all the senses), as when water comes-to-be out of, or passes away into, air; for air is pretty well imperceptible. But if, in these circumstances, any property belonging to a pair of contraries persists in being the same in the thing which has come-to-be as it was in the thing which has passed-away — if, for instance, when water comes-to-be out of air, both are transparent or cold — that into which it changes is not necessarily another property of this thing; otherwise the change will be «alteration». For example, the musical man passed-away and an unmusical man came-to-be, but the man persists as identically the same. Now if musicality (and unmusicality) were not in itself a property of man, there would be a coming-to-be of the one and passing-away of the other; therefore, these are qualities of a man, but the coming-to-be and the passing-away of a musical man and of an unmusical man; but, in fact, musicality (and unmusicality) are a quality of the persistent identity. Consequently such changes are «alteration».

When, therefore, the change from one contrary to another is quantitative, it is «growth and diminution»; when it is change of place, it is «motion»; when it is a change of property (or quality), it is «alteration»; but when nothing persists of which the resulting state is a property or an accident of any kind, it is a case of coming-to-be and the contrary change is a passing-away. Matter, in the chief and strictest sense of the word, is the substratum which admits of coming-to-be and passing-away; but the substratum of the other kind of change is also in a sense matter, because all the substrata admit if certain kinds of contrariety. Let this, then, be our decision on the question about coming-to-be, whether it exists or not and how it exists and about «alteration» [58].

For our purposes, the most important point of this entire chapter is found in Aristotle's understanding of change: alteration ἀλλοίωσις is a change of *quality*, while coming-to-be/passing-away γένεσις/φθορά represents a change of *the thing as a whole*. Hence Aristotle's fundamental distinction on the nature of change sheds some important light on the tension between continuity and discontinuity in being, matter and indeed, all living things.

Lastly, Aristotle held that nothing can cause its own γένεσις and φθορά. All κίνησις (which is most often translated into English as «movement»,

---

[58] ARISTOTLE, *De generatione et corruptione*, 319 b 6–320 a 8.

although «change» gets closer to Aristotle's primary meaning) can be traced back to an Unmoved Mover.

> From what has been said, it is evident that coming-to-be and passing-away take place and why this is so, if there is to be movement, there must, as has been explained elsewhere in an earlier treatise, be something which causes movement and if movement is to go on always and, if it is to be continuous, that which causes it must be one and the same and unmoved, ungenerated and unalterable [...][59].

Aristotle's famous Unmoved Mover, by its very nature, was not susceptible to change or alteration of any kind. As the one who set the cosmos in motion, he remained free from the world's ongoing process of passing-away and coming-into-being[60]. This significant insight, one which represents a fundamental pillar of Aristotle's metaphysics, was of course readily adopted by Jews and Christians in order to explain the incorruptible, immutable and transcendent nature of God.

4.4 *Astronomy*

From the beginning of recorded history, human beings have been telling stories about the sky and looking to it to give meaning and structure to their lives. The cyclical motion of the heavenly bodies reflects an extraordinary harmony and regularity of movement, a remarkable orderliness which is so often lacking in the course of human events. The regular return of the sun at dawn, the rising of the full moon on a certain day, or the particular appearance of a planet immediately after sunset — these and other similar events helped human beings develop a uniform notion of time. In this way, the steady movement of the heavenly bodies aided in bring a certain regularity down to earth: every recorded civilization in antiquity adopted its own particular calendar with a unique partition of hours, days, months and years. The Greeks of course were not indifferent to this celestial phenomena and from the earliest

---

[59] ARISTOTLE, *De generatione et corruptione*, 337 a 19-21.

[60] Did Aristotle posit the existence of only one unmoved mover, or many? Scholars are still discussing the stages of development of his theology, as well as his final teaching on the unmoved mover as first cause. This debate, although quite fascinating, lies outside the scope of this excursus. For further reading, see W.K.C. GUTHRIE, *Aristotle*, 252-276.

period recognized a certain order in the universe. It was for this reason that
they named the universe ὁ κόσμος, their word for good order or behavior[61].

Greek mythology as recorded in Homer and Hesiod helps shed some light
on what the ancient Greeks believed about the heavens. They imagined an
underworld below the earth, heavens above it and a cosmic axis which
oriented the whole universe. Over time, thanks largely to the contributions of
the philosophers, mathematical ideas were introduced to the discussion[62]. By
the time of Socrates, then, the Greeks had established a common language with
which they could describe celestial phenomena and speculate as to both its
origins and purpose.

The founder of scientific astronomy in Greece was Eudoxus of Cnidos
(c.408-355 B.C.)[63]. A contemporary of Plato, he had studied at the academy
and learned Pythagorean astronomy. Later, he traveled extensively in the East,
spending a total of sixteen months in Egypt under the tutelage of learned
priests. He gained a great deal of knowledge about Egyptian observations and
had an observatory built for himself between Heliopolis and Cercesura. Once
back in his native Cnidos, he had another observatory built where he studied
the star Canopus. Although he never traveled to Mesopotamia, he was familiar
with many ancient theories which had their origin in Persian, Chaldean, or
Babylonian astronomy.

Eudoxus' most important achievement, however, was entirely his own. His
theory of the homocentric spheres insured him a lasting place in the history of
science. In order to account for the erratic trajectory of the planets (for the
observer on earth, of course, they seem to progress, stop and then sometimes
go in reverse), he came up with a mathematical explanation in order «to save
the phenomena», to use his own expression. Thus he proposed the existence
of twenty-seven concentric spheres, each turning at a particular speed on a
particular axis. In this way he explained the motion of the heavenly bodies. His
theory of homocentric spheres is truly brilliant, for it was the first genuine
attempt to explain the movement of the stars and planets with the help of
mathematics. Although his data was imperfect and his calculations imprecise,
nevertheless Eudoxus is rightly remembered as one of the greatest astronomers
of antiquity and indeed, of all time.

---

[61] See E.C. KRUPP, *Beyond the Blue Horizon*, 275.
[62] See E.C. KRUPP, *Beyond the Blue Horizon*, 278-279.
[63] See G. SARTON, *Ancient Science*, 447-449.

Euxodus was a younger contemporary of Plato and the two certainly had an effect on each other during their time at the Academy. While the former constructed his theories on observations and rationalism, the latter based his astronomic knowledge on out-of-date Pythagorean theories which agreed with his philosophy. Nevertheless, Plato's astronomy did make its mark in the ancient world, not only in the fourth century B.C. but also with the rise of neo-Platonism in the Byzantine period[64].

In the *Republic*, Plato attempted to show how human beings could construct a moral and political system. In the *Timaeus*, he tries to link such an ideal republic to the organization of the cosmos[65]. This is Plato's account of the generation of time and the creation of the celestial bodies.

Time, then, came into existence along with the Heaven, to the end that having been generated together they might also be dissolved together, if ever a dissolution of them should take place; and it was made after the pattern of the Eternal Nature, to the end that it might be as like thereto as possible; for whereas the pattern is existent through all eternity, the copy, on the other hand, is through all time, continually having existed, existing and being about to exist. Wherefore, as a consequence of this reasoning and design on the part of God, with a view to the generation of Time, the sun and moon and five other stars, which bear the appellation of «planets», came into existence for the determining and preserving of the numbers of Time. And when God had made the bodies of each of them He placed them in the orbits along with the revolution of the Other was moving, seven orbits for the seven bodies. The Moon He placed in the first circle around the Earth, the Sun in the second above the Earth; and the Morning Star and the Star called Sacred to Hermes He placed in those circles which move in an orbit equal to the Sun in velocity, but endowed with a power contrary thereto; whence it is that the Sun and the Star of Hermes and the Morning Star regularly overtake and are overtaken by one another. As to the rest of the stars, were one to describe in detail the positions in which He set them and all the reasons therefor, the

---

[64] «The success of Plato's astronomy, like that of his mathematics, was due to a series of misunderstandings: the philosophers believed that he had obtained his results by the aid of his mathematical genius; the mathematicians did not like to discuss the same results because they ascribed them to his metaphysical genius. He was speaking in riddles and nobody dared to admit that he did not understand him for fear of being considered a poor mathematician or a poor metaphysician. Almost everybody was deceived, either by his own ignorance and conceit or by his subservience to fatuous authorities. The Platonic tradition is very largely a chain of prevarications» (G. SARTON, *Ancient Science*, 451).

[65] See G. SARTON, *Ancient Science*, 421.

description, though but subsidiary, would prove a heavier task than the main argument which it subserves. Later on, perhaps, at our leisure these points may receive the attention they merit[66].

For Plato, then, the universe can be compared to a living body composed of four elements, there being no distinction between the matter that makes up earthly or heavenly bodies. He asserts that the properties of matter can be matched to geometrical principles[67]. The soul of the cosmos is similar to that of a human being, since both are divine and immortal. As for the planets and stars, they represent the most magnificent representations of the eternal Ideas. In this sense, they are similar to the gods. The movements of the stars is an expression of divine mathematics which can be glimpsed in music and the theory of numbers. When a human being dies, his soul returns to his native star[68].

In the meantime, the homocentric theory of Eudoxus had been adopted by the two great minds of the Lyceum, Callippus and Aristotle. The former had opted to specialize in astronomic research, while the latter preferred his own research into zoology, all the while developing his expertise in logic and philosophy. Callipus of Cyzicos (born in c.370 B.C., his date of death is uncertain) had most probably met Eudoxus in his youth, the great man having made a profound impression on him[69]. At any rate, Callipus was thoroughly familiar with his master's scientific teaching when he settled in Athens at the beginning of Alexander's reign in 336. In an effort to improve the homocentric theory, he added seven more spheres, thus arriving at a total of thirty-three concentric spheres in his understanding of the cosmos. Each of these rotated on its own axis and at its own rate. Yet again, a Greek scientist was able «to save the phenomena».

By following in the footsteps of these great astronomers, Aristotle would attempt to do the same. Not content with their geometric solution, Aristotle came up with a mechanical one that he thought solved the problem of the erratic movement of the planets. For him, there are three kinds of movement in space: 1) rectilinear, 2) circular and 3) mixed. This notion of the movement of bodies had a profound effect on his theories in astronomy, as we shall see

---

[66] PLATO, *Timaeus*, 38 B–E.
[67] PLATO, *Timaeus*, 53 Cff.
[68] PLATO, *Timaeus*, 42 B.
[69] See G. SARTON, *Ancient Science*, 508.

below. What follows is a brief presentation of Aristotle's teaching on the heavens, based in large part on his own work which bares that name[70].

Aristotle shared the belief of his age with regard to the nature and purpose of the celestial bodies. Rather than considering the stars and planets to be made up of inorganic and inanimate matter, as of course we do today, the master of the Lyceum believed that they enjoyed the best and most independent life of all the bodies in the universe. Hence the heavenly bodies are not merely alive, but they also unchanging and therefore, eternal.

> The fact is that we are inclined to think of the stars as mere bodies or units, occurring in a certain order but completely lifeless; whereas we ought to think of them as partaking of life and initiative[71].

For Aristotle, then, the heavens and the heavenly bodies are composed of the fifth element, ether, whose natural movement is circular and whose matter is free from change and corruption[72].

A brief and helpful summary of Aristotle's cosmology is found at the beginning of the first Book of *Meteorologica*. Here is his understanding of the matter which makes up the heavens and the earth.

> We have previously laid down that the there is one element from which the natural bodies in circular motion are made up and four other physical bodies produced by the primary qualities, the motions of these bodies being twofold, either away from or towards the centre. These four bodies are fire, air, water and earth: of them fire always rises to the top, earth always sinks to the bottom, while the other two bear to each other a mutual relation similar to that of fire and earth — for air is the nearest of all to fire, water to earth. The whole terrestrial region, then, is composed of these four bodies and it is the conditions which effect them which, we have said, are the subject of our inquiry. This region must be continuous with the motions of the heavens, which therefore regulate its whole capacity for movement: for the celestial element as source of all motion must be regarded as first cause. (Besides, the celestial element is eternal and moves in a path that is spatially endless but always complete, while the terrestrial bodies have each their distinct and limited regions). Fire, earth and the kindred elements must therefore be regarded as the material cause of all sublunary events (for we

---

[70] See G. SARTON, *Ancient Science*, 509-511.

[71] ARISTOTLE, *De caelo*, 292 a 19-22.

[72] For concise and informative presentations on Aristotle's theory of the heavens, cf. G. SARTON, *Ancient Science*, 509-511 and M.J. CROWE, *Theories of the World*, 26-27.

call the passive subject of change the material cause): while the driving power of the eternally moving bodies must be their cause in the sense of the ultimate source of their motion[73].

There is, therefore, a sharp distinction between the elements in the celestial and terrestrial realms. Ether is not found in the sublunary regions since it is more divine than the four terrestrial elements.

From all these premises therefore it clearly follows that there exists some physical substance besides the four in our sublunary world and moreover that it is more divine than and prior to, all these. The same can also be proved on the further assumption that all motion is either natural or unnatural and that motion which is unnatural to one body is natural to another and the motions of up and down are natural or unnatural to fire and earth respectively; from these it follows that circular motion too, since it is unnatural to these elements, is natural to some other [...]

Thus the reasoning from all our premises goes to make us believe that there is some other body separate from those around us here and of a higher nature in proportion as it is removed from the sublunary world[74].

In spite of their many differences, however, ether is similar to the terrestrial elements in as much as both can produce living creatures. There are heavenly bodies and earthly bodies and the quality of the former far excels that of the latter due to the striking difference in the make-up of their respective elements.

Even though the celestial element is found by definition only in the heavens, we must not conclude that it is somehow immaterial or incorporeal. In Aristotle's universe, the contrary is true. For him, ether is in fact a physical substance[75]. In short, ether is not, in our modern usage of the term, «ethereal».

---

[73] ARISTOTLE, *Meteorologica*, I. II.

[74] ARISTOTLE, *De caelo*, 269 a 30–269 b 17.

[75] «The overriding motive for the postulation of the fifth substance, the aether, was to give a physical foundation to the basic assumption of the incorruptibility and stability of heavenly phenomena, in contrast to the perpetual change and fluctuation of sublunar events. Within the strongly classified dynamical system of Aristotle this could only be achieved through the uniqueness attributed to the physical and kinetic properties of aether. This was easily arranged from the physical point of view by assigning to this substance those qualities of an unchangeable, immutable, sublime material that are lacking in the four other elements which are constantly being destroyed and regenerated. The aether was in fact the embodiment of that highest degree of perfection attainable by matter which can be achieved only in the celestial region» (S. SAMBURSKY, *The Physical World of Late Antiquity*, 124).

Superior in nature to the terrestrial elements due to its divine and hence indestructible nature, ether was to the ancients a material element present in the cosmos[76]. Thanks to its superior qualities, Aristotle calls ether «the first of the elements» τὸ πρῶτον τῶν στοιχείων (*Heavens* 298 b 6) and «the primary body» τὸ πρῶτον σῶμα (*Heavens* 270 b 21)[77]. Moreover it is also important to note that, when speaking of ether, Aristotle uses the words «element» and «body» as synonyms. It is the element which composes the heavenly bodies and so it is not possible to speak of one without mentioning the other.

Hence in Aristotle's model of the cosmos we have a further development of the theory of homocentric spheres. If we were to take an imaginary trip through the universe, going outward from its center towards its outermost edge, we would first encounter the fixed levels of the sublunary world, namely, the four spheres for earth, water, air and fire. Next we would find the celestial realm composed of ether. First comes the «inner heavens» which are composed of interconnecting concentric spheres whose movement is eternal and continuous. Again going outward from the earth, we find first the moon, then Mercury, Venus, the sun, Mars, Jupiter and lastly Saturn[78]. Beyond these heavenly bodies lies the «first heaven» or outermost sphere in which the fixed stars are located. Beyond this last sphere lies the ultimate source of all movement, the Unmoved Mover, who moves the first heaven yet himself remains unmoved.

But what precisely does Aristotle understand by the word «heaven»? He gives three different meanings, each of which must be distinguished from the other two.

This therefore remains to be demonstrated, that our world is composed of the whole sum of natural perceptible body. Let us first establish what we mean by *ouranos* and in how many senses the word is used, in order that we may more clearly understand the object of our questions. (1) In one sense we apply the word *ouranos* to the substance of the outermost circumference of the world, or to the natural body which is at the outermost circumference of the world; for it is customary to give the name of *ouranos* especially to the outermost and

---

[76] Cf. ARISTOTLE, *De caelo*, 269 a 31ff., 270 a 12ff. and 270 b 10ff.

[77] It is not accurate to speak of ether as being the fifth element, as some modern writers do. For Aristotle, ether represents the first element since it is closer in nature to the divine than those four elements which are found on earth.

[78] See E.C. KRUPP, *Beyond the Blue Horizon*, 185.

uppermost region, in which also we believe all divinity to have its seat. (2) Secondly we apply it to that body which occupies the next place to the outermost circumference of the world, in which are the moon and the sun and certain of the stars; for these, we say, are in the *ouranos*. (3) We apply the word in yet another sense to the body which is enclosed by the outermost circumference; for it is customary to give the name of *ouranos* to the world as a whole[79].

Hence the Greek word οὐρανός has three different meanings. There is no single word in English which conveys all three senses and so we must alternate between «world» or «the heavens» or «sky» in an attempt to grasp Aristotle's meaning. We must keep in mind, however, that for Aristotle all three meanings are closely interconnected in as much as the substance in the sky which composes the heavens is the οὐρανός.

Thus for Aristotle, heaven is a divine body.

Now since there exists no circular motion which is the opposite of another, the question must be asked why there are several different revolutions although we are far away from the object of our attempted inquiry, not in the obvious sense of distance in space, but rather because very few of their attributes are perceptible to our senses. Yet we must say what we can. If we are to grasp their cause, we must start from this, that everything which has a function exists for the sake of that function. The activity of a god is immortality, that is, eternal life. Necessarily, therefore, the divine must be in eternal motion. And since the heaven is of this nature (*i.e.* is a divine body), that is why it has its circular body, which by nature moves forever in a circle[80].

In addition, ether's motion is always circular and so is that of the stars, since they are composed of it.

It falls to us next to speak of the bodies called stars, of what elements they are composed and what are their shapes and movements. The most logical and consistent hypothesis is to make each star consist of the body in which it moves, since we have maintained that there is a body whose nature it is to move in a circle. Thus we adopt the same line of argument as those who say that the stars are of fire, for their reason is that they call the uppermost body fire and think it

---

[79] ARISTOTLE, *De caelo*, 278 b 8-22. In a note, Guthrie (transl.) points out that the «certain of the stars» ἔνια τῶν ἄστρων is a reference to the planets, since the fixed stars are in the first heaven.

[80] ARISTOTLE, *De caelo*, 286 a 3-13.

logical that each individual thing should consist of those elements in which it has its being.

The heat and light which they emit are engendered as the air is chafed by their movement. It is the nature of movement to ignite even wood and stone and iron, *a fortiori* then that which is nearer to fire, as air is. Compare the case of flying missiles. These are themselves set on fire so that leaden balls are melted and if the missiles themselves catch fire, the air which surrounds them must be affected likewise. These then become heated themselves by reason of their flight through the air, which owing to the impact upon it is made fire by the movement. But the upper bodies are carried each one in its sphere; hence they do not catch fire themselves, but the air which lies beneath the sphere of the revolving element is necessarily heated by its revolution and especially in that part where the sun is fixed. That is the reason for the heat experienced as it gets nearer or rises higher or stands above our head. Let this suffice for the point that the stars are neither made of fire nor move in fire[81].

In this way, Aristotle was able to explain how the movement of the heavenly bodies affects the uppermost level of the sublunary world and hence all life on earth.

As for the more complex motion of the planets, as opposed to the stars, Aristotle made this assertion.

Considering that the primary body has only one motion, it would seem natural for the nearest one to it to have a very small number, say two and the next one three, or some similar proportionate arrangement. But the opposite is true, for the sun and moon perform simpler motions than some of the planets, although the planets are farther from the centre and nearer the primary body, as has in certain cases actually been seen; for instance, the moon has been observed, when half-full, to approach the planet Mars, which has then been blotted out behind the dark half of the moon and come out again on the bright side[82].

For Aristotle, the orbits of the sun, moon and planets cause meteorological phenomena as well as the generation of animals.

In all cases, as we should expect, the times of gestation and formation and of lifespan aim, according to nature, at being measured by «periods». By a «period» I mean day and night and month and year and the times which are measured by these; also the moon's «periods» which are: full moon and waning moon and the

---

[81] ARISTOTLE, *De caelo*, 289 a 11-35.
[82] ARISTOTLE, *De caelo*, 291 b 32–292 a 7.

bisections of the intervening times, since these are the points at which it stands in a definite «aspect» with the sun, the month being a joint period of both moon and sun. The moon is a «principle» on account of its association with the sun and its participation in the sun's light, being as it were a second and lesser sun and therefore is a contributory factor in all processes of generation and perfecting. As we know, it is heat and cooling in their various manifestations which up to a certain due proportion bring about the generation of things and beyond that point their dissolution;   and the limits of these processes, both as regards their beginning and their end, are controlled by the movements of these heavenly bodies. Just as we observe that the sea and whatever is of fluid nature remains settled or is on the move according as the winds are at rest or in motion, while the behaviour of the air and the winds in turn depends upon the period of the sun and moon, so too the things which grow out of them and are in them are bound to follow suit (as it is only reasonable that the periods of things of inferior standing should follow those which belong to things of higher standing) since even the wind has a sort of lifespan — a generation and a decline. And as for the revolution of these heavenly bodies, there may very well be other principles which lie behind them. Nature's aim, then, is to measure the generations and endings of things by the measures of these bodies, but she cannot bring this about exactly on account of the indeterminateness of matter and the existence of a plurality of principles which impede the natural processes of generation and dissolution and so are often the causes of things occurring contrary to Nature[83].

In spite of the fact that the celestial realm is composed of ether and the terrestrial realm is composed of earth, water, air and fire, nevertheless the first element exerts a powerful influence on the lower four. Aristotle and his contemporaries knew that the moon caused the tides and had some impact on the gestation period of animals. Although the exact reasons were still a mystery to them, they realized that it had something to do with the moon's orbit.

It would seem that in spite of the different spheres and elements which compose the cosmos, there is a true harmony to the whole. The living bodies in the outer spheres do in fact influence the living bodies in the lower spheres. In fact, for Aristotle there is an analogy to be made between planets and human beings as well as between the sun, moon and earth on the one hand and animals and plants on the other.

---

[83] ARISTOTLE, *De generatione animalium*, 777 b 17–778 a 9.

With these considerations in mind, we must suppose the action of the planets to be analogous to that of animals and plants. For here on earth it is the actions of mankind that are the most varied and the reason is that man has a variety of goods within his reach, wherefore his actions are many and directed to ends outside themselves. That which is the best possible state, on the other hand, has no need of action. It is its own end, whereas action is always concerned with two factors, occurring when there is on the one hand an end proposed and on the other the means towards that end. Yet the animals lower than man have less variety of action than he and plants might be said to have one limited mode of action only; for either there is only one end for them to attain (as in truth there is for man also), or if there are many, yet they all conduce directly to the best. To sum up, there is one thing which possesses, or shares in, the best, a second which reaches it immediately by few stages, a third which reaches it through many stages and yet another which does not even attempt to reach it, but is content merely to approach near to the highest. For example, if health is the end, then one creature is always healthy, another by reducing, a third by running in order to reduce, a fourth by doing something else to prepare itself for running and so going through a large number of motions: another creature cannot attain to health, but only to running or reducing. To such creatures one of these latter is the end. To attain the ultimate end would be in the truest sense best for all; but if that is impossible, a thing gets better and better the nearer it is to the best. This then is the reason why the earth does not move at all and the bodies near it have only few motions. They do not arrive at the highest, but reach only as far as it is within their power to obtain a share in the divine principle. But the first heaven reaches it immediately by one movement and the stars that are between the first heaven and the bodies farthest from it reach it indeed, but reach it through a number of movements[84].

What then are we to make of this difficult text? Guthrie, in a note on this enigmatic argument, explains it in the following way[85]. First, we must remember that this analogy is similar to the relation between the First Mover and the first heaven. This primary analogy is outside the present comparison, but it is presumed for the sake of the argument. The First Mover exhibits no movement because it is equal to the good; the first heaven exhibits simple movement because it is nearest to the good. Now with this in mind, we can turn again to Aristotle's text as quoted above. The analogy could be summa-

---

[84] ARISTOTLE, *De caelo*, 292 b 0-25.
[85] See W. GUTHRIE, *Aristotle*, 208.

rized in this way: Human beings are to the planets as the animals and plants are
to the sun, moon and the earth. In other words, on the one hand human beings
and planets exhibit many motions; their complex movement allows them to
reach the good in different ways and at several removes. Animals and plants
and the sun, the moon and the earth, on the other hand, exhibit simple
movement or none at all; their relative inactivity is due to the fact that they
have no hope of attaining the highest good and so they must be content with
those lesser goods within their reach.

The movement of the planets fascinated Aristotle and he was always keen
to try to explain their motion and nature.

The first principle and primary reality is immovable, both essentially and
accidentally, but it excites the primary form of motion, which is one and eternal.
Now since that which is moved must be moved by something and the prime
mover must be essentially immovable and eternal motion must be excited by
something eternal and one motion by some one thing; and since we can see that
besides the simple spatial motion of the universe (which we hold to be excited
by the primary immovable substance) there are other spatial motions — those of
the planets — which are eternal (because a body which moves in a circle is
eternal and is never at rest — this has been proved in our physical treatises);
then each of these spatial motions must also be excited by a substance which is
essentially immovable and eternal. For the nature of the heavenly bodies is
eternal, being a kind of substance; and that which moves is eternal and prior to
the moved; and that which is prior to a substance must be a substance. It is
therefore clear that there must be an equal number of substances, in nature
eternal, essentially immovable and without magnitude; for the reason already
stated.

Thus it is clear that the movers are substances and that one of them is first and
another second and so on in the same order as the spatial motions of the heavenly
bodies. As regards the number of these motions, we have now reached a question
which must be investigated by the aid of that branch of mathematical science
which is most akin to philosophy, i.e., astronomy; for this has as its object a
substance which is sensible but eternal, whereas the other mathematical sciences,
e.g., arithmetic and geometry, do not deal with any substance. That there are
more spatial motions than there are bodies which move in space is obvious to
those who have even a moderate grasp of the subject, since each of the non-fixed
stars has more than one spatial motion[86].

---

[86] ARISTOTLE, *Metaphysica*, 1073 a 23-b 10.

It is important to note that Aristotle uses two different terms to describe the planets. In the first reference above he uses the word πλανήτης, which could be rendered in English as «the wandering one». In the second reference, Tredennick translates ἕκαστον…τῶν πλανωμένων ἄστρων as «each of the non-fixed stars». Perhaps a better translation would be «each of the wandering stars». The point is simply that, for Aristotle and the ancients in general, the planets represented a particular kind of star. This being the case, in antiquity both terms were used synonymously to describe them. Unlike their more perfect counterparts in the outermost sphere which remained stable with respect to one another, the planets moved across the evening sky, changing their position as they moved through the signs of the zodiac over the passage of time.

Many people in ancient Greece made a clear connection between the planets and the gods[87]. This was due to the influence of the Babylonians, who had closely associated their gods with the planets as far back as the end of the third millennium before Christ. This custom would in turn be adopted by the Romans, who of course gave the names of their own divinities to the seven wandering bodies in the sky. In fact, the name of each day of the week in our present calendar attests to the god for which it was named. For the ancients, then, the planets represented far more than moving objects in the sky. For most people, they were divinities who regularly intervened in the lives of human beings and hence influenced the course of human events. In this sense, then, the ancients were not so much concerned with the nature of the planets and stars in themselves; rather, their real interest lay in the study of how the heavenly bodies affected their own lives on earth. The study of and belief in astrology represented a common and familiar practice in ancient Greece as well as in the Roman Empire[88]. Thus the modern distinction between

---

[87] See E.C. KRUPP, *Beyond the Blue Horizon*, 173-192. In addition to ancient Babylon and Greece, Krupp also discusses the legends of ancient Egypt, India and China. Each of these peoples associated the planets with its own deities. In this way, every civilization constructed its own unique cosmology which nevertheless had much in common with those of other ancient cultures. The similarities between them are truly astounding.

[88] «Wer glaubt schließlich nicht an die Sterne, an ihre Macht, das Menschenleben zu gestalten oder doch wenigstens seine Wege anzudeuten? Der Neupythagoreer Nigidius Figulus, zur Zeit des Caesar, ist ihr Adept so gut wie der gleichzeitige Polyhistor Varro. Der düstre große Psycholog unter den römischen Historikern, Tacitus, kommt ihr in unsicher schwankender Überlegung weit entgegen. Man könnte kein Ende finden, wollte man alle die Berichte über ihre Bedeutung für die römischen Großen und Kaiser

astronomy and astrology did not exist in antiquity and it is safe to state that most people in the Hellenistic world were far more concerned with the latter than with the former[89].

If it is clear to even the most casual observer that the planets shine differently from one another, then how did the ancients explain this phenomenon? Aristotle's solution was quite ingenious. In order to account for the planets' varying degrees of brilliance, he posited the theory of the declining purity of ether in the planetary spheres.

So much then for the difficulties involved — let us now give our own statement of the matter with reference both to what we have already said and to our future discussions. We maintain that the celestial region as far down as the

---

zusammenstellen. Der Komet, der nach Julius Caesars Ermordung am Himmel erscheint, gilt allem Volk als das sidus Julium, als der sichere Beweis für die Aufnahme des großen Diktators unter die weltbeherrschenden Gestirne; aber der junge Oktavian, sein Erbe, sieht in der himmlischen Erscheinung zugleich die Verkündigung seiner eigenen Größe. Im Leben des Kaisers Tiberius spielt die Astrologie bis zu seinem Ende eine besonders verhängnisvolle Rolle; verhängnisvoll nicht für ihn allein, sondern nicht minder auch für die Senatoren, die sich von den Himmelskundigen belehren ließen, daß die Sterne dem Tiberius eine Rückkehr von seiner Ausfahrt nach Kampanien versagten, und in trügerische Sicherheit gewiegt nicht ahnten, daß er noch volle elf Jahre dort im freiwilligen Exil leben und sie um ihr Leben zittern lassen werde. Die Sprüche der Astrologen waren oft nicht minder zweideutig und gefährlich als die der alten Orakel, die so manches Reich zerstört hatten. Aber ihr unheimlicher Doppelsinn verminderte nicht, sondern erhörte vielmehr den Glauben an ihr Untrüglichkeit. Die Kaiser haben oftmals die Astrologen verfolgt und aus der Hauptstadt verbannt. Aber sie konnten ihrer selbst so wenig entraten wie die übrige vornehme römische Gesellschaft, von deren Damen so manche keine Meile vor die Stadt fahren und keine Mahlzeit zu sich nehmen wollte, ohne ihren astrologischen Kalender zu befragen, den sie am planetengeschmückten Armband (Abb. 1) mit sich herumtrug» (F. BOLL – C. BEZOLD – W. GUNDEL, *Sternglaube und Sterndeutung*, 26-27).

[89] «In contrast to Babylonian celestial divination, astrology depended for its existence on the concept of celestial influence and on the geocentric Aristotelian cosmos. The influence of the heavenly bodies on the sublunar region was given physical justification through Aristotelian physics. According to Ptolemy, the motion of the ether, the 5th (celestial) element, through the 8 celestial spheres penetrated to the sublunar elements (earth, air, fire, water) and affected their change. This constituted the mechanism of astrological causation, not the will of the gods (Ptolemy Tetr. I.2). Astrology's claim that the motions of the celestial bodies were not only indications but also actual causes of change on earth shows astrology to be antithetical to divination, which depends solely on the will of the deity to provide signs» (F. ROCHBERG-HALTON, «Astrology in the Ancient Near East», 506).

moon is occupied by a body which is different from air and from fire, but which varies in purity and freedom from admixture and is not uniform in quality, especially when it borders on the air and the terrestrial region. Now this primary substance and the bodies set in it as they move in a circle set on fire and dissolve by their motion that part of the lower region which is closest to them and generates heat therein[90].

If we keep in mind Aristotle's notion of the hierarchy of being, this theory will soon become very intelligible. This is based on his concept of value/worth τιμή. If we were to make a return trip through Aristotle's universe, this time proceeding from the outermost boundary towards the center of the earth, we would notice bodies which manifest an ever decreasing degree of divinity. Thus they also decrease in worth, permanence and the other attributes associated with them. It is important to remember that this concept of τιμή is rather common in Aristotle's philosophy.

In fact, in his argument for the existence of ether, Aristotle posits that it is of a higher worth than the four elements of the terrestrial realm.

> Thus the reasoning from all our premises goes to make us believe that there is some other body separate from those around us here and of a higher nature in proportion as it is removed from the sublunary world[91].

The Greek reads τιμιωτέραν ἔχον τὴν φύσιν, which could also be translated as «of a more valuable nature». In other words, the upper part of the heavens exemplifies honor, perfection and indissolubility, while the lower part stands for the opposite. Hence that which is of the earth exemplifies dishonor, imperfection and dissolubility.

It is clear from our survey of the astronomy of ancient Greece that the dominant model in celestial theory was the doctrine of concentric spheres[92]. First proposed by Eudoxus and later improved on by Callippus and Aristotle, this theory put the earth at the center of the cosmos. In the third century B.C., two astronomers were to challenge this view. Aristarchus of Samos proposed his heliocentric hypothesis and Apollonius of Perga put forward his twin models of epicycles and eccentric circles. Both of these represent mathematical models to explain the retrograde motion of the planets. Yet Aristotle's ideas

---

[90] ARISTOTLE, *Meteorologica*, 340 b 4-14.
[91] ARISTOTLE, *De caelo*, 269 b 14-17.
[92] See G.E.R. LLOYD, *Greek Science after Aristotle*, 53-74.

continued to influence astronomers throughout the Hellenistic period and well beyond. The geocentric view of the universe was still adopted by most scientists and it remained the prevalent doctrine throughout antiquity. The Aristotelian notion that the heavenly bodies had to move in circles, the perfect form of movement, prevented scientists from applying the geometry of ellipses to their observations. Such an undertaking would have to wait until the publication of Kepler's findings many centuries later. Ptomely, writing in the second century A.D., would only repeat and confirm the doctrines of Aristotle: the earth and the heavenly bodies are spherical, the latter being composed of ether, the most homogenous element and the earth remains at rest in the center of the universe[93].

In conclusion, the astronomy of the entire Hellenistic period is entirely dominated by the doctrines of Aristotle. Although some (like Apollonius of Perga) tampered somewhat with the prevailing doctrine of the homocentric spheres, the Aristotelian system basically remained intact throughout the Hellenistic period, the Middle Ages and well into the Italian Renaissance. In fact, it remained the prevailing teaching on the organization of the entire universe until the sixteenth century. Only then, and at great risks to their own lives and reputations, were Copernicus, Galileo and Kepler able to disprove it. These three men, through their great courage, conviction and fearlessness, displaced the Aristotelian model and thereby ushered in the beginning of modern astronomy.

5. 1Cor 15,35-44a in Light of Ancient Greek Science

Thanks to the insights gained from this excursus into ancient Greek science, we are now in a good position to return to 1 Corinthians 15 and apply some of these discoveries to our exegesis of vv. 35-44a. Of special interest to us are the scientific theories prevalent in the Hellenistic world that most probably influenced Paul. These suppositions would have allowed him to describe the nature of the spiritual body which is created when the dead are raised.

We begin with a investigation into the verb σπείρω[94]. Since it occurs seven times in 1 Corinthians 15,35-44a, it clearly represents a crucial term for Paul in this subunit. In his article on this word, Schulz gives four different meanings

---

[93] See G.E.R. LLOYD, *Greek Science after Aristotle*, 113-135.

[94] Cf. BAUER, «σπείρω» and S. SCHULZ, «σπέρμα, σπείρω», in *ThWNT*; and W. HACKENBERG, «σπείρω», in *EWNT*.

for σπείρω: 1) «to sow», «to sow seed»; 2) «to sow (e.g., a field)»; 3) «to scatter», «to disseminate», or «to disperse»; and 4) «to generate», «to beget»[95]. In their exegesis of 1 Corinthians 15,35-44a, scholars have for the most part opted for the first meaning of the word and interpreted it literally in vv. 36-38 and metaphorically in the application. Hence, according to this reading, in vv. 42-44a the human body is understood as a seed sown in the ground at burial so as to be raised like a plant at the moment of the resurrection of the dead.

But is there another way of explaining the meaning of this text? In our initial exegesis of the subunit, we saw how vv. 36-38 presents an A A' B B' structure. In the movement from A, v. 36, to A', v. 37, we saw how Paul's use of the καί consecutivum serves to coordinate both statements by using one so as to demonstrate the other. If we interpret ὃ σπείρεις in v. 36 as meaning «what you generate», then the demonstration that Paul is making becomes much clearer. In other words, the verb in this verse could refer to the act of sexual intercourse while the relative pronoun could denote human semen[96]. Then in v. 37, Paul continues his argument by proposing the example of the different kinds of grain: here the verb refers to the act of sowing grain while the relative pronoun would then denote the grain itself. Hence the translation would read «Fool! Just as what you generate does not come to life unless it dies, so what you sow is not the body which is to be, but a naked grain, perhaps of wheat or of some other kind». Understood in this way, v. 36 would then flow far more smoothly from v. 35, which after all asks two questions about the fate of the human body. Paul turns to the example of the seed precisely because of its visibility and easily recognizable nature. Although one can observe the transformation of a grain of wheat, the growth that takes place in the womb remains imperceptible to the human eye. To the ancients this

---

[95] See S. SCHULZ, «σπέρμα, σπείρω», in *ThWNT* who lists several examples of this meaning in the works of Sophocles, Euripides, Plato and Aeschylus.

[96] This would not be the first time in 1 Corinthians that Paul would have referred to sexual activity. In fact, the topic of sexual immorality, πορνεία, is mentioned in 5,1.9.10.11; 6,9.13.15.16.18; 7,2. Over the course of the letter, the Apostle has charged his addressees with many vices; sexual immorality seems to appear at the top of the list. By opting for a euphemism at this point in his argument on the resurrection of the dead, Paul highlights the biological nature of the act by accentuating what human procreation shares in common with the reproduction of plants. In this way he is also able to avoid a discussion of the moral implications of the sexual act, a topic already sufficiently addressed in chs. 5–7. Given the eschatological tone of 1Cor 15, a digression of this kind would have been entirely out of place.

hidden activity no doubt represented a profound and truly unfathomable mystery.

In the excursus we saw how ancient Greek scientists proposed all kinds of theories to explain the reproduction of living things. Today most of them strike us as silly or even nonsensical, false assumptions which could never be taken seriously in our age. Aristotle, Theophrastus and Galen clearly held conflicting hypotheses on the topic of reproduction. On the one hand, Aristotle theorized that plants were generated spontaneously[97] and that the very nature of certain kinds of plants could be altered[98]. On the other hand, in his *De partibus animalium* he emphasizes the fact that each kind of σπέρμα produces a particular body[99]. Since Aristotle's theories on reproduction[100] (conflicting though they might be) pretty much dominated the scientific stage of the Hellenistic world, anyone in the first century dealing with issues related to

---

[97] «The same sort of thing is found in plants too: some are formed our of seed, others as it might be by some spontaneous activity of Nature — they are formed when either the soil or certain parts in plants become putrescent, since some of them do not take shape independently on their own, but grow upon other trees, as for instance the mistletoe does» (ARISTOTLE, *De generatione animalium*, 715 b); and «Seed-bearing plants come up in still another way when some spontaneous growth arises somewhere from the collecting of a pool and from decomposition (or rather when a natural alteration occurs). Now it is evident that generation through the seed is common to all; and if some are generated in both ways, spontaneously as well as by seed, there is no absurdity: so some animals similarly come from two sources, both from other animals and from the earth» (THEOPHRASTUS, *De causis plantarum*, I 1.2).

[98] «Some plants, we are told, are transformed into a different type when they grow old, like nuts. They say too that the catmint changes into the sweet-smelling variety and the hypericum if cut and planted by the sea will become thyme. They also say that corn and flax change into other species. The deadly nightshade which grows in Persia becomes fit to eat if transplanted to Egypt or Palestine. Similarly almonds and pomegranates change from their natural poorness to a better condition under cultivation. Pomegranates improve when pig manure is put on their roots and by drinking sweet cold water; almonds when nails are fastened into them and when gum exudes from the holes for a long space of time. By such treatment many wild plants become cultivated» (ARISTOTLE, *Scripta minora. De plantis*, 821 a).

[99] «because in fact we do not find any chance creature being formed from a particular seed, but A comes from a and B from b; nor does any chance seed come from any individual» (ARISTOTLE, *De partibus animalium*, 641b). In his discussion on the same verse, Gillman also quotes the same passage from Aristotle. See J. GILLMAN, «Transformation», 326.

[100] For a superb presentation on Aristotle's theories of reproduction, see G.E.R. LLOYD, «Aristotle's Zoology and his Metaphysics», 381-388.

biology would have had to reason with these scientific categories. Hence in his discussion of the reproduction of plants, animals and human beings in 1 Corinthians 15, Paul seems to have adopted Aristotle's concept of the one-to-one connection between seed/semen and the body that is created.

That ὃ σπείρεις in v. 36 could refer to human generation is also supported by the excerpt which we considered from Aristotle's *De generatione animalium*[101]. As this passage makes clear, the physical part of the semen of animals and human beings was believed to dissolve and evaporate in order for it to generate offspring. It passes away so that it can be transformed into something new. In other words, the embryo is produced by the semen but not really from it. For Aristotle, the father's semen is both the formal cause and the efficient cause, the power that triggers the reproductive process, while the mother's menstrual blood is the material cause, since she contributes the matter which forms the embryo.

In the second century we find a convincing attack on this theory in Galen's treatise *De semine*. For him, the semen does in fact provide essential matter in the reproductive process; it is not merely the efficient cause of procreation. Given Galen's attack on those physicians and philosophers who misrepresented Aristotle, we may assume that in the first century there was indeed great confusion in medical circles around the whole question. If this was the case with the learned men of the day, we can only imagine the conflicting and confusing ideas which must have circulated among common folk. Although it is true that ancient scientists and physicians did not use the verb «to die» with respect to the generation of semen, nevertheless this kind of passing away may certainly be considered as a kind of death. It would be easy to imagine that once Aristotle's theories became popularized and misrepresented (as Galen's treatise proves), some people might say that the semen had to die if the embryo is to take shape in the womb. Moreover, given his penchant for dualism, as

---

[101] «Consider now the physical part of the semen. (This it is which, when it is emitted by the male, is accompanied by the portion of soul-principle and acts as its vehicle. Partly this soul-principle is separable from physical matter — this applies to those animals where some divine element is included and what we call Reason is of this character — partly it is inseparable.) This physical part of the semen, being fluid and watery, dissolves and evaporates; and on that account we should not always be trying to detect it leaving the female externally, or to find it as an ingredient of the fetation when that has set and taken shape, any more than we should expect to trace the fig-juice which sets and curdles milk. The fig-juice undergoes a change; it does not remain as a part of the bulk which is set and curdled; and the same applies to the semen» (ARISTOTLE, *De generatione animalium*, 737).

well as the eschatological tone of the entire passage, the Apostle chose the verb «to die» in this context so as to highlight in a more forceful way the antithesis between life and death.

In light of all this, therefore, v. 36 could allude to this concept taken from Aristotle: the male does not contribute matter to the embryo but instead represents the formal and efficient causes in procreation. In other words, along with most of his contemporaries, Paul most probably accepted Aristotle's hematogenic doctrine (i.e., semen originates in a man's blood) as an explanation of the coming-into-being of sperm along with the Greek philosopher's doctrine of embryology[102]. Thus the scientific theories of the great philosopher would harmonize beautifully with the theology of the Apostle. Given all of the above, we may safely conclude that Paul had solid scientific, philosophical and theological reasons to insist on his teaching that God alone creates the human body, both natural and spiritual. That in fact was our exegesis of v. 38, «But God gives it a body as he has chosen and to each kind of seed its own body». It would seem then that every act of conception would entail for the Apostle a divine intervention of sorts. God is conceived as the active partner in the creative process, while the man and woman serve more as instruments of the divine initiative.

After having considered the two possible interpretations of σπείρω in vv. 36-37, we must also take a closer look at Paul's treatment of the connection between the σπέρμα and the body as stated in v. 38b. Just as before with the verb σπείρω, Paul is also playing on the word σπέρμα here, since in Greek it can denote either seed or semen. We saw above in the excursus how σπέρμα clearly denotes the seed of a plant in the botanical texts of Aristotle and Theophrastus. This is also the case in the Bible, for example in Gen 1,11 (LXX). The question that we have to answer next is, Which of the two does it denote in v. 38b?

---

[102] Aristotle greatly influenced the Stoic doctrines of spermatogenesis, the medical school of the pneumatics (founded in the first century A.D.), as well as many Jewish authors of the period. Van der Horst has demonstrated that the hematogenic doctrine of semen was known in educated Jewish circles, showing how Aristotelian terminology is used or alluded to in 1 Enoch 15,4, Wis 7,1-2, 4 Macc 13,20 and Philo's *Questiones ad Genesim* 3.47, as well as in John 1,13. In addition, his article also gives ample evidence of just how much Greek ideas, especially those of Aristotle, influenced rabbinic embryology. See P.W. VAN DER HORST, «Sarah's Seminal Emission», 290-301, where the various Greek and Jewish theories are discussed in detail.

In our study of the structure of the text, we saw how according to the A A' B B' pattern of the verses, v. 36 is connected to v. 38b while v. 37 is linked to v. 38a. In other words, Paul makes two distinct statements in v. 38 about God's creative power, the first pertaining to grain and the second to σπέρμα. First, the Apostle claims that God gives a body to the grain as he chooses (the pronoun αὐτῷ takes the place of the noun κόκκον from v. 37). Second, he asserts that God gives to each one of the σπερμάτων its own body. If σπερμάτων denotes seeds in v. 38b, then Paul would simply be repeating what he had just said in v. 38a. But if on the other hand σπερμάτων denotes semen, then Paul would be introducing a new and significant nuance to his argument. In this way he would be broadening his discussion to include a treatment of animal life and in this way prepare for the second example which comes next in vv. 39-41. Given the unfolding of the first analogy in vv. 36-38, as well as the list of four semen-producing animals that immediately follows in v. 39, it makes more sense to conclude that σπερμάτων denotes semen in v. 38b. In other words, in as much as it refers back to the man who generates in v. 36, it clearly denotes human semen; while in as much as Paul is already anticipating the point that he wants to make with regard to each kind of flesh, it denotes «each kind of semen», i.e., the semen of human beings, animals, birds and fish[103].

---

[103] In her study of Paul's use of analogy in Rom 7,1-6, J. Little has pointed out how the Apostle tends to add on new ideas in the midst of his analogizing rather than stopping and pulling together the diverse strands of his argument. Disagreeing with C.H. Dodd, who believed that Paul suffered from a defect of imagination, she comes to Paul's defense. «In point of fact, the defect Paul suffers from in the writing of this passage is, if anything, an excess of imagination which propels him through the above-noted succession of ideas so rapidly that he has neither the time nor the opportunity to bring his images to completion. Nor is it entirely certain that he could do so, even were he so inclined, inasmuch as he wished to employ the analogy in two directions at once, both backward in relation to v. 1 and forward in relation to the rest of the pericope. To put the matter analogically, he is trying to burn the candle at both ends simultaneously and it is by no means clear that such a procedure can be carried out in a neat and tidy fashion» (J.A. LITTLE, «Paul's Use of Analogy», 90). These observations on Paul's penchant for presenting a quick succession of ideas while analogizing also hold true with regard to 1Cor 15,36-38. Paul begins the passage with a reference to human semen and procreation in v. 36, he quickly moves on so as to point out the visible change perceivable in various grains in vv. 37-38a and then he returns to his point about semen in v. 38b. By referring to «each kind of semen» in v. 38b, the Apostle has broadened his argument so as to prepare the ground for the example of earthly bodies that follows. This is a good example of what Little calls Paul's «sequential»

After having considered the scientific information relevant to the first example in vv. 36-38, we can now consider the data which concerns the second in vv. 39-41. We have already seen how Paul simply states that «There are celestial bodies and there are terrestrial bodies» (v. 40a). In this elementary and straightforward declaration, the Apostle reveals the Aristotelian background to his view of the cosmos. In fact, as we saw in the excursus on astronomy, this distinction between the terrestrial and celestial realms is quite typical of Greek science and it was to influence western science for centuries to come[104]. As such, it represents a scientific and theological position quite common in the Hellenistic age, one that most probably would have been thoroughly familiar to the Corinthians. In short, we may safely claim that Paul completely shared in the scientific world view of his contemporaries with regard to the composition of the cosmos.

In addition, not only are there heavenly and earthly bodies, but the quality of the ether which composes the first far excels that of the sublunary elements which make up the second[105]. To put this in Paul's own language, «the glory

---

rather than «integrative» thought.

[104]«In the end, Aristotle's cosmos continued to dominate human thought throughout the ancient world and scholastic periods right up to the sixteenth century. Nor is this surprising, seeing that it was eminently qualified to maintain this position both in the Ancient World and after the rise of Christianity. In Aristotle's philosophy the cosmos is a sublime manifestation of the rule of order in the universe. The idea was as well suited to the Greek mentality, in which the concept of order blended with those of beauty and perfection as expressed in artistic creation, as to the basic creed of the monotheistic religions which regard the cosmic order as the work of the Creator and the expression of His will. The teleological idea therefore endured as a guiding principle in the explanation of nature, being woven into the pattern of mediaeval religious thought. Long life was likewise assured to the Aristotelian antithesis between heaven and earth, rooted as it was in star-worship, of which spiritual traces are to be found throughout the Greek period. In the theology of the monotheistic creeds this antithesis reappeared anew in the location of God and his angels in the heavens, in the pure region of Aristotle's eternal movements» (S. SAMBURSKY, *The Physical World of the Greeks*, 103-104).

[105]«From all these premises therefore it clearly follows that there exists some physical substance besides the four in our sublunary world and moreover that it is more divine than and prior to, all these. The same can also be proved on the further assumption that all motion is either natural or unnatural and that motion which is unnatural to one body is natural to another and the motions of up and down are natural or unnatural to fire and earth respectively; from these it follows that circular motion too, since it is unnatural to these elements, is natural to some other [...] Thus the reasoning from all our premises goes to make us believe that there is some other body separate from those around us here and of

of the celestial is one and the glory of the terrestrial in another» (v. 40b). Hence the point which the Apostle is making by means of this second example underscores the radical discontinuity between the matter and glory of earthly bodies and the matter and glory of heavenly ones. Given this fact, it is obvious that the glory of the sun, moon and the stars is far superior to that of earthly human beings, animals, birds and fish. This radical discontinuity is not due primarily to their different position in the universe, although this of course is the case; rather, it is due to the difference in their fundamental material composition. Earthly bodies are made up of perishable and changing elements while heavenly bodies are made up of the imperishable and unchanging element, ether. In short, by means of this second example, Paul highlights this radical separation which divides these two realms, a division which is due to the profoundly different matter found in each.

In our exegesis of the text before the excursus, we saw how Paul manages to join the chronological point of the first example (i.e., that God is able to achieve a profound and genuine transformation in his creatures by calling them through death to life) to the material point of the second (i.e., that there is a qualitative difference between earthly and heavenly bodies due to their location in the universe and this, due to their material constitution). In the application in vv. 42-44a, Paul has taken the before/after point of the first example and combined it with the earthly/ heavenly point of the second. In this he accentuates the transforming and discontinuous nature of the spiritual body that results thanks to the act of resurrection. This has in fact been his fundamental intention all along. In short, Paul has proven that God can raise a dead, natural body into a living, spiritual one through the resurrection of the dead.

In vv. 42-44a, Paul repeats the verb σπείρεται four times. Just as before, we must ask ourselves how he is using this verb. By saying «It is sown», what metaphor is the Apostle employing here? Since the context clearly shows that he is referring to the human body, it is logical to turn first to the fourth meaning of the word as presented by Schulz and translate it as «it is generated or begotten». The findings from Aristotelian biology on the dissolution and evaporation of semen also support this choice. Paul is not speaking of grain here, nor is he comparing a corpse to a seed sown in the ground at burial so as to be raised like a plant at the moment of the resurrection of the dead. Rather,

---

a higher nature in proportion as it is removed from the sublunary world» (ARISTOTLE, *De caelo*, 269 b).

«it is sown» refers to the origin of the natural body during the act of intercourse. In these four antitheses, the Apostle is contrasting the origin of the
natural body (which is formed during the act of intercourse through the sowing
of semen) to the origin of the spiritual body (which is formed at the moment
of resurrection through the act of being raised from the dead). The natural body
is sown into a world marked by perishability, dishonor and weakness; like the
physical component of semen, this earthly world is passing away and will soon
come to an end. In contrast, the spiritual body is raised at the resurrection into
a world marked by imperishability, honor and power; this heavenly world is
coming to be and will last for ever. The contrast becomes especially clear
when we consider the understood agents of these verbs. If the natural body is
created by God after the seed is sown by man, the spiritual body is raised by
God without any intermediary role of man. Thus the Apostle is highlighting the
difference between the impotence of men and the omnipotence of God.

Paul's point then is this: what human beings cannot do, God can. Although
men play an active role in the sowing of the seed, they play no role at all in the
giving of the natural body nor in the raising of the dead. It is God who gives
the natural body (v. 38) and it is God who raises up the spiritual one (v.44a).
In fact, throughout this subunit, the Apostle has been telling the creation story
by means of his argument from reason. This will of course become explicit in
the next subunit when the Apostle develops his midrash of Genesis 2,7. But
even at this point in his argument his true intentions have become clear. The
listing of creatures in reverse biblical order in vv. 39-41 represents a subtle
backwards movement towards the origin of living things. From the sixth, to the
fifth, to the fourth day of creation, it is as if Paul were counting down to the
very moment when God first began his work of creation. The act of raising is
therefore presented as one which is entirely divine; completely independent
of human agency and activity, God alone brings the dead to life and gives them
a spiritual body.

We saw in the excursus how Greek philosophers had reflected on the
antithesis between γίγνεσθαι, «to come to be», and its antithesis
φθείρεσθαι, «to perish», «to be destroyed». In their attempt to understand the
visible world, they expressed how matter underwent an ongoing process of
creation and dissolution over time. Like those before him, Aristotle also
proposed his own philosophy of matter and change; these findings are

presented most succinctly in his work *De generatione et corruptione*[106]. For him, alteration ἀλλοίωσις is a change of quality, while coming-to-be/passing-away γένεσις/φθορά represents a change of the thing as a whole[107]. Paul, like these Greek philosophers before him, also finds himself face to face with the whole ontological problem of change. Given the destruction of the natural body and the raising of the spiritual one, the Apostle is attempting to answer the question, Is the change produced by the resurrection one of alteration, or is it better described as a kind of coming-to-be and passing-away? Since the Apostle has taken great pains to emphasize the whole notion of discontinuity, a mere alteration of the human body must be immediately excluded from our consideration.

Hence we are left with the other option, that of a kind of coming-to-be and passing-away. That Paul is in fact speaking about a new creation seems clear, given how the theme of creation permeates the entire second half of 1 Corinthians 15. As for things passing away, this passage is also filled with repeated occurrences of either the noun φθορά, perishability, (in v. 42 and v. 50) and its cognate adjective φθαρτός, perishable, (in v. 53 and v. 54) or its opposite, ἀφθαρσία, imperishability, (in vv. 42, 50, 53, 54) and its cognate

---

[106] «In the second part of his book *On Generation and Corruption* Aristotle propounds the main principles of his theory of matter. There he explains the transition from element to element by the interchange of qualitative factors in a given combination. Obviously fire is produced from air when moisture is changed into dryness and earth from fire if heat is replaced by cold and so on. Aristotle similarly examines other pairs of opposites such as hard-soft, rough-smooth, dense-rare and their role in the differentiation of the primary bodies. The history of physics has proved that all this theory of absolutely opposed qualities, even when presented with dialectical brilliance in the form of thesis and antithesis, leads nowhere» (S. SAMBURSKY, *The Physical World of the Greeks*, 91).

[107] «When, therefore, the change from one contrary to another is quantitative, it is "growth and diminution"; when it is change of place, it is "motion"; when it is a change of property (or quality), it is "alteration"; but when nothing persists of which the resulting state is a property or an accident of any kind, it is a case of coming-to-be and the contrary change is a passing-away. Matter, in the chief and strictest sense of the word, is the substratum which admits of coming-to-be and passing-away; but the substratum of the other kind of change is also in a sense matter, because all the substrata admit of certain kinds of contrariety. Let this, then, be our decision on the question about coming-to-be, whether it exists or not and how it exists and about "alteration"» (ARISTOTLE, *De generatione et corruptione*, 320 a).

adjective, ἄφθαρτος[108]. Given all this data, we may conclude that Paul is in fact describing the resurrection as a kind of coming-to-be and a passing-away. In other words, when the natural body is raised, it is changed as a whole and transformed into the spiritual body. That is why he stresses the reality of discontinuity and otherness so forcefully throughout the chapter. What passes away is the earthly matter which makes up the natural body; what comes to be is the heavenly matter which composes the spiritual one. In this way it becomes possible for the human body to inherit the Kingdom of God and the imperishable (v. 50). Therefore, thanks to traditional Greek philosophical terms as well as common examples from the visible creation, Paul presents his addressees in Corinth with a persuasive argument that most any educated person in the Hellenistic world could comprehend.

In conclusion, Paul ends his argument from reason in the same way he began it. In vv. 36-38 he had contrasted the human activity of sowing, σὺ ὃ σπείρεις and ὃ σπείρεις...σπείρεις, to God's activity in the giving of the natural body, ὁ δὲ θεὸς δίδωσιν αὐτῷ...ἠθέλησεν. In vv. 42-44a he again returns to the human act of sowing, σπείρεται, but this time he contrasts it to the divine act of raising, ἐγείρεται, i.e., the giving of the spiritual body. The subunit as a whole, therefore, conveys a profound theological truth which Paul wants to make very clear to his addressees in Corinth. That which man sows cannot come to life through human power alone. A more exact translation of this Greek verb in v. 36 would read «it cannot make-life», οὐ ζῳοποιεῖται. Not only are human beings both physically and spiritually impotent in this life, but they are also incapable of generating true life for themselves in the age to come. Thus the Apostle contrasts divine strength and potency to human weakness and impotency: God raises the dead to new life and grants them a spiritual body in imperishability, in glory and in power. As we shall see in our detailed study of the next subunit, God alone is the giver of true, eschatological life through the agency of his «life-making Spirit», πνεῦμα ζῳοποιοῦν (v. 45b). It is to this passage that we now turn.

6. 1Cor 15,44b-49 as a Distinct Subunit

As we saw above in the overview of chapter fifteen, 1 Corinthians 15,44b-49 represents the central member of the A B A' structuration and as such it

---

[108] Cf. G. HARDER, «φθείρω, φθορά, φθαρτός», in *ThWNT* and T. HOLTZ, «φθείρω, ἀφθαρσία, ἄφθαρτος, φθαρτός, φθορά», in *EWNT*.

forms a distinct subunit in the chapter[109]. In these crucial verses, Paul develops his argument from Scripture. He develops a midrash of Genesis 2,7, thereby establishing a biblical basis for his understanding of the two kinds of bodies enjoyed by human beings. He begins this new subunit with a conditional sentence, «If there is a natural body, there is also a spiritual one» (44b). By means of a complex comparison of the two Adams, Paul proves the main point of the subunit: a human being has a natural body for earthly life and a spiritual body for heavenly life. Moreover, this extraordinary transformation occurs thanks to the action of the «life-giving Spirit» (v. 45b). By dealing with the question of the first Adam's creation and the last Adam's resurrection and new creation, the apostle displays a keen interest in the makeup and composition of the human body, the limits and possibilities of human action as well as the natural and supernatural existence of human beings as designed by their Creator.

6.1 *Human Body Language*

The Greek noun for body, σῶμα, occurs forty-six times in 1 Corinthians, more so than in any other New Testament book. Its frequency in this particular letter proves that it represents a very significant term for Paul, one which the Apostle wants to clarify and explain very carefully to his addressees. It is evident that for Paul, τὸ σῶμα always means the «physical body», that is, the material, corporeal part of a living being[110]. The Apostle uses the word in both the literal and figurative senses, yet the basic meaning of σῶμα does not change. Although this simple and straightforward definition is accepted by

---

[109] In his commentary, Weiss claims that vv. 44b-49 is a subdivision whose purpose is to show «daß wir wirklich auf ein σῶμα πνευματικόν hoffen dürfen» (J. WEIß, *Der erste Korintherbrief*, 373). Bousset entitles the same subdivision «Die Wirklichkeit eines himmlischen Leibes» (BOUSSET, «Der erste Brief an die Korinther», 160). Similarly, another exegete also recognizes that vv. 44b-49 forms a subunit. «Les versets 44*b* et 49 encadrent une unité littéraire dont le premier forme l'énoncé fondamental et le second, le sommet ainsi que la conclusion. Ils offrent maints traits communs aux versets respectifs *I Cor.*, 21 et 22» (R. MORISSETTE, «L'Antithèse entre le "psychique" et le "pneumatique"», 108). Lastly, J. Murphy-O'Connor argues that these verses address the whole question of the existence of the resurrection body. «Paul deals with two associated questions. What is the resurrected body like (vv 35-44a)? What reasons is there to think that such a body really exists (vv 44b-49)?» (J. MURPHY-O'CONNOR, «The First Letter to the Corinthians», 813).

[110] For an excellent defense of this thesis, see R.H. GUNDRY, *Sōma in Biblical Theology*, 1976.

most people in everyday conversation, that is unfortunately not the case with certain exegetes. Since Bultmann, many scholars have maintained that, when used of a human being, σῶμα can also mean «the whole person»[111]. This is simply not true and the presence of this definition has merely confused matters in New Testament scholarship.

A correct understanding of σῶμα is especially important for the proper exegesis of chapter fifteen. As we saw above in our overview of his argument, Paul is intent on answering his imaginary interlocutor with regard to the bodily condition of the dead who will be raised: «With what kind of *body* do they come?» (v. 35). Although the Apostle's response is complex and intricate, the essential point throughout vv. 35-58 is that God remains infinitely free and omnipotent vis-à-vis his creation. With regard to the seed that is sown and dies, «God gives it a body as he has chosen and to each kind of seed its own body» (1Cor 15,38). God expresses his boundless creativity in the universe through the diversity of beings he has created. Plants, animals and human beings, the sun, the moon and the stars — all these creatures have bodies, whether they are terrestrial or celestial and each differs from the other in appearance according to God's loving plan. By appealing to nature in this way, Paul asks his interlocutor to reconsider his appraisal of the Creator's handiwork. If God can do all this with such splendor, can he not also create a new body for the dead when he raises them to eternal life?

In vv. 44b-49, the Apostle now addresses his main subject of interest: the human body. Just as there are dissimilar earthly and celestial bodies in the cosmos, so too there is a diversity of bodies with regard to human beings. God has created a particular kind of body for human life on earth, the σῶμα ψυχικόν and another kind of body for human life in heaven, the σῶμα πνευματικόν. Since the Corinthians clearly were confused as to the precise nature of these different bodies, the entire unit is designed to explain these terms to them in greater detail. Paul was keenly aware of the fact that a body was intimately connected to the environment for which it was created, whether for earth or for heaven[112]. A move from one milieu to another clearly entails

---

[111] For the history behind the rise of this incorrect definition, see R.H. GUNDRY, *Sōma in Biblical Theology*, 3-8. For articles which include it, cf. E. SCHWEIZER, «σῶμα», in *ThWNT* and in *EWNT*.

[112] Contemporary philosophy has been fascinated with this question of the body understood as «a being in the world». One twentieth century philosopher who brilliantly elaborated a theory of the body is Merleau-Ponty. «Le corps est le véhicule de l'être au

a requisite change of bodies. Thus, if the natural body is to enter the heavenly realm, it must first be completely transformed into a new substance, that is, into a spiritual body. It is for this reason that Paul discusses both natural and supernatural human bodies in this pericope. Keeping in mind that Paul is basically concerned with «human body language» in these verses, we can now turn to a brief discussion of the antithetical structure of the passage.

6.2 Antithetical Parallelism

Paul composed this subunit in a series of opposing parallel components, a rhetorical feature which is called antithetical parallelism. He did this in order to underscore the sharp contrast between that which is characteristic of earthly bodies as opposed to heavenly ones. In this subunit, Paul contrasts words and clauses, the effect of which serves to accentuate the discontinuity between the earthly realm and the heavenly one. These opposing components were labeled A B in our initial analysis of the concentric nature of the passage.

The subunit's first example of antithesis is found in the contrast between the natural and the spiritual body. This distinction sets the tone for all the others which follow[113]. Just as Paul contrasts the ψυχικόν to the πνευματικόν in

---

monde, et avoir un corps c'est pour un vivant se joindre à un milieu défini, se confondre avec certains projets et s'y engager continuellement» (M. MERLEAU-PONTY, La Phénoménologie de la perception, 97).

[113] In recent years, scholars have attempted to determine the precise background to the ψυχικόν-πνευματικόν terminology in 1Cor Some would say that this distinction finds its origin in certain interpretations of Gen 2,7 current in Hellenistic Judaism. For defenders of this thesis, cf. J. DUPONT, Gnosis, 172-80 and B.A. PEARSON, The Pneumatikos-Psychikos Terminology in 1 Corinthians, 11-12, 17-21. Nevertheless, in response to this position, Horsley points out that the ψυχικόν-πνευματικόν terminology does not occur anywhere in Philo or in other Hellenistic Jewish writings. He admits that although Dupont and Pearson are incorrect in their attempt to account for this terminology in contemporary Hellenistic literature, nevertheless they have helped to lead the argument in the right dirsection. «The pneumatikos-psychikos language is part of or parallel to a fundamental contrast between two types of human being, heavenly and earthly, immortal and mortal, which Paul argues against polemically in 1 Cor 15,44-54. This same fundamental cosmological-soteriological contrast is found in Philo's writings generally, but particularly in the explanations of the two types humanity based on Gen 1,27 and 2,7a, respectively. Only the specific terminology, pneumatikos-psychikos, is missing. It would appear, then, that the Corinthians used pneumatikos-psychikos along with the rest of these terms to make the same basic contrast between people of different levels of spiritual ability and attainment, different religious types of people, for whom the heavenly anthrōpos and the earthly

v. 44 and v. 46, so also he opposes their nominal cognates, the ψυχή and the πνεῦμα, in v. 45. This last verse also contains the comparison between the first and last Adam: the first is living while the last is life-giving. V. 47 continues the Adam analogy. In this verse Paul contrasts the substance of which each one is made: the first human being is made of earth and the second one is made of the firmament of heaven. The contrast is developed in v. 48, the first is characteristic of dust and the second is characteristic of heaven. Just as there is one of dust, so too there are those of dust; just as there is one of heaven, so too there are those of heaven. The striking contrast of clauses continues into the subunit's final verse where Paul goes on to play with the tense of the verb «to bear». By opposing the aorist subjunctive to the present indicative in this way, the Apostle proposes a new form of ethical behavior to the Corinthians, one which is entirely different from their previous form of conduct.

In short, through the sustained use of antithetical parallelism throughout the subunit, Paul underscores the discontinuity between this passing world and the eschatological world that has already dawned. Thanks to Jesus' resurrection from the dead, the natural order of existence is yielding to the spiritual one, the powers of this world are giving way to the power of the Spirit. This rhetorical device serves to drive home Paul's principal point with added force. If a natural body is to enter the spiritual realm, it must be changed into its antithesis, that is, a spiritual body. Now that we are aware of this important point, we can move on to consider a brief overview of the Apostle's argumentation. This will help prepare us to understand better the detailed exegesis that follows.

6.3 Paul's Argumentation within the Subunit

The Apostle's argument in vv. 44b-49 flows logically from verse to verse. When discussing the limits of the passage, we saw above how this subunit begins immediately after Paul has declared, «It is sown a natural body, it is raised a spiritual body». After having stated his belief in the resurrection of bodies, Paul can now declare the thesis of the new subunit, «If there is a

---

anthrōpos were paradigmatic symbols in Philo» (R.A. HORSLEY, «Pneumatikos vs. Psychikos», 280). For further information on the gnostic or Philonic influence on this passage in 1Cor, these three articles provide a fine *point de départ* for further reading in a field which lies beyond the scope of this present work.

natural body, there is also a spiritual one» (v. 44b). He desires to narrow his previously general discussion of different kinds of bodies to a specific consideration of the human body. The Apostle is very keen to answer the two questions he first asked in 1 Corinthians 15,35, «How are the dead raised? With what kind of body do they come?» In the analogy of the seed in the previous section, Paul had stated that «God gives it a body as he has chosen and to each kind of seed its own body» (v.38). In order to convince his skeptical addressees that there is indeed such a thing as a spiritual body, Paul now turns to the Pentateuch for help. In Genesis 2,7, the well-known description of the creation of Adam, the Apostle finds the essential information he needs.

With this text clearly in mind, Paul now narrates his account of two parallel creation stories in 1 Corinthians 15,44b-49. It is important to note, however, that he does not relate the narrative in the same order as it is presented in the Bible. In fact, Paul tells the story backwards! By means of an elaborate midrash of Genesis 2,7, he presents his own version of the first creation story in order to develop his own unique account of the second creation story[114]. In this way, he uses Genesis 2,7 as a kind of paradigm which allows him to explain and emphasize the material composition of the natural and spiritual bodies of human beings. This pivotal verse which represents the essential core of 1 Corinthians 15,44b-49 allows Paul to reach an obvious conclusion: in the first creation, God created a natural body out of earthly matter through his breath of life. In other words, Adam became a living creature thanks to God's breath which was blown into him. By v. 49, the Apostle has convincingly

---

[114] «Going back to the idea of two creations in 1Cor 15,45, we might paraphrase Paul's thought by saying: In the first creation man lives contingently by the breath of God breathed into him which will one day return to God when, too, his mortal body will return to dust. In the last creation, man will live completely by the very Spirit of God, the very source of life, as the risen Christ, the first fruits of this creation now already does. The inauguration of the first creation is described in Gn 2,7, which Paul first quotes and then paraphrases to point out the essential differences of the final creation» (B. SCHNEIDER, «The Corporate Meaning and Background of 1 Cor 15,45b», 154). It is thanks to Schneider that I was able to recognize the backwards reading of the two parallel stories. Nevertheless, although he recognizes that Paul is discussing the nature of earthly bodies, he fails to apply this insight with regard to the nature of heavenly bodies. In my opinion, this is one of the central points of the entire passage, for with this insight Paul constructs his argument for the existence of a particular kind of heavenly body, namely, the spiritual one.

answered the question he had first posed in v. 35, «With what kind of body do they come?»

We start with Paul's version of the first creation story. In v. 45a he begins with the formed, animate creature. The first Adam is a living being who was given a natural body by God (Gen 2,7c). Next, he passes over the clause which states that God breathed into Adam's nostrils the breath of life (Gen 2,7b). Lastly, in v. 47a he concludes that the first human being is made out of earth and is of dust (Gen 2,7a). In other words, Paul starts with the finished product, Adam's natural body and then emphasizes the matter of which it is made, namely, earth. This backwards movement of the familiar and well-known Genesis story serves to accentuate the nature of Adam's body, which is one of the points that Paul wants to underscore in this passage.

Next we turn to Paul's narration of the second creation story. Again he tells the story backwards, moving from the existing creature back to the matter from which it was made. In v. 45b he begins with the last Adam who became a life-giving Spirit. This is an allusion to Genesis 2,7c and b: from 2,7c he gets the name Adam and from 2,7b he uses the πνοὴν ζωῆς as a point of departure, changing it into πνεῦμα ζῳοποιοῦν. Lastly, he concludes in v. 47b that the second human being is made out of heaven. Again Paul has started with the finished product, the last Adam's spiritual body and then emphasizes the matter from which it is made, namely, heaven. Similarly, this way of telling the creation story backwards serves to underscore the heavenly nature of the spiritual body. By using his midrash of Genesis 2,7 as the essential nucleus for this passage, Paul succeeds in creating an intricate text by weaving the first and second creation stories together. The result, as we saw above, represents a detailed and elaborate backwards telling of the two creation stories, the first being used as a model for the second[115].

In this way, Paul successfully achieves the goal of this complex subunit. What then are the Apostle's conclusions with respect both to the first and last

---

[115] I am grateful to Schneider who helped me recognize the «backward» reading of Gen in relation to the «forward» reading of 1Cor 44b-49. He recognizes a chiasm and sees in v. 45b a reference to Ez 37,1-14. «A confrontation of Paul's argument from Genesis with the text itself presents a chiasmus:

1 Cor 15,45a — Gen 2,7c (quoted with adaptation)
    v. 45b —   v. 7b (midrashic ref. to Ez exploited)
    (v. 46 is parenthetical)
      vv. 47-49 —   v. 7a (alluded to)» (B. SCHNEIDER, «The Corporate Meaning and Background of 1 Cor 15,45b», 157).

Adam, as well as to all those who are like them? In the first creation, God creates a natural body out of earthly matter through his life-giving breath; in the second creation, God creates a spiritual body out of heavenly matter through his life-giving Spirit[116]. The products of the two creations are of course distinct in as much as the natural body is temporal and perishable while the spiritual body is eternal and imperishable. It is precisely this discontinuity, this difference with respect to the material composition of the bodies that Paul seeks to emphasize in this subunit and indeed, throughout 1 Corinthians 15,35-58. With these observations kept in mind, we are now ready to undertake a close reading of the text.

---

[116] In Genesis itself, there is a very close connection between God's breath and God's spirit. Cf. «Then the Lord said, "My spirit (רוּחִי, LXX τὸ πνεῦμά μου) shall not abide in man for ever, for he is flesh, but his days shall be a hundred and twenty years"» (Gen 6,3) and «Everything on the dry land in whose nostrils was the breath of life (רוּחַ חַיִּים, LXX πνοὴν ζωῆς) died» (Gen 7,22). We shall examine this semantic relationship in greater detail below in the section devoted to a close reading of the text. For now it is enough to note that Paul (along with other Jews and Christians of his era) believed that God creates natural bodies through the agency of his breath/spirit. In light of this, Paul seeks to convince his addressees in Corinth that God creates spiritual bodies through the agency of his Holy Spirit.

CHAPTER II

A Close Reading of 1Cor 15,44b-49

1. 1Cor 15,44b

After having considered an overview of Paul's argumentation in the passage, we are now in a position to begin the close reading of the text. Here is the text of v. 44b.

εἰ ἔστιν σῶμα ψυχικόν, ἔστιν καὶ πνευματικόν.
«If there is a natural body, there is also a spiritual one».

– εἰ ἔστιν. The particle εἰ, «if», introduces the protasis of a first class conditional sentence[1]. We shall consider the characteristics of this kind of conditional after we have examined the next word in the clause, the verb ἔστιν. What is essential to note is that in this clause, as well as in the following one, ἔστιν conveys the notion of existence; it is best translated as «there is»[2]. By means of this double affirmation of existence, «There is a natural body; there is a spiritual body», Paul provides a positive response to his opponents' twofold denial as posited earlier in the chapter. «Now if Christ is preached as raised from the dead, how can some of you say that there is no (οὐκ ἔστιν) resurrection of the dead? But if there is no (οὐκ ἔστιν) resurrection of the dead, then Christ has not been raised» (1Cor 15,12-13).

---

[1] For more general information on the particle εἰ in conditional sentences, cf. ZERWICK § 299-334; BDR § 371-76; HS § 280-85. For the particle itself, see G. LÜDEMANN, «εἰ», in *EWNT*. Of its 507 occurrences in the NT, Paul uses the word 181 times, far more often than any other author.

[2] For other examples of this verb when it is used to express existence, see BAUER, «εἰμί», I.1.

Thus in v. 44, Paul echoes back to his insistence that there is indeed such a thing as the resurrection of the dead. This time, however, he focuses on the issue of the existence of the spiritual body by forcefully affirming its reality. Thus in chapter fifteen, the fourfold repetition of ἔστιν understood as «there is» serves to underscore the ontological nature of the Apostle's argument in the subunit as a whole.

Considered in its entirety, this kind of sentence is commonly referred to as a «Simple Conditional» by Greek grammarians[3]. Appearing approximately three hundred times in the New Testament and most especially in Paul's letters, its syntactic form may be described as «εἰ + indicative, indicative». But what does a first class conditional mean? What is its purpose? It expresses a logical connection between the protasis and the apodosis within the sentence[4]. In this instance, Paul is emphasizing the logical correlation between the object of the protasis, i.e. the natural body and the object of the apodosis, i.e. the spiritual body. This syntactic connection reminds us of Paul's purpose in vv. 35-44a with regard to the reality of earthly and celestial bodies. In that subunit, Paul discussed the many different kinds of bodies that characterize creatures in general; in this subunit, he focuses on the particular example which interests him most of all: human beings and the two different kinds of bodies that are specific to them.

Given these important insights into the nature of the first class conditional sentence, as well as the meaning of the verb ἔστιν, we are now in a position to continue our analysis of the remaining terms in v. 44b. A detailed exegesis of σῶμα, ψυχικόν, and πνευματικόν will show that Paul is interested in demonstrating the marked discontinuity between the earthly body and the resurrected one. Let us now prove this by examining these critical words more closley.

– σῶμα. We begin our study of this noun by surveying some of the important texts in 1 Corinthians where Paul uses σῶμα. In the course of our discussion on these passages, it will quickly become clear that throughout the letter, Paul consistently understands «physical body» as the singular meaning of σῶμα. This analysis will help us later when we investigate the precise nature of the spiritual body and its relationship to the Holy Spirit.

---

[3] Cf. ZERWICK § 303-05; BDR § 372; HS § 281.
[4] For the meaning of first class conditional sentences in the NT, see J.L. BOYER, «First Class Conditions», 75-114.

Let us begin by examining the literal meaning of σῶμα. Paul uses σῶμα thirty-nine times in 1 Corinthians in order to designate the material part of the human being[5]. Clearly this literal use of the noun represents the overwhelming majority of examples in the letter. It is interesting to note that the bulk of these occurrences are concentrated in chapters six, twelve and fifteen. Since it is not necessary to examine every single case individually, let us limit our study to a few examples from each of these chapters.

In chapter six, Paul is clearly speaking of the physical body as understood literally when he chastises those Corinthians who may have had sexual relations with prostitutes. Obviously one has sex by means of the body and its members, not by means of the mind or the soul. He reproves them by asking, «Do you not know that your bodies are members of Christ? Shall I therefore take the members of Christ and make them members of a prostitute? Never! Do you not know that he who joins himself to a prostitute becomes one body with her? For, as it is written, "The two shall become one flesh"» (1Cor 6,15-16). Since the Christian has already given his body to Jesus Christ, his Lord, he is not free to take it back and then give it away to a prostitute to be profaned. The Apostle next goes on to remind his addressees of the inherent dignity of the human body, especially now that they have become Christians. «Do you not know that your body is a temple of the Holy Spirit within you, which you have from God? You are not your own; you were bought with a price. So glorify God in your body» (1Cor 6,19-20). From this passage we learn that the body is so important that Paul considers it to be the very temple of the Holy Spirit. Thus for the Apostle, the Holy Spirit dwells in the body in the same way that a Greek god was thought to have dwelled in a temple. In the Greco-Roman world, people commonly believed that the presence of the god transformed the building into a sanctuary suitable for proper worship[6]. Paul

---

[5] Cf. 1Cor 5,3; 6,13 (2x).15.16.18 (2x).19.20; 7,4 (2x).34; 9,27; 12,12 (3x).14.15 (2x).16 (2x).17.18.19.20.22.23.24.25; 13,3; 15,35.37.38 (2x).40 (2x).44 (3x).

[6] «A. Greek Temples. By the 8th century B.C.E. the Greeks had begun to build temples to their gods. The typical Archaic *temenos* was an enclosed area containing a rectangular building facing a high, raised rectangular altar (*bomos*). The Greek temple, *naos*, was considered the dwelling place of the divinity and the main chamber of the *naos*, the *cella*, was used for display of the cult statue of the god. Sometimes temples also included a separate chamber, *adyton*, whose use was restricted to priests or priestesses. The major religious ceremonies, however, did not take place in the temple, but at the altar outside [...] The architecture of the Greek sanctuary was determined by the needs of the cult. Because the area of the sanctuary was though to be sacred, certain standards of purity were required

adopts this rather familiar notion and applies it to the Christian. It is in the believer's own body that God's Spirit now dwells and this indwelling divine presence serves to make the body a kind of sanctuary in which God can truly be glorified. This passage from 1 Corinthians is essential for a correct Christian understanding of the worth and significance of the human body. The Apostle sees a strong link between the Christian's inherent dignity as a temple of the Holy Spirit and the moral obligation he has to preserve that dignity intact. Hence this passage provides a significant ethical principle for Christian action in the present life. Not only during his life on earth does the believer's body remain a temple of the Holy Spirit, but also in the life to come. In fact both the natural body and the spiritual body are capable of radiating God's glory: the first, only once it has been inhabited by the Holy Spirit, but in an obscure way; the second, once it has been clothed with immortality, in a radiant and brilliant way. Freed from sin and corruption, the spiritual body will be the fitting and flawless vessel through which human beings will glorify God. We shall return to this passage later when we consider the relationship between the spiritual body and the eternal indwelling of the Holy Spirit.

In chapter twelve Paul returns to a discussion of the body, but this time he chooses to emphasize the fact that τὸ σῶμα is composed of parts. «For just as the body is one and has many members and all the members of the body, though many, are one body, so it is with Christ» (1Cor 12,12). The Apostle next goes on to list the parts of the body, each of which provides an irreplaceable contribution to the workings of the whole. The foot (v. 15), the hand (v. 15), the ear (v. 16) and the eye (v. 16) represent the various members of the

---

of worshippers. Inscriptions at the entrance to sanctuaries often prohibited from entry those who had recently participated in a funeral, assisted at a childbirth, or engaged in recent sexual intercourse. Basins of water were placed at the entrance of the sanctuary so that those about to worship could perform a ritual purification by sprinkling water before entering the sacred area [...] B. Roman Temples. The Latin word *templum* is related to the Greek word *temenos* and referred originally to an open space marked off for observation of the sky and the taking of auspices and divination. Eventually the word *templum* referred to the piece of land dedicated to a god and used for religious ritual. A *templum* could include a building, *aedes*, an altar and votive dedications. The *aedes* functioned like the Greek *naos* and housed the statue of the god. The architecture of Roman temple buildings, in fact was influenced by Greek models. Some temples were open to all, others were subject to restrictions based on gender or social status. Some temples belonged to private religious associations or *collegia*; many of these included cooking and dining facilities for the banquets of the members» (S. GUETTEL COLE, «Temples and Sanctuaries: Greco-Roman Temples», 380-381).

human body. Whether honorable or less honorable, each of them is united to the others thanks to God's loving, creative design.

For a last set of examples to demonstrate the literal sense of σῶμα, we now consider chapter fifteen. We have already seen that the second half of this chapter dedicated to the resurrection serves to respond to Paul's question as posed in 15,35, «But some one will ask, "How are the dead raised? With what kind of body do they come?"» The ensuing discussion explicitly focuses on the various types of bodies as fashioned by the Creator. As regards to the bare kernel to be sown, Paul insists that God has the power to transform it as he wills: «But God gives it a body as he has chosen and to each kind of seed its own body» (1Cor 15,38). He goes on to affirm that there are celestial as well as terrestrial bodies (1Cor 15,40), each with its own glory. In fact, we have seen that this assertion is essential for Paul's argument. By means of this extensive consideration of the various types of bodies, Paul has been building up to the crucial point of his entire argument: the natural body will be transformed into the spiritual body at the time of the resurrection of the dead. But this fundamental change must be clarified and explained. Paul strongly insists on the difference in order to prove his point that the glorious and imperishable spiritual body does not resemble the weak and perishable natural one. Lest his addressees misunderstand the mystery of the resurrection, the Apostle asserts with great conviction that he is not referring to the reanimation of the natural body. On the contrary, if the present body of human beings is to become eternal and imperishable, it must be completely changed.

We saw above that by using the metaphor of sowing, Paul had concluded one subunit by affirming «It is sown a natural body, it is raised a spiritual body» (1Cor 15,44a). He begins the next subunit with the present verse in question: «If there is a natural body, there is a spiritual one» (1Cor 15,44b). In short, it is obvious that the σῶμα under discussion in 1 Corinthians 15,44 can only refer to the physical body as understood in the literal sense of the term.

Elsewhere in the letter, Paul uses σῶμα metaphorically seven times[7]. The Apostle speaks of the body in the figurative sense in order to describe the newly-formed social body made up of the baptized. In light of this sacrament of initiation, Christians are now joined to Christ and to one another in a new community. Paul expresses this most eloquently in chapter ten. «The cup of blessing which we bless, is it not a participation in the blood of Christ? The

---

[7] Cf. 1Cor 10,16-17; 11,24.27.29; 12,13.27.

bread which we break, is it not a participation in the body of Christ? Because there is one bread, we who are many are one body, for we all partake of the one bread» (1Cor 10,16-17). The Apostle returns to this image of the community later in the letter when he states «For by one Spirit we were all baptized into one body — Jews or Greeks, slaves or free — and all were made to drink of one Spirit» (1Cor 12,13). Before going on to treat the variety of gifts and the diversity of roles in the Church, Paul first reminds the Corinthians of their recent incorporation into Christ: «Now you are the body of Christ and individually members of it» (1Cor 12,27).

In addition to referring to the Church, σῶμα is also used in the figurative sense to refer to the eucharistic elements. In his teaching on the Lord's Supper, Paul explains that the bread and wine sacramentally become the body and blood of Christ. «For I received from the Lord what I also delivered to you, that the Lord Jesus on the night when he was betrayed took bread and when he had given thanks, he broke it and said, "This is my body which is for you. Do this in remembrance of me"» (1Cor 11,23-24). It is for this reason that the Christian has an obligation to share in the Lord's Supper in a worthy manner: when he eats the eucharistic bread and drinks from the sacred cup he in fact partakes of the body and blood of Christ. Sacred table-fellowship demands virtuous and righteous behavior on the part of the believer. Unruly and selfish conduct during the eucharist is completely unacceptable since it profanes «the body and blood of the Lord» (1Cor 11,27).

In conclusion, τὸ σῶμα is always understood by Paul to mean the physical body. Whether understood literally or figuratively, the word always keeps this basic, primary meaning. Given the overall unfolding of Paul's argument in 1 Corinthians 15, σῶμα must also be understood literally in this subunit. Nevertheless, the presence of two modifying adjectives draws attention to the fact that there are two different kinds of bodies in question. It is to these crucial terms that we now turn our attention.

– ψυχικόν. There are only six occurrences of the Greek adjective ψυχικός in the New Testament; the four which appear in the Pauline corpus are limited to 1 Corinthians and thus interest us in a special way[8]. The word may be translated into English as «natural», «earthly», or «worldly». Unfortunately, none of these English adjectives adequately conveys the etymological connection of ψυχικός to its nominal cognate, ψυχή, which means «soul» or «being». Used

---

[8] Cf. E. SCHWEIZER, «ψυχικός», in *ThWNT*; A. SAND, «ψυχικός», in *EWNT*.

to describe a human being or a human body, this Greek adjective characterizes humanity's natural existence apart from the Holy Spirit.   It is interesting to note that the Apostle uses ψυχικός in antithetical parallelism with πνευματικός. In all four of the word's occurrences in 1 Corinthians, both of these adjectives appear together. Paul clearly presents these two adjectives as opposites in order to express his understanding of the two distinct types or modes of human life which he wants to depict in this subunit.

The word ψυχικός first occurs in the Apostle's teaching on God's Spirit at the beginning of the letter. «The natural human being (ψυχικὸς δὲ ἄνθρωπος) does not receive the gifts of the Spirit of God, for they are folly to him and he is not able to understand them because they are spiritually discerned» (1Cor 2,14). Since he knows only the things of this earth and has not received the Holy Spirit or the Spirit's gifts, it is simply impossible for the natural human being to know spiritual things. In contrast, Paul goes on to claim «But the spiritual one (ὁ δὲ πνευματικός) judges all things, but is himself to be judged by no one» (1Cor 2,15). Since he has received the Holy Spirit and the Spirit's many gifts, the spiritual human being has the capacity to judge, discern and comprehend spiritual gifts. In this passage, then, the natural human being refers to the non-Christian, someone who knows only «a wisdom of this age» (1Cor 2,6). In contrast, the spiritual human being is the Christian, someone who has «a secret and hidden wisdom of God» (1Cor 2,7) and «the mind of Christ» (1Cor 2,16).

The next three occurrences of ψυχικός are found in chapter fifteen. We have already seen that the previous subunit ends with the assertion «It is sown a natural (ψυχικόν) body, it is raised a spiritual body» (1Cor 15,44a) and the present subunit begins «If there is a natural (ψυχικόν) body, there is also a spiritual one» (1Cor 15,44b). Paul is speaking about the kind of body the Christian has both before and after the resurrection of the dead; in this verse he is no longer contrasting the believer to the non-believer[9]. The Apostle has

---

[9] «En *I Cor.*, II, 14ss, l'antithèse entre ψυχικός et πνευματικός porte sur deux catégories d'hommes qui existent maintenant et se distinguent en première ligne quant à leur *attitude religieuse*; dans XV, 44 à 46 il s'agit au contraire de deux *conditions anthropologiques* successives. Paul songe, en ce dernier passage, à la vie "pneumatique" en son expression plénière — celle de ressuscité — , tandis que son attention se porte, au chapitre II, sur les prémices de celle-ci, déjà accordées moyennant l'effusion de l'Esprit qui fait connaître les mystères de la sagesse divine (cf. v. 12)» (R. MORISSETTE, «L'Antithèse entre le "psychique" et le "pneumatique"», 101).

been principally concerned with the body since v. 35 where he raised the question, «How are the dead raised? With what kind of *body* do they come?» In light of this, the opposition between ψυχικόν and πνευματικόν in v. 44 can be traced to Paul's desire to contrast the believer's natural body which must die (since it was sown into a world marked by perishability and corruption) and his spiritual body which is raised to eternal life. In other words, the Apostle finds it necessary to emphasize the difference between the present body and the future one. At birth, a human being receives a body which is appropriate for life on earth; later, at the resurrection of the dead, he will receive a different kind of body which is appropriate for life in heaven. This conclusion is corroborated two verses later when Paul spells out the order of events. «But it is not the spiritual which is first but the natural (τὸ ψυχικόν) and then the spiritual» (1Cor 15,46). «The natural», that is, the natural *body*, appears first. Only later, at the resurrection of the dead, does the spiritual body arise. Paul insists on this sequence in order to make clear the fact that the first Adam possesses the first kind of body (the natural one), while the second Adam, the risen Christ, possesses the second kind (the spiritual one).

In short, the «natural body» (σῶμα ψυχικόν) as presented in this subunit refers to the Christian's body as it exists in this life. This body is of course no different from the body of non-believers. At the time of death, it is placed into the grave where it awaits the moment of the resurrection when «the trumpet will sound and the dead will be raised imperishable and we shall be changed» (1Cor 15,52). In the moment of transformation, the natural body will become the spiritual body through God's all-powerful intervention. By the use of antithetical parallelism, therefore, Paul seeks to underscore discontinuity in 1 Corinthians 15,44b-49, the natural body will be replaced by the spiritual body at the resurrection of the dead.

As regards to the whole question of continuity, we may assume that there is a basic correlation in as much as the particular body that dies is the same one that will be raised and transformed. But Paul prefers to remain silent on this point. His central idea is that the natural will cease to exist since it is not suitable to the post resurrection state of the believer. Since it is of the earth, the natural is not suitable for the realm of the Spirit. It must be changed, since «flesh and blood cannot inherit the kingdom of God, nor does the perishable inherit the imperishable» (1Cor 15,50).

We have already noted the etymological connection of ψυχικός to the noun ψυχή, «soul» or «being». But what precisely is the relation between these two cognates? We face the same difficulty with regard to πνευματικός and πνεῦμα, the other set of cognates that concern us in this subunit. If we are to answer this important question, it seems clear that we must first understand the function and meaning of the Greek suffix -ικός. Only in this way can we appreciate the use of the adjectives in v. 44 and the nouns in v. 45. With this purpose in mind, let us now turn to a brief excursus dedicated to this critical ending.

Although -ικός is one of the most common adjectival endings in the Greek language, there is little agreement as yet among exegetes over its precise function. In the beginning of the century, Robertson and Plummer held that this suffix communicates an ethical of dynamic sense with respect to the cognate noun[10]. Later, Clavier maintained that it indicates dependence or direction[11], while in a recent book Harris claims that its aim is functional or ethical[12]. But if these interpretations were true for all adjectives ending in -ικός, how then should we understand common words like βασιλικός, ἐθνικός, or λογικός? Is it really accurate to say that this suffix conveys the sense of «being led or directed by» the king, the nation, or the Logos? A brief glimpse at a few examples in the New Testament would suffice to prove that this interpretation is obviously inaccurate. If we are to gain any insights at all into the exact

---

[10] Robertson and Plummer make an important point in their exegesis of the word σαρκίνοις in 1Cor 3,1. «The word is chosen deliberately and it expresses a shade of meaning different from σαρκικός, placing the state of the Corinthians under a distinct aspect. The termination -ινος denotes a *material* relation, while -ικος denotes an *ethical* or dynamic relation, to the idea involved in the root» (A. ROBERTSON – A. PLUMMER, *The First Epistle of St. Paul to the Corinthians*, 52).

[11] «(ii) Ψυχικόν. La désinence "κόν", la même que dans σαρκικόν, semble indiquer que cette épithète ne désigne pas une composition, une formation psychique, in ψυχή, mais une dépendance ou une direction. Une nuance péjorative y est-elle également attachée? Il faudrait, dans ce cas, que "psychique" eût pris un sens éthique analogue à celui de "charnel", et opposé à "pneumatique". Qu'il y ait une antithèse dans notre texte, cela paraît évident; mais il n'est pas certain qu'elle se ramène à l'antagonisme de σάρξ et de πνεῦμα dans κατὰ σάρκα — κατὰ πνεῦμα, ou dans σαρκικός — πνευματικός. Il serait imprudent de se prononcer sans autre témoin. (iii) Πνευματικόν. La même désinence "κόν", dont le sens général a été déja précisé, semble écarter, à première vue, la notion d'une substance "pneumatique", dont serait constitué le nouveau corps. Il s'agirait plutôt d'une orientation différente, d'une direction, d'une inspiration [...]» (H. CLAVIER, «Brèves remarques sur la notion de σῶμα πνευματικόν», 345-346).

[12] «because Greek adjectives ending in -*ikos* carry a *function* or *ethical* meaning, it is preferable to understand *pneumatikos* in the sense "animated and guided by the spirit [*pneuma*]," with the spirit as the organizing or governing principle» (M.J. HARRIS, *From Grave to Glory*, 195).

meaning of -ικός, it would seem best to consult the work of Greek philologists. Let us now consider the findings of three scholars who have studied this problem in great detail.

Moulton's ground breaking work on word composition was taken up and completed by his editor, W. H. Howard, who was responsible for the chapter on suffixes[13]. He divides denominative adjectives in -ικός into two kinds. The first type dates to the Homeric period and it consists of those words which describe ethnic groups. Examples include Ἑβραϊκός, Ἑλληνικός, Ἰταλικός and Ῥωμαϊκός. The second type can be traced to the classical period. At that time the suffix was extended through the creation of words like φυσικός and μαντικός. Howard remarks that in these cases the suffix was joined to the -ι- stem of the noun. First a favorite of the Ionian sophists and then used commonly by Attic writers, -ικός had made a valuable contribution to the Greek language by the fifth century B.C. At this point its other meaning became apparent: «belonging to», «pertaining to», «with the characteristics of»[14]. If we again use βασιλικός as an example, the term now makes sense in light of this definition. βασιλικός means «belonging to the king» or «royal». Lastly, Howard lists four adjectives from the New Testament which form an important group: σαρκικός, ψυχικός, πνευματικός and σωματικός. It is interesting to note that these four terms appear primarily in Paul's genuine letters. They belong to the same semantic field in as much as they explain and specify his notion of the human body.

In his monumental study on the function and meaning of the suffix in Plato, A. N. Ammann came up with very similar findings[15]. In addition to expressing membership in a particular ethnic group or city state, -ικός primarily indicates possession. Ammann presents an impressive analysis of the four hundred and twenty-nine words created by the philosopher which end in this suffix. A couple examples include ἀνθρωπικός, «zum ἄνθρωπος "Menschen" gehörig, menschlich» and ἀστρονομικός, «was zu einem Sternkundiger (ἀστρονόμος) und seinem Wissensgebiet gehört». For Plato, then, the suffix exhibits a classifying and categorizing function throughout his work. It represents a helpful tool for the philosopher as he sought to define the complex nuances of his thought.

---

[13] See J. H. MOULTON and W.F. HOWARD, *Accidence and Word-Formation*, § 157.
[14] This represents the principal meaning still held today. See BDR §113.2.
[15] See A.N. AMMANN, *-ΙΚΟΣ Bei Platon*, § 70-75.

Lastly, we consider two important works of one of this century's major philologists, Pierre Chantraine. In an early book on the formation of the noun, Chantraine points out that -ικός made a great contribution to the formation of new vocabulary in ancient as well as Koine Greek[16]. The suffix was a favorite of the Sophists in particular and the cultivated and well educated in general. Through the use of many diverse examples, he shows that medical, scientific and philosophical prose is filled with adjectives ending in -ικός. The phenomenon is especially striking in the works of Plato and Aristotle. Chantraine confirms the findings of Howard when he demonstrates that the adjective's suffix means that which concerns or belongs to its nominal cognate. A few terms coined by Aristotle will provide some helpful examples[17]: ἐλαϊκός, «qui concerne l'olivier», cf. ἐλαία; σιτικός, «qui concerne le blé», cf. σῖτος (le mot est attesté chez plusieurs écrivains de la κοινή); and λιθικός, «qui concerne les picrres», cf. λίθος. This is only a sampling of the seven hundred or so derivatives in -ικός created by the philosopher.

Yet it was not until 1956 that Chantraine published his definitive study on the suffix. In a seventy-five page study entitled «Le suffixe grec -ικός», he undertook a comprehensive and systematic analysis which treats the entire history of the Greek language[18]. After presenting the origin of the suffix in Homer, Chantraine defines its function by giving abundant examples as found in the works of the historians and philosophers. Agreeing with Ammann, he also recognizes that the suffix's strength lies in its ability to classify ideas in a methodological way[19]. He proves convincingly that the suffix has indeed made a significant contribution to the enrichment of the Greek language. In his summary of the essential function of -ικός, Chantraine insists again that this suffix signifies belonging to a group or to a category. This data supports his earlier findings, namely, that -ικός is primarily used to express possession. As for the most creative contributors to the development of this very functional and significant suffix, Chantraine readily admits that Plato and Aristotle were by far the most seminal authors. He credits this to the great precision required for their intellectual method which is constructed on dialectic and dichotomy[20].

---

[16] See P. CHANTRAINE, *La Formation des noms*, § 317-321.

[17] See P. CHANTRAINE, *La Formation des noms*, § 321.

[18] See P. CHANTRAINE, *Études sur le vocabulaire grec*, 97-171.

[19] See P. CHANTRAINE, *Études sur le vocabulaire grec*, 141.

[20] «On a déjà dit que c'est le développement de la pensée des sophistes ou, si l'on préfère, des philosophes, qui a donné au suffixe une extension inattendue. L'examen des

Thanks to the scholarly contribution made by these Greek philologists, we are now in a position to return to our study of the adjectives in v. 44. These very important findings allow us to draw the following conclusion: the ψυχικός is that which concerns, belongs to, or is characteristic of the ψυχή, while the πνευματικός is that which concerns, belongs to, or is characteristic of the πνεῦμα. Hence by extension, the σῶμα ψυχικόν is that body which concerns, belongs to, or is characteristic of the ψυχή, while the σῶμα πνευματικόν is that body which concerns, belongs to, or is characteristic of the πνεῦμα. Hence the suffix reveals the close relationship that exists between each pair of cognates, a connection that must be kept in mind both for exegesis and for translation. Nevertheless, -ικός by itself does not disclose the exact meaning of these adjectives. That information can only be determined through further investigation into the precise meaning of their nominal cognates.

What then does Paul understand by ψυχή and πνεῦμα? Only once this question is answered shall we be able to comprehend what he means by ψυχικός and πνευματικός. We must investigate these nouns in great detail in our study of the following verse. For now it is enough to note that ψυχή and πνεῦμα in v. 45 stand in opposition to one another, just like ψυχικός and πνευματικός do in v. 44. This contrast is essential for Paul since he is asserting that there is a fundamental difference between the two Adams. Although it is not the only characteristic that distinguishes them, the differing corporeal nature of the two men in question certainly represents one of the essential points of the subunit.

Given everything that has been said above, how then are we to translate ψυχικός into English? As we noted in our study of the word σῶμα, the noun itself already means «physical body». So when the RSV and NRSV translate ψυχικός as «physical», they advance a misleading interpretation. If Paul had wanted to modify the noun by describing it as «physical», he would have used the common Greek adjective φυσικός to convey that meaning. He did not, since to do so would have implied that somehow the body is material in this

---

dialogues de Platon que nous avons choisis comme examples, le *Sophiste* et le *Politique*, a illustré la valeur catégorisante de -ικός. C'est la dialectique, avec sa démarche d'analyse le plus souvent dichotomique, qui a dégagé la fonction essentielle du suffixe et s'est d'autre part trouvée à l'origine de son immense diffusion. On pourrait relever également chez Aristote un grand nombre d'adjectifs de ce type. La science d'Aristote visait essentiellement à établir une classification des notions; or le suffixe -ικός constituait l'instrument approprié à cet objet» (P. CHANTRAINE, *Études sur le vocabulaire grec*, 151).

world and immaterial in the next[21]. The NAB and NJB capture this point when they correctly translate ψυχικός as «natural». In contrasting the σῶμα ψυχικόν to the σῶμα πνευματικόν, Paul is comparing the original, natural kind of human body as God first created it on earth to the spiritual body of the risen Lord who now dwells in heaven. The first is concerned with or is characteristic of the ψυχή while the second is concerned with or is characteristic of the πνεῦμα. At present, only Christ has this spiritual body. Yet at the last trumpet, the body of every Christian will be transformed into a spiritual body so that he may fully come to «bear the image of the one of heaven» (1Cor 15,49).

– ἔστιν καὶ πνευματικόν. These three words make up the apodosis of the first class condition which begins the subunit. By means of this clause, Paul draws out the logical conclusion from the evidence he has just provided. Accepting the existence of the natural body as a given, the Apostle now informs his addressees that «there is also a spiritual one», (the noun «body» being understood). The καί in this clause acts as an adverb; it serves to accentuate Paul's claim that there is in fact another kind of body that the Corinthians do not yet know[22]. The sentence as a whole provides an excellent example of a typological argument. Through the use of antithetical parallelism, Paul creates a tension between both clauses in this conditional sentence which, as we have seen, continues through the whole passage that follows. In this way, the Apostle composes a simple yet brilliant introduction to the whole subunit. Right from the start, he focuses the attention of his addressees on the bodies of the two individuals who will be named explicitly in v. 45, the first Adam and the last Adam.

---

[21] «What should be noticed is that Paul, contrasting the two bodies, uses particularly the words "natural" (*psychikon*) and "spiritual". If Paul wanted to teach that the resurrection-body will not be a body of flesh, he would certainly have used another word than *psychikon*. In Paul's writings the most common counterpart of "spirit" is "flesh", and if he meant to say that this present body is a flesh-body in distinction from the resurrection-body as a spirit-body, the apostle would have used his favorite words "carnal", "fleshly", or "fleshy" (*sarkikon* or *sarkinon*). The fact that Paul avoids all of these adjectives and instead uses *psychikon* proves that he wants to prevent the Corinthians (and the Church of all ages) from thinking that there is no resurrection hope for this present body of flesh» (J.A. SCHEP, *The Nature of the Resurrection-Body*, 200).

[22] See W. RADL, «καί», in *EWNT*.

In our preceding discussion on the natural body, we had already begun to examine the term πνευματικόν. It is now time to scrutinize this very important word in greater detail. Given the etymological link between πνευματικόν and πνεῦμα, a close study of this adjectival form will help shed some valuable light on our investigation into the Holy Spirit's action in the resurrection of the dead.

The word πνευματικόν means «spiritual»; it occurs twenty-six times in the New Testament and nineteen times in the genuine letters of Paul. It is interesting to note for our present purposes that over half of the total occurrences of the word, fifteen to be exact, are found in 1 Corinthians[23]. Unlike ψυχικόν, πνευματικόν poses no problems for the translator; the English adjective «spiritual» both captures its exact meaning as well as underscores it etymological connection to «Spirit», its nominal cognate.

The first distinction that must be made concerns the Apostle's use of this adjective. He employs it either as a substantivized or attributive adjective. In most cases, πνευματικός occurs as a substantivized adjective, with or without the definite article. As we saw above, this is the case of 1 Corinthians 2,15. «The spiritual human being (ὁ πνευματικός) judges all things, but is himself to be judged by no one». The πνευματικοί know God's saving deeds thanks to the Holy Spirit[24]. In addition, Paul uses the neuter noun πνευματικά to describe those gifts given by the Holy Spirit. «Make love your aim and earnestly desire the spiritual gifts (πνευματικά), especially that you may prophesy» (1Cor 14,1)[25].

In the remaining occurrences of the adjective, πνευματικός is used as an attributive adjective to describe the noun it modifies. This is the case in chapter ten with regard to Paul's warning against idolatry. «and all ate the same spiritual (πνευματικόν) food and all drank the same spiritual (πνευματικόν) drink. For they drank from the spiritual (πνευματικῆς) rock which followed them and the rock was Christ» (1Cor 10,3-4). The reference is of course to Israel's miraculous meals in the desert: her food and drink came from a

---

[23] Cf. E. SCHWEIZER, «πνευματικός», in *ThWNT*; J. KREMER, «πνευματικός», in *EWNT*.

[24] For other references to the πνευματικοί in Paul's letters, cf. 1Cor 2,13; 3,1; 14,37; and Gal 6,1.

[25] For other references to πνευματικά, cf. Rom 15,27; 1Cor 2,13; 9,11; and 12,1.

supernatural source[26]. It is precisely this supernatural origin that Paul wishes to emphasize in the subunit that concerns us. In 1 Corinthians 15,44, πνευματικόν appears twice as an attributive adjective in order to modify σῶμα. By claiming that there is also a «spiritual body», the Apostle teaches that, like the manna and water in the desert, this body also has a supernatural origin. The Apostle underscores his point concerning the spiritual body's creation yet again by repeating πνευματικόν twice in v. 46, «But it is not the spiritual which is first but the natural and then the spiritual». If weremember that the σῶμα πνευματικόν signifies that body which is concerned with or characteristic of the πνεῦμα, then it would seem reasonable to speculate that the Holy Spirit plays an essential role in the creation of the spiritual body. But before this can be proven, however, we must study the noun πνεῦμα very closely to see if the context allows us to draw this conclusion. With this task in mind, we are now ready to proceed with the analysis of the next verse.

2. 1Cor 15,45

Given its reference to the life-giving Spirit, this crucial verse on the two Adams lies at the heart of our study on the Spirit's agency in the resurrection of the dead. For centuries it has presented exegetes with a challenging *crux interpretum*. As with the preceding verse, we will now examine all the key words of v. 45 as part of the close reading of the text.

οὕτως καὶ γέγραπται, Ἐγένετο ὁ πρῶτος ἄνθρωπος Ἀδὰμ εἰς ψυχὴν ζῶσαν· ὁ ἔσχατος Ἀδὰμ εἰς πνεῦμα ζῳοποιοῦν.
«So it is written, "The first human being Adam became a living being"; the last Adam became a life-giving Spirit».

– οὕτως καὶ γέγραπται. The first three words of this verse present a formulaic introduction to the Scriptural quotation that follows. The adverb οὕτως is used frequently by Paul; it is found thirty-one times in 1 Corinthians and seventeen times in Romans. οὕτως can either refer to what has come before, in which case it is best translated as «thus»; or, as in the case of v. 45,

---

[26] For another example of πνευματικός used as an attributive adjective, see Rom 1,11, «spiritual gift». For the unique example of πνευματικός when used as a predicate adjective, see Rom 7,14, «the law is spiritual». In both cases, Paul is teaching that both the spiritual gift he wishes to share as well as the Mosaic law are supernatural in origin. They do not owe their existence to human beings.

it can refer to what follows, in which case it may be translated as «so» or «as follows»[27].

The verb γέγραπται is the perfect passive form of γράφω, a common verb that appears sixty-two times in the genuine letters of Paul and eighteen times in 1 Corinthians. Paul frequently employs it as a way of presenting a passage from Scripture[28]. For example, there are two typical occurrences in the first chapter of the letter: «For it is written (γέγραπται γάρ), "I will destroy the wisdom of the wise and the cleverness of the clever I will thwart"» (1Cor 1,19) and «therefore, as it is written (καθὼς γέγραπται), "Let him who boasts, boast of the Lord"» (1Cor 1,31). In this way Paul puts forward his own interpretation of Genesis 2,7, the scriptural text which follows and to which we now turn.

– Consistent with the antithetical argument begun in the previous verse, v. 45 constitutes an antithesis built on the Adam-Christ typology. The first half, devoted to Adam, introduces a midrash pesher[29] of Genesis 2,7 (LXX), the proof text for Paul's argument; the second half, devoted to Christ, presents the Apostle's own words which parallel the Genesis text. In order to exegete this verse thoroughly, it would be best to proceed in three successive steps. First, we have to focus on v. 45a, namely, Paul's midrash pesher. How exactly does it differ from the Septuagint? What did Paul add and why? Second, we must examine the sentence as a whole in order to grasp its parallel structure. In doing so, we shall discover that Paul composed the verse in such a way that the elements of v. 45a are perfectly balanced with those of v. 45b. After having completed this work, we will then be in a position to undertake our third task, namely, the word by word analysis to which we are now accustomed. Only in this way can the richness of this passage be fully appreciated.

---

[27] See H. BALZ, «οὕτω, οὕτως», in *EWNT*.

[28] A study of Paul's exegetical method, although fascinating, would take us too far afield. For some essential literature on the subject, see the bibliography in the article by H. HÜBNER, «γραφή, ῆς, ἡ , γράφω», in *EWNT*.

[29] A midrash pesher is a biblical quotation that is both a citation as well as an interpretation. A good example of a midrash pesher can be found in 1Cor 14,21. «In the law it is written, "By men of strange tongues and by the lips of foreigners will I speak to this people and even then they will not listen to me, says the Lord"». Here the Apostle has liberally adapted a passage from Is 28,11-12, following exactly neither the LXX nor the MT. To address his own concerns, Paul changes the word order and leaves out a good portion of the original text. He modifies Gen 2,7 in a similar manner.

Let us begin by focusing on the first half of the verse, the midrash pesher. How does it compare to the Septuagint? What are the similarities and differences? In as much as the Apostle's whole argument is constructed on this proof text, a close examination of v. 45a will help shed more light on the subunit as a whole.

In order to make a sharp contrast between these two texts, let us place them in parallel lines to facilitate the comparison.

Gen 2,7 (LXX)καὶ ἐγένετο ὁ   ἄνθρωπος   εἰς ψυχὴν ζῶσαν.
1Cor 15,45a   ἐγένετο ὁ πρῶτος ἄνθρωπος ᾿Αδὰμ εἰς ψυχὴν ζῶσαν·

It is clear that in his pesher, Paul adds only two words, the adjective πρῶτος and the name ᾿Αδαμ. But why did he make these additions? It would seem that by means of the adjective «first», the Apostle carefully sets the stage for the Adam-Christ typology that follows. Paul is quite consistent here. The antithetical argument of the previous verse had focused on two different kinds of bodies. In his pesher, the antithesis now becomes typological: Paul concentrates on the two different types of human beings as embodied by their representatives, Adam and Christ. As for the addition of the name «Adam», the use of the proper noun points to humanity's singular ancestor, the man whom God first formed from the dust of the earth[30]. In this way, Paul personalizes his argument by moving it beyond the more scientific discussion of the various sorts of seeds and bodies (as developed before in his argument from reason). In this subunit the talk is no longer of birds and fish (v. 39) or the sun and the moon (v. 41), but of a real human being formed by God and granted the breath of life. For Paul, then, «the first human being Adam» not only possesses the first natural body, but he also stands as the first natural human being. Adam perfectly exemplifies the prototype of all who were to follow him in the natural order of life.

We are now in a position to turn to the second task and examine the sentence as a whole. If we place both parts of the verse side by side in parallel lines, the syntactic structure of the sentence can be examined more readily. Once arranged in this way, the correspondence between the two halves is rather striking.

---

[30] «(1) By means of the introduction of πρῶτος, "first," "man" is given a typological interpretation. (2) By means of the insertion of "Adam," his character as "primal man" is indicated» (H. CONZELMANN, *1 Corinthians*, 284).

1Cor 15,45 οὕτως καὶ γέγραπται,
Ἐγένετο ὁ πρῶτος ἄνθρωπος Ἀδὰμ εἰς ψυχὴν   ζῶσαν·
ὁ ἔσχατος   Ἀδὰμ εἰς πνεῦμα ζωοποιοῦν.

Note that the verb ἐγένετο and the noun ἄνθρωπος appear only in the first line. Although omitted in the second, these words are nevertheless clearly implied. No doubt Paul left them out for stylistic reasons, since their presence would have made the sentence unnecessarily ponderous and repetitive. The only words that are repeated are the definite article ὁ and the proper noun Ἀδάμ. Note also how the remaining words match up into opposing pairs. In this way the Apostle contrasts ὁ πρῶτος to ὁ ἔσχατος, ψυχήν to πνεῦμα and ζῶσαν to ζωοποιοῦν. The choice of these adjectives, nouns and participles is not accidental; Paul selected them with great care in order to make his point. Moreover, the syntax of the sentence is quite important. By placing them at the end of each line, Paul puts added emphasis on the nouns and the participles: The first Adam became a being that is *living*, while the second Adam became a Spirit that is *life-giving*. The final position of these verbal forms shows that they represent the important action words of the verse.

What then can we conclude from these findings? It seems clear that Paul composed the verse in such a way so as to place the emphasis on the second line. Through his midrash pesher, the Apostle changed the text of Genesis 2,7 in v. 45a so that it would resemble what he really wanted to write in v. 45b. The nouns ψυχή and πνεῦμα refer back to their cognate adjectives in v. 44, ψυχικόν and πνευματικόν. These too have been chosen with great care to fit into the context. The first Adam is the bearer of the natural body, while the last Adam is the bearer of the spiritual one. Hence, through his own exegesis of the Pentateuch, Paul demonstrates the cardinal doctrine of the gospel he preaches: the resurrection body truly does exist. In other words, there is such a thing as a spiritual body because in fact the risen Christ possesses one. The entire verse has been carefully crafted so that the Adam-Christ typology proves the central point of the subunit, namely, «there is also a spiritual body» (v. 44b).

After studying both the midrash pesher and the parallel structure of this crucial verse, we are now ready to undertake a detailed investigation of each word. Let us now turn to this task.

– Ἐγένετο...εἰς. Occurring six hundred and sixty-seven times, the verb γίνομαι is one of the most common words in the New Testament. In the genuine letters of Paul it is found one hundred and eighteen times, forty-one times in 1 Corinthians. For Paul it has three principle meanings: 1) «to happen», «to take place», 2) «to become», «to originate», 3) «to be made, created, or born». In addition, Paul sometimes uses it as a synonym of εἰμί[31].

Let us start with the third meaning, since it is relatively rare in the Pauline corpus. Two examples are found in a single verse in Galatians: «But when the time had fully come, God sent forth his Son, born (γενόμενον) of woman, born (γενόμενον) under the law», (Gal 4,4). As for the first meaning, «to happen», this occurs quite frequently in Paul's letters. For example, when speaking about his own rights the Apostle insists «But I have made no use of any of these rights, nor am I writing this that it may happen (γένηται) in my case» (1Cor 9,15). And as for the use of γίνομαι as a synonym of εἰμί, we find a good example in the passage where Paul speaks of becoming all things to all people. «To the Jews I became (ἐγενόμην) as a Jew, in order to win Jews; to those under the law [I became] as one under the law — though not being myself under the law — that I might win those under the law» (1Cor 9,20). In other words, with the Jews Paul *is* a Jew and with the Gentiles Paul *is* a Gentile. Having become someone and being someone are closely linked in meaning in this verse.

After having examined these diverse meanings, we are now ready to examine the second meaning of γίνομαι, «to become». Paul had already used γίνομαι earlier in the letter to express the notion of change or alteration. In chapter three, the Apostle admonishes the Corinthians by telling them, «Let no one deceive himself. If any one among you thinks that he is wise in this age, let him become (γενέσθω) a fool that he may become wise» (1Cor 3,18). The change in question is a mental one: transformed by the folly of the cross, the disciple is now turned into a fool for Christ.

Another example of γίνομαι which shows a radical change of nature can be found in 2 Corinthians. In urging his addressees to be reconciled to God, Paul teaches that «For our sake he (God) made him (Christ) to be sin who knew no sin, so that in him we might become (γενώμεθα) the righteousness of God» (2Cor 5,21). In order to express the mystery of salvation, Paul speaks of two extraordinary transformations: the sinless Son of God is made into the embodiment of sin, while sinners are changed into the very righteousness of God. The perspective natures of each one are essentially changed through the intervention of God the Father.

---

[31] Cf. F. BÜCHSEL, «γίνομαι», in *ThWNT*; W. HACKENBERG, «γίνομαι», in *EWNT*.

It is this sense of a fundamental change of being that the verb expresses in 1 Corinthians 15,45a. Paul is citing the creation passage from Genesis: from the dust of the earth, Adam became (ἐγένετο) a human being. The first man was changed at the moment of his creation, as the Genesis text makes quite clear. Dust ceased to be dust and was transformed into a human being; what was once lifeless suddenly and miraculously came to life. Thus, when Paul asserts that Adam became a living being, he means that a fundamental transformation occurred in his very nature. A real alteration took place in the very act of creation which radically transformed his former condition as dust into his new condition as man.

Lastly, it is interesting to not that ἐγένετο [...] εἰς discloses the Hebrew original behind the Septuagint of Genesis 2,7. Both the Greek of this verse as well as Paul's pesher in 1 Corinthians 15,45a provide a literal and unidiomatic translation of the Masoretic Text, as they follow the Hebrew original word for word. The verb «to become» in Hebrew is of course expressed by combining the verb «to be», היה and the preposition ל. It is precisely this Hebrew idiom that we discover in Genesis 2,7 (LXX) and v. 45a with the words ἐγένετο [...] εἰς. After the verb γίνομαι we would expect a predicate nominative, but due to Semitic influence, instead we have the preposition εἰς followed by its object in the accusative case[32]. Hence both ψυχήν and πνεῦμα as well as the participles that modify them are all in the accusative in v. 45.

– ὁ πρῶτος. The adjective πρῶτος occurs one hundred and fifty-six times in the New Testament. The common term for «first», there are seven occurrences in 1 Corinthians of which three are found in the present subunit[33]. By repeating the word in v. 45, v. 46 and v. 47, Paul emphasizes that Adam came first in time. In fact, as we noted in the overview of the sentence, πρῶτος forms an antithesis with ἔσχατος, its opposite. In this way the Apostle makes a clear contrast between the different Adams he is describing: chronologically speaking, one is «the first» while the other is «the last». The word also signals the presence of a sequence: since these two human beings are types, there are also others who find their origin in them. The existence of this succession is

---

[32] «In place of the predicate nominative we find, not indeed in contradiction with the spirit of Greek, but, in Biblical usage at least, fairly certainly owing to Semitic influence (Hebrew *le*), after γίνεσθαι and εἶναι (or rather, ἔσεσθαι, which is closer in sense to γίνεσθαι), εἰς with the accusative and especially in O.T. quotations [...]» (ZERWICK § 32). Cf. BDR § 145.1 and HS § 184gδ.

[33] Cf. W. MICHAELIS, «πρῶτος», in *ThWNT*; H. LANGKAMMER, «πρῶτος», in *EWNT*.

stated explicitly in v. 48 when Paul speaks of two groups of people, «those who are of dust» and «those who are of heaven». In v. 45a, however, Paul primarily wants to insist that Adam was in fact the first example of a natural human being.

– ἄνθρωπος. The noun ἄνθρωπος means «human being» understood as a living creature distinct from other living beings (plants, animals, angels, or heavenly bodies) and from God. The word is quite common in the New Testament, occurring five hundred and fifty-one times in all; found ninety-five times in the genuine Pauline letters, in 1 Corinthians it occurs thirty-one times. We should note that Paul employs the noun only in the literal sense. Moreover, in the plural, ἄνθρωποι is used to refer to people[34]. A study of this essential term, limited though it may be, is essential if we are to achieve any insights into Pauline anthropology. What precisely is Paul's understanding of the human being? What is his philosophy of the human person? How does he conceive of the human being in relation to God? Unfortunately, a thorough and complete answer to these questions would require a systematic study of all the passages in the Pauline corpus which contain the word ἄνθρωπος, a daunting task which is clearly beyond the scope of this present work. Instead, for the purposes of this dissertation, let us significantly narrow our field of vision by focusing only on 1 Corinthians. How does Paul employs the word ἄνθρωπος in this letter and most especially, in the subunit we are currently examining?

First of all, Paul divides living creatures into categories in conformity with the prevailing notions of Hellenistic science. Like his contemporaries, the Apostle considered human beings as creatures who belong to a unique species distinct from all others. In the previous subunit, Paul took care to catalog human beings along with other creatures that have earthly bodies: «Not all flesh is alike, but there is one flesh for human beings, another for animals, another for birds and another for fish» (1Cor 15,39)[35]. Paul next adds that the

---

[34] Cf. J. JEREMIAS, «ἄνθρωπος», in *ThWNT*; A. SAND, «ἄνθρωπος», in *EWNT*.

[35] We noted above that these animals are not listed in biblical order. According to Genesis, God first created the fish and the birds, then the animals of the earth and then human beings. See Gen 1,20-31 for the complete account of the fifth and sixth days of creation. So why then did Paul reverse the biblical order of these creatures? Since the Greeks categorized animals differently, it seems that he is appealing to his addressees' own concepts of natural science. It would have pleased the Corinthians to begin the list with human beings, the most perfect of animals and then move on to a consideration of the less perfect animals. Yet again, Paul shows himself to be very familiar with the scientific

appearance of these earthly bodies is different from heavenly ones. After having given this overview of the various kinds of bodies, Paul now focuses on the one creature who represents the hinge between earth and heaven: the human being. He is similar to the animals in this life, in as much as his natural body is also composed of earthly matter; he will be similar to the celestial beings in the next life, in as much as his spiritual body will be composed of heavenly matter.

Not only are human beings distinct from plants and other animals, they are also different from angels. «For I think that God has exhibited us Apostles as last of all, like human beings sentenced to death; because we have become a spectacle to the world, to angels and to human beings» (1Cor 4,9). Throughout the letter, Paul is very much aware of the heavenly and earthly realms, the cosmos being composed of both. If human beings are capable of seeing heavenly beings, then the reverse is also true. Angels are also in a position to observe human beings and scrutinize their conduct.

Most of all, however, human beings are distinct from God. The human condition is marked by mortality, dishonor and weakness. The folly of human pride and hubris represents a commonplace in Greek literature; this significant theme permeates both their drama and philosophy and hence it was certainly familiar to Paul and the Corinthians. In contrast, God's condition is marked by immortality, glory and power. «For the foolishness of God is wiser than human beings and the weakness of God is stronger than human beings» (1Cor 1,25). Paul teaches that God's wisdom was made manifest in the crucified Christ, yet the wise of this world reject it as folly. By rejecting the gospel, human beings show themselves to be the prideful sinners that they are. God for his part thoroughly rejects these human standards and fulfills his own loving designs: «God chose what is low and despised in the world, even things that are not, to bring to nothing things that are, so that no human being might boast in the presence of God. He is the source of your life in Christ Jesus, whom God made our wisdom, our righteousness and sanctification and redemption» (1Cor 1,28-30). This passage summarizes Paul's basic understanding of God the Father: He is the one who creates life, both natural and spiritual and the one who sent Jesus Christ as humanity's redeemer. True boasting then resides only in God:

---

categories of Hellenism. «Man is the only one of the animals known to us who has something of the divine in him, or if there are others, he has most. This is one reason why we ought to speak about man first and another is that the shape of his external parts is better known than that of other animals» (ARISTOTLE, *De partibus animalium*, 656a7-10).

«therefore, as it is written, "Let him who boasts, boast of the Lord"» (1Cor 1,31).

In addition, human beings can also be divided into two different groups. In our discussion of the adjective ψυχικόν, we noted that Paul speaks of the natural human being and the spiritual human being (cf. 1Cor 2,14-15). The former has not received the gifts of the Spirit while the latter has. As a result, the spiritual one is able to judge all things. This touches upon one of the problems Paul is facing as author of this letter: How is he to address the Corinthians, as natural or as spiritual human beings? Is he to feed them with mere milk, or nourish them with solid food? Paul judges that they are not yet ready for the substantial nourishment he has to offer them, since they are still of the flesh and «behaving like ordinary human beings» (1Cor 3,3). By using the expression κατὰ ἄνθρωπον in this verse, Paul is pointing out that the Corinthians' behavior is contrary to God's will. It is important to note that Paul associates this charge with another, namely, that they are still «of the flesh» (σαρκικοί). To be «of the flesh» means to think and act in way that is hostile to God. κατὰ ἄνθρωπον is pejorative in as much as it implies a restriction to the human way of thinking and behaving. This is another way for Paul to describe human folly in comparison to divine wisdom which knows no such limitations.

After having surveyed some of the ways in which Paul employs the term, we are now in a good position to return to 1 Corinthians 15. ἄνθρωπος is an indispensable term in v. 45, since this entire subunit is meant to define for a Greek audience what it means to be a human being. One of Paul's aims here is in fact primarily anthropological; for him, God has intended that human beings should share in divine life, living on earth in this life and in heaven forever in the next. He adopts the philosophical categories of the Greek world (especially σῶμα, ψυχή and πνεῦμα) in order to reinterpret human nature in light of Old Testament revelation. In other words, Paul addresses the Corinthians in a philosophical language familiar to them (as well as to most people in the Greco-Roman world of the first century), all the while exegeting the creation text from Genesis. As a Jew of the Diaspora, Paul knows the cultural mindset of his Corinthian addressees very well. Yet he develops his understanding of the word ἄνθρωπος, not by quoting Plato or Aristotle, but by interpreting Genesis 2,7 for his Gentile addressees. In short, the Apostle to the Gentiles has redefined Greek philosophical concepts thanks to the wisdom of the Pentateuch. Like some other saints that have come after him, Paul enters into a complex intellectual discussion through the Corinthians' door and then takes them out through his own.

– Ἀδάμ. In contrast to Jewish literature of the first century, the New Testament makes very few references to Ἀδάμ, the first human being[36]. There are only nine occurrences of his name in all, five of which are found in the genuine letters of Paul: 1 Corinthians 15,22, 45 (2x) and Romans 5,14 (2x). For Paul, as well as for his contemporaries, Adam was an historical figure. In 1 Corinthians 15,22, the Apostle points out that «in Adam all die»; in this way Paul holds Adam responsible for the human race's bondage to death. But since he was the first man created by God, Adam also represents humanity's progenitor[37]. It is precisely in this sense that Paul uses Ἀδάμ in the typological argument in v. 45. The first Adam designates the reality of the old humanity while the last Adam designates the reality of the new. The first Adam possesses a natural body, the one created for human existence on earth. In this way the Apostle emphasizes the fact that Adam is one with the other creatures in this world. The presence of this proper noun (absent in Genesis 2,7) reveals that he did not merely want to speculate on the nature of the human being. By referring to an historical person in this way, he personalizes his argument, thus making it more compelling thanks to the introduction of a famous and well known character onto the scene.

– ψυχήν. The noun ψυχή is used quite infrequently by Paul: it occurs only eleven times in his genuine letters and only in this verse in 1 Corinthians[38]. The word designates a human «life», «being or person», «mind», or «soul». Since this is one of the terms which Paul took from Genesis 2,7 (LXX) and kept in his midrash pesher, it is worth our while to investigate the meaning of ψυχή in

---

[36] Cf. J. JEREMIAS, «Ἀδάμ», in *ThWNT*; B. SCHALLER, «Ἀδάμ», in *EWNT*.

[37] In his article on this v., Schneider rightly insists that Paul is primarily emphasizing the sense of corporate personalities rather than two individual men. «Such a corporate-person meaning for *'o anthrōpos, hā'ādām* in Gen 2,7 and also here in v. 45 by reason of the whole argument in vv. 42-46 is the only natural one. It may have been just because of the ambiguous meaning of the Hebrew *'ādām*, at once both a generic term and a proper name, that Paul here inserts the Hebrew form after its Greek translation *anthrōpos* in his citation of Gn 2,7c in v. 45a and uses it alone in v. 45b instead of writing simply *'o prōtos anthrōpos* — *'o eschatos anthrōpos* much as he does just two verses later (in v. 47, *'o prōtos anthr.* — *'o deuteros anthr.*)» (B. SCHNEIDER, «The Corporate Meaning and Background of 1 Cor 15,45b», 151-152).

[38] Cf. E. SCHWEIZER, «ψυχή», in *ThWNT*; A. SAND, «ψυχή», in *EWNT*.

light of its usage in the Septuagint. Before that, however, let us see how the Apostle employs this noun in his other letters.

For the most part, ψυχή simply denotes a human «life». For example, in describing his ministry in Thessalonica, Paul declares that he and his helpers are willing to give their energy and lives for the gospel. «So, being affectionately desirous of you, we were ready to share with you not only the gospel of God but also our own lives (ψυχάς), because you had become very dear to us» (1Th 2,8). Another example is found in Philippians. When Paul refers to Epaphroditus risking his life for the gospel, he writes «for he nearly died for the work of Christ, risking his life (τῇ ψυχῇ) to complete your service to me» (Phil 2,30). The word is used in a very similar way in Romans when Paul sends personal greetings to his friends in Rome. He speaks about his own life having been saved by Prisca and Aquila «who risked their necks for my life (ὑπὲρ τῆς ψυχῆς μου), to whom not only I but also all the Churches of the Gentiles give thanks» (Rom 16,4). Earlier in the letter, he had mentioned attempts on the life of the prophet Elijah whom he quotes from 1 Kings. Here again we find the noun ψυχή. «Lord, they have killed your prophets, they have demolished your altars and I alone am left and they seek my life (τὴν ψυχήν μου)» (Rom 11,3).

The ψυχή can also denote the «human being» or «person» understood in his entirety. We find this in the beginning of 2 Corinthians when Paul explains to his addressees the reasons for the delay of his visit to them. «But I call God to witness against me (τὴν ἐμὴν ψυχήν); it was to spare you that I refrained from coming to Corinth» (2Cor 1,23). Two more examples are found in Romans. When describing God's righteous judgment, Paul makes this prophecy. «There will be tribulation and distress for every human being (ἐπὶ πᾶσαν ψυχὴν ἀνθρώπου) who does evil, the Jew first and also the Greek» (Rom 2,9). Later, in the hortatory section of the letter, Paul gives these instruction concerning obedience to rulers. «Let every person (Πᾶσα ψυχήν) be subject to the governing authorities. For there is no authority except from God and those that exist have been instituted by God» (Rom 13,1).

There is also one reference of ψυχή which is best translated by the English word «mind». In the following passage from Philippians, ψυχή conveys the sense of a group's aim or intention. «Only let your way of life be worthy of the gospel of Christ, so that whether I come and see you or am absent, I may hear of you that you stand firm in one spirit, with one mind (μιᾷ ψυχῇ) striving side by side for the faith of the gospel» (Phil 1,27).

Lastly, Paul also employs ψυχή to denote the human «soul». We find an instance of this in his final greetings to the Thessalonians. «May the God of peace himself sanctify you wholly; and may your spirit and soul (ἡ ψυχή) and body be kept sound and blameless at the coming of our Lord Jesus Christ» (1Th 5,23). The final example of ψυχή for denoting the soul is found in 2 Corinthians when Paul tells his addressees of his great concern for them and makes this promise. «I will most gladly spend and be spent for your souls (ὑπὲρ τῶν ψυχῶν ὑμῶν). If I love you the more, am I to be loved the less?» (2Cor 12,15). This seems to denote the eternal, immaterial part of the human being.

Given these four choices, does ψυχή denote a human life, being, mind, or soul in 1 Corinthians 15,45a? Before we can answer this question, we first have to turn to a brief overview of the word's usage in Genesis 2,7 (LXX). This investigation will assist us in arriving at a more accurate answer, since we of course are dealing with the text which the Apostle himself used in order to compose his own midrash.

The Greek ψυχή represents a systematic translation of the Hebrew noun נֶפֶשׁ throughout the Pentateuch[39]. The noun is derived from the verb ψύχω, «to blow», and it designates either breath or the vital force as understood as breath. The authors of Septuagint stayed very close to the original Hebrew understanding of the word which can denote life, that which lives and dies, feelings, the living being and the I. They never understood ψυχή as meaning the soul, the immaterial part of the human being which is opposed to the body. Nevertheless, what the translators intended was one thing and what Greek readers understood was another. Most readers in the Greco-Roman world probably received the word as charged with its ontological meaning as described by the classical philosophers[40]. In his exegesis of this passage from Genesis, Philo claims that πνεῦμα is the essence of ψυχή, the divine, ethereal particle. Church Fathers like Theodore and Augustine later rejected this notion of the soul understood as an emanation of God.

---

[39] For an excellent exegesis of ψυχή in Gen 2,7 (LXX), see M. ALEXANDRE, Le Commencement du livre Genèse I-V, 236-237. This brief investigation into the meaning of ψυχή in the Septuagint is based on her insights.

[40] «Au mot ψυχή les lecteurs associèrent aisément des définitions et représentations philosophiques (dualisme platonicien âme/corps, tripartition aristotélicienne des fonctions de l'âme: végétative, sensitive, intellectuelle, âme souffle corporel des stoïciens, tripartition intellect/ âme/corps du moyen platonisme, etc.), de même que les problématiques liées à ces conceptions (immortalité première et dernière de l'âme? préexistence? inanimation du corps humain, etc.)» (M. ALEXANDRE, Le Commencement du livre Genèse I-V, 243).

How then are we to understand ψυχή in v. 45a? Through his exegesis of Genesis, the Apostle teaches that Adam was created by God as a complete living being, a human person understood in his entirety. Given this, it makes sense for us to translate ψυχή as «being» since in our modern languages this word conveys the sense of entirety and wholeness best of all[41].

– ζῶσαν. As a participial form of the verb ζῶ, «to live», ζῶσαν modifies the noun ψυχήν and describes Adam as «a living being». The verb occurs one hundred and forty times in the New Testament, although there are only three occurrences in 1 Corinthians[42]. In each case it refers to the living of one's natural, biological life on earth.

The verb first appears in chapter seven where Paul is teaching about marriage. He tells the Corinthians that marriage ties are indissoluble. «A wife is bound to her husband as long as he lives (ζῇ). If the husband dies, she is free to be married to whom she wishes, only in the Lord» (1Cor 7,9). Hence, living is obviously understood as the condition of physical activity which ceases with death. A bit later, when speaking about his privileges, Paul reminds the Corinthians that he has the right to live from his ministry as an apostle. Those who serve in the Temple enjoy the food from the Temple. «In the same way, the Lord commanded that those who proclaim the gospel should get their living by the gospel (ἐκ τοῦ εὐαγγελίου ζῆν)» (1Cor 9,14). In other words, Paul has the right to make his living from preaching the gospel, but he has freely made no use of it. He too needs to eat and drink, to sustain his physical life, in order to continue on with his apostolic ministry.

The last occurrence of the verb is found in v. 45a. It too refers to a human being's biological existence, as the pesher taken from Genesis obviously shows. Adam was once mere inanimate dust, but now he has come to life through God's creative act. Since Adam received his breath from God his Creator, human life has to be understood primarily as a divine gift. In addition, the context makes it clear that Paul is referring to the kind of living enjoyed by the natural body. By asserting in this way that Adam is a living being, the Apostle is also implying that the first man experiences the same perishability and mortality common to all life on earth. Negatively put, the breath that was

---

[41] Cf. the NAB, NIV, RSV and NRSV, which translate ψυχή as «being», and the NJB which translates it as «soul».

[42] Cf. R. BULTMANN, «ζῶ», in *ThWNT*; L. SCHOTTROFF, «ζῶ», in *EWNT*.

given to Adam will one day be taken away from him. Hence his natural living is marked by finitude and circumscribed by death.

– Having completed our close study of all the terms in v. 45a, we are now in a good position to proceed with the exegesis of v. 45b. But before we continue with the word by word analysis of this text which deals with the last Adam, we must first return to the verb ἐγένετο. We noted above in our discussion on the sentence as a whole that ἐγένετο serves as the principal verb of both parts of v. 45. If this is true, then the verb must also keep its same meaning in both parts; it must mean «become» in v. 45b as well. Before we go on then, we must take some time and consider the meaning of ἐγένετο with respect to «the last Adam». This is an essential task if we are to achieve a proper understanding of both v. 45b considered as a whole as well as Paul's conception of the Spirit's role in the resurrection of the dead.

What then does Paul mean when he states that the last Adam *became* a life-giving Spirit? Later, when we discuss the meaning of the expression πνεῦμα ζῳοποιοῦν, we shall be in a better position to consider in greater detail just what the last Adam became. For now, however, we must focus on the verb ἐγένετο and consider the act of change itself. When precisely did this extraordinary event happen with regard to the last Adam? The aorist tense clearly points to a past event. Although Paul does not say so explicitly, the context of chapter fifteen certainly points to the moment of Jesus' rising from the dead. This wondrous exaltation represents the fundamental doctrine which the Apostle wishes to proclaim to his addressees in Corinth. «For I delivered to you as of first importance what I also received, that Christ died for our sins in accordance with the scriptures, that he was buried, that he was raised on the third day in accordance with the scriptures and that he appeared to Cephas, then to the twelve» (1Cor 15,3-5).

For Paul, then, the last Adam became a life-giving Spirit at his resurrection. When God raised him from the dead, the situation of the Son of God was radically altered. The earthly Jesus became the risen Jesus, the suffering servant became the glorious Messiah. Unlike Adam, Christ's *nature* did not change, but his *state* most certainly did. He had passed from this world to the next in order to dwell at the right hand of the Father; he left this earthly existence and took up his heavenly one. In this way, the humble condition that marked Jesus' life on earth, especially as characterized by his passion and death on the cross, was transformed into the glorified state that marks his risen life in heaven. Thus the verb ἐγένετο retains the meaning «to become» in

v. 45b, but we must be very careful in our interpretation of the transformation in question. For the Apostle, Christ's nature as a divine person did not change, but the material components of his human body most certainly did. The resurrection marks the moment of extraordinary metamorphosis when Jesus' earthly lowliness gave way to his glorious, heavenly splendor.

This interpretation of ἐγένετο in v. 45 is supported by Paul's teaching in his other letters. The hymn in Philippians also speaks of Jesus' humility as servant and glorification as Lord. The Son of God freely took on the form of a slave in order to save humanity. «He humbled himself and became obedient unto death, even death on a cross. Therefore God also highly exalted him and bestowed on him the name which is above every name» (Phil 2,8-9). The humbled state of Jesus' life on earth was changed when God exalted him and gave him the name above all others. This exaltation is of course a clear reference to Christ's resurrection. In other words, Jesus was highly exalted when God the Father raised him from the dead. Since he lives and reigns with the Father, Jesus is worthy of worship and praise by everyone «in heaven and on earth and under the earth» (Phil 2,11). The Son of God is now known for what he truly is, namely, as the glorified Lord of all creation.

The contrast between Christ's pre- and post-resurrection condition is one of the themes that concerns Paul at the beginning of Romans. There he summarizes Jesus' lowly state when he refers to his birth into the people of Israel. By earthly reckoning, Jesus «was descended from David according to the flesh» (Rom 1,3) and as such was a Jew born into the Jewish nation. Any opinion which considers Christ's birth as the beginning of his glorification has no place in Paul's theology. Instead, Paul teaches that he «was declared to be Son of God in power according to the Spirit of holiness by resurrection from the dead, Jesus Christ our Lord», (Rom 1,4). In this passage as well, Paul clearly considers Jesus' resurrection as the pivotal moment in the Son of God's existence. In his pre-resurrection state, he is known as a descendant of David, the anointed servant of God. In his post-resurrection state, he is known as Son of God in glory and power. Again we notice the transition between the earthly and heavenly realms. Jesus Christ did not change in nature, but his state, status and condition most certainly did change. Thanks to God's loving intervention through the act of resurrection, Jesus now enjoys a new relationship with the Father. Paul develops this in greater detail later in Romans: «We know that Christ, being raised from the dead, will never die again; death no longer has dominion over him. The death he died, he died to sin, once for all, but the life he lives, he lives to God. So you also must consider yourselves dead to sin and alive to God in Christ Jesus» (Rom 6,9-11). All of these passages help to lend more proof in defense of our exegesis of ἐγένετο in 1 Corinthians 15,45, it was at the time of his resurrection (and not at his birth on earth, nor at his begetting before time began) that the last Adam became a life-giving Spirit.

– ὁ ἔσχατος ᾿Αδάμ. In our previous discussion on the name ᾿Αδάμ, we observed that the first Adam designates the reality of the old humanity while the last Adam designates the reality of the new. While the first Adam possesses a natural body, the one created for human existence on earth, the last Adam possesses a spiritual body, the one created for eternal life in heaven. Just as the first man was the progenitor of the old humanity, so too the last man is the prototype of the new[43].

The adjective ἔσχατος, «last», directly modifies «Adam», there being no repetition of the noun «human being» in v. 45b. It nicely balances with πρῶτος of v. 45a, thus reinforcing yet again the subunit's antithetical parallelism. ἔσχατος appears fifty-two times in the New Testament[44]. The term is clearly eschatological, occurring five times in Paul and only in 1 Corinthians[45].

Two of the occurrences refer to the Apostle's self-understanding. In contrast to the Corinthians who are puffed up with pride, Paul accentuates his humility by counting himself among the weak, foolish and despised: «For I think that God has exhibited us apostles as last (ἐσχάτους) of all, like men sentenced to death; because we have become a spectacle to the world, to angels and to men» (1Cor 4,9). When commenting on the Easter appearances, Paul insists that he was the last to see the risen Christ: «Last (ἔσχατον) of all, as to one untimely born, he appeared also to me» (1Cor 15,8). In this way the Apostle insists that he is at the end of a series; standing along with the other apostles, he considers himself to be the last in line.

---

[43] «Moreover, Jesus is also related to the whole of humanity for Paul; he has become, in fact, the founder of a new humanity. This is the implication of Paul's doctrine of Jesus Christ as "the last Adam" (1 Cor 15,20-49; Rom 5,12-14). Jesus for Paul is the last, the eschatological Adam whose obedience has canceled out the disobedience of the first and introduced a new humanity, freed from the tyranny of sin and death. As last Adam, Jesus is, or represents, all people as they are obedient to God. In him, representatively, the broken unity of mankind is objectively restored» (W.D. DAVIES, «From Tyranny to Liberation», 207).

[44] Cf. G. KITTEL, «ἔσχατος», in *ThWNT*; J. BAUMGARTEN, «ἔσχατος», in *EWNT*.

[45] Cf. 1Cor 4,9; 15,8.26.45.52.

Paul also uses this term to describe the timing of the last things. With Christ's resurrection, the end time has already begun and the powers of this world will ultimately be conquered by the Son of God. Of all Christ's enemies, «The last (ἔσχατος) enemy to be destroyed is death» (1Cor 15,26). So also in v. 45, by calling Christ «the last Adam», Paul asserts that he is the last man of the old humanity and hence the first of the new. In addition, we find the eschatological musical instrument mentioned in the next subunit: «in a moment, in the twinkling of an eye, at the last (ἐσχάτῃ) trumpet. For the trumpet will sound and the dead will be raised imperishable and we shall be changed» (1Cor 15,52). The last here refers to the change which will occur at the end time. On this note Paul brings to a close his eschatological excursus in 1 Corinthians.

Lastly, we should note what Paul does not say in this verse. Although it is clearly understood that the person in question is in fact Jesus Christ, no where in v. 45 (or in this subunit, for that matter) does the Apostle use the name «Jesus» or any christological title. In this chapter's first Adam-Christ typology, Paul made the two characters quite explicit. «For as by a human being came death, by a human being has come also the resurrection of the dead. For as in Adam all die, so also in Christ shall all be made alive» (1Cor 15,21-22). He mentions Christ by name because the purpose of that subunit is in fact christological: «But in fact Christ has been raised from the dead, the first fruits of those who have fallen asleep» (1Cor 15,20). His theological approach highlights Christ's victory over the powers of this world and God's ultimate victory over all his enemies, especially death. This is not Paul's objective in the present subunit, however. Here he is presenting his addressees with anthropological proof for the resurrection of the dead. As a result, the biblical text he chose deals with the creation of the first human being, while his own vocabulary remains focused on human body language.

In short, in 1 Corinthians 15,44b-49 Paul is interested in the last Adam's human body, especially in as much as it serves as a prototype for those who will follow him. Since the Apostle is describing the creation of the natural and spiritual body, Paul's exegesis of Genesis remains decidedly anthropological. It would do an injustice to the text to find in this subunit a christological pronouncement of any kind. For this reason Paul does not use the title «Christ» at all. Instead he speaks of «the last Adam», who is, of course, Christ. This nuance beautifully summarizes the aim and intent of the subunit, underscoring in a remarkable way the common ground all human beings share with Jesus, their brother.

– πνεῦμα. This significant noun appears forty times in 1 Corinthians. Its frequency clearly demonstrates that it is a very important term in the letter, and as such, one that is decisive for a proper understanding of both Paul's anthropology and theology. The first task confronting us is to determine whether πνεῦμα refers to the human spirit or the Holy Spirit[46]. When we translate the term, should it be written as «spirit» or «Spirit» in English? Once we have studied other passages in the letter, we shall then be in a good position to comprehend how Paul employs πνεῦμα in v. 45b.

Let us begin with those references in 1 Corinthians which refer to the human spirit. The first occurrence is found in chapter two. «For who knows a person's thoughts except the spirit (τὸ πνεῦμα) of the person which is in him?» (1Cor 2,11a). Spirit here is another way of describing the human mind. Another example is found at the end of chapter four, where Paul tells his addressees about his upcoming visit. After admonishing them, he asks, «What do you wish? Shall I come to you with a rod, or with love in a spirit (πνεύματί τε πραΰτητος) of gentleness?» (1Cor 4,21). This spirit can be understood as Paul's attitude or disposition towards the Corinthians; it is clearly an example of the anthropological use of the word since it expresses the Apostle's psychological state. Immediately after this verse, we have several more references to the spirit at the start of chapter five. In this passage, Paul is chastising the Corinthians for condoning the fact that a man in the Church is living with his father's wife. The text speaks of both Paul's and this man's spirit. «For though absent in body I am present in spirit (τῷ πνεύματι) and as if present, I have already pronounced judgment in the name of the Lord Jesus on the man who has done such a thing. When you are assembled and my spirit (τοῦ ἐμοῦ πνεύματος) is present, with the power of our Lord Jesus, you are to deliver this man to Satan for the destruction of the flesh, that his spirit (τὸ πνεῦμα) may be saved in the day of the Lord Jesus» (1Cor 5,3-5). This appears to be another way of expressing a human being's psychological and spiritual dimension. Lastly, another example of this anthropological use of the term is found in chapter seven where Paul praises the advantages of the unmarried life for both men and women. In contrasting the unmarried to the married woman, he has this to say. «[...] And the unmarried woman or girl is anxious about the affairs of the Lord, how to be holy in body and spirit (τῷ πνεύματι); but the married woman is anxious about worldly affairs, how to

---

[46] Cf. BAUER, «πνεῦμα», 3, 3b and 5; E. SCHWEIZER, «πνεῦμα», in *ThWNT*.

please her husband» (1Cor 7,34). The spirit in this case refers to the woman's internal psychological condition, as opposed to her external bodily appearance.

In the overwhelming majority of cases in the letter, however, πνεῦμα designates a power extrinsic to human beings. This πνεῦμα is of course the Holy Spirit. Most often, Paul simply refers to him as «Spirit», as in this first reference to him in the letter: «And my speech and my message were not in plausible words of wisdom, but in demonstration of Spirit (πνεύματος) and of power» (1Cor 2,4); or «the Spirit», as in these verses from chapter twelve: «To each is given the manifestation of the Spirit (τοῦ πνεύματος) for the common good. To one is given through the Spirit (διὰ τοῦ πνεύματος) the utterance of wisdom and to another the utterance of knowledge according to the same Spirit (τὸ αὐτὸ πνεῦμα)» (1Cor 12,7-8). In addition, the Apostle also calls him «the Spirit of God». In his teaching on the wisdom of God, Paul explains that God's thoughts are incomprehensible to human beings. «So also no one comprehends the thoughts of God except the Spirit of God (τὸ πνεῦμα τοῦ θεοῦ)» (1Cor 2,11a). And later, when comparing the Church to a temple, Paul questions his addressees, «Do you not know that you are God's temple and that the Spirit of God (τὸ πνεῦμα τοῦ θεοῦ) dwells in you?» (1Cor 3,16). Lastly, on two occasions the Apostle refers to the Spirit as «the Holy Spirit». In urging the Corinthians to glorify God in their bodies, Paul asks them, «Do you not know that your body is a temple of the Holy Spirit (ἁγίου πνεύματος) within you, which you have from God?» (1Cor 6,19). Lest anyone doubt that the Holy Spirit is in fact God's Spirit, Paul clearly equates them in his teaching on the spiritual gifts. «Therefore I want you to understand that no one speaking by the Spirit of God ever says «Jesus be cursed!» and no one can say «Jesus is Lord» except by the Holy Spirit» (1Cor 12,3). In short, whether Paul calls him «Spirit», «the Spirit», «the Spirit of God», or «the Holy Spirit», the Apostle is always speaking about the divine Spirit who is extrinsic to Christians yet nevertheless dwells in them. It is this one Spirit who gives spiritual gifts to believers, knows and reveals the mind of God, sanctifies Christians by uniting them together in the Church, the Body of Christ and guides and instructs all believers in prayer. The Apostle's highly developed pneumatology expresses in various ways the power and presence of the πνεῦμα who was bestowed by God on all who believe in Christ.

With this overview in mind of Paul's use of πνεῦμα in 1 Corinthians, we are now in a good position to make a judgment about the word in v. 45b. Does it refer to the human spirit or the Holy Spirit? Given the anthropological nature of the subunit, we might be tempted to conclude the former. But this option has to be excluded because of the context. v. 45b describes the genesis of the last Adam; this eschatological event is clearly beyond the realm of mere human activity. The word cannot have an anthropological sense here, nor can it refer to the human mind or soul. Rather, the context clearly shows that πνεῦμα must denote the Holy Spirit. For Paul, the formation of the spiritual body and the recreation of the last Adam could only occur through divine intervention. Only God can transform the natural body and make it suitable for eternity; only God can change earthly matter and make it heavenly. What is essential to note in this verse is that Paul ascribes this divine activity to the πνεῦμα, portraying him as «life-giving». As the gift *par excellence* of the eschatological age, the Spirit is God's power to renew and restore the sinful world. He is the agent of the resurrection, in as much as God recreates the natural body through him. For this reason Paul speaks of the resurrected body as «spiritual»: it has been formed by the Spirit so as to dwell eternally in the spiritual realm, heaven. This eschatological force to recreate the dead and clothe them with immortality is succinctly expressed by the modifying participle to which we now turn.

– ζῳοποιοῦν. The present participle of the verb ζῳοποιέω, «to make alive», «to give life», modifies the noun Spirit. There are only eleven occurrences of ζῳοποιέω in the New Testament, seven of which are in Paul's letters. In all these cases this verb refers to the giving of eschatological life and is connected with the resurrection of the dead[47]. It occurs twice in Romans and we shall indeed study those passages in great detail in PART TWO. For now, however, let us begin by examining the three occurrences of ζῳοποιέω in 1 Corinthians, all of which are found in chapter fifteen.

Earlier in the chapter Paul had made an obvious reference to the resurrection on the last day, «For as in Adam all die, so also in Christ shall all be made alive» (1Cor 15,22). This is a fine example of the theological passive: Paul is teaching that God will grant risen life to all who are in Christ. God is in fact the origin of this eternal life and the one who freely bestows it. A similar point is made again later in the chapter, when Paul is discussing the natural, biological life which thrives after death. «[...] What you sow does not come to life unless it dies» (1Cor 15,36). The Apostle develops this thought by specifying the giver just two verses later: «God gives it a body as he has chosen» (1Cor 15,38). From these two references we can conclude that Paul

---

[47] Cf. R. BULTMANN, «ζῳοποιέω» in *ThWNT*; L. SCHOTTROFF, «ζῳοποιέω», in *EWNT*.

clearly understands God the Father as the primary giver of eschatological life. Once he gave natural life to his creatures; at the resurrection of the dead, he will grant them supernatural life as well.

The role of the Spirit in this divine activity is made clear in v. 45b when he states «the last Adam became a life-giving Spirit». It is essential to note that the participle in question modifies Spirit, not the last Adam. Hence, not only the Father, but also the Spirit gives resurrected life to the dead. It is «the last Adam» who receives his spiritual body through the agency of the Spirit at the moment of his resurrection. If there were any doubts about the Spirit's role as subject of this eschatological action, we need only consider one final reference, this time from 2 Corinthians. There Paul states quite explicitly, «for the written code kills, but the Spirit gives life» (2Cor 3,6). In this verse, the Spirit is presented as subject of the verb, as doer of the action. That is also the case for the participle that modifies Spirit in v. 45b. Paul calls him the «life-giving Spirit», thereby summing up in two words the heart of his pneumatology.

In 1 Corinthians 15,38ff., Paul presents the Father as the creator of natural and celestial bodies; all natural and heavenly life finds its origin in him. In v. 45b, however, he envisages the Spirit as the creator of the spiritual body; all eschatological life springs from «the life-giving Spirit» who forms the eternal body of the last Adam. Although at first glance these statements may seem contradictory, they in fact convey a significant nuance in Paul's thought. By raising up his Son through the agency of the Holy Spirit, the Father has inaugurated the last days of this transient world. The new world has already begun in Christ, the first man to be raised from the dead, the crucial turning point of the new creation[48]. Moreover, Paul presents the Holy Spirit as the agent of risen life because he is life itself: he is the very life of the Father and the Son now poured out into the world. Thus, while remaining intimately connected to his theology and christology, Paul's pneumatology is nevertheless quite independent from them. According to the Apostle, the Spirit too plays a very significant role in the resurrection of the dead.

---

[48] Paul's argumentation in this v. (and indeed throughout 1Cor 15) holds true precisely because of the Christ-event: Jesus in fact passed from this earth to heavenly glory at his resurrection. Thus the Apostle, a witness of the risen Christ, reasons here in a profoundly christological manner. «Paolo formula l'antitesi "primo Adamo – ultimo Adamo" (primo Uomo "terreno" – ultimo Uomo "celeste") a partire dal testo di *Gn* 2,7, riletto sulla base del suo incontro con il Risorto» (M. TEANI, *Corporeità e Risurrezione*, 248).

At this point, it is worthwhile to recall our previous discussion on the meaning of the suffix -ικός. The πνευματικός is that which is characteristic of the Spirit. Thus when Paul teaches that the risen body is spiritual, he means that it has been created by God through the agency of the Spirit and formed for heaven, the ideal and appropriate environment for the new creation. Nothing in the text allows us to understand πνευματικός as meaning immaterial or intangible, as some contemporary readers of the Bible might be tempted to. The whole context of the subunit stresses the point that a different kind a of matter is at stake here and Paul will develop this idea momentarily. Moreover, just as the last Adam received his spiritual body thanks to the Spirit's agency, so too those who follow him will receive their spiritual bodies from the Spirit as well. Since this is precisely the theme that will concern Paul at the end of the subunit, we shall return to this point below when we study vv. 48-49.

3. 1Cor 15,46

Continuing the method of exegesis we have used with the preceding two verses, we will now examine v. 46. Here is the text.

ἀλλ᾽ οὐ πρῶτον τὸ πνευματικὸν ἀλλὰ τὸ ψυχικόν,
ἔπειτα τὸ πνευματικόν.
«But it is not the spiritual which is first but the natural and then the spiritual».

After his midrash pesher of Genesis 2,7, Paul now returns to the thesis he made in v. 44b which pertains to natural and spiritual bodies. He is still primarily concerned with the question that dominates the second half of chapter fifteen, the one he first raised in v. 35, «How are the dead raised? With what kind of *body* do they come?» Just as in v. 44, so also in v. 46, the adjectives πνευματικόν and ψυχικόν are neuter in gender since they modify σῶμα. Hence the spiritual and the natural can only refer to the two kinds of bodies that lie at the heart of the discussion in this whole passage.

So why then does Paul repeat all this here? This verse should not be misconstrued as somehow being parenthetical or superfluous. It would seem that the Apostle wants to insist forcefully on the order of events: the spiritual body does not come first; rather, first comes the natural body and only later comes the spiritual body. This is entirely consistent with the sequence of creation as explained in the previous verse. In the beginning God created the first Adam and then, to mark the start of the end time, he recreated the last Adam. Yet again, Paul is contrasting the different bodies for the sake of his dialectical argument. This point is made very clear through his use of ἀλλά, the first word of this verse in question.

– ἀλλά. An adversative particle which means in most cases either «but», or when following a negation, «rather», «on the contrary». The first translation is appropriate for the verse we are presently studying. Employed primarily by Paul and John in the New Testament, ἀλλά occurs seventy-two times in 1 Corinthians. These are the only two occurrences of the word in this subunit, although it appears eight times in chapter fifteen. In short, ἀλλά in Greek is used to underscore an emphatic difference between two clearly contrasting positions[49].

The ἀλλ' οὐ/ἀλλά of v. 46 serves to stress the chronology of creation. In this sense, Paul is repeating the point he has already made before. «But each in his own order: Christ the first fruits, then (ἔπειτα) at his coming those who belong to Christ» (1Cor 15,23). In other words, the natural and the spiritual bodies have been created in their own order, too: first the natural and then the spiritual have come to exist by the will of the Creator.

– ἔπειτα. The repetition of ἔπειτα in v. 46 is also quite significant. This adverb, best translated into English as «then», occurs sixteen times in the New Testament, ten times in Paul's authentic letters and six times in 1 Corinthians. It is used to indicate a sequential or temporal relationship[50]. This adverb clearly expresses a temporal significance in the two occurrences we are studying. In v. 23ff. appears the series ἀπαρχή – ἔπειτα – εἶτα, while in v. 46 we find πρῶτον – ἔπειτα.

In short, Paul emphatically emphasizes the temporal sequence of bodily creation for his addressees: first the natural body is created, then the spiritual one and only in that order. It would seem that this insistence serves a very strong rhetorical purpose. Perhaps Paul found the need to correct the erroneous view shared by some of the Corinthians who may have believed that their bodies were already spiritual. The Apostle teaches them that they still have their natural bodies in this world and that they will only receive their spiritual ones in the world to come. In other words, God made the spiritual body for heaven and not for earth.

---

[49] Cf. BDR § 448,1; HS § 252,1; W. RADL, «ἀλλά», in *EWNT*.

[50] See H. BALZ, «ἔπειτα», in *EWNT*.

4. 1Cor 15,47

We are now ready to examine the fourth verse of this subunit dedicated to the two Adams. Here is the text of v. 12.

ὁ πρῶτος ἄνθρωπος ἐκ γῆς χοϊκός, ὁ δεύτερος ἄνθρωπος ἐξ οὐρανοῦ.
«The first human being is made of earthly matter, characteristic of dust; the second human being is made of heavenly matter».

After having clarified the confusion concerning the correct sequence of events in the creation of natural and spiritual bodies, Paul next takes up the difficult question of the matter that composes them. What material are these bodies made of? What substance are they formed of? In order to answer these questions, the Apostle returns to the story of Adam's creation in search of some answers. Paul is continuing the midrash begun in v. 45, freely changing the order and even the composition of words of Genesis 2,7. He does this in order to contrast the matter which constitutes the first human being, the first Adam, to the matter which constitutes the second human being, the last Adam. Before we begin our close examination of the verse's significant words, we must first compare Paul's text to the Septuagint in order to appreciate what he changed in the course of his midrash.

Gen 2,7a (LXX) καὶ ἔπλασεν ὁ θεὸς τὸν ἄνθρωπον χοῦν ἀπὸ τῆς γῆς...
1Cor 15,47a   ὁ πρῶτος ἄνθρωπος   ἐκ γῆς χοϊκός,

In the Septuagint text of Genesis, note the occurrence of the noun χοῦν, dust. Interpreting this verse quite literally, the Jews believed that the first human being really was made up of dust taken from the earth. The prepositional phrase ἀπὸ τῆς γῆς expresses the origin of the dust, the place where it first comes fRom With this in mind, now let us consider Paul's text. He changes the verse from Genesis in a fundamental way in the course of his exegesis. Note that he writes a verbless clause beginning with ὁ πρῶτος ἄνθρωπος, just as in v. 45. Next, he changes the preposition ἀπό to ἐκ and lastly, he adds the adjective χοϊκός to replace the noun χοῦς. In the exegesis that follows, we shall have to make sense of all of these changes and propose some convincing explanations for them.

– ὁ πρῶτος ἄνθρωπος ἐκ γῆς. The first point to notice is that we are dealing with a verbless clause. What verb should be supplied here and where? The verb «to be» is the most obvious possibility and it is chosen by most modern translators. Although this is perfectly acceptable, another real possibility is to understand the verb in the Genesis text that Paul left out, namely, «to form». Hence it would also be accurate to translate the clause with or without the past participle: «The first human being is [formed] of earth».

– ἐκ. We must now make sense of ἐκ, the preposition which Paul chose so as to replace the Septuagint's ἀπό. Why did he make this change? ἐκ followed by the noun γῆς presents a fine example of the *genitivus materiae*[51]. This kind of genitive seeks to answer the question, «What kind of matter is it?» In other words, Paul is explaining that the first human being is formed of earth, that earth is the very substance which composes his natural body[52]. Given this understanding of the preposition, it is obvious then that Paul does not intend to explain Adam's place of origin. He is not saying that the first human being comes from earth, as opposed to the sun or the moon. Rather, Paul is still concerned with Adam's somatic existence; for this reason, he describes the matter of which his body is made. Let us now take a closer look at the noun in question.

– γῆς. The word γῆ occurs two hundred and fifty times in the New Testament, especially in the gospels and Acts. It can be translated as «earth», «soil», «ground», or «land», but as always, care must be taken so that the right English word is employed in any given context. In spite of its frequency elsewhere, it is a very rare word for Paul. There are only six occurrences in all of his genuine letters, with three of them found in 1 Corinthians. γῆ can refer either 1) to the matter itself, in which case earth is synonymous with soil and ground, or 2) to that place in the cosmos which is contrasted to heaven and thus stands in relation to God[53]. Let us now examine those references in the Pauline corpus where the noun appears.

The word is primarily used by Paul to denote that place which is part of the universe yet different from heaven. Often, when the words «heaven and earth» are used together, it is a biblical way of referring to the entire cosmos. We see this in the word's first occurrence in 1 Corinthians, where Paul is speaking about food offered to idols. «For although there may be so-called gods in heaven or on earth (εἴτε ἐν οὐρανῷ εἴτε ἐπὶ γῆς)» (1Cor 8,5). In other

---

[51] For an explanation of this particular use of the genitive case, cf. G. LÜDEMANN, «ἐκ», in *EWNT*; BDR § 167.1; HS § 161.

[52] Bauer shares this interpretation and explains 1Cor 15,47 in this way: «v. Stoff, aus dem etw. gefertigt ist» (BAUER, «ἐκ», 3-h).

[53] Cf. H. SASSE, «γῆ» in *ThWNT*; A. KRETZER, «γῆ», in *EWNT*.

words, these so-called gods are thought to exist somewhere in the cosmos. It is significant to note that the next four occurrences of γῆ are all contained in quotations from the Old Testament. Each of them understands the earth as a part of God's creation and hence belonging to him. In his exhortation to charity in chapter ten, Paul quotes from Psalm 24,1 and declares «For the earth is the Lord's and everything in it» (1Cor 10,26). Similarly, in Romans the Apostle cites the Old Testament to show that God's word has not failed and that there is no injustice on God's part. «For the scripture says to Pharaoh, "I have raised you up for the very purpose of showing my power in you, so that my name may be proclaimed in all the earth (ἐν πάσῃ τῇ γῇ)"» (Rom 9,17). A bit further, in a quotation from the prophet Daniel he states «for the Lord will execute his sentence upon the earth (ἐπὶ τῆς γῆς) with rigor and dispatch» (Rom 9,28). Lastly, he cites a passage from Psalm 18,5 to explain the universal spread of the gospel. «But I ask, have they not heard? Indeed they have; for "Their voice has gone out to all the earth (εἰς πᾶσαν τὴν γῆν) and their words to the ends of the world"» (Rom 10,18).

What then shall we make of γῆ in v. 47? Since none of the five occurrences quoted above refers to the soil or ground, can we make a convincing case for that sense here? Yes, in as much as the preposition ἐκ holds the key to the answer. In four of the above examples, Paul follows an accurate reading of the Old Testament text he is quoting, remaining consistently faithful to the Greek of the Septuagint. The same can be said of the rather common expression «in heaven and on earth» found in 1 Corinthians 8,5. But in v. 47, Paul purposely alters the text from Genesis and in so doing, he also changes the sense of the original passage. This was his way of focusing on the material element which God used to form the first man. This emphasis serves the purpose of the subunit taken as a whole and prepares the way for his discussion of the last human being which characterizes the second half of the verse. Given all this data, therefore, we may conclude that γῆ refers to that matter which is synonymous with soil or ground.

We next have to deal with the rather significant adjective which modifies the first human being. Paul obviously feels the need to describe Adam in greater detail. Is he still referring to the substance of his body, or could he have something else in mind?

– χοϊκός. There are only four occurrences of the adjective χοϊκός in the entire New Testament and all four are found in the subunit we are studying. It appears once in v. 47, twice in v. 48 and once in v. 49. Since we are unable to examine other references in the Pauline corpus for the purpose of comparison, we must try to make sense of this word given the present context. What does Paul intend by this term?

The first point that should be made is that χοϊκός appears in Greek literature for the first time in this verse[54]. Afterwards many of the Fathers cite it, especially in their commentaries on this passage[55], but the word simply is not found before Paul. Therefore we can conclude with certainty that χοϊκός is a Pauline neologism. But why did Paul feel the need to create it and what does it mean?

To answer this question, we need only recall our previous research into the meaning of adjectives ending in -ικός. The nominal cognate is χοῦς, the Greek word for dust and the term that is found in the Septuagint passage that Paul is quoting fRom Paul takes the noun and transforms it into an adjective by adding -ικός, thus adapting it to serve his purpose. If we remember from our research that this suffix means «to belong to», «concern», «be characteristic of», then we shall able to propose an accurate translation. Hence χοϊκός means that which belongs to, concerns, or is characteristic of χοῦς. It does not mean that which is made of dust, just as βασιλικός does not refer to something which is made of a king. Unfortunately there is no English word that precisely translates this sense. The adjective «dusty» comes close, but that really describes something which is covered with dust rather than something that is characteristic of it. Perhaps the best solution is to use the expression «characteristic of dust», since this avoids the notion that the object in question is composed of a dusty substance.

What then does it mean to be characteristic of dust? It conjures up images of something fleeting or temporary, like dust in the wind, something which is here right now but gone in just a moment. The fact that Paul uses χοϊκός to modify the first human being is quite significant. In other words, the Apostle wants to show that Adam is characteristic of dust in as much as he is ephemeral and passing. As a creature his life is marked but feebleness, frailty and mortality. Paul is merely highlighting the point he has already made in vv. 42-43 with regard to the body that is sown in perishability, dishonor and weakness. He is teaching that the first Adam is subject to decay and death

---

[54] Cf. E. SCHWEIZER, «χοϊκός», in *ThWNT*; H. BALZ, «χοϊκός», in *EWNT*.

[55] The word is used by Athanasius, Basil, Clement of Alexandria, John Chrysostom, Epiphanius, Eusebius, Gregory of Nazianzus, Gregory of Nyssa, Irenaeus, Macarius, Nemesius, Origen, John Philoponus and Photius.

since he has a natural body and shares in the passing nature of the earth. For this reason Paul creates a neologism and calls him χοϊκός, «characteristic of dust».

We discovered in the course of our research into the function of -ικός that this suffix was a favorite of the Greek philosophers. Plato and Aristotle each created hundreds of neologisms in order to categorize new terms in their philosophical and scientific texts. Paul is doing the same thing in this subunit. Since the Greek language did not already possess the adjective which could best convey the meaning he desired, Paul coined χοϊκός to fit his understanding of the passing nature of the first human being. Adam is χοϊκός in as much as he is weak and perishable. A frail mortal in this passing world, he is a creature made of earth and formed for life on earth. Given his earthly nature then, it is impossible for him to leave this world and pass to heaven. For that to happen, a human being would have to be changed and fitted in a new way for the heavenly realm. A new creation would have to occur, but this time he would have to be made of heavenly matter. And this is precisely the case of the second human being whom Paul examines next.

– ὁ δεύτερος ἄνθρωπος. The adjective δεύτερος, Greek for «second», modifies the noun ἄνθρωπος which appears for the third time in the subunit. Paul now turns his attention back to the eschatological human being whom he had earlier called «the last Adam» in v. 45. That Paul changed ἔσχατος for δεύτερος in v. 47 is rather significant: δεύτερος emphasizes the idea of newness which goes beyond the condition of the first Adam mentioned in the first half of the verse[56].

δεύτερος occurs forty-three times in the New Testament, five times in Paul's genuine letters and twice in 1 Corinthians. The adjective is mostly used as a numeral to mark the second occurrence of an event. We see this in the word's other appearance in the letter. «And God has appointed in the Church first apostles, second (δεύτερον) prophets, third teachers, then workers of miracles, then healers, helpers, administrators, speakers in various kinds of tongues» (1Cor 12,28). Paul uses it in the same way in 2 Corinthians when speaking about his second visit among them. «I warned those who sinned before and all the others and I warn them now while absent, as I did when present on my second (τὸ δεύτερον) visit, that if I come again I will not spare them» (2Cor 13,2).

---

[56] See L. OBERLINNER, «δεύτερος», in *EWNT*.

In v. 47, however, δεύτερος adopts a different nuance by stressing something that is brand new. This human being is not merely the last in the line of earthly people, which is the assumption of v. 45. Rather, by calling him «the second human being», Paul is suggesting that he exceeds the first due to his glorious resurrection from the dead. Hence he represents a new prototype for humanity, a new possibility for human beings to live in the eschatological age. What the first man could not do for those who came after him, this second man can thanks to the crucial role he plays in salvation history. In him, humanity at last discovers a reason to hope in heaven.

– ἐξ οὐρανοῦ. The noun οὐρανός appears quite frequently in the New Testament. It is found two hundred and seventy-four times in all, the largest concentration found in Matthew with its eighty-two occurrences. In addition, the noun is used ninety-four times in the plural due to the influence of Hebrew. In the authentic letters of Paul, however, the word occurs only eleven times, with just two references in 1 Corinthians.

οὐρανός is an extremely difficult word to define, in as much as it joins together both the physical and metaphysical dimensions of the universe[57]. Since the scientific revolution at the start of the modern age, humanity has clearly distinguished between the two, placing that which can be observed into the realm of the scientific and that which cannot be into the realm of the spiritual or religious. This artificial division still underpins the ruling philosophy of contemporary society and represents the roots of secularism in the west. As we saw in the excursus on ancient science, such a clear and distinct separation would have been unthinkable in the Greco-Roman world of the first century. For Paul and his contemporaries, οὐρανός, οὐράνιος and ἐν οὐρανοῖς refer in a general way to all that has power over human beings and cannot be controlled by them. These terms denote that which is «above» earthbound humanity, that which is entirely beyond human authority and jurisdiction. Spatial and temporal categories are combined in their cosmology in a way that is completely foreign to our own.

With this complex worldview in mind, we can now attempt a more complete definition of the term. οὐρανός refers to the firmament, the vault of heaven, or sky understood as an empirical point of reference. This is the place above the earth which forms a part of the created universe and composes its highest

---

[57] Cf. H. TRAUB, «οὐρανός, οὐράνιος, ἐπουράνιος», in *ThWNT*; U. SCHOENBORN, «οὐρανός, οὐράνιος», in *EWNT*.

region. οὐρανός also refers to heaven, the place of God's sacred dwelling and the home of the saints. Again, it is important to remember that our modern desire to separate the physical from the metaphysical was entirely foreign to the ancients. Our first task then is to study the other references in Paul's letters that contain the word οὐρανός before we examine how it is used in v. 47. Perhaps the best way of going about this would be to categorize the references according to grammatical number. We begin by analyzing those passages that present οὐρανός in the plural and then we shall consider those that present the word in the singular.

There are only three passages that list οὐρανός in the plural. Paul teaches the Philippians that, in contrast to the enemies of the cross of Christ, the saints will inherit an eternal reward. «But our commonwealth is in heaven[s] (ἐν οὐρανοῖς) and from it we await a Savior, the Lord Jesus Christ» (Phil 3,20). Heaven is also where Christ now lives until he comes to earth again. Paul praises the Thessalonians for they have come to serve God «and to wait for his Son from the heavens (ἐκ τῶν οὐρανῶν), whom he raised from the dead, Jesus who delivers us from the wrath to come» (1Th 1,10). Paul also gives a similar message to the Corinthians. «For we know that if the earthly tent we live in is destroyed, we have a building from God, a house not made with hands, eternal in the heavens (ἐν τοῖς οὐρανοῖς)» (2Cor 5,1).

The remaining eight passages all use οὐρανός in the singular. In describing to the Thessalonians his doctrine concerning the Lord's return, Paul teaches that the living will not precede the dead at the parousia. «For the Lord himself will descend from heaven (ἀπ' οὐρανοῦ) with a cry of command, with the archangel's call and with the sound of the trumpet of God. And the dead in Christ will rise first» (1Th 4,16). When writing to the Galatians about the one gospel of Christ, Paul curses those who preach something contrary to what they have already received. «But even if we, or an angel from heaven (ἐξ οὐρανοῦ), should preach to you a gospel contrary to that which we preached to you, let him be accursed» (Gal 1,8). Turning next to 1 Corinthians, we now come to a passage that we already studied in our previous discussion on the noun γῆ. «For although there may be so-called gods in heaven (ἐν οὐρανῷ) or on earth — as indeed there are many gods and many lords» (1Cor 8,5). The word comes up again in 2 Corinthians when Paul boasts of his visions and revelations. «I know a man in Christ who fourteen years ago (whether in the body or out of the body I do not know, God knows) was caught up to the third heaven (ἕως τρίτου οὐρανοῦ)» (2Cor 12,2). In the letter to the Romans, Paul also mentions heaven in the section on the sinfulness of the Gentiles. «For the wrath of God is revealed from heaven (ἀπ' οὐρανοῦ) against all ungodliness and wickedness of men who by their wickedness suppress the truth» (Rom 1,18). Lastly, in the section devoted to the salvation of Israel in Romans, we find our final reference to the term in a brief quotation from Deuteronomy. «But the righteousness based on faith says, Do not say in your heart, "Who will ascend into heaven (εἰς τὸν οὐρανόν)?" (that is, to bring Christ down)» (Rom 10,6).

We have now completed a survey of nine of the passages that include οὐρανός in the authentic Pauline corpus, both in the plural and in the singular. We are now in a fine position to take a closer look at the two remaining passages, 2 Corinthians 5,2 and 1 Corinthians 15,47. Both of these passages are quite similar in as much as they present the prepositional phrase ἐξ οὐρανοῦ as an example of the *genitivus materiae*. In other words, ἐξ in both of these cases is to be explained in the same way as ἐκ γῆς was in v. 47a.

We begin with the passage from 2 Corinthians. At the beginning of chapter five, Paul describes the human body as an earthly tent that will be replaced after death by an eternal building made by God. He conceives of the earthly body as a kind of house that a person lives in during his life and moves out of at the time of his death. «Here indeed we groan and long to put on our heavenly dwelling (τὸ οἰκητήριον ἡμῶν τὸ ἐξ οὐρανοῦ)» (2Cor 5,2). The heavenly house is next compared to an article of clothing that someone puts on and wears, «so that by putting it on we may not be found naked» (2Cor 5,3). Hence τὸ οἰκητήριον ἡμῶν τὸ ἐξ οὐρανοῦ is Paul's way of describing the heavenly substance with which believers will clothe themselves in the eschatological life. He does not mean that it *comes* out of heaven, but rather, that it is *made* of heaven, that it is composed of heavenly substance. Could this heavenly dwelling be anything other than the spiritual body that Paul speaks about in 1 Corinthians 15? They must indeed be one and the same.

After this extensive survey of the ten other occurrences of this word in the Pauline corpus, we are now able to examine ἐξ οὐρανοῦ in v. 47b. This prepositional phrase is meant to contrast with ἐκ γῆς of v. 47a, thus insuring the subunit's antithetical parallelism. v. 47b is the Apostle's way of narrating the new genesis which has now begun with Jesus' resurrection from the dead. In the beginning, God formed the first man from the earth and granted him a natural body; at the moment of Jesus' resurrection from the dead, God formed the second man from the firmament of heaven and granted him a spiritual body. In a word, then, the whole point of v. 47 is to contrast earthly matter to heavenly matter. Paul does this in order to show that there is a particular substance which is proper to each part of the cosmos, one an earthly kind and the other a heavenly kind. This crucial distinction reinforces his point on the necessity for the change of bodies: the natural body is appropriate for this earthly life and a spiritual body is appropriate for eschatological heavenly life.

Before we leave this verse, we must say a final word about what is missing in this clause. χοϊκός, the final word of v. 47a, does not have a counterpart in v. 47b. Why would Paul have left its antithesis unexpressed? The answer lies in the next verses where Paul makes a forceful contrast between χοϊκός and ἐπουράνιος. The Apostle most probably left this particular verse unfinished since he intended to draw out the implications of this dialectic in the verses that conclude the subunit.

5. 1Cor 15,48

Building on Paul's discussion of the origin of the two Adams, this verse extends the argument so as to include those who belong to Adam and Christ. Let us now turn to the exegesis of this text.

οἷος ὁ χοϊκός, τοιοῦτοι καὶ οἱ χοϊκοί,
καὶ οἷος ὁ ἐπουράνιος, τοιοῦτοι καὶ οἱ ἐπουράνιοι·
«As is the one like dust, so are those who are like dust;
and as is the one like heaven, so are those who are like heaven».

In vv. 45-47, Paul took great pains to develop his exegesis of Genesis 2,7. Now that he has put forward and clarified his first Adam – last Adam analogy, he goes on to broaden his argument so as to include the Corinthians. In v. 47 he teaches that the first and second human beings represent the prototypes of all those who belong to them. The Apostle is thinking in corporate terms here. Those who descend from the first Adam resemble their forefather in earthly matters; those who descend from the last Adam resemble theirs in heavenly matters. The verse is perfectly balanced so as to underscore the contrast between ὁ χοϊκός and ὁ ἐπουράνιος. If we keep in mind the thesis which Paul made in v. 44b, v. 48 certainly suggests that those like the first Adam share his natural body and those like the last Adam will share his spiritual one. In fact the whole question of bodies is basic to the point of these different ancestries. The proverb, «Like father, like son», captures the sense of this verse in a nutshell.

– οἷος ὁ χοϊκός, τοιοῦτοι καὶ οἱ χοϊκοί. The pronouns οἷος and τοιοῦτοι serve to introduce and connect the four verbless clauses of v. 48. Serving a correlative function, they may be translated «as..., so..». We find another example of this in 2 Corinthians when Paul defends himself and his ministry against his enemies. «Let such people understand that as (οἷοί) we are in word through letters when absent, so (τοιοῦτοι) we also are in action when present» (2Cor 10,11). The Apostle's point of course is this: as is the one who is characteristic of dust, so too are those who are characteristic of dust. We saw above in our exegesis of the adjective χοϊκός that this term refers to humanity's weak and perishable nature. We may translate it as «earthly» as long as we keep this notion of frailty and mortality in mind. Nevertheless, given the fact that no one has yet coined the term «dustic», «like dust» captures the sense of the Greek word better and will have to do in English.

– καὶ οἷος ὁ ἐπουράνιος, τοιοῦτοι καὶ οἱ ἐπουράνιοι·. The word that interests us in v. 48b is the adjective ἐπουράνιος, the parallel to χοϊκός from v. 48a. ἐπουράνιος occurs nineteen times in the New Testament, six times in Paul's authentic letters and five times in 1 Corinthians 15. In classical Greek this adjective was used to describe the gods who live in heaven and it is found in Homer, Plato, Philo and Josephus[58]. ἐπουράνιος conveys the sense of belonging to heaven and so it may be translated «heavenly», or «like heaven», or «of heaven». Before we can study its meaning in v. 48, we first have to survey the other occurrences of ἐπουράνιος in the Pauline corpus.

The only place where this word is found outside of 1 Corinthians is in Philippians. In this letter it is used as a noun which refers to heavenly things or bodies. «that at the name of Jesus every knee should bow, that of heavenly bodies (ἐπουρανίων) and of earthly bodies and of subterranean bodies» (Phil 2,10). The action of genuflecting, a gesture of respect in the ancient world, is performed by every creature in the cosmos. Paul is not using a metaphor here. He understands these beings as having bodies with movable members and thus with their knees they adore and worship the Lord Jesus. Hence the heavenly powers also recognize Christ's universal lordship.

This important connection to bodies, both earthly and heavenly, is precisely the point of the second half of 1 Corinthians 15. The word ἐπουράνιος is used twice in this chapter: first it modifies the noun body and then it stands alone, just as in Philippians. «There are both heavenly bodies (σώματα ἐπουράνια) and earthly bodies; but the appearance of the heavenly ones (τῶν ἐπου-

---

[58] Cf. H. TRAUB, «οὐρανός, οὐράνιος, ἐπουράνιος», in *ThWNT*; O. MICHEL, «ἐπουράνιος», in *EWNT*.

ρανίων) is one thing and that of the earthly ones is another» (1Cor 15,40). One of the principal purposes of vv. 35-44a is to demonstrate the contrast between earthly and heavenly bodies. Again, the Apostle is not using metaphor here. The celestial beings were commonly believed to have bodies and that is certainly Paul's assumption in this verse.

Now that we have examined the other passages that contain this adjective, we are ready to scrutinize the three final examples of ἐπουράνιος in v. 48 and v. 49. This contrast between earthly and heavenly things serves as a preparation for Paul's whole discussion on the natural and the spiritual body as developed in this passage. We must remember that in this part of the subunit Paul is contrasting the adjectives χοϊκός to ἐπουράνιος. The first, on account of the -ικός suffix, conveys the meaning «belonging to», «concerning», or «being characteristic of» dust. The second, on account of the -ιος suffix, conveys the meaning «of», or «belonging to»[59]. Therefore, given the parallel structure of the verse, we may conclude that both terms are meant to express those characteristics which belong to the substance in question: if χοϊκός is characteristic of dust and hence is like earth, i.e., mortal, then ἐπουράνιος is that which belongs to heaven and hence is like heaven, i.e., eternal.

6. 1Cor 15,49

Here is the sixth and final verse of the subunit. With the exegesis of v. 49, we conclude our close reading of the text.

> καὶ καθὼς ἐφορέσαμεν τὴν εἰκόνα τοῦ χοϊκοῦ, φορέσωμεν καὶ τὴν εἰκόνα τοῦ ἐπουρανίου.
> «Just as we have borne the image of the one like dust, let us also bear the image of the one like heaven».

– καὶ καθὼς. A very common word, καθώς occurs one hundred and eighty-two times in the New Testament. Paul uses it often in his letters, a total of seventy times and it appears nineteen times in 1 Corinthians. καθώς most often serves as a subordinating conjunction whose function is to make a

---

[59] «*Denominative adjectives.*—This very numerous class consists of adjectives formed from the stems of nouns by means of the suffix -ιος with the meaning "of, or belonging to." Thus δοκίμιος (<δοκιμή<δόκιμος<δέκομαι), τίμιος (<τιμή), κόσμιος (<κόσμος)» (J.H. MOULTON – W.F.HOWARD, *Accidence and Word-Formation*, § 135.3).

comparison with what follows. It is best translated as «just as»[60]. An important feature to notice is that καθώς often makes a connection between a figure from the Old Testament with one from the New. For example, Paul compares Abraham to the faithful people of his generation who have embraced the gospel. «Thus (Καθώς) Abraham "believed God and it was reckoned to him as righteousness." So you see that it is people of faith who are the sons of Abraham» (Gal 3,6-7). Καθώς also appears in reference to the Old Testament in Romans, «And as (καὶ καθώς) Isaiah predicted, "If the Lord of hosts had not left us children, we would have fared like Sodom and been made like Gomorrah"» (Rom 9,29) as well as earlier in 1 Corinthians, «the women should keep silence in the Churches. For they are not permitted to speak, but should be subordinate, as even (καθὼς καί) the law says» (1Cor 14,34). In v. 49, therefore, Paul is obviously comparing Adam, his principal character from the Old Testament, to Christ, his principal one from the New. By doing so, the Apostle is underlining the continuity between the word of God as revealed in the Law, Prophets and the Writings, to the gospel which is now revealed in Jesus Christ. He teaches that God is consistent in all his plans and enjoys the infinite power to create as he wills. For as he will tell the Romans in his gospel to them, «But it is not as though the word of God had failed». (Rom 9,6). The Almighty has the ability to create a new type of human being even in light of the sin, rebellion and death of Adam's race.

– ἐφορέσαμεν. The verb φορέω appears six times in the New Testament and only twice in Paul's authentic letters. Its basic sense, «to bear», «to wear», refers to carrying something forward or to keep on carrying something. Hence it came to be used to describe how certain individuals wear clothing, bear something, or carry weapons[61]. For example in Romans, the governing authority is said to carry the sword for the sake of public order: «for he is God's servant for your good. But if you do wrong, be afraid, for he does not bear (φορεῖ) the sword in vain; he is the servant of God to execute his wrath on the wrongdoer» (Rom 13,4). As for the two examples of the noun in v. 49, these refer to the bearing of images. As such, φορέω in this context represents a metaphor for putting on an article of clothing.

We must now make sense of the verb's tense. Although ἐφορέσαμεν is obviously in the aorist, that does not mean that it should be translated into the

---

[60] Cf. BDR § 453; HS § 287a; W. RADL, «καθώς», in *EWNT*.

[61] Cf. K. WEISS, «φορέω», in *ThWNT*; H. BALZ, «φορέω», in *EWNT*.

simple past tense in modern languages. This is an example of the gnomic aorist which is commonly used in axioms, proverbs and sayings[62]. Blass and Debrunner point out that in this case, the present perfect tense is appropriate for translation since it expresses the notion of a past action which continues into the present. Hence the text in v. 49 is best translated as, «Just as we *have borne*.»

But what does the verb mean in this context? Paul is about to use the same metaphor in vv. 53-54 with the verb ἐνδύω. «To bear the image of someone» means to put him on (as one would a garment) and so resemble him. Here again we see that the image of the human body is not far from the Apostle's mind, for at Adam's creation he put on a natural body. This is what he will explain by his choice of the verb's object, εἰκών, which immediately follows.

– τὴν εἰκόνα τοῦ χοϊκοῦ. The noun εἰκών appears twenty-three times in the New Testament. There are only seven occurrences in Paul's letters, three of which are found in 1 Corinthians. The word refers to an «image» or «likeness», and it is used both literally and figuratively[63]. Even though the word is relatively infrequent, nonetheless it exhibits a wide range of meaning. In order to understand what Paul means by εἰκών in v. 49, let us begin by examining the other occurrences of the word.

We start with the literal use of the term. In the Synoptics, Caesar's image on the coin is called an εἰκών[64]. The term is also used this way in Revelation where it refers to the cultic image that is worshiped by apostates. This is in line with the oldest Greek usage of εἰκών as referring to a statue of a god. Paul uses this word in the literal sense only once. In his condemnation of the sins of the Gentiles at the beginning of Romans, the Apostle quotes Ps 105,20 (LXX) in a midrash. «And they exchanged the glory of the immortal God for images resembling (ἐν ὁμοιώματι εἰκόνος) a mortal human being or birds or animals or reptiles» (Rom 1,23). Exegetes differ in the explanation of ἐν ὁμοιώματι εἰκόνος, but perhaps the best solution is to consider εἰκών as an epexegetical genitive and then translate it as «images representing or resembling».

The remaining five occurrences in Paul's letters are all metaphorical, yet each expresses a unique shade of meaning. We begin with the only other

---

[62] Cf. ZERWICK § 256; BDR § 333; and HS § 1991.
[63] Cf. G. KITTEL, «εἰκών», in *ThWNT*; H. KUHLI, «εἰκών», in *EWNT*.
[64] Cf. Mk 12,16; Mt 22,20; Lk 20,24.

reference in 1 Corinthians: «For a man ought not to cover his head, since he is the image (εἰκών) and glory of God; but woman is the glory of man» (1Cor 11,7). It is not our concern here to develop Paul's understanding of women's subordinate role at worship: it would seem that this unit is a typical midrash of the time and must be taken as such. What does concern us is his conception of a man as an «image of God». It would seem that Paul uses this as an anthropological attribute, a kind of category that conveys man's inherent dignity and value.

The next metaphorical meaning refers to Christ as the image of God. Paul defends the «veiled» manner of his preaching of the gospel against his Corinthian attackers and speaks to them about those who are perishing. «In their case the god of this world has blinded the minds of the unbelievers, to keep them from seeing the light of the gospel of the glory of Christ, who is the image of God (εἰκὼν τοῦ θεοῦ)» (2Cor 4,4). The Apostle's addressees are deficient in their perception and fail to see Christ for who he truly is. Thus the Apostle reminds them of Christ's true nature in light of the revelation made known to them through the gospel.

The remaining three references all present believers as the image of Christ. At the end of the previous unit in 2 Corinthians, Paul speaks about the new glorious relation which now exists between Christians and Christ. «And we all, with unveiled face, beholding the glory of the Lord, are being changed into the same image (τὴν αὐτὴν εἰκόνα) from one degree of glory to another; for this comes from the Lord who is the Spirit» (2Cor 3,18). Since one day believers will also share in glory, they too will be resemble Christ and share in his likeness. Hence εἰκών describes Christ's nature. It should not be understood as a mere copy, but rather, as an original.

Paul employs εἰκών in the same way in Romans when he defines the purpose of God's election of believers. «For those whom he foreknew he also predestined to be conformed to the image of his Son (τῆς εἰκόνος τοῦ υἱοῦ αὐτοῦ), in order that he might be the first-born among many brothers» (Rom 8,29). This process of being conformed to Christ's image has already begun thanks to the gift of the Spirit who dwells in them. This great salvific event will only be completed at the eschaton with the bodily resurrection of the dead. Hence we discover once again the already – not yet tension in Paul's eschatology. At any rate, Paul's primary concern here has to do with Christ's relationship to believers and not his relationship to God.

Lastly, we reach the two final occurrences of εἰκών in v. 49. After having developed the antithesis of the first and second human beings through his midrash on Genesis and after having extended this notion to include their representative roles for the rest of humanity, Paul now specifies the nature of the resemblance in the subunit's last verse. «The image of the one like dust» of v. 49a obviously refers to the first Adam, ὁ χοϊκός. All those connected to Adam, their representative and forefather, bear his εἰκών. In other words, those who bear the image of the first Adam share in his natural condition, one which is subject to decay and death. They are frail and mortal precisely because of the natural body which each one possesses, it being the hallmark of earthly existence for all human beings in this passing life.

– φορέσωμεν. Much ink has been spilt over this last verb in v. 49. Did Paul intend φορέσομεν, the future indicative, or φορέσωμεν, the aorist subjunctive? There is still no consensus among exegetes at this point. Metzger and his committee opted for the future tense in spite of the scant evidence in its favor[65]. We must do some textual criticism of our own before arriving at an informed and conclusive decision.

We begin with the evidence for the future indicative. It is supported by B I 38 88 206 218 242 630 915 919 1149 1518 1872 1881 Lect cop[sa] eth Irenaeus Origen Aphraates Ephraem Cyril[3/5] Theodoret Gennadius-Constantinople Cosmas[1/3] Ps-Oecumenius and Theophylact, as well as Tischendorf, Westcott-Hort, von Soden, Vogels and the majority of modern commentators.

The evidence for the aorist subjunctive, however, is far more convincing. It is supported by P[46] ℵ A C D G K P Ψ 0243 33 81 104 181 326 330 436 451 614 629 1241 1739 1877 1962 1984 1985 2127 2492 2495 Byz it[ar,d,dem,e,f,g,x,z] vg cop[bo] goth Marcion Theodotus Iranaeus[lat] Clement Tertullian Origen[gr,lat] Cyprian (Methodius) Ambrosiaster Hilary Caesarius-Nazianzus Basil Priscillian Gregory-Elvira Gregory-Nyssa Ambrose Macarius Epiphanius Chrysostom Cyril[2/5] Euthalius Ps-Athanasius Cosmas[2/3] Maximus-Confessor and John-Damascus.

Given this information, it becomes clear that the external evidence clearly leans in favor of φορέσωμεν thanks to its nearly universal testimony in the early Church[66]. So why then did the United Bible Societies Committee opt for

---

[65] «Exegetical considerations (i.e., the context is didactic, not hortatory) led the Committee to prefer the future indicative, despite its rather slender external support» (METZGER, 569).

[66] St. Peter Chrysologus also understood the hortatory subjunctive as the better reading in this verse. «"Therefore, even as we have borne the likeness of the earthly, let us bear also the likeness of the heavenly." Let it be granted that all this was a necessity: that we, formed

φορέσομεν? It would seem that they determined that the internal evidence calls for the future indicative. By doing so, they allowed the prevailing opinion of exegetes at that moment to determine the correct biblical text. This was a regrettable mistake. The hortatory subjunctive not only enjoys the majority of witnesses but it also represents the more difficult reading in this context. If the future were original, however, it would be very difficult to explain why a scribe would have changed it to the subjunctive and that this mistake should have caught on, only to become the overwhelmingly predominant reading. For all these reasons, therefore, φορέσωμεν is by far the better reading and we accept it as the original.

– καὶ τὴν εἰκόνα τοῦ ἐπουρανίου. What then does Paul mean when he says «let us also bear the image of the one like heaven»? He certainly cannot be urging them to put on the spiritual body, since this will happen only at the end of time. This is the whole point of his argument in vv. 23-28 and vv. 50-57. Rather, the Apostle is exhorting them to adopt the Spirit-filled life of the last Adam even now during their earthly existence. This is not an impossible duty, nor is it a goal beyond their reach. Those who bear the image of the last Adam already partly share in his supernatural condition thanks to the Spirit whom believers received at baptism. They are already called through their life in the Spirit to resemble him now in their natural bodies. At the eschaton they will come to resemble him completely when they at last put on their spiritual bodies. In heaven they will be imperishable and immortal when they at last share a spiritual body like his. Hence this final verse of the subunit brilliantly sums up Paul's eschatology: the last time has indeed already begun, but it has not yet arrived in its entirety. This will only happen at the general resurrection of the dead, when the natural body is changed into the spiritual one, «in a

---

from earth, could not produce heavenly fruits; that, born from concupiscence, we could not avoid concupiscence; that we, born from the powerful attractions of the flesh, had to carry the base load of its attractions; that we, accepted into this world for our home, were captive to its evils. Yes, let us who have been reborn to the likeness of our Lord (as we mentioned), whom a Virgin conceived and the Spirit enlivened and modesty carried and integrity brought to birth and innocence nourished and sanctity taught and virtue trained and God adopted as His sons — let us bear the image of our Creator in a perfect reproduction. Let it be a reproduction not of that majesty in which He is unique, but of that innocence, simplicity, meekness, patience, humility, mercy and peacefulness by which He deigned to become and to be one with us» (P. Chrysologus, *Selected Sermons*, 201-202).

moment, in the twinkling of an eye, at the last trumpet» (v. 52). Thus Christ's last enemy will be destroyed and death will be vanquished forever.

7. The Rhetoric of the Subunit

We saw above in the section entitled «Antithetical Parallelism» (Chapter I, 6.2) how Paul composed this subunit in a series of opposing parallel segments. By contrasting words and clauses in this way, the Apostle stresses the discontinuity between the first Adam and the last Adam, the earthly realm and the heavenly one. There are in fact three types of parallelism recognized by scholars: antithetical, synonymous and mixed[67]. Given the violent and tumultuous world of the first century, it is not at all surprising to find a writer like Paul using this rhetorical device in order to convey his own perception of the dawn of the eschatological age[68]. Let us take another look at the subunit as a whole, paying special attention to the conjunctions and particles that highlight Paul's rhetoric.

V. 44b offers an excellent example of antithetical parallelism. In this, the thesis statement of the subunit, both clauses of this conditional sentence serve as contrasting statements. Just as Paul had compared the earthly bodies to the heavenly ones in the previous pericope, so here he wants to compare the natural human body to the spiritual one.

After the familiar introduction for a Scriptural passage οὕτως καὶ γέγραπται, Paul again compares two clauses in the following verse. v. 45a is dedicated to the first human being Adam while v. 45b is dedicated to the last Adam. In this way, Paul accentuates the differences between them, as seen by these opposing pairs: πρῶτος – ἔσχατος, ψυχήν – πνεῦμα and ζῶσαν – ζῳοποιοῦν. The contrast helps to underscore Paul's principal point, namely, that there exists a striking discontinuity between the two. By contrasting πνεῦμα ζῳοποιοῦν to ψυχὴν ζῶσαν, the Apostle compares the Holy Spirit, that which is life itself, to a living creature, that which receives life.

Next, we see that the conjunction ἀλλά introduces v. 46a as well as v. 46b. This strong adversative, along with ἔπειτα, insists on the order of creation of the bodies. In the second half, Paul echoes back to the contrast he first made in the thesis through the ψυχικόν – πνευματικόν antithesis.

---

[67] Cf. BDR § 485, § 489-90; HS § 294z-bb.
[68] See MOULTON, *A Grammar*, vol. IV by N. TURNER, 96-97.

V. 47 not only continues the midrash pesher begun in v. 45, but it also mirrors that verse's structure. Paul repeats ὁ πρῶτος ἄνθρωπος, this time contrasting it to ὁ δεύτερος ἄνθρωπος. Moreover, with the help of the preposition ἐκ, he compares their radically different material natures: the first is made ἐκ γῆς and the second ἐκ οὐρανοῦ. By emphasizing the material component of their natures, the Apostle reinforces the physical character of their respective bodies. As we demonstrated in the close reading of the text, the spiritual body should not be seen as composed of Spirit, but rather, characterized by Spirit. Just as God formed Adam out of earthly matter so he could live on earth, so too at the resurrection God formed the last Adam out of heavenly matter so he could live in heaven. Thus Paul manages to link this verse to what has come before and so prepare his addressees for what follows.

V. 48 is held together by the repetition of the pronouns οἷος [...] τοιοῦτοι in both clauses. Again this serves to contrast two more opposing pairs, ὁ χοϊκός – ὁ ἐπουράνιος and οἱ χοϊκοί – οἱ ἐπουράνιοι. The parallelism so carefully fashioned by Paul is now extended to include all those who take after their given progenitor. If to be «dustic» means to be weak and mortal, then to be heavenly means to be imperishable and immortal. Since each Adam is considered to be the progenitor of his particular kind of humanity, then each one stands as the exemplary representative of the many who follow.

Lastly, v. 49 closes out the subunit on a hortatory note. As the final verse in the subunit, it recapitulates everything that has come before. After the introductory words καὶ καθώς, Paul presents his last set of contrasting clauses. The opposing pairs ἐφορέσαμεν – φορέσωμεν and τοῦ χοϊκοῦ – τοῦ ἐπουρανίου emphasize for the last time the striking contrast between the natural and supernatural realms. The use of this rather uncommon verb highlights the ethical point of the sentence. If ἐφορέσαμεν refers to our natural behavior as people like dust, then φορέσωμεν refers to our spiritual behavior as people like heaven. Paul is exhorting the Corinthians to put on Christ, to take on his image in their lives, to think and behave as he did. Although decidedly eschatological, this action is not reserved for the parousia. Rather, Christian living ought to start now and thereby become the hallmark of all who hope to resemble «the one like heaven», the last Adam. If all people already bear the image of the one like earth, the first Adam, the Apostle now exhorts the Corinthians to be true to their vocation and bear the image of the one like heaven.

CHAPTER III

Theological Reflections on 1Cor 15,44b-49

1. The Human Body, Natural and Spiritual

Our exegesis of the subunit has sought to highlight Paul's fundamental anthropological concern in 1 Corinthians 15,35-58. Intent on proving the existence of the spiritual body, the Apostle grounds his complex demonstration both on reason as well as on the Genesis account of the creation of the natural body. In the reflections that follow, we shall take seriously Paul's teaching on the σῶμα, both natural and spiritual and in so doing, attempt to articulate just what his doctrine on the human being might mean for Christians today.

When God formed Adam from the earth, he created the first man as a living being. What does it mean to be a living being with a natural body? Like Adam before us, we too are made up of material taken from the world in which we live. We too have been given the gift of life through God's loving and creative intervention. Thus every human being by his very nature finds himself in solidarity with all the created world (with which he shares its materiality) and with God (from whom he enjoys the gift of life). If over the centuries Christians have come to see themselves more and more as souls temporarily trapped in bodies — due no doubt to the pervasive influence of Platonism in western thought — Paul's instructive teaching in 1 Corinthians presents us with a challenging corrective. His message was certainly intended to be taken that way by his own addressees.

As human beings we live in the here and now, linked to particular places and cultures and generations, all the while taking up space in certain determined localities. And yet, thanks to our minds and our souls, we can indeed transcend our bodily limitations and restrictions. We relate to people in other eras and civilizations and we are able to commune with God in prayer and meditation. What then does it mean to have a natural body? On the one hand, as human beings we cannot be reduced to the matter that constitutes us. It is too much to say that we are bodies, for to do so would downplay the intellectual and spiritual dimensions of our being. On the other hand, human beings cannot be conceived of without bodies, since the material element makes up an essential part of who we are. But if it is true that as human beings we have bodies, nonetheless we must affirm that the ownership of our bodies represents a unique kind of possession. We do not have bodies in the same way that we have books or cars or other things. These possessions are extrinsic to us in a way that our bodies are not and never could be.

How then are we to understand the singular relationship each of us has with his own body? Paul's anthropology manages to do justice to our humanity in as much as he preserves the mystery of what it means to be human. He does not attempt to evacuate the tensions which we just considered. For him, the complete salvation of the human being necessarily entails the redemption of the natural body. If this were not the case, God would not really be God at all. But God in fact shows his sovereign and omnipotent power over his creation and over us in particular, precisely by saving our bodies from the decay and corruption caused by death. In raising the dead to eternal life, God shows himself victorious over humanity's principal enemies, sin and death. In the final analysis, Paul's theology of the body says much more about God than it does about us: the divine plan for the world will not end in failure. As creator and redeemer, God reigns as supreme Lord over all.

Unlike those philosophies that conceive of the human being as somehow separate from the body, the biblical image of man is far more *terre à terre*, if you will forgive the pun. If today he were asked an opinion on the matter, Paul, basing his teaching on that of Genesis, would most probably describe the human being as an ensouled body. The history of our lives, be they long or short, be they happy or tragic, is intimately bound up with the history of our bodies. We are living organisms subject to all the biological and physical laws of the universe. And thanks especially to the insights of Freud and Jung, in our century we have also become aware of the many psychological and sociological forces that determine our lives. In an overwhelming way today, personal freedom is at times restricted and at other times fostered by the countless influences that affect and often circumscribe the parameters of our existence. This is especially true in the field of medicine, where the continuing progress of technology forces us to ask ourselves more and more what it means to be a human being[1].

Hence the limited and frail condition which characterizes our lives as creatures brings us face to face with our reality as ensouled bodies in the world. Our corporeal existence in fact springs from the bodily union of our parents, who themselves have fulfilled the Lord God's command to them: «And God blessed them and God said to them, "Be fruitful and multiply and fill the earth and subdue it; and have dominion over the fish of the sea and over the birds of the air and over every living thing that moves upon the earth"» (Gen 1,28). We do not determine our coming into being, nor do we usually determine our own death. From the very moment of our conception, we begin our lives in solidarity with all other human beings, who like us, share in the natural history of the body's development, decline and death. This solidarity extends to all other living things as well, since God has made us stewards of his creation.

From the divine command to be fruitful and multiply springs a fundamental ethic: human beings must act in a way that is consonant with their dignity as creatures made in the image of God; they must respect, treasure and promote life, both human life and that of all other living things. In a very real way, every discussion of moral Christian behavior must be constructed on this solid foundation, whether in the field of interpersonal ethics (e.g., sexuality) or social ethics (e.g., warfare, health care, or the promotion of justice). Conscious of our own mortality, we are also aware of our indebtedness to those who have come before us as well as our responsibility to those who will come after us. Since our history flows from and into theirs, we have a compelling obligation before God to protect and safeguard all creation, especially our fellow human beings.

---

[1] Over the past thirty years, bioethicists have been struggling over two competing concepts of what it means to be a human person. Is a person defined by the presence or absence of certain capacities (i.e., the ability to make autonomous decisions), or rather, is it the natural history of the embodied self that makes the person? This debate continues to rage today and the outcome is far from certain. It seems clear that Paul's anthropology would certainly favor the latter understanding of what it means to be human. Christian ethicists must keep in mind the biblical vision of the human being understood as an embodied being with a natural body alive in the world. For both a fine overview of the status questionis and a convincing defense of the thesis that the person is someone who has a history, see G. MEILAENDER, «Terra es animata», 25-32.

It is obvious that this biblical image of the human being flies in the face of the post-Enlightenment concept of man which conceives of him as fully autonomous, independent and self-sufficient. Yet we who live at the end of the second millennium, standing in the shadow of Hiroshima and Auschwitz, should know better by now. Our autonomy is at best illusory, our independence can only be fully insured in fellowship and our self-sufficiency finds its fullest expression only in loving service to others. This Christian vision of life, firmly based on the Lord's command to love God with all our heart and love our neighbor as ourself, will always remain countercultural in both tone and message; it will continue to present a major stumbling block to people today as well. The proclamation of the gospel calls everyone to repentance and belief in the Good News that God's reign has indeed begun in the person of Jesus Christ. Our age, perhaps more so than any other in humanity's history, desperately needs to discover the Bible's vision of human worth and dignity. As a global society, the world today needs to encounter the Lord God of Genesis who created everything out of love and declared it all to be good. Conscious all the while of our capacity to commit evil, we proclaim our faith in Jesus Christ our redeemer, Lord of all creation, victor over sin and death.

As Christians, we are called by God to embrace the passing nature of our lives. The world itself is marked by change and transition and as living beings we fully share in its temporal and passing quality. Like the first Adam, we too are χοϊκός, «characteristic of dust». Yet by living fully in the natural body, we both embrace the earth and at the same time transcend it. As pilgrims in this passing world, active in loving service to our neighbor, we nevertheless keep our eyes focused on the world to come with great faith. Inextricably linked to the world's history until it reaches its final consummation in Christ, we nevertheless wait in hope for our eternal abode with God.

These remarks on Christian hope lead us next to inquire into the composition and characteristics of the spiritual body. What can we hope to be like when we are raised from the dead? What will our risen bodies be made of? Or, to repeat Paul's question in 1 Corinthians 15,35, «With what kind of body do they come?» Although we shall never get a truly satisfactory answer in this life, many scholars have speculated on this matter over the ages. What follows is a brief presentation of some of the exegetes in our century who maintain that the σῶμα πνευματικόν is made up of some kind of matter.

At the beginning of the century, Bousset, a German exegete, recognized that Paul was describing two different kinds of matter in v. 47. Over the years, however, his exegesis was ignored or rejected by other scholars (particularly

Bultmann and Schweizer) in favor of their own interpretation of the text. Bousset rightly recognized that Paul was contrasting an earthly substance to a heavenly one. For him, the body of the first Adam is composed of a material substance which is earthly, while the body of the last Adam is composed of a material substance which is heavenly[2].

Several years later Bousset broached the subject again, this time describing the spiritual body as one composed of a heavenly substance of light[3].

More recently, other exegetes have developed this notion of the material nature of the spiritual body in light of their study of 1 Corinthians 15. For example, Brandenburger claims that the body of the last Adam is formed from a heavenly substance, perhaps even out of πνεῦμα itself[4]. In a recent work

---

[2] «Seiner Herkunft nach ist der erste Mensch von der Erde und daher auch aus irdischem Stoff, der zweite Mensch ist seiner Herkunft nach himmlisch und — dürfen wir im Sinne des Paulus hinzusetzen — deshalb auch von himmlischem Stoff. Ihm steht eben dabei der erhöhte Christus in seinem Leibe voller Lichtherrlichkeit vor Augen. Wir beachten hier, wie für Paulus Leibliches und Geistiges in unmittelbarer Wechselwirkung mit einander stehen: die niedrige sinnliche Beschaffenheit des ersten Menschen hängt mit seiner irdischen Stofflichkeit zusammen; und wiederum: kein höheres geistiges Dasein ohne die entsprechende leibliche Grundlage» (W. BOUSSET, «Der erste Brief an die Korinther», 161).

[3] «Wir sahen bereits soeben, wie Paulus, wenn er von σάρξ spricht, nicht nur an die materielle Beschaffenheit des Menschen denkt, wie für ihn die σάρξ eine Innenseite, eine ψυχή hat, so daß die Begriffe σαρκικός identisch werden. Umgekehrt aber ist das Pneuma bei ihm nicht etwas rein Geistiges, das als solches dauernd und ohne somatische Grundlage für sich bestehen könnte. Am deutlichsten kommt das in seiner Eschatologie zum Ausdruck. Er kann es sich gar nicht anders kenken, als daß dem Pneuma in seiner eschatologischen Vollendung eine leibliche Grundlage zu Teil wird. So erklärt sich seine Hoffnung auf das σῶμα πνευματικόν (I. Kor. 15,44 vgl. Rö. 8,10f. 19.23. II Kor. 5,1ff.). Wenn er in diesem Zusammenhang von der δόξα des zukünstigen Leibes spricht, so ist zuzugeben, daß dieser Begriff bei ihm schwankt zwischen einer mehr geistigen Auffassung (Herrlichkeit, Ehre I. Kor. 15,40.43) und einer naturhaften (Lichtglanz). Aber es kann kaum geleugnet werden, daß er bei der δόξα doch auch wieder und wieder an die seine himmlische Lichtsubstanz denkt, wie sie den Gestirnen eignet). Ihm ist es selbstverständlich, daß der erhöhte Herr eine himmlische Leiblichkeit, ein σῶμα τῆς δόξης, besitzt. Er hat diese δόξα Gottes einst vor Damaskus auf dem Antlitz Christi leuchten sehen (II. Ko. 4.6), und die Christen sollen in der Vollendung σύμμορφοι τῆς εἰκόνος τοῦ υἱοῦ werden (Rö. 8,29 Phil 3,21)» (W. BOUSSET, Kyrios Christos, 124).

[4] «Die christologischen Aussagen der VV.45 und 47 enthalten eine Reihe von Schwierigkeiten. Der himmlische Mensch ist in V.49 wegen der futurischen Formulierung mit Sicherheit der Auferstandene in pneumatischer Leiblichkeit. Das muß dann aber von diesem Zielgedanken her nicht weniger für V.48 und ebenfalls für die auffallende Formulierung "der zweite Mensch (ist) vom Himmel" in V.47b gelten. Worauf diese

which examines the connection between the Spirit and spiritual gifts in the Church, Ellis maintains that the spiritual body is made of «immortal living matter»[5]. Similarly, Harris underscores the transformation from mortal bodies to «resplendent bodies» in his description of the σῶμα πνευματικόν[6]. All of the scholars referred to above recognize that, in one way or another, the spiritual body is made of a material substance which is not of this world.

So what precisely is the spiritual body like? Our exegesis of the subunit, based on some of the data gleaned from the excursus on ancient Greek astronomy, allows us to conclude that Paul believed it to be some kind of heavenly body. What kind of matter is it made of? This is a question which no doubt fascinated the Corinthians and it has fascinated every generation of Christians ever since. For Paul and his contemporaries, the existence of heavenly matter was simply a given. They found in the Aristotelian doctrine of ether, the fifth element, the fitting element which could make up the risen body. It seems very likely that Paul is alluding to this celestial substance in this passage of the letter.

How then are we to make sense of these findings for us today? Although Aristotelian categories dominated scientific paradigms until modern times, they have obviously been replaced by the findings of contemporary physics. We now know that the elements which make up the earth are the same as those

---

Formulierung hinauswill, zeigt das Gegenüber V.47a: Wie der erste Mensch bei seiner Erschaffung von der Erde genommen wurde und darum aus Erdsubstanz besteht (ἐκ γῆς χοϊκός), so besteht der Auferstandene bzw. sein Leib aus der Substanz der Himmelswelt, eben aus Pneuma. Die Formulierung ist nicht glücklich, wird doch Christus bei der Auferweckung nicht wie Adam überhaupt erst erschaffen. Aber die Auferweckung Christi dürfte als Schöpfungsakt Gottes verstanden sein (vgl. Röm 4,17), als Wiederverleihung von Leben oder Neuschöpfung. Erst seitdem gibt es nach diesem Text den Himmelsmenschen als zweiten Menschen» (E. BRANDENBURGER, «Alter und neuer Mensch», 207-208).

[5] «The initial coming of the Spirit, also called "the firstfruits" (ἀπαρχή) or "sealing" (σφραγίζειν) or "down-payment" (ἀρραβών), anticipates and assures the final work of the Spirit at the last day. The connection between these two events is first seen in the individual person of Jesus. The Spirit who came upon Jesus after his baptism was apparently also considered to be active in his resurrection from death in which Jesus' body became the first bit of earth to be transformed into immortal-living mater» (E.E. ELLIS, *Pauline Theology*, 33).

[6] «Just as Christ has a spiritual body, so his "descendants" will have spiritual bodies. Through a radical transformation, bodies that at present bear all the marks of frailty and mortality will become resplendent bodies bearing the impress of Christ's likeness (Php 3,20-21; cf. 1 Jn 3,2, "we shall be like him")» (M.J. HARRIS, *From Grave to Glory*, 224).

which make up the planets, the sun and the stars. Nevertheless Paul's point still holds true. Given his insistence on the discontinuity between this world and the world to come, we may conjecture that the spiritual body is surely not composed of any of the elements in the universe. Since this new substance (substances?) clearly remains beyond the realm of our experience, it cannot be the object of scientific study. As descendants of the first Adam and as inhabitants of the world created for him, we cannot hold or touch it, measure or quantify it. Rather, the spiritual body is composed of a new kind of substance which is appropriate to the world to come. God has made for the last Adam (and will make for those who follow him, as 1 Corinthians 15,48 makes clear) a new kind of matter with which to form his new creation. This element will be eternal, glorious and indestructible. Since matter by definition takes up space, the heavenly material which makes up the risen body is also spatial. We conclude from all this that heaven is in fact a place for bodies and not merely a repository for souls[7].

If we consider the meaning of the term πνευματικός once again, we shall unearth a few more insights into the reality of the risen body. We saw above in our word study that this adjective, thanks to its valuable suffix -ικός, means that which belongs to, pertains to, or is characteristic of the Spirit. Since God creates the risen body through the Holy Spirit, the Spirit now dwells in it in a perfect and complete way. Hence for Paul, the spiritual body belongs to the Holy Spirit in as much as he dwells in it completely. This dwelling of the Spirit in the human body, already begun in baptism, reaches perfection at the parousia. Yet since the risen body lives in the spiritual realm, heaven, the converse also holds true: the spiritual body dwells perfectly in God's Holy Spirit. Thus heaven is that eternally abiding place located in the very heart of the most Blessed Trinity.

Moreover, the spiritual body is characteristic of the Holy Spirit in as much as that which is proper to the Holy Spirit is also proper to the spiritual body. In the Apostle Paul, therefore, we discover for the first time a profound motif which would leave an indelible mark on Christian theology, the *admirabile commercium*: God has created and redeemed the world out of love, sharing his

---

[7] «If (and in so far as) we cannot think of the physical nature and concreteness of the risen and real person (even in accordance with what was experienced with regard to the risen Christ) in any other way than together with a definite spatial and local determination, we must think of heaven as a place and not merely as a "state"» (K. RAHNER, «The Resurrection of the Body», 214-215).

divine nature with us so that we may become what he is. God brings his saving work to completion in the universe through the agency of the Holy Spirit. Since God's Spirit is eternal, then so too is the spiritual body; since he is glorious, so too is this body; and since he is utterly free, so too is this body. If the Holy Spirit is understood as God's eternal loving power poured out into creation, then the spiritual body is formed of an eternal living substance which best receives that divine love. If you will, it becomes the perfect repository for that perfect divine love.

In our discussion of the natural body, we touched upon some of the tensions which mark our lives as ensouled bodies in space. Although our bodies connect us to a particular time and place in the world, our minds and souls nevertheless remain free to transcend the here and now, if only in a partial and imperfect way. This extraordinary ability sets us apart from all other creatures and as such it fittingly characterizes the uniqueness of the human condition. In the life to come, however, this tension will be definitively resolved in the eternity of heaven. In his spiritual body, Jesus Christ experiences a definite spatial and local determination that knows no bodily limitations or restrictions. The same will be true of all who will come to resemble the man of heaven at the resurrection. Our bodies will then fully experience the freedom that our minds and souls already partially enjoy in this life.

But how can this be? How can that which is material not be limited by time and space? From this side of the grave we cannot comprehend such a reality. Yet in spite of our limited knowledge, Paul's teaching should not be watered down: in the risen life we shall in fact have bodies and those bodies will indeed be spiritual. Given the profound nature of the mystery we are contemplating, perhaps it is best to ponder the reality of the spiritual body in light of the mystery of the Incarnation of the Son of God. To ask how the spiritual body is truly characteristic of the Spirit (thus truly divine) and still truly a material body (thus truly human) is similar to asking how Jesus Christ can be truly divine and truly human. How are we to make sense of the mystery of God become man for us? If in faith we believe that the infinite God became a finite creature and died for us on the cross, should it be any easier for us to believe that a finite creature can become divinized by grace and recreated for eternal life? In the final analysis, all our reflections on the fascinating subject of the resurrection body — our anthropology and pneumatology, our theology and christology — must maintain the dynamic tensions here described and then, with great faith in God's word, affirm the unfathomable profundity of the mystery.

How then will this glorious change come to pass? The Apostle is content to attribute the raising of the dead and the creation of the spiritual body to God's omnipotent power and so too should we[8]. If God was able to create the world in the beginning, he certainly is able to recreate it in the end. If the all-powerful God can create natural bodies, then he can also create spiritual ones. This is precisely the logic which governs the Apostle's argumentation throughout the second half of 1 Corinthians 15. God is truly so powerful in fact that even the dead are alive to him. But if the answer to the how still leaves us somewhat dissatisfied, perhaps we could pause for a moment and meditate on the why instead. Why did God raise his Son from the dead and promise to do the same for us? It would seem that the only answer to this question could be found in God's infinite love for his Son Jesus and indeed, for all his creation. In Christ, God truly desires to communicate his very being with us, to share his life and his love with us forever. Since on account of sin the natural body cannot fully reflect his glory, God freely transforms it into a spiritual body which can. God's love reaches its perfection in the perfection of his creatures. In the final analysis, the only acceptable answer to the whole question of the existence of the spiritual body is to be found in God's omnipotent and eternal love for us who are to be divinized through the agency of the Holy Spirit.

2. The Life-Giving Spirit

Every Sunday at mass, Catholics around the world proclaim together the Church's belief in the one triune God. After professing our faith in God the Father and God the Son, we go on to state our belief in the third person of the most Blessed Trinity, «We believe in the Holy Spirit, the Lord and Giver of Life». This explicit belief in the Lordship of the Spirit and his activity as giver of life is firmly grounded in New Testament roots, especially in Paul's letters. These brief reflections on the Holy Spirit will focus in a general way on the

---

[8] «One way of coping with the problem which some people adopt without too much fuss is to press the point that the divine initiative effects the risen life. God can use his sovereign power as he wills (1 Corinthians 15,38). He is able to create man (1 Corinthians 15, 45, 48, 49) and through the resurrection bring him into new creation, a Spirit-dominated, heavenly existence (1 Corinthians 15,44ff.). God can bring about such a radical, definitive post-mortem transformation, while somehow preserving the continuity with the earthly life of the ante-mortem person. Despite some incomprehensibility, belief in resurrected life is rendered possible through a sense of God's absolute power» (G. O'COLLINS, *The Easter Jesus*, 114-115).

Spirit's relationship with all of creation, but most especially with Christians in whom he dwells[9]. In light of the data we amassed in our close reading of the subunit, we shall concentrate our attention on the Holy Spirit as he manifests himself to us as believers. This approach will allow us to pull together some diverse insights into the economic Trinity (i.e., the exterior activity of the triune God who manifests himself in the world and its history), thereby helping us to come to a deeper understanding of Paul's profound and deeply mysterious pneumatology.

In the course of our close reading we noted that at various points in the letter the Apostle speaks of the πνεῦμα in various ways. He refers to him as «Spirit», «the Spirit», «the Spirit of God», «the Holy Spirit», and the «life-giving Spirit». We saw that for Paul, the πνεῦμα gives spiritual gifts to believers, knows and reveals the mind of God, sanctifies Christians by uniting them together in the Church, the body of Christ and guides and instructs all believers in prayer. But it is the final epithet that presently attracts our attention. What does the Apostle mean when he speaks of the «life-giving Spirit»? Exactly what kind of life does the Spirit give?

We noted above in our close reading of the text that there are only eleven occurrences of ζῳοποιέω in the New Testament, seven of which are found in Paul's letters. In all these cases ζῳοποιέω refers to the giving of eschatological life and as such it is associated with the resurrection of the dead on the last day. Thus we are correct in understanding the life-giving Spirit as God's loving power that grants eternal life to the dead by transforming their natural bodies into spiritual ones. Given this, the life in question here must be conceived of solely in eschatological terms, since it is clearly a new kind of life that is granted to Christians at the end of time, as 1 Corinthians 15,50-58 also makes quite clear.

Thanks to the dispute over spiritual gifts with his opponents at Corinth, the Apostle was able to articulate the relationship between his pneumatology and

---

[9] How do we begin to understand the economy of the Holy Spirit? One approach is presented by neo-scholastic theology which prefers to emphasize the notion of the general indwelling of the Trinity in the soul of the believer. Another approach would underscore the Holy Spirit's personal indwelling in the soul. Pauline pneumatology would support the second interpretation, as we shall see more clearly in our exegesis of Rom 8,9-13 in Part Two. For some background on this fascinating discussion, see J.J. O'DONNELL, *The Mystery of the Triune God*, 88-91.

his christology in a clearer way[10]. Let us first consider what this life-giving Spirit did for the last Adam and then examine his activity in the life of believers. In this way we shall remain true to Paul's argument in 1 Corinthians 15,44b-49 where he went to such great lengths to insist that the last Adam is but the first of a new kind of humanity.

In our exegesis of 1 Corinthians 15,45b, we paid very close attention to the fact that the verb «became» must be supplied from the first half of the verse. That this is indeed so led us to conclude that the last Adam became a life-giving Spirit at his resurrection. We saw how in his rising from the dead, Christ's *nature* did not change, but his *state* most certainly did. Jesus left this earthly existence and took up his heavenly one, thus abandoning his condition of earthly lowliness in favor of his heavenly splendor. This glorious event came to pass because God created for him a spiritual body through the agency of the Holy Spirit. In other words, the life-giving Spirit of God overshadowed him in such a powerful and extraordinary way that his body was recreated and transported into the eternal realm. Thanks to this transforming action of the Holy Spirit, Jesus Christ now dwells forever in heaven in the fullness of his glorified humanity. This exaltation occurred thanks to his very nature as God's Son. Given his divine status, therefore, it is also true that Christ is now filled with the Spirit in a truly unique and unrepeatable way[11]. In fact Paul insists on Christ's singularity as «the first fruits of those who have fallen asleep» (1Cor 15,20). Moreover, since he represents the beginning of this new creation, he henceforth becomes the source and font of the Spirit for all others. Since it is through him that the life-giving Spirit is available to believers, the Spirit is now

---

[10] «The dispute with pneumatic enthusiasm leads to clarification of the relationship between pneumatology and Christology, eschatology, anthropology and ecclesiology. The denial of physical resurrection resulted from an overvaluation of participation in $zo\bar{e}$, "life," via possession of the spirit and from an undervaluation of the difference between *soma* (sic) *psychikon*, "physical body," and *soma* (sic) *pneumatikon*, "spiritual body." The enthusiasts saw transformation in mystical terms as incorporation into the exalted body of Christ. Paul concurs that *zoopoioun*, "being made alive," does take place in the sphere of the Christ but maintains that it does so in the future resurrection. Accordingly, being in Christ is conceived historically. It has its beginning in baptism in Christ and is consummated in the resurrection with Christ» (F.W HORN, «Holy Spirit», 275).

[11] «Pour dire le devenir du Christ à la résurrection, Paul a recours à l'expression *zôiopoioun* qui implique le fait du *sôma pneumatikon*, mais le dépasse. Cette expression manifeste l'originalité du Christ; il n'est pas simplement, comme on pourrait le dire d'un chrétien "mort et ressuscité", devenu *sôma pneumatikon*» (J.P. LÉMONON, «Le Saint Esprit dans le corpus paulinien», in *DBS*, XI, 291).

christologically known to us. In fact, the life-giving Spirit is so fully and completely Christ's Spirit that Paul can state that the last Adam «became» that Spirit at his resurrection. We are correct in concluding from all this that the Apostle does not confuse the identities of the two divine persons; rather, in a succinct way he seeks to express the truly mysterious manner in which they collaborate together in the economy of salvation.

After studying how the life-giving Spirit was active in the life of the last Adam, let us now turn to a consideration of his work with regard to believers. Against those who claimed that they already enjoyed a fully-realized spiritual being (and in the process denied the existence and dignity of the natural body), Paul adamantly preached that the fullness of the spiritual life will be achieved only at the parousia. For the Apostle, only when God creates the spiritual body through the agency of the Holy Spirit will the Christian participate completely in eternal life. Fulfilling his role in the economy of salvation, it is the Holy Spirit who communicates divine life to the believer. Yet as amazing and extraordinary as his gifts are, the Spirit does not merely communicate life, love or salvation to those who believe. It is more accurate to say that the Spirit constitutes these gifts within us[12]. Thus as far as Christians are concerned, the life-giving Spirit both creates their spiritual body and divinizes them at the same time. It is he who deifies human beings by transforming them in an utterly perfect way into the image of the last Adam, thus bringing to perfection the Father's loving plan of salvation for all who believe in Jesus Christ.

This brief study of pneumatology has led us to understand the life-giving Spirit as God's loving power which grants eternal life to the dead by transforming their natural bodies into spiritual ones. With regard to Jesus, the last Adam, the life-giving Spirit created his spiritual body yet did not divinize him, since he was already divine by nature. With regard to Christians, the life-giving Spirit both creates their spiritual bodies and divinizes them. «and as is the one like heaven, so are those who are like heaven» (1Cor 15,48b): what Christ becomes by his divine nature, we become by his divine grace. Centuries ago in the East, Christian thinkers grasped this very significant insight into God's mysterious dealings with us and with the world. We in the twentieth

---

[12] «the biblical identification of our life in grace with the very Spirit of God, which was grasped in the early theology of divinization, can again take on its original vivid sense of divine immanence. The Spirit does not simply cause our holiness or love but *constitutes* it within us. The Spirit is God's full infinity of being in the "mode of coming to be" in the creature» (E.J. DOBBIN, «Trinity», in *NDT*).

century need to rediscover and promote this theology of divinization and make it more understandable for people today. The Second Vatican Council, placed under the aegis of the Holy Spirit by Pope John XXIII, teaches in *Lumen Gentium* and *Gaudium et Spes* how the Spirit is at work both in and beyond the Church. In this way, the Council started to redress the divisions caused by overly polemical theologies which led to the schism with the East and the Protestant Reformation in the West[13]. Many other developments in the Church since the end of the Council (e.g., the restoral of the epiclesis in the eucharistic prayer, the charismatic movement, the catechumenate seen as an entry into new life in the Spirit) give ample witness to the renewed action of the Spirit and his presence in the lives of many Christians today.

3. On Bearing the Image of Christ

In the previous two reflections we focused on some of the ramifications which derive from the eschatological character of Paul's thought. We considered how 1 Corinthians 15,44b-49 develops two important questions that are very dear to the Apostle: his anthropology (in as much as the subunit narrates the creation of the bodies of the first and last Adam) and his pneumatology (in as much as it also discloses the extraordinary effects of the agency of the life-giving Spirit on the new creation). In this essay, we shall concentrate instead on a different topic, yet one which nevertheless remains closely associated with these first two: Paul's ethics[14]. What does the Apostle have to say about the ethical life of Christians? What does he mean by the exhortation «Just as we have borne the image of the one like dust, let us also bear the image of the one like heaven» (1Cor 15,49)? Given the restricted scope of this short essay, we shall not attempt to examine Paul's specific moral

---

[13] «Reflecting in 1973 on what the Council had achieved, Pope Paul VI presciently remarked: "The Christology and particularly the ecclesiology of the Council must be succeeded by a new study of and devotion to the Holy Spirit, precisely as the indispensable complement to the teaching of the Council." Paul VI's desire has been realized, in part, by the growing number of studies devoted to the theology of the Holy Spirit, to "pneumatology"; and by the increasing awareness that authentic reform in the church must move beyond the merely institutional or intellectual to the depths of transformation which only the Spirit can reveal and empower. Significant in this regard is the issuance by Pope John Paul II, on Pentecost Sunday 1986, of an encyclical dedicated to the Holy Spirit and entitled "The Lord and Giver of Life" (*Dominum et Vivificantem*)» (R.P. IMBELLI, «Holy Spirit», in *NDT*).

[14] Cf. P. PERKINS, «Ethics (NT)», 652-665; W. SCHRAGE, «Ethics in the N.T», 281-289.

teaching, whether on virginity, marriage, divorce, homosexuality, the role of women in the Church, the relations between Christians and governing authorities, etc.[15]. Instead, our focus will be limited to a rather brief consideration of the foundations of Paul's ethics. What grounds the Apostle's moral theology and what does it say to us today?

Let us begin by returning to a rather significant observation we made in our close reading of the subunit. The exhortation in 1 Corinthians 15,49b sets this verse off from what preceded it; in this way it serves as a conclusion to the passage considered as a whole. Given this, if we examine vv. 44b-49 again, we note that it can be subdivided in still another way. The first and much longer section of the subunit, vv. 44b-49a, consists of statements written in the indicative mood, while the second and shorter part, v. 49b, is made up of the exhortation to moral behavior in the subjunctive mood. In fact this two-fold division of the passage is revelatory of Paul's conception of the two essential dimensions of the gospel of Jesus Christ[16]. As such, it is firmly rooted in the eschatological dialectic that typifies his entire way of reasoning.

Another example of moral exhortation used to conclude doctrinal instruction can be found in the very last verse of 1 Corinthians 15. In v. 58 Paul writes, «Therefore, my beloved brothers, be steadfast, immovable, always abounding in the work of the Lord, knowing that in the Lord your labor is not in vain». In light of Paul's teaching on the resurrection of the dead and the hope that awaits them, the Corinthians are now called to live out their faith in Jesus Christ in the here and now. This work will not be easy. Paul is aware that it will be laborious and difficult and it is precisely for this reason that he desires to exhort them. The moral life is never a given; it must be lived out day by day in the face of difficult trials and challenges.

Yet perhaps the most obvious example of this aspect of the Apostle's method of reasoning is demonstrated in Romans. The extensive segment in the indicative, the doctrinal section (1,16-11,36), is followed by the briefer

---

[15] See V.P. FURNISH, *The Moral Teaching of Paul*, 29-139.

[16] «Paul understands these two dimensions of the gospel in such a way that, though they are not absolutely identified, they are closely and necessarily associated. God's *claim* is regarded by the apostle as a constitutive part of God's *gift*. The Pauline concept of grace is *inclusive of* the Pauline concept of obedience. For this reason it is not quite right to say that, for Paul, the imperative is "based upon" or "proceeds out of" the indicative [...] The Pauline imperative is not just the result of the indicative but fully integrated to it» (V.P. FURNISH, *Theology and Ethics in Paul*, 224-225).

segment devoted to the demands of the Christian moral life, the hortatory section (12,1-15,13). We may conclude from this that Paul's moral teaching constitutes an integral part of his preaching of the gospel and not merely some kind of superfluous addition to his argumentation.

In addition to the structural dialectic we find in 1 Corinthians 15,44b-49, there is another dialectic that is also firmly rooted in the eschatological contrast which typifies his thought. This subunit demonstrates the very close link in Paul's theology between the human body and the Holy Spirit. People in the Greco-Roman world would have expected that the material and perishable in creation would have nothing to do with God's eternal, imperishable Spirit, that the two should remain completely separated from one another. For the Apostle, nothing could be farther from the truth. In his theology of the new creation begun in the Christ-event, Paul manages to synthesize this dialectic in a truly marvelous and extraordinary way.

In order to prove the existence of the spiritual body, the Apostle went to great lengths to fuse his theology of the body to his theology of the Spirit. Paul's anthropology and pneumatology are not merely entwined in 1 Corinthians 15,44b-49, but elsewhere in his letters as well[17]. In fact, it is accurate to claim that Paul's theology of the body leads to his moral theology. For this reason, his ethical teaching truly constitutes a body-ethics[18]. This is so because for him the body is the temple of the Holy Spirit. «Do you not know that your body is a temple of the Holy Spirit within you, which you have from God? You are not your own; you were bought with a price. So glorify God in your body» (1Cor 6,19-20). Although it is weak, perishable and dishonorable (1Cor 15,42-43), the natural body truly becomes sanctified by the indwelling of God's Spirit. Thus without the Holy Spirit, the morally upright life would simply be an impossibility for the Christian.

This connection between the gift of the Holy Spirit and the call to moral behavior was not first made by Paul, the Old Testament having already developed this correlation between God's Spirit and ethics[19]. For his part, the Apostle clearly expanded and further elaborated this insight inherited from his

---

[17] This statement applies above all to Rom 8,9-13, as the exegesis in the next part will make clear.

[18] See L.E. KECK, *Paul and His Letters*, 105-109. In spite of the fact that Keck incorrectly maintains that the σῶμα means the entire self, Keck's insight (i.e., that Paul's ethics is body-ethics) is truly a brilliant one.

[19] Cf. Ezek 36,26-27; Ps 51,12-13; Wis 1,5.

Jewish heritage in light of his faith in Christ. Earlier in the letter, he described how the Christian is liberated from a sinful past and freed for a new life in God: «But you were washed, you were sanctified, you were justified in the name of the Lord Jesus Christ and in the Spirit of our God». (1Cor 6,11). Thanks to the gift of the Spirit received in baptism, it really is possible for the Christian to live a new life free from bondage to sin.

Not only that, but in fact the Christian has been given the obligation to live a morally upright life. He is called to live out in his body the righteousness he has received in Christ. Although Paul will go on to develop the ramifications of life in the Spirit more fully in Romans 8, he had already expressed this crucial idea several years before in his letter to the Galatians. In living out his moral life, the Christian is guided by the promptings of the Holy Spirit as he follows his Lord in faith: «For through the Spirit, by faith, we wait for the hope of righteousness. For in Christ Jesus neither circumcision nor uncircumcision is of any avail, but faith working through love» (Gal 5,5-6). This unit in Galatians ends with another fine example of ethical exhortation to believers: «If we live by the Spirit, let us also walk by the Spirit» (Gal 5,25). We note again that the indicative is followed by the imperative: the love which God has shown to humanity in Christ now calls for a response on the part of believers[20]. Thanks to the Holy Spirit who dwells in them, Christians are enabled to love as God loves. Divine love elicits and empowers a loving human response; human love responds in kind, originating in and flowing from divine love. It would seem then that Paul was not the first to work out a synthesis, after all: it was God who first spanned the seemingly unbridgeable abyss between himself and humanity in the cross of Jesus Christ.

If we return again to Paul's exhortation, we note that it is phrased in the first person plural: «Let us bear». The plural form is in fact quite revelatory, since Paul is stressing the communal nature of our transformation in Christ. The first and last Adam each represent the beginning of a new race of human beings.

---

[20] «for Paul the power of the New Age is *love* — not just love in general, but *God's* love, the love through which God has created all that is, in which God wills that it be sustained and by which God acts to redeem it. For Paul the decisive *event* of God's love is Christ's death. There he finds established that powerful, redeeming love by which the world is reconciled to God and by which those who are open to receive it participate in the new creation (II Cor. 5,14-20; Rom 5,6-11). This is love, *God's* love, to which faith is a response and by which faith itself is empowered to express itself in the believer's life (Gal 5,6, assuming a double reference in the verb: faith rendered active by God's love and expressed in the believer's love)» (V.P. FURNISH, *The Moral Teaching of Paul*, 25).

While it is true that in 1 Corinthians 15,44b-49 Paul primarily conceives of the individual believer as a member of humanity, nevertheless he never loses sight of the fact that he is also a member of the Church. He had already developed this point earlier in the letter when he treated the whole question of the body of Christ in chapter twelve. «Now you are the body of Christ and individually members of it» (1Cor 12,27). It is then as members of the Church, as members of a community of faith, that we come to bear the image of Christ. Paul's particular exhortations in chapter seven to certain individuals in Corinth must be examined in light of his ecclesiology. Since we are members of the Body of Christ, we Christians do not work out our salvation as autonomous individuals but rather as solidaristic members of a faith community. As Church we come to resemble Christ in this life and as Church we will resemble him perfectly in the life to come. The transformation of our bodies both now and in the future must always be considered in light of the building up of all the other members that compose the body of Christ.

Lastly, let us consider more closely the image motif which Paul employs in 1 Corinthians 15,49. What precisely does he mean by urging the Corinthians to «bear the image of the one like heaven»? As we saw in the close reading, he entreats them and himself along with them, to conform themselves now to the likeness of the last Adam who awaits the saints in heaven. Thanks to the presence of the Spirit in their lives, it is already possible for believers to resemble Christ in a partial and imperfect way. On the last day they will come to resemble him completely when they put on their spiritual bodies at the resurrection of the dead. The moral exhortation to become Christlike in this life serves to drive us forward in hope as we await the eschatological likeness promised us in the next. But what is truly amazing about Paul's teaching here is a hint of the theme of divinization which we considered above. If Christ is the image of God[21] and if Christians come to bear the image of Christ, then glorified Christians are also the image of God. While Jesus Christ is the unique Son of God by his nature, Christians become God's sons and daughters by his grace. God is transforming us into what he is so that we may inherit the Kingdom he has prepared for us. In short, Paul is urging us to behave in a way that befits our dignity as children of God and heirs of God's glory and majesty.

In conclusion, even though the Apostle concentrates on the life to come in

---

[21] «Christ as image of God clearly describes eschatological humanity. This image, now visible completely only in Christ, will one day be given to the believer» (R. SCROGGS, *The Last Adam*, 99).

1 Corinthians 15, he never fails to remind his addressees that they are called to follow Christ in the world today. If the life-giving Spirit creates the spiritual body at the parousia, the Holy Spirit sanctifies and empowers Christians so as to help them in their day-to-day moral behavior on earth. Whether Paul calls him the life-giving Spirit or the Holy Spirit, whether he is speaking of divinization in the age to come or sanctification in the age that is passing away, it is the one unique Spirit that changes and transforms Christians. The Holy Spirit is the eschatological link that joins earth to heaven and connects the present to the future. He unites sinners to God by welcoming them into the body of Christ, the Church; he brings God to believers by dwelling in their hearts as in a temple. In bearing the image of their Lord and Savior, Christians in fact come to participate in God's great salvific deed accomplished in Christ and actualized by the Holy Spirit who dwells in them.

PART TWO

**ROMANS 8,9-13
THE INDWELLING SPIRIT
AND BELIEVERS IN CHRIST**

INTRODUCTION

In chapter eight of Romans, Paul develops his famous and beloved understanding of life in the Spirit for all those who are called to be heirs of God and fellow heirs with Christ (Rom 8,17). Thanks to his death and resurrection, Jesus Christ has rescued human beings from sin, death and the law (Rom 8,1-2). A new age has begun for humanity because God has made manifest his saving righteousness in the Christ-event. By pouring forth his love into the lives of believers through the Holy Spirit (Rom 5,5), God empowers Christians to live according to the Spirit both now and in the age to come. In fact, this fundamental point represents a significant development in Paul's notion of the consequences of righteousness: we are now justified by Christ's blood and one day we shall be saved by his life (Rom 5,9-10).

Part Two is dedicated to an exegetico-theological study of Romans 8,9-13. In the course of our inquiry, we shall see how Paul develops his understanding of the contrast between life according to the flesh and life according to the Holy Spirit. Thanks to God's loving mercy, what was once impossible has now occurred in Christ: human beings, destined to die because of sin, are now filled with the Holy Spirit, the source of eternal life for all who are justified. In the present age, the on-going struggle between death and life is played out within the human body, the temple of the Holy Spirit. Since the Spirit dwells in Christians and thereby sanctifies them through his divine presence, he is the pledge of new life today and risen life in the future. In fact the Apostle teaches that at the end of time, God will manifest his saving righteousness by raising the dead to life at the general resurrection. This definitive saving act of God will occur by the agency of his life-giving Spirit poured out in Jesus Christ.

Our way of proceeding will parallel the approach we adopted in Part One on 1 Corinthians 15. Chapter IV examines Romans 8,9-13 as a literary and semantic subunit. After studying the context and defining the limits of the passage, we shall then examine some of the subunit's more significant characteristics. Composed of six conditional sentences, this pericope employs chiasm as well as antithetical, synonymous and mixed parallelism. In this way Paul illustrates his major themes and concerns in a very forceful way. In addition to these principal stylistic features, the Apostle reiterates and rephrases his well thought-out beliefs, thus giving the passage a coherent sense of symmetry. This variation on a theme strikes the right balance between continuity and progression in his argument. In short, Paul's dense yet moving style serves to highlight the profound and mysterious theological message he wished to convey to the Roman Church.

Chapter V then proposes a close reading of Romans 8,9-13. Every significant word will be examined in order to see how it makes sense both in the subunit and in the chapter as a whole. Reference will be made to other passages in Romans, as well as to the other genuine letters of Paul, so as to present a keener sense of how the given term is used by the Apostle. This section concludes with a brief discussion of the subunit's rhetoric by highlighting the presence of different kinds of parallelism in the text.

Lastly, Chapter VI offers some final theological reflections on the subunit. It presents some considerations which serve to summarize the exegesis, all the while pointing the way to Part Three, the book's conclusion. The first reflection develops Paul's theology of sin and death. Although sin has enslaved and dominated humanity since Adam (Rom 5,12-14), its control over sinners has at last been broken by Christ. The second reflection focuses on the Apostle's profound assertion in Romans 8,10, «the Spirit is life». For Paul, the Spirit is both God's life as well as new life for humanity; he is both the pledge and guarantee that God is truly working out the definitive redemption of humanity through the Christ-event. Just as in his eschatological teaching to the Corinthians, so also here Paul's pneumatology holds profound implications for his theology of the human body and the resurrection. And finally, the third reflection considers some rather fascinating implications which arise from the Apostle's teaching on eschatology. The whole of creation has already entered into the last phase of its existence; through the agency of the Holy Spirit, one day it too will come to share in the eschatological glory of God's sons and daughters.

CHAPTER IV

Rom 8,9-13 as a
Literary and Semantic Subunit

Chapter eight forms a distinct section in Romans. It brings to a conclusion the unit begun in chapter five through its emphasis on the role of the Holy Spirit. Its tone is quite different from Rom 7,7-25, a pericope in which Paul is concerned with the role of the Jewish law (in spite of its divine origin, the law is incapable of delivering the faithful from the power of sin), as well as from Rom 9,1ff., where he returns to the complex question of Israel's salvation[1].

Paul begins chapter eight with a *subpropositio*: «There is therefore now no condemnation for those who are in Christ Jesus. For the law of the Spirit of life in Christ Jesus has set you free from the law of sin and death» (Rom 8,1-2). This statement is true for the Apostle because the Spirit of life has been given to us. Without a doubt, the most significant word of chapter eight is in fact πνεῦμα. It occurs twenty-one times in this chapter, more often than in any other in the New Testament. In comparison, πνεῦμα is found only five times in Romans 1-7 and eight times in Romans 9-16. Due to its striking frequency,

---

[1] For further information on the structure of Rom 5–8, see J.-N. ALETTI, «La présence d'un modèle rhétorique en Romains», 1-24. The *dispositio* of Greek rhetoric represents the dominant literary model in Rom 5–8. Many exegetes had already noticed that 5,1-11 corresponds to 8,31-39; in fact, these two passages begin and end this major unit of the dogmatic section of Rom Aletti presents this outline of Paul's argumentation, 22.

    5,1-11 *exordium*
    5,12-21 *narratio*
    5,20-21 *propositio*
    6,1.15; 7,7; 8,1-2 secondary *propositiones*
    6,1–8,30 *probatio*
    8,30-39 *peroratio*

an in-depth study of this pivotal term will be essential task in our close reading of the text in Chapter V.

1. **Rom 8,9-13 in its Context**

Romans 8 can be divided into six smaller subunits. In the first subunit, vv. 1-8, Paul contrasts the two ways: life according to the flesh as opposed to life according to the Spirit. In the very first verse he makes a sharp break with chapter seven by declaring, «There is therefore now no condemnation for those who are in Christ Jesus». In other words, Christians no longer live under the dispensation of condemnation since Christ has set us free. The Apostle leaves behind his description of the war that rages between the law of God and the law of sin which he had earlier developed in Romans 7,21-25. Instead, he makes broad, general statements and demonstrates how the Spirit enables moral Christian living by empowering Christians to live with their minds set on the mind of the Spirit.

In the second subunit, vv. 9-13, Paul goes one step further by giving an application of his argument. He now applies this comprehensive teaching to Christians who are alive in the Spirit. He does so by revealing that the Holy Spirit dwells within our mortal bodies and not merely within our minds. He contrasts the human body that will die because of sin to the Spirit who guarantees life because of righteousness. This subunit ends with v. 13 where Paul concludes with a personal admonition to the Romans: if you live according to the flesh you will die, but if you live according to the Spirit you will live.

In the third subunit, vv. 14-17, the Apostle provides some additional consequences of his reasoning by developing the relationship between the Spirit and the children of God. He asserts that Christians are able to call God Father thanks to the Spirit who dwells in them. In addition to being God's children, Christians are also heirs of God and fellow heirs with Christ.

In the fourth subunit, vv. 18-25, Paul focuses on the eschatological glory that is to be revealed in all creation. He contrasts the future liberty of the children of God to their present reality as hopeful individuals who already enjoy the first fruits of the Spirit.

In the fifth subunit, vv. 26-30, the Apostle explains how the Spirit helps Christians in their weakness and intercedes for them before God. All God's children are predestined to share in the image of his Son and in so doing, share in his eschatological glory.

Finally, in the sixth subunit, vv. 31-38, Paul praises God for the love which has been revealed to us in Christ Jesus our Lord. In these final verses there is no mention of the Spirit; since this subunit is primarily theological and christological in purpose, it serves as a fitting conclusion to the argument which Paul began in chapter five.

In addition, if we use the terms of rhetorical criticism to guide us, there is in fact another way of dividing Romans eight. According to this delineation, there are three general divisions. The first part, vv. 1-17, is introduced by the *subpropositio* from v. 1, «There is therefore now no condemnation for those who are in Christ Jesus»[2]. The second part, vv. 18-30, begins with the *subpropositio* from v. 18, «I consider that the sufferings of this present time are not worth comparing with the glory that is to be revealed to us». The third and last subunit, vv. 31-39, represent the *peroratio* of Romans 5–8, as we noted above.

2. Rom 8,9-13 as a Distinct Subunit

Romans 8,9-13 represents a very important subunit in the chapter. In this brief passage Paul condenses into a few short lines his teaching on Christ's resurrection, our own eschatological resurrection and the Spirit's role in these events. Before turning to a close reading of these five verses, we must first consider some preliminary comments on the subunit as a whole[3].

---

[2] «The style of 8:1-17 is intriguing. Paul writes in an objective *proclaiming* style. Christians must know and had better realize that Jesus' death and resurrection have brought them life (see the past tenses in vv. 2,3,11 and 15), that they no longer are "according to the flesh" or "in the flesh" (see vv. 5,8 and 9) and the Spirit, or Christ, dwells in them (see vv. 9,10,11 and 15). All this is given them by way of information. However the style is also *exhortative*. Christians can no longer "live according to the flesh" (very clearly in vv. 12-13). One could therefore call the real change effected by the Christ event — of which the presence of the Spirit is the result — only a somewhat provisional or still incomplete victory. There remains the possibility that Christians do not live according to their new status. Apparently, in a first function, the description of "the life according to the flesh" calls attention to the manner in which Christians have lived in an unregenerate state. One must be duly informed. Nonetheless this description is intended, above all, to avert the danger that still threatens every Christian. The message that we are in Christ and have the Spirit is the basis for exhortation and is, in a certain sense, itself already admonition and warning» (J. LAMBRECHT, *The Wretched "I" and its Liberation*, 97).

[3] Most commentators (cf. Achtemeier, Barrett, Barth, Best, Black, Cranfield, Dunn, Heil, Käsemann, Michel and Morris) divide the passage differently since they consider v. 12

2.1 *Six Conditional Sentences*

The first important characteristic to note is that this passage is composed of six conditional sentences. The particle εἴπερ begins the protasis of the first condition in v. 9, while the more usual particle εἰ begins the five conditions that follow in vv. 9, 10, 11 and 13[4]. The occurrence of six conditions in such quick succession is yet further evidence that these verses should be treated as a distinct subunit in chapter eight. The content as well as the grammatical construction of these sentences prove that they indeed belong together[5].

---

as the start of a new subunit. One reason is because v. 12ff. is clearly hortatory in nature and differs from the doctrinal teaching of vv. 9-11. Another reason why some divide the passage there is that Paul sometimes uses the word ἀδελφοί (which appears in v. 12) to mark the beginning of a new subsection. cf. Rom 7,1.4; 9,3; 10,1; 11,25; 12,1. But «brothers» occurs eighteen times in the letter. Is this sufficient reason to insist that v. 12 must start a new subunit? Also, that v. 12 is in fact hortatory is undeniable, but does this necessarily mean that it must begin a new passage?

In order to decide whether vv.12-13 concludes what comes before or begins what follows, it is more important to study the expression Ἄρα οὖν, the first two words of the verse. In addition to v. 12, Ἄρα οὖν occurs 7 times in Romans (5,18; 7,3; 7,25; 9,16.18; and 14,12.19); it may be translated as «so», «so then», or «accordingly». In all seven cases, it is used to conclude an argument, to sum up what has just been said. It is never used to begin a new point or introduce a new subunit. The occurrence in 7,25, the last one before 8,12, offers a good example of how Paul employs it: here he is obviously ending his argument in ch. seven. Thus in light of the presence of the expression Ἄρα οὖν we conclude that vv. 12-13 completes what comes before and so should be considered together with vv. 9-11. Although this is certainly the minority position, nevertheless it is found in the literature. «This verse [v. 13] and v. 12 conclude the preceding discussion and form a transition to the next section» (J.A. FITZMYER, «The Letter to the Romans», 853).

In short, Rom 8,12-13 acts as a hortatory conclusion which ends the doctrinal presentation of Rom 8,9-11 and points the way to Paul's next point: the relationship between the Spirit and God's children.

[4] For more general information on the particle εἰ in conditional sentences, cf. ZERWICK § 299-334; BDR § 371-76; HS § 280-85. For the particle itself, see G. LÜDEMANN, «εἰ», in *EWNT*. Of its 507 occurrences in the NT, Paul uses the word 181 times, far more often than any other author.

[5] It should be noted that the third subunit, vv. 14-17, also ends with conditional sentences, just as the second subunit does. V. 17 is composed of two first class conditions: «and if children, then heirs. Heirs of God and fellow heirs with Christ, if in fact (εἴπερ) we suffer with him in order that we may also be glorified with him». Hence the uncommon word εἴπερ, first used in v. 9 to begin the series of conditionals of one subunit, now brings the following subunit to a close in v. 17. In addition, v. 9 and v. 17 are also linked thanks to the occurrence of Χριστοῦ which can be found in both.

The precise meaning of a first class conditional sentence has been vigorously debated by grammarians for more than a century. Its syntactic form can be described as «εἰ + indicative, indicative», or in shorthand, «εἰ p,q» where «p» stands for the protasis and «q» for the apodosis[6]. This kind of conditional sentence appears approximately three hundred times in the New Testament, occurring quite often in the Pauline corpus. It is commonly called the «Simple Condition»[7]; it indicates a logical connection between protasis and apodosis without any reference to the reality, truth, or actuality of the statement itself[8]. Many exegetes assume that this construction implies truth and as a result they incorrectly translate εἰ as «since». Such an approach is simply wrong[9].

An attentive reading of the text reveals the Paul inverted the first conditional sentence of the subunit. But why? He most probably did so on account of the preceding verse. In v. 8 the Apostle mentions those who are in the flesh and he begins v. 9 with a clause that parallels it: «You are not in the flesh». By beginning the sentence in this way, Paul connects this subunit to what has come before. The net result is that the apodosis is emphasized; in so doing Paul stresses his main point of the whole subunit, namely, «You are in the Spirit».

But why use conditional sentences at all? In Romans 8,9 Paul states «You are not in the flesh, but in the Spirit, if indeed God Spirit dwells in you. If anyone does not have Christ's Spirit, this one does not belong to him». Here Paul is not saying by his use of the first class condition that they belonged to, or did not belong to, Christ[10]. We know from the context that they do in fact

---

[6] See L.W. LEDGERWOOD, «What Does the Greek First Class Conditional Imply?», 101.

[7] Cf. ZERWICK § 303-305; BDR § 372; HS § 281.

[8] For the meaning of first class conditional sentences in the NT, see J.L. BOYER, «First Class Conditions», 75-114.

[9] «Bible students should not be taught that εἰ p,q means "since p,q." Exegetes should be honest in their hermeneutics and should refrain from stating or implying in an exegesis of a passage that the Greek conditional εἰ p,q itself implies that p is true. Nor should an exegete state that εἰ p,q does not imply doubt like English "if p,q" can and that it would be better translated with "since p,q." In those cases where one wishes to make a point that the proposition p is not being called into question, it should be demonstrated that the context implies that the proposition p is true or that the participants in the communication knew that p was true in fact» (L.W. LEDGERWOOD, «What Does the Greek First Class Conditional Imply?», 118).

[10] See L.W. LEDGERWOOD, «What Does the Greek First Class Conditional Imply?», 78.

belong to him and that they do indeed have the Spirit, since Paul has said as much in the beginning of the chapter: «There is therefore now no condemnation for those who are in Christ Jesus» (Rom 8,1) and «in order that the righteous requirement of the law might be fulfilled in us who do not walk according to the flesh but according to the Spirit» (Rom 8,4). The Apostle uses the first class condition in v. 9 to insist on the logical connection between the protasis and apodosis. If the first is true, then it is reasonable to accept that the second is also true[11]. In short, Paul states that an individual's belonging to Christ depends upon his possession of the Holy Spirit. The same reasoning follows for vv. 10-13. If we accept the protasis as true, then it is also reasonable to accept the apodosis as also being true. The two clauses in each of these six conditional sentences fit together, and their combined effect underscores and encourages the reader's role in the argumentation. It is as if Paul were inviting his addressees to reflect on every if-clause, decide upon its truthfulness and then assent to its corresponding conclusion. Thus in this way readers today are invited to follow the Apostle's method of reasoning, yet all the while they remain free to accept or reject each successive clause along the way. Their freedom is engaged in the very act of following Paul's grammatical construction; this underscores their freedom to believe the content of these verses as well.

The Apostle is in fact reasoning in such a way as to convince his addressees in Rome of the profound truth and theological accuracy of his insights into the gospel of Jesus Christ. His position could be paraphrased in the following way. You accept as true that God raised Jesus' mortal body from the dead. And you are right, because God truly did. Now, also accept as true that one day he will also raise your mortal bodies from the dead and that you will live with him forever. Such is the force of the first class conditional sentences in this passage.

---

[11] «In summary, what does a first class conditional sentence in NT Greek mean? It means precisely the same as the simple condition in English, "If this...then that..." It implies absolutely nothing as to the "relation to reality." It is saying that the result (the apodosis) is as sure as the condition (the protasis). It is as forceful device of language which leaves the judgment and convictions of the hearer with regard to the truthfulness of the supposition to prove or disprove and to enforce the truth of the conclusion. These statements can be made of every one of the 300 NT examples and are equally true of every one of them. It is the verdict of a usage study of this grammatical construction» (J.L. BOYER, «First Class Conditions», 82).

2.2 *Variation on a Theme*

A close examination of the subunit's structure reveals another significant feature. Paul repeats the clause «the Spirit [...] dwells in you» three times: 1) «if the Spirit of God dwells in you» (Rom 8,9); 2) «If the Spirit of the one who raised Jesus from the dead dwells in you» (Rom 8,11); 3) «through his Spirit who dwells in you» (Rom 8,11). The repetition of this theme underscores the purpose of this subunit in Romans 8. Paul is intent on teaching that the Holy Spirit dwells in believers, in fact, that the very presence of this indwelling Spirit is what distinguishes them as Christians. In other words, to be a Christian means to have the Spirit of Christ. The Spirit's presence profoundly influences the lives of Christians both in this life (since the believer lives his Christian life as one led by the Spirit, v. 14) as well as in the life to come (since the Spirit as the agent of the resurrection is also necessary for salvation, v. 11). In short, what is essential for the Apostle is eternal life with God, not death and absence from him.

Paul in fact describes the Spirit in various ways throughout the subunit. The word appears without any modifiers three times: «in the Spirit» (v. 9); «the Spirit» (v. 10); and «by the Spirit» (v. 13). These occurrences mark the beginning, middle and end of the subunit. Paul also understands the Spirit in relation to God: «the Spirit of God» (v. 9); and «the Spirit of the one who raised Jesus from the dead» (v. 11). There are also two occurrences where the Spirit is portrayed in relation to Christ: «the Spirit of Christ» (v. 9); and «through his Spirit» (v. 11). It should be noted from the outset that no where in the passage does Paul use the term «Holy Spirit». This term appears six times in Romans (5,5; 9,1; 14,17; 15,13.16.19) but never once in chapter eight. Nevertheless, in the exegesis that follows we shall prove that all occurrences of «the Spirit» in Romans 8,9-13 do in fact refer to the Holy Spirit.

Although Paul goes to great lengths to characterize the mysterious relationships between the Spirit and the Father, the Spirit and the Son, as well as the Father and the Son, never does the Apostle confuse them. Each divine person is distinct and different yet related to the other two in a profoundly mysterious way. In the course of the exegesis, it will become very clear that for Paul these individuals are in fact divine. Although the Apostle does not refer to the members of the Trinity as «Persons», nonetheless we can already glimpse in his letters the origins of this crucial Church dogma. For now it is enough to note that Paul describes trinitarian relations in terms connected to human salvation; in other words, his primary concern lies with the economic

Trinity. He focuses on how the three divine persons relate to human beings on earth and bring to completion their extraordinary plan of salvation «through his Spirit who dwells in you» (Rom 8,11).

2.3 *Paul's Argumentation within the Subunit*

The Apostle's argument within the unit flows logically from verse to verse. After having contrasted in a general way the two opposing ways of life in Romans 8,2-8, Paul now applies his understanding in a personal way to his addressees. «You are not in the flesh, but in the Spirit, if indeed God's Spirit dwells in you. If anyone does not have Christ's Spirit this one does not belong to him» (Rom 8,9). With this verse the Apostle reintroduces pronouns into his argument. He personalizes his reasoning by using ὑμεῖς, a personal pronoun placed at the start of the verse for the sake of emphasis. Moreover, Paul insists that «God's Spirit» dwells ἐν ὑμῖν, yet again underlining the divine presence in his listeners.

The reference to Christ and the prepositional phrase ἐν ὑμῖν are repeated in v. 10, thus connecting it to what has come before. The verse itself can be divided into three parts. 1. εἰ δὲ Χριστὸς ἐν ὑμῖν, 2. τὸ μὲν σῶμα νεκρὸν διὰ ἁμαρτίαν and 3. τὸ δὲ πνεῦμα ζωὴ διὰ δικαιοσύνην. In the first part, Paul is personally addressing the Romans, but then abandons his use of personal pronouns in parts two and three. He now presents five nouns with or without the definite article (τὸ σῶμα, ἁμαρτίαν, τὸ πνεῦμα, ζωὴ and δικαιοσύνην) and one adjective (νεκρόν) in order to make a broad statement. Thus the second and third part of this verse should be understood as a general Pauline conviction. The essential point here is that Paul is contrasting two parallel clauses, the first introduced by μέν and the second by δέ. With this example of parataxis, the Apostle emphasizes the opposition between the three elements of the first clause to the three in the second: σῶμα and πνεῦμα, νεκρόν and ζωή and ἁμαρτίαν and δικαιοσύνην. It is essential to recognize this contrast in Paul's argument if we are to grasp the meaning of the verse correctly.

In Romans 8,11 Paul then goes on to apply this general statement: «If the Spirit of the one who raised Jesus from the dead dwells in you, the one who raised Christ Jesus from the dead will give life to your mortal bodies also through his Spirit who dwells in you». The Apostle arrives at a conclusion with reference to his listeners in Rome. The prepositional phrase with the personal pronoun returns again and is repeated twice: ἐν ὑμῖν serves as a conclusion to both clauses. Paul has now applied his general teaching to the situation at hand, making his conclusion specific and personal for the Romans. If the Spirit dwells in them, then God will give them life as he did to Jesus.

In v. 12 Paul formulates a negative conclusion from the information he presented in his argumentation in vv. 1-8 and in his application in vv. 9-11. He starts the verse with the words «So then», and in this way begins an exhortation to the Romans, his brothers in Christ. It is interesting to note that he uses the personal pronoun «we», thereby including himself in his own entreaty. The verse is a bit awkward since it seems unfinished. Paul explains that we are not debtors to the flesh, to live according to the flesh and then leaves his thought incomplete. He leaves the reader free to draw his own positive conclusion by supplying a phrase like «but to the Spirit to live according to the Spirit». Given the flow of his argumentation, such a deduction is clearly implied by Paul.

Romans 8,12 in fact represents the hinge of the passage. Up until this point in the subunit, Paul has been carefully presenting his teaching on the Spirit and the resurrection. In fact, vv. 9-11 make up the first half of the subunit. These verses, in addition to the opening verses of the chapter, constitute Paul's teaching. But in v. 12-13 we have something new. These two final verses propose the exhortation which often follows Paul's teaching[12]. We are in debt to God and as a result we are no longer free to live our lives according to the flesh. Christians now have a duty to live according to the Spirit.

In v. 13, the final verse of the subunit, the Apostle juxtaposes two conditional sentences. He does this in order to emphasize the two major possibilities for every human being: death or life. Both these terms have eschatological significance for Paul, and the allusion to Deuteronomy 11,26ff would not have escaped the first Christians of Rome. The subunit closes on a very uplifting note. If you choose to live in the Spirit, then you will live with God forever.

---

[12] In ch. III we already considered this technique of Paul's in our theological refections on 1Cor 15, «On Bearing the Image of Christ». Here we note its presence in Romans. See especially Rom 6,1-14, which is constructed in a way that is very similar to Rom 8,9-13. The first part, Rom 6,1-11, consists of teaching on baptism and Christ's victory over sin and death. The second part, vv. 12-14, offers pure exhortation. By observing this transition from argument to exhortation in Paul's rhetoric, we gain a crucial insight into the Apostle's method of reasoning. First the Apostle teaches Christian doctrine and then he urges believers to live in a manner consistent with their calling. Thus for Paul it is never sufficient merely to know what is right: a Christian has to live the moral life through his righteous ethical action.

CHAPTER V

A Close Reading of Rom 8,9-13

1. **Rom 8,9**

After having studied the text in its context and after having seen an overview of Paul's argumentation in the subunit, we are now ready to begin the close reading. As in Part One on 1 Corinthians, the exegesis will proceed verse by verse. Here is the text of v. 9.

> ὑμεῖς δὲ οὐκ ἐστὲ ἐν σαρκὶ ἀλλὰ ἐν πνεύματι, εἴπερ πνεῦμα θεοῦ οἰκεῖ ἐν ὑμῖν. εἰ δέ τις πνεῦμα Χριστοῦ οὐκ ἔχει, οὗτος οὐκ ἔστιν αὐτοῦ.
> «You are not in the flesh but in the Spirit, if indeed God's Spirit dwells in you. If anyone does not have Christ's Spirit, this one does not belong to him».

– ὑμεῖς. The verse begins with the personal pronoun «you», second person plural; it occurs seven times in Romans[1]. After having made some general statements in Romans 8,1-8 which refer to those who live according to the Spirit and to those who live according to the flesh, Paul now personalizes his argument in v. 9. He communicates to the Romans directly, in light of their distinct situation, applying to them in a particular way what he has just said about humanity in a general way.

The is the first time in chapter eight that Paul has used the pronoun ὑμεῖς. In verse two he used the second person singular form, σε, as a way of addressing each individual personally[2]. In that verse, Paul was focusing on the

---

[1] Cf. Rom 1,6; 6,11; 7,4; 8,9; 9,26; 11,30; 16,17.

[2] The choice of this pronoun presents a textual problem. The ancient witnesses offer four different readings: με, ἡμᾶς, σε and no object pronoun at all. The first reading, με, could be due to an assimilation to the first person singular pronoun that was used above in

individual as a representative of the group, in this case the Roman Church. He did this to emphasize his point, a technique he uses elsewhere in the letter[3]. In v. 9, however, Paul uses the second person plural form in order to accentuate his particular teaching to the Romans. In v. 13, the end of the subunit, Paul will employ four verbs in the second person plural (ζῆτε, μέλλετε, θανατοῦτε and ζήσεσθε). There the subject pronoun is unexpressed, which of course typifies normal Greek syntax. Nevertheless, the use of ὑμεῖς (whether expressed or unexpressed) in the first and last verses of the subunit serves as an inclusion to the passage, thus rendering its tone more personal and intimate for Paul's addressees.

– δὲ οὐκ ἐστέ. «You are not». The verb εἰμί is conjugated in the present indicative to agree with the subject pronoun ὑμεῖς. Paul is here making a statement of fact about the Roman Christians. Note that it is a double statement which begins by asserting what they are not and ends by affirming what they are. The Apostle first expresses himself negatively and then positively in order to emphasize the actual condition of his addressees[4].

– ἐν σαρκί. The phrase is translated as «in the flesh». The expression had just been used in Romans 8,8; thus it serves as a connection to what has come before in the argument. It sums up what Paul has already stated and refers the reader back to vv. 5-8. In order to understand this expression, we first have to

---

The ancient witnesses that support this are A C D K and P. The second reading, ἡμᾶς, could be an assimilation to the first person plural pronoun used in 8,4. The textual witnesses includes Ψ, showing that there is very poor attestation for this reading. As for no object at all, only Origen among the Church Fathers knew this reading. Hence we are left with σε, which indeed has the best witnesses: ℵ B G 1739 it syr Tertullian Ambrosiaster Ephraem Chrysostom Pelagius Augustine. This is the reading accepted by ALAND, yet given a D rating, i.e. a very high degree of doubt.

[3] Cf. Rom 2,1.3-5.17-27; 9,19-20; 10,9; 11,17-24; 13,3-4; 14,4.10.15.20-22.

[4] «In disjunctive propositions, it is a Semitic peculiarity to express one member negatively so as to lay more stress on the other, saying "not A but B" where the sense is "not so much A as B" or "B rather than A". A well-known example is Hos 6,6, where the author himself indicates the sense of the idiom by the parallel second member: "I desire mercy and *not* sacrifice; and the knowledge of God *more than* holocausts". In the NT cf. 1Cor 1,17 οὐ γὰρ ἀπέστειλέν με Χριστὸς βαπτίζειν ἀλλὰ εὐαγγελίζεσθαι, Mt 10,20 οὐ γὰρ ὑμεῖς ἐστε οἱ λαλοῦντες ἀλλὰ τὸ πνεῦμα; Jo 12,44 Ὁ πιστεύων εἰς ἐμὲ οὐ πιστεύει εἰς ἐμὲ ἀλλὰ εἰς τὸν πέμψαντά με, cf. also Mk 9,37; Lk 10,20; Jo 7,16. This idiom reflects the same mentality as that which uses "hate" to say "love less" (cf. Lk 14,26 with Mt 10, 37)» (ZERWICK § 445.d).

identify the various meanings of the word σάρξ and then deal with its use in this prepositional phrase.

The noun σάρξ means «flesh»; it appears thirteen times in Romans 8,1-13 and twenty-six times in the letter as a whole. Appearing in antithetical parallelism to πνεῦμα, the word's frequency in chapter eight shows us that it represents a key term in Paul's argument on life in the Spirit. σάρξ primarily refers to a power which enslaves humanity by holding it in bondage to sin and death, thus alienating it from God. In Romans the word has two principal meanings[5].

First of all, Paul employs the word σάρξ in order to describe the relationship between human beings of the same extended family or bloodline. In Romans 1,3 the Apostle first uses the word in this way in the phrase κατὰ σάρκα when he describes God's Son as one «descended from David according to the flesh». In other words, Jesus is of the lineage of David and so both individuals belong to the same family. He uses σάρξ in the same way in Romans 4,1 when he describes the relationship between Jews and «Abraham, our forefather according to the flesh». Jews are related to one another κατὰ σάρκα since they have the same ancestor. The word also has the same meaning in Romans 9,3 where Paul speaks of τῶν ἀδελφῶν μου τῶν συγγεμῶν μου κατὰ σάρκα, «my brethren, my kinsmen by race», as well as in Romans 9,5.8. Later, in Romans 11,14, Paul again refers to his fellow Jews as μοῦ τὴν σάρκα, «my fellow countrymen». In these verses (as well as in Philippians 3,3-4 which also refers to the people of Israel), σάρξ denotes kinship, the physical relationship that joins the members of a klan or nation together as a group. Moreover, the term can also convey kinship with all human beings and not merely a particular people. An example of this is found in Romans 8,3, where the second use of σάρξ in the verse has this meaning. When Paul says «God [...] sending his own Son in the likeness of sinful flesh and for sin» he is referring to Christ's corporeal solidarity with humanity. In addition, this idea of physical relationship is also found in the use of the word in 1 Corinthians 15,39 where the Apostle teaches that there are different kinds of flesh, «one kind for human beings, another for animals, another for birds and another for fish». σάρξ,

---

[5] Cf. E. SCHWEIZER, «σάρξ», in *ThWNT*; A. SAND, «σάρξ», in *EWNT*. «d. menschliche Natur, d. irdische Herkunft» (BAUER, «σάρξ», 4,); «*Nach paul. Vorstellung* bes. ist *d. Fleisch das willenlose Werkzeug der Sünde* u. dieser so unterworfen, daß sich, wo Fleisch ist, auch alle Erscheinungsformen der Sünde finden müssen und in der Sarx nichts Gutes wohnen kann» (BAUER, «σάρξ», 7).

therefore, is the term used when Paul joins together many human beings or animals of the same species and considers them as a group.

For the most part, however, σάρξ has a far more negative connotation in the Pauline letters. The Apostle understands the flesh as that power belonging to this world which holds humanity in bondage to sin and death. It enslaves human beings by drawing them away from God, thereby seducing them to walk in ways contrary to God's will.

This pejorative use of σάρξ is found throughout Romans 8. Paul uses the expression ἐν ὁμοιώματι σαρκὸς ἁμαρτίας, «in the likeness of sinful flesh», to underscore his teaching that Christ has indeed taken on our human nature. The word appears in connection with sin and the law in v. 3, in antithesis to πνεῦμα in vv. 4-6, as well as in antithesis to God in vv. 7-8. This contrast between flesh and Spirit continues into the present subunit and finds expression in v. 9 and vv. 12-13. Galatians 5,17 spells out this antithesis most succinctly: «For the desires of the flesh are against the Spirit and the desires of the Spirit are against the flesh; for these are opposed to each other». In short, the σάρξ is that power of this world which is opposed to God. The enemy of human nature, its desires are inherently hostile to «the Lord Jesus Christ» (Rom 13,14).

After having defined the word, we must now deal with its use in the phrase ἐν σαρκί. «In the flesh» appears four times in Romans, in 7,5; 8,3. 8. 9. This is an example of the sociative use of the preposition ἐν[6]. The expression «to be in the flesh» means to be in the sphere of the flesh, to be allied or associated with it. The phrase is basically synonymous with κατὰ σάρκα, «according to the flesh», as found in Romans 8,4.5. 12 and 13. «To be in the flesh» means to live according to that power which is hostile to God, to set one's mind against God's law, to follow one's sinful passions as a fallen human being. It is interesting to note that the word σάρξ no longer appears in chapter eight after v. 13; its numerous occurrences in the first half of the chapter, however, serve to act as a foil to Paul's primary concern: a presentation of his vision of new life in the Spirit.

–ἀλλά. This is an adversative particle which in most cases means «but», or when following a negation, «rather», «on the contrary». The second case applies in v. 9. Used primarily by Paul and John in the New Testament, ἀλλά occurs sixty-nine times in Romans. This is the only occurrence of the word in this

---

[6] See ZERWICK § 116-117.

subunit, although it appears eight times in Romans 8. Its presence in v. 4 and v. 9 testifies to the flesh/Spirit antithesis that constitutes the backbone to Paul's argument. It is used to contrast what has already been said in a negative way («You are not in the flesh...») to what will now be said in a positive one («...but you are in the Spirit»). Thus ἀλλά emphasizes the difference between two contrasting positions[7].

– ἐν πνεύματι. In Part One of this book, we already considered the crucial role the Spirit plays in the formation of the spiritual body as presented by the Apostle in 1 Corinthians 15. As then, so now, we must begin with a discussion of the noun's two principal meanings. Where in Romans does πνεῦμα designate the human spirit and where does it designate the Holy Spirit? Lastly, after gaining more insights into the word's significance for Paul, we shall also consider the meaning of the prepositional phrase ἐν πνεύματι.

πνεῦμα appears thirty-four times in Romans. By far the largest concentration of the word appears in chapter eight, where, as we noted already, it occurs twenty-one times. πνεῦμα is clearly a critical term in this subsection. The first task confronting the exegete is to determine whether it refers to the human spirit (e.g., Paul's own spirit, as in Rom 1,9) or to the Holy Spirit (as in Rom 5,5; 9,1; 14,17; 15,13.16.19). How then are we to understand πνεῦμα in Romans 8,9-13? Should it be written as «spirit» or «Spirit»?

Of the twenty-one listings in Romans 8, only one clearly refers to the human spirit. In v. 16 we read, «it is the Spirit himself bearing witness with our spirit that we are children of God». This reference to τῷ πνεύματι ἡμῶν, «our spirit», is most enlightening. It highlights the distinction in Paul's mind between God and the human being and yet it also conveys the fact that they cooperate with one another in a mysterious way. This anthropological use of πνεῦμα can also be found in 1 Corinthians 7,34 and 2 Corinthians 7,1, where Paul speaks of «the body and spirit» as the two constitutive elements which make up a human being. 2 Corinthians 2,13, Galatians 6,18 and Philippians 1,27; 4,23 offer other occurrences of πνεῦμα which denote the human spirit.

In the majority of the other occurrences of the word in Romans 8, however, πνεῦμα refers to a force or being extrinsic to human beings. This πνεῦμα given by God clearly refers to the Holy Spirit. In a few instances such as v. 10 and v. 15, exegetes are divided in their judgment over the designation of this

---

[7] Cf. BDR § 448,1; HS § 252,1; W. RADL, «ἀλλά», in *EWNT*.

word[8]. But as we shall see below, even in these disputed passages πνεῦμα is best understood as «Holy Spirit».

For Paul, the Spirit is above all «the Spirit of holiness» present at Jesus' resurrection (Rom 1,3) and at ours (Rom 8,11). He is the divine power (Rom 15,13.19) that sanctifies human beings and transforms creation (Rom 8,23). Having liberated humanity from «the law of sin and death» (Rom 8,2), he now achieves, secures and guarantees the freedom «of the children of God» (Rom 8,16). He is the «Spirit of Sonship» (Rom 8,15) who allows Christians to call God «Abba! Father!» Mediating «with sighs too deep for words» (Rom 8,26) in order to help Christians in their prayer, «the Spirit intercedes for the saints according to the will of God» (Rom 8,27). By his dwelling in us (Rom 8,9.11), the Spirit provides an endless source of «life and peace» (Rom 8,6) to those who walk in his ways (Rom 8,4). Thanks to the righteousness gained for us by Jesus Christ, «God's love has been poured into our hearts through the Holy Spirit which has been given to us» (Rom 5,5). Paul calls him alternately «the Holy Spirit» (Rom 5,5; 9,1; 14,17; 15,13.16.19), the «Spirit of God» (Rom 8,9. 14) and the «Spirit of Christ» (Rom 8,9), yet all these epithets refer to the one and the same Spirit who «bears witness with our spirit that we are children of God» (Rom 8,16). Paul presents the Father, Son and Spirit as distinct, divine individuals who work in concert for the salvation of humanity (Rom 5,1-5; 8,14-17)[9]. When Paul asks the Roman Christians to pray for him, he invokes all three in his request.

I appeal to you, brothers, by our Lord Jesus Christ and by the love of the Spirit, to strive together with me in your prayers to God on my behalf, that I may be

---

[8] In v. 15 Paul states, «For you did not receive the Spirit of slavery to fall back into fear, but you have received the Spirit of sonship [...]». Both occurrences of πνεῦμα link this verse to the opening verse of the subunit which speaks of «the Spirit of God». These are clear references to the Holy Spirit. In the first clause Paul affirms that the Holy Spirit is most definitely not the «Spirit of slavery». It is a negative statement which defines the nature of the Holy Spirit: he does not enslave. In the second clause Paul continues his teaching with a positive statement on his divine nature. The «Spirit of sonship» makes us sons who are able to cry, «Abba! Father!». In short, Paul is clearly defining the same reality through the use of contrasting clauses. In this case, that individual is the third person of the Blessed Trinity.

[9] We noted above that although the word «person» is never used by Paul to describe the Father, Son, or Spirit (the term was adopted only much later in the articulation of the dogma on the three distinct persons of the Trinity), nevertheless Paul's teaching here clearly serves as the basis for subsequent Church doctrine on the question.

delivered from the unbelievers in Judea and that my service for Jerusalem may
be acceptable to the saints, so that by God's will I may come to you with joy and
be refreshed in your company. The God of peace be with you all. Amen. (Rom
15,30-33)

In short, as the eschatological power poured out by the risen Christ, the Spirit
represents God's agent for the glorification of believers and the recreation of
the whole world.

We must now devote some attention to the phrase ἐν πνεύματι. As with
the expression «in the flesh», this is another example of the sociative use of the
preposition ἐν[10]. «To be in the Spirit» means to be in the sphere of the Spirit[11].
Here Paul reminds his addressees that they are in fact intimately connected
with the Holy Spirit who was poured into their hearts (Rom 5,5). They are
closely associated with him since they «set their minds on the things of the
Spirit» (Rom 8,6) and «walk according to the Spirit» (Rom 8,4). In short, this
phrase expresses the deep and profound communion which exists between the
believer and God's Spirit.

– εἴπερ. The protasis of this first class condition begins with the word εἴπερ,
a conjunction which means «if in fact» or «if indeed». Elsewhere in the New
Testament, εἴπερ is also found in Romans 3,30; 8,17; 1 Corinthians 8,5; 15,15
and 2 Thessalonians 1,6. This particle serves to highlight the basis for the
conclusion of the conditional sentence[12].

---

[10] «In Biblical usage the value of ἐν seems to be very ill defined and often to be very far
indeed from the local sense [...] The question has a certain importance when one wishes to
understand what Paul means by saying sometimes that we are in Christ, or in the Spirit and
at others that Christ, or the Spirit, is in us. Indeed the distinction in Paul's mind between
the two notions seems to be so small, not to say non-existent, that he explains and as it
were defines the one by the other: Rom 8,9, "you are not in the flesh but in the Spirit, if the
Spirit of God dwells in you." So he is "in the Spirit," in whom the Spirit is, or as the
Apostle goes on to say, who "has the Spirit": "but if anyone have not the Spirit of Christ,
the same is not of Him" [...] Thus ἐν (not without Semitic influence) is practically reduced
to the expression of a general notion of association or accompaniment, which would be
rendered in English by "with" [...]» (ZERWICK § 116-117).

[11] See BAUER, «ἐν», I, 5d.

[12] Cf. H. BALZ, «εἴπερ» in EWNT; BDR § 454,2; HS § 252,19 and 280b.

– πνεῦμα θεοῦ. The phrase «Spirit of God» is found three times in the letter, appearing in Romans 8,9.14 and 15,19[13]. θεοῦ presents us with an example of the subjective genitive. Since this grammatical form is used to convey possession, Paul is indeed speaking about the Spirit that belongs to God[14]. For Paul, the Holy Spirit is in fact God's Spirit; namely, the Apostle conceives of the Spirit first of all in theological terms. By doing so he underscores the continuity between his teaching and the Old Testament's understanding of the God of Israel[15]. Paul affirms Jewish monotheism by insisting that the Spirit who dwells in the minds and hearts of Christians is in fact the same Spirit who has his origin in the one «living and true God» (1Th 1,9).

From the beginning to the end of Romans, God and the things of God emerge as a dominant Pauline concern[16]. A study of this fundamental term will disclose some key insights into Paul's gospel. The word θεός occurs one hundred and fifty three times in Romans, eighteen times in chapter eight, but only once in the subunit 8,9-13[17]. God is «the God and Father of our Lord

---

[13] In the latter verse the textual evidence is questionable. Should we read «Spirit of God», «Spirit», «Holy Spirit», or «Holy Spirit of God»? Although there is some confusion over the correct text, the earliest witness (Papyrus 46 from the second and third centuries) reads πνεῦμα θεοῦ. That is why Metzger and his committee prefer this reading. For further information, see the discussion in METZGER, 537. More examples of πνεῦμα θεοῦ in the authentic letters of Paul may be found in 1Cor 2,11.12.14; 3,16; 6,11; 7,40; 12,3; 2Cor 3,3; Phil 3,3; and 1Th 4,8. In the deutero-Pauline literature, see Eph 4,30.

[14] Cf. ZERWICK § 36-39; BDR § 163; HS § 160.

[15] The phrase πνεῦμα θεοῦ occurs nine times in the LXX: cf. Gen 1,2; 48,38; Num 23,7 (N.B. the phrase is not found in the Hebrew); 24,2; 1Sam 10,10; 19,9.20.23; and 2Chr 24,20. In Gen 1,2 it refers to the Spirit of God at work in creation. In all the other occurrences, however, πνεῦμα θεοῦ is used to describe how God's Spirit is found in, or comes upon, a human being. For example, in Num 24,2 we read how the Spirit of God was in Balaam: «[...] καὶ ἐγένετο πνεῦμα θεοῦ ἐν αὐτῷ». Note that this is similar to how Paul uses the phrase in his letters. Another example is found in Gen 41,38, where Pharaoh is looking for a man who has the Spirit of God in him. The LXX reads «καὶ εἶπεν Φαραω πᾶσιν τοῖς παισὶν αὐτοῦ Μὴ εὑρήσομεν ἄνθρωπον τοιοῦτον, ὃς ἔχει πνεῦμα θεοῦ ἐν αὐτῷ;». Note how the expression «ἔχει πνεῦμα θεοῦ ἐν αὐτῷ resembles Paul's idiom in 8,9: πνεῦμα θεοῦ [...] ἐν ὑμῖν and πνεῦμα Χριστοῦ οὐκ ἔχει. In short, Paul is being true to the Old Testament's notion of God's Spirit dwelling in a human being when in Rom 8 he describes a Christian's new life in the Holy Spirit.

[16] Cf. H. KLEINKNECHT, «θεός», in ThWNT; H. DIETER, «θεός», in EWNT.

[17] The genitive form τοῦ θεοῦ occurs seventy-one times in Romans. Although not all of these occurrences present examples of the subjective genitive, the overwhelming majority of them do. For example, Paul uses the subjective genitive in describing the qualities of

Jesus Christ» (Rom 15,6) as well as «our Father» (Rom 1,8). In the Spirit of sonship, Christians pray to him by exclaiming, «Abba! Father!» (Rom 8,15). God is Creator, the one «who gives life to the dead and calls into existence the things that do not exist» (Rom 4,17). He is also the efficient cause of the resurrection, both for Christ and for all human beings: he «raised from the dead Jesus our Lord» (Rom 4,24; 6,4; 8,11; 10,9) and «will give life to your mortal bodies also» (Rom 8,11). The God of «the covenants» (Rom 9,4) of Israel, he is also «the God of Gentiles» (Rom 3,29) «since God is one» (Rom 3,30). He has made manifest his «eternal power and divinity» (Rom 1,20), «his purpose» (Rom 8,29; 9,11) and his «will» (Rom 1,10; 15,32) to all those who believe in his plan of salvation achieved «at the appointed time» (Rom 5,6) by Jesus Christ, his Son.

– οἰκεῖ. The verb οἰκέω, meaning to live, to dwell (intrans.), or to inhabit (trans.), is conjugated to agree with the subject πνεῦμα θεοῦ. It occurs nine times in the New Testament: five times in Romans, three times in 1 Corinthians and once in 1 Timothy.

The intransitive meaning of οἰκέω is found in 1 Corinthians and Romans. In his teaching on marriage, Paul instructs the Corinthians in these words.

> To the rest I say, not the Lord, that if any brother has a wife who is an unbeliever and she consents to live (οἰκεῖν) with him, he should not divorce her. If any woman has a husband who is an unbeliever and he consents to live (οἰκεῖν) with her, she should not divorce him. (1Cor 7,12-13)

Thus, Paul uses the verb to describe the cohabitation of a married couple. In Romans, however, he uses οἰκέω when explaining how sin dwells in a human being.

> So then it is no longer I that do it, but sin which dwells (ἡ οἰκοῦσα) within me. For I know that nothing good dwells (οἰκεῖ) within me, that is, in my flesh. I can

---

God. The three most important are «the wrath of God» (1,18; 2,8; 3,5; 4,15; 5,9; 9,22), «the righteousness of God» (1,17; 3,5.21-22.25-26; 10,3) and «the love of God» (5,5; 8,39). In addition, Paul speaks of «the gospel of God» (1,1.16; 15,16), «the Son of God» (1,4), «the glory of God» (3,23; 5,2; 15,7); «the law of God» (7,22.25), «the children of God» (8,16), «the word of God» (9,6), «the mercy of God» (9,16), «the riches and wisdom and knowledge of God» (11,33), «the Kingdom of God» (14,17) and «the will of God» (15,32). This list of examples is not meant to be exhaustive; it does serve to demonstrate, however, the extensive presence of this pattern throughout the letter.

will what is right, but I cannot do it. For I do not do the good I want, but the evil I do not want is what I do. Now if I do what I do not want, it is no longer I that do it, but sin which dwells (ἡ οἰκοῦσα) within me. (Rom 7,17-20)

The question of indwelling sin dominates the end of Romans 7. Intimately connected with the flesh, sin tyrannizes the home of the one whom it has mastered.

In Romans 8, Paul uses οἰκέω again, but this time to characterize the reign of the Spirit. «The Spirit of God dwells (οἰκεῖ) in you» (Rom 8,9) and «the Spirit of the one who raised Jesus from the dead dwells (οἰκεῖ) in you» (Rom 8,11) describe how the Holy Spirit transforms the spiritual life of a Christian. The expression «the Spirit of God dwells (οἰκεῖ) in you», also found in 1 Corinthians 3,16, is used there in a similar way[18].

The transitive use of the verb, meaning to inhabit, is found only in 1 Timothy 6,16 where the author presents his depiction of heaven: «who alone has immortality and dwells in unapproachable light» (φῶς οἰκῶν ἀπρόσιτον). Perhaps the presence of a direct object in this final example provides us with subtle proof that this text does not come from one of Paul's authentic letters. As we have noted, the Apostle seems to prefer the intransitive followed by a prepositional phrase.

– ἐν ὑμῖν. The phrase ἐν ὑμῖν occurs seven times in Romans as a whole and three times in this subunit[19]. In the introductory comments on the subunit under the section «Variation on a Theme», we noticed how the presence of personal pronouns lends a more familiar, more intimate tone to Paul's argument. The fact that this prepositional phrase is repeated four times in only three verses serves to underscore the Apostle's ardent desire to address the Romans directly. This aim is no doubt linked to Paul's sincere wish, expressed so beautifully at the start of the letter, that «we may be mutually encouraged (συμπαρακληθῆναι ἐν ὑμῖν) by each other's faith, both yours and mine» (Rom 1,12). He recognizes the Spirit's presence in them and wants to be edified by their faith in Jesus Christ. As with the phrases ἐν σαρκί and ἐν πνεύματι that precede it, ἐν ὑμῖν expresses the general notion of

---

[18] See O. MICHEL, «οἰκέω», in *ThWNT*.
[19] Cf. Rom 1,12.13; 8,9.10.11(2x); 12,3.

association[20]. Given the sociative use of the preposition, the phrase may be translated as «in you», or «with you».

– Lastly, it is necessary to make a concluding comment on the protasis «if indeed God's Spirit dwells in you». Paul had already developed his notion of the Spirit's indwelling in his earlier correspondence with the Corinthians, as we noted in Part One above. Reminding them of their sanctity, Paul asks «Do you not know that you are God's temple and that God's Spirit dwells in you? (τὸ πνεῦμα τοῦ θεοῦ οἰκεῖ ἐν ὑμῖν;) If any one destroys God's temple, God will destroy him. For God's temple is holy and that temple you are» (1Cor 3,16-17). Later in the letter, he repeats the theme: «Do you not know that your body is a temple of the Holy Spirit within you (ναὸς τοῦ ἐν ὑμῖν ἁγίου πνεύματός), which you have from God? You are not your own» (1Cor 6,19). Clearly then, Paul is making the same point again in Romans. The Holy Spirit, by his dwelling in Christians, transforms them into God's temple. Note well that Paul does not refer to their minds or to their souls, but rather to their bodies, τὸ σῶμα ὑμῶν. It is in fact the human body that is indwelt by the Spirit of God. Since this crucial point has major ramifications for his teaching on the resurrection of the body, Paul will return to this question later in the subunit. For the Apostle, the «Spirit of sanctification» (Rom 1,4) fulfills one of his divine tasks by making Christians holy; thanks to this saving action, believers become fitting and acceptable temples of the most high God.

– εἰ δέ τις. The second conditional sentence of Romans 8,9 begins with the words εἰ δέ τις, «If any one»; this of course indicates the start of the protasis of another first class condition. The personal pronoun ὑμεῖς in the first sentence is now replaced by the indefinite pronoun τις in the second. Paul does this in order to make a general point in his argument. This is the only occurrence of εἰ τις in Romans, although it is a common way for the Apostle to begin an «If-clause» in his other letters.

εἰ τις occurs twenty-six times in the Pauline corpus, most often in 1 Corinthians where the combination is found thirteen times. A few examples will help us gain insight into Paul's method of reasoning: «If any one destroys God's temple, God will destroy him. For God's temple is holy and that temple you are» (1Cor 3,17); «If any one imagines that he knows something, he does not yet know as he ought to know. But if one loves God, one is known by him»

---

[20] See ZERWICK § 116-117.

(1Cor 8,2-3); «If any one does not recognize this, he is not recognized» (1Cor 14,38); «Therefore, if any one is in Christ, he is a new creation; the old has passed away, behold, the new has come» (2Cor 5,17).

Along with Romans 8,9, the syntax of these first class conditions can be described as «If p,q» where both clauses contain verbs in the indicative mood. There are first class conditions, however, whose apodosis contains a verb in the imperative mood: «Let no one deceive himself. If any one among you thinks that he is wise in this age, let him become a fool that he may become wise» (1Cor 3,18); «To the rest I say, not the Lord, that if any brother has a wife who is an unbeliever and she consents to live with him, he should not divorce her. If any woman has a husband who is an unbeliever and he consents to live with her, she should not divorce him» (1Cor 7,12-13); «Look at what is before your eyes. If any one is confident that he is Christ's, let him remind himself that as he is Christ's, so are we» (2Cor 10,7).

We may conclude from these examples that Paul employs the first class condition with the indefinite pronoun τις in the protasis to articulate general principles of reasoning or conduct which are applicable to everyone. It is fascinating to note that Paul uses the same syntactical structure («εἰ p,q») both to teach and prove a point as well as to exhort and command. As we have noted already on several occasions, these two different functions are very closely connected for the Apostle.

– πνεῦμα Χριστοῦ. This is the only occurrence of the expression «Spirit of Christ» anywhere in the Pauline corpus. As we saw above in our discussion of πνεῦμα θεοῦ, the case of Χριστοῦ provides another example of the use of the subjective genitive in order to convey possession. Paul continues his description of the Holy Spirit: in addition to belonging to God, the Spirit also belongs to Christ. He is truly Christ's Spirit. The Apostle is still identifying the Spirit, as in the previous sentence, but this time he uses christological terms to do so: the Holy Spirit is now revealed and given to us through Christ. The Son is of God (Rom 1,3), while the Spirit is of God and the Son (Rom 8,9). Hence both Son and Spirit are intimately united by their origin in God the Father, yet different because the Spirit is of Christ but Christ is not of the Spirit. In their origin they are distinct yet equal, since they are both of God; in their mission they are similar yet different, since there is only one Christ who saves and there is only one Spirit who sanctifies. The new eschatological life won for humanity through the Christ-event is now mediated to us through Christ's Spirit[21].

The term Χριστός is clearly indispensable for Paul, since he uses it two hundred and sixty six times in his genuine letters. It appears sixty-six times in Romans, with chapter eight showing nine occurrences and the present subunit, three. When speaking of Jesus as Messiah of the Jews, Paul uses Χριστός in the titular sense: «to them belong the patriarchs and of their race, according to the flesh, is the Christ» (Rom 9,5). For the most part, however, Χριστός is employed as if it were another name for Jesus. Paul speaks of «Jesus Christ» eighteen times[22] and «Christ Jesus» fourteen times[23] in Romans. The double form of the name appears in the introduction, in important doctrinal passages (such as chapter eight, where «Christ Jesus» is found five times), as well as in the conclusion. Regardless of the order of the words or the presence or absence of an article, Paul understands Jesus the Christ as the universal Savior of both Jews and Gentiles[24].

πνεῦμα Χριστοῦ follows closely after the phrase πνεῦμα θεοῦ from the previous clause. Paul is building up his argument, using different terms to demonstrate that God is present and active in human beings. He understands Christ as the one human being who stands in the place of God. Both Christ and God are intimately united by their joint connection to the Spirit, yet they are different because God is purely divine and hence invisible (Rom 1,20) while Christ is «descended from David according to the flesh and designated Son of God in power according to the Spirit of holiness by his resurrection from the dead» (Rom 1,3-4). Thanks to his double descent, Christ is God's Son, sent by the Father to proclaim God's gospel (Rom 1,1) as well as our brother with whom we cry «Abba! Father!» (Rom 8,15). Christ plays a singular role in human salvation, since he alone is the one «whom God put forward as an expiation by his blood» (Rom 3,25) and who later «was raised from the dead by the glory of the Father» (Rom 6,4). He is of God yet in complete solidarity

---

[21] «As in his christology, so too in his references to the Spirit, Paul is interested in the functional role played by the latter in human salvation. If Christ opened up to human beings the possibility of new life, to be lived in him and for God, it is more accurately the "Spirit of Christ" that is the mode of communicating this dynamic, vital and life-giving principle to human beings» (J.A. FITZMYER, «Pauline Theology», 1396).

[22] Cf. Rom 1,1.4.6.7.8; 3,22; 5,1.11.15.17.21; 7,25; 13,14; 15,6.30; 16,20.25.27.

[23] Cf. Rom 2,16; 3,24; 6,3.11.23; 8,1.2.11.34.39; 15,5.16.17; 16,3.

[24] See W. GRUNDMANN, «Χρίω, Χριστός», in ThWNT.

with human beings, save sin. For this reason Christ is God's unique mediator, since the Father acts for the salvation of humanity «through the redemption which is in Christ Jesus» (Rom 3,24). As Son of God and our redeemer, Christ is fully divine; as Son of David and our brother, Christ is fully human. In conclusion, throughout Romans the Apostle is fascinated by the mystery of Christ and for this reason his Good News of salvation is chiefly christological in nature.

– οὐκ ἔχει. In Romans, the verb «to have» occurs twenty-five times. In Romans 8,9 it is conjugated to agree with τις, the subject of the sentence. ἔχω has several different meanings: «to have, own, or possess», «to hold», and «to enjoy». Since we are in fact dealing with the language of possession, the verb's first meaning is appropriate here: «he does not have». It is interesting to notice that both here and in Romans 8,23 (the verb's only other occurrence in chapter eight) ἔχω has «Spirit» as a predicate object: «the Spirit of Christ» (v. 9) and «the first fruits of the Spirit» (v. 23). It is also important to note that references to having the Spirit are rare in the New Testament[25]. For Paul, not having the Spirit means not thinking in accordance with the mind of the Spirit (Rom 8,5) and not walking in his ways (Rom 8,4). Since the mind of the Spirit is life and peace (Rom 8,6), one who lacks the Spirit also lacks his life and his peace. Such a one opts instead for hostility to God (Rom 8,7).

– οὗτος οὐκ ἔστιν αὐτοῦ. The apodosis of the condition is expressed negatively, hence it corresponds to the negative protasis of the same conditional sentence. It may be translated as «this one is not of him» or «this one does not belong to him». The demonstrative pronoun οὗτος refers to its antecedent τις in the protasis. Both pronouns serve as the subject of their respective clauses. The personal pronoun αὐτοῦ refers back to Christ, its antecedent in the first clause. Why then does Paul use the genitive case here? When followed by the genitive, the verb εἰμί indicates possession[26]. This represents yet another example of the language of possession we have encountered throughout the verse. Thus, the clause «this one is not of him» is equivalent to «this one is not a Christian», i.e., not a spiritual being[27].

---

[25] Cf. H. HANSE, «ἔχω», in *ThWNT* and E. LARSSON, «ἔχω», in *EWNT*.

[26] Cf. ZERWICK § 36-39; BDR § 162,7; HS § 159b; H. BALZ, «εἰμί», in *EWNT*.

[27] Paul also develops this notion of belonging to Christ in his other letters. Evidently members of the early Church were greatly preoccupied with belonging to someone, which was tantamount to adhering to his party or faction. Paul explains in 1Cor 1,11-12, «For it

We must now make sense of the complete conditional sentence «If any one does not have the Spirit of Christ, this one does not belong to him». After having just explained the difference between the two opposing ways of living, Paul now addresses a specific Church about the way they live their lives. He is not conjecturing on the hypothetical difference between a Christian and a non-Christian; rather, he is explaining to Christians that only when their behavior is influenced by the Spirit can they claim to belong to Christ. The hortatory point of the subunit must be kept in mind here. «To have the Spirit of Christ» means to give witness to the Spirit's presence by what one does — not just by what one thinks or says. It means to provide evidence of «the things of the Spirit» (Rom 8,5) for all to see by allowing the Spirit to act freely in one's life. In fact, this is precisely what Paul will spell out when he says «For all who are led by the Spirit of God are sons of God» (Rom 8,14). Such moral living is never automatic for any Christian; one must choose again and again to cooperate with the Spirit as one follows Christ as a disciple. It is not a decision made once and for all; it must be renewed on a daily basis. After a brief teaching on the new life ensured by Christ's resurrection, Paul will return to his parenesis at the end of the subunit and explain to the Romans how this is to be done.

2. Rom 8,10

Here is the text that we are about to exegete.

εἰ δὲ Χριστὸς ἐν ὑμῖν, τὸ μὲν σῶμα νεκρὸν διὰ ἁμαρτίαν, τὸ δὲ πνεῦμα ζωὴ διὰ δικαιοσύνην.

«If Christ is in you, although the body [was, is, will be] dead because of sin, the Spirit is life because of righteousness».

---

has been reported to me by Chloe's people that there is quarreling among you, my brethren. What I mean is that each one of you says, "I belong to Paul," or "I belong to Apollos," or "I belong to Cephas," or "I belong to Christ"». Note again how in these exclamations like «ἐγὼ δὲ Χριστοῦ» the genitive case is used to convey possession. Cf. 1Cor 3,23, «ὑμεῖς δὲ Χριστοῦ, Χριστὸς δὲ θεοῦ»; 1Cor 15,23, «ἔπειτα οἱ τοῦ Χριστοῦ ἐν τῇ παρουσίᾳ αὐτοῦ»; 2Cor 10,7, «εἴ τις πέποιθεν ἑαυτῷ Χριστοῦ εἶναι, τοῦτο λογιζέσθω πάλιν ἐφ' ἑαυτοῦ ὅτι καθὼς αὐτὸς Χριστοῦ οὕτως καὶ ἡμεῖς»; Gal 3,29, «εἰ δὲ ὑμεῖς Χριστοῦ, ἄρα τοῦ Ἀβραὰμ σπέρμα ἐστέ, κατ' ἐπαγγελίαν κληρονόμοι»; and Gal 5,24, «οἱ δὲ τοῦ Χριστοῦ [Ἰησοῦ] τὴν σάρκα ἐσταύρωσαν σὺν τοῖς παθήμασιν καὶ ταῖς ἐπιθυμίαις».

Before undertaking an in-depth study of the individual words in this verse, a preliminary remark concerning its syntactical structure is in order. Romans 8,10 is in fact composed of three verbless clauses: 1) εἰ δὲ Χριστὸς ἐν ὑμῖν, 2) τὸ μὲν σῶμα νεκρὸν διὰ ἁμαρτίαν and 3) τὸ δὲ πνεῦμα ζωὴ διὰ δικαιοσύνην. The first task at hand is to decide which verb or verbs to supply in order to fill in this lacuna. The most logical choice for the copula is of course the verb εἰμί. Grammarians confirm that it can be omitted in certain circumstances, such as in proverbs, impersonal expressions, questions, exclamations, or simple statements[28]. Paul sometimes leaves out the verb «to be» in the protasis of conditional sentences. This criterion, then, would allow us to supply the verb «is» in the first clause. Moreover, the context allows us to use εἰμί in all three clauses since it was the last verb to be used by the Apostle in Romans 8,9[29]. We are therefore justified in supplying ἔστιν as the appropriate conjugated form of the verb in v. 10. Hence the text would appear in this way: εἰ δὲ Χριστὸς [ἔστιν] ἐν ὑμῖν, τὸ μὲν σῶμα [ἔστιν] νεκρὸν διὰ ἁμαρτίαν, τὸ δὲ πνεῦμα [ἔστιν] ζωὴ διὰ δικαιοσύνην.

After having justified the use of the verb «to be» in each of these clauses, we must now pay attention to the clauses as such. The first clause is obviously the protasis since it is introduced by εἰ. The second contains the particle μέν while the third has the particle δέ. Since μὲν – δέ clauses go together, they both form the apodosis of the conditional sentence. Hence it is the apodosis that needs to be examined in greater detail. μέν is sometimes used in correlation with δέ to begin a concessive clause[30]. That would leave us free to begin the second clause with the conjunction «although». The skeleton of the entire sentence would then look something like this: «If 1, although 2, 3». The full force of the apodosis now falls on the third clause which in fact emphasizes Paul's principal point. Thus the complete sentence in English reads like this: «If Christ is in you, although the body is dead because of sin, the Spirit is life because of righteousness».

---

[28] Cf. BDR § 127; HS § 256d.

[29] «Bei Paulus fehlt nicht selten d. Verbum, wenn es aus d. Zusammenhang zu ergänzend ist: εἰ Χριστὸς ἐν ὑμῖν (erg. ἐστιν), τὸ μὲν σῶμα νεκρόν (erg. ἐστιν) *wenn Christus in euch ist, ist d. Leib tot* 8,10. εἰ τέκνα (erg. ἐστέ) *wenn ihr Kinder seid, so* [...] 8,17. εἰ χάριτι (γέγονεν), οὐκέτι ἐξ ἔργων 11,6 und öfter» (BAUER, «εἰ», I,1a). See G. LÜDEMANN, «εἰ», in *EWNT*.

[30] Cf. ZERWICK § 467; BDR § 447,2a; HS § 252,34.

The presence of the μὲν – δέ clauses reveals an important feature of Paul's Greek style. The Apostle often juxtaposes opposing words, phrases and sentences to emphasize a contrast in meaning. His antithetical style, in part derived from Hebrew and marked by the Greek of the LXX, typifies the black and white reasoning of his society[31]. In Romans 8,10 the two opposing μὲν – δέ clauses are short, concise and mysterious; set so close to one another in this way, they present a fine example of antithetical parallelism. The cryptic form of the apodosis serves to convey the inscrutable content of Paul's doctrine. He abruptly contrasts that which is human, mortal and disposed to sin («although the body is dead because of sin») to that which is divine, immortal and disposed to God's will («the Spirit is life because of righteousness»). The succinct phrasing manages to contrast the inexpressible mysteries symbolized by the words. Thanks to its style and content, this verse represents an enigmatic masterpiece.

The terse contrast presented in Romans 8,10 beautifully reflects the antithetical style of its surroundings. Paul makes a stark opposition between his argument in Romans 7,7-25, where he develops the law's inability to save, and Romans 8,1-13, where he contrasts life according to the flesh to life according to the Spirit. The words «sin» and «law» dominate in the first passage, while «Spirit», a word not found in chapter seven, reigns supreme in the second. «Death» and «body» are more or less equally distributed in both sections. «Flesh», however, is clearly concentrated in Romans 8,1-13; this is because it serves as a foil to the «Spirit», the most important term in the whole chapter.

In these passages, the Apostle is contrasting two main characters in this part of the letter: sin, humanity's foe and adversary and the Spirit, humanity's ally and intercessor. While sin deceives and kills (Rom 7,11), «working death in me through what is good» (Rom 7,13), «the Spirit is life because of righteousness»

---

[31] «In a world torn by violence, it is little wonder if authors took naturally to an antithetical style and contrasted heaven and earth, light and darkness, life in Christ and death in sin, spirit and flesh, faith and unbelief, love and hate, truth and error, reality and appearance, longing and fulfillment, past and present, present and future» (N. TURNER, Vol. 4 of *A Grammar* by J.H. MOULTON, 96). Turner offers the following passages as examples of antithetic parallelism with μὲν – δέ clauses in Paul's letters: «to those who by patience in well-doing seek for glory and honor and immortality, he will give eternal life; but for those who are factious and do not obey the truth, but obey wickedness, there will be wrath and fury» (Rom 2,7-8) and «For the word of the cross is folly to those who are perishing, but to us who are being saved it is the power of God» (1Cor 1,18).

(Rom 8,10). Sin produces death, the Spirit dispenses life. Paul presents them as opposing forces which inhabit human beings, either for evil or for good. The verb «to dwell» [οἰκέω] occurs three times in chapter seven: «sin dwelling in me» (Rom 7,17); «nothing good dwells within me, that is in my flesh» (Rom 7,18); and «sin dwelling in me» (Rom 7,20). In the next chapter, Paul repeats this triple refrain, but this time, with the Spirit as subject: «if indeed God's Spirit dwells in you» (Rom 8,9); «If the Spirit [...] dwells in you» (Rom 8,11); and «through his Spirit who dwells in you» (Rom 8,11)[32]. Thus for Paul, there are only two possibilities for a human being: either he is indwelt by sin or indwelt by the Spirit. If the former dwells in him, then he will die; if the latter dwells in him, then he will live.

With the data gained from this word study, we may conclude that having the Spirit represents an absolutely essential component in the life of a Christian. Without the Spirit, «the law of sin which is in my members» (Rom 7,23) impels a person to «walk according to the flesh» (Rom 8,4) on the way to death. With the Spirit, however, the Christian comes alive in a brand new way. His body is no longer a slave to sin, but it now becomes the temple of God's Spirit. In fact this divine indwelling produces two principal effects. In the present, the Christian can live a life pleasing to God. He can «walk according to the Spirit» (Rom 8,4) and «by the Spirit» put to death the deeds of the body (Rom 8,13). This was previously impossible as long as sin remained the dominating power: «For I know that nothing good dwells within me, that is, in my flesh. I can will what is right, but I cannot do it. For I do not do the good I want, but the evil I do not want is what I do» (Rom 7,18-19). Moreover, in the future, «the body of death» (Rom 7,24) (which as a servant of the law of sin could not hope to inherit eternal life) can now look forward to the general resurrection of the dead: «he who raised Christ Jesus from the dead will now give life to your mortal bodies also». (Rom 8,11). In short, the indwelling of the Spirit produces profound and enduring consequences in the present as well as in the future for every Christian.

Lastly, we can sum up the difference between these two chapters by contrasting two of Paul's own assertions. In chapter seven he affirms «I am

---

[32] We have already studied the meaning of the verb οἰκέω in the close reading of 8,9. It is interesting to note that this verb occurs five times in Rom, only in chs. 7 (3 x) and 8 (2 x). In addition, 8,11 uses the verb «to dwell» twice, but with two different verbs. The first is οἰκέω, while the second is ἐνοικέω (its only occurrence in Rom). We will return to this detail later in the close reading of 8,11.

carnal [σάρκινος], sold under sin» (Rom 7,14). This rather desperate and hopeless situation has now been radically altered, thanks to «the law of the Spirit of life in Christ Jesus» (Rom 8,2). That is why Paul can declare with great confidence, «But you are not in the flesh, you are in the Spirit, if in fact the Spirit of God dwells in you» (Rom 8,9). Having been liberated from a virtual state of slavery, Christians can now rejoice in their current status as vessels of the Spirit. The essence of Paul's teaching celebrates the new-found freedom enjoyed by all who have been redeemed by the Lord Jesus Christ.

As with the preceding verse, we shall now examine all the key words of Romans 8,10 as part of the close reading of the text.

– εἰ δὲ Χριστὸς ἐν ὑμῖν. The protasis repeats the word «Christ» which was already expressed in the preceding sentence, thus helping to connect Romans 8,10 to what has come before. The first noun of the clause is in fact very important. At the beginning of the subunit, Paul had already made two references to «Christ Jesus». In Romans 8,1 he states that for those «in Christ Jesus» there is no condemnation and in Romans 8,2 he refers to the law of the Spirit of life «in Christ Jesus». In fact, Paul often uses the phrase «in Christ» to express the mysterious communion between believer and Lord[33]. In v. 10, however, Paul reverses the sides of the equation by employing the more unusual expression «Christ is in you»[34]. If we keep in mind that the preposition ἐν indicates association[35], then it is clear that both expressions are synonymous. Hence, «Christ is in you» is equivalent to «You are in Christ». Both express the mysterious way in which Christ shares in our life and we in turn share in his.

Paul uses rather surprising language in his description of Christ and the Spirit in this subunit. Both terms seem to be equivalent ways of describing God's relationship with Christians. There is a thematic common denominator

---

[33] For «in Christ», cf. 9,1; 12,5; and 16,7. For «in Christ Jesus», cf. 3,24; 6,11; 8,1.2; 15,17; and 16,3; for «in Christ Jesus our Lord», cf. 6,23 and 8,39. The expression is also quite common in the other authentic letters of Paul. «In Christ/Christ Jesus/Christ Jesus our Lord» occur 13 times in 1Cor, 8 times in 2Cor, 9 times in Gal, 9 times in Phil, 3 times in 1Th and 4 times in Philem. It does not occur in 2Th.

[34] This notion of Christ's being in believers occurs in two other passages in the Pauline corpus. Cf. 2Cor 13,5 and Gal 2,20. It is interesting to note that the verb «to be» is also unexpressed in the first example above. This formulation is in fact very similar to the one found in the first clause in Rom 8,10.

[35] See ZERWICK § 116-118.

in Romans 8,9-13, in these verses Paul introduces a new life-giving principle in the Christian that replaces the flesh. He varies his language by calling it either «Spirit» (v. 9), or «Spirit of God» (v. 9), or «Spirit of Christ» (v. 9), or simply «Christ» (v. 10), or again «the Spirit» (v. 10), or «the Spirit of the one who raised Jesus from the dead» (v. 11), or «his Spirit» (i.e. Christ's, v. 11), or «by the Spirit» (v. 13). By modifying his description in this way, Paul strives to express the unfathomable way in which divine life manifests itself in the lives of Christians. Ultimately he is trying to convey the inexpressible, namely, how God dwells in human beings[36]. The variety of terms employed further accentuates the mysterious nature of the divine indwelling.

– τὸ σῶμα. The Greek noun for «body» is found thirteen times in Romans, with three occurrences in this subunit (Romans 8,10.11.13). As we saw above in our study of 1 Corinthians 15, it is an essential term for Paul when he speaks of the resurrection of the dead. In Romans, as in 1 Corinthians before it, τὸ σῶμα always means the «physical body». The Apostle also uses the word in both its literal and figurative senses, but the term's basic meaning always remains the same.

Our discussion of this noun begins with a presentation of texts from Romans where Paul uses σῶμα. As we examine both the literal and the figurative senses of the word, we will discover a consistent use of the meaning «physical body». Then we shall have to explain the presence of the definite article in Romans 8,10. Why «the» body, as opposed to «your» or «our» body? Finally, there is a shift in Romans 8,9-11 from σάρξ to σῶμα and again back to σάρξ. Is this change significant and if so, what does Paul intend by it?

We begin with the literal meaning first. In the overwhelming majority of cases, Paul uses σῶμα in Romans to designate the physical body as such. The word is used this way in Romans 1,24 with reference to the impure acts of the Gentiles: «to the dishonoring of their bodies among themselves»; in Romans 4,19 with reference to Abraham, «He did not weaken in faith when he considered his own body»; in Romans 6,6.12 where Paul speaks of the body under the power of sin, «We know that our old self was crucified with him so that the sinful body might be destroyed»; and «Let not sin therefore reign in your mortal bodies, to make you obey their passions»; in Romans 7,4 with an illusion to Jesus' bodily death, «Likewise, my brethren, you have died to the law through the body of Christ»; in Romans 7,24 when Paul speaks of his body

---

[36] Cf. R. PENNA, *Lo Spirito di Cristo*, 251ff.; and J.D.G. DUNN, *Romans 1-8*, 430.

that will die, «Who will deliver me from this body of death?» in Romans 8,23 with reference to physical redemption, «we ourselves, who have the first fruits of the Spirit, groan inwardly as we wait for adoption as sons, the redemption of our bodies»; in Romans 12,1 with reference to a physical sacrifice, «I appeal to you, therefore, brothers, by the mercies of God, to present your bodies as a living sacrifice, holy and acceptable to God, which is your spiritual worship»; and finally in Romans 12,4 with a simple use of the physical sense, «For as in one body we have many members». The term also has this straight-forward, literal meaning in other letters of Paul, such as in 1 Corinthians 6,15; 12,12-27 and 2 Corinthians 12,2-3.

σῶμα may also be used in the figurative sense. It can mean the community or the social body, as it does in Romans 12,5, «so we, though many, are one body in Christ and individually members one of another». As we saw in Part One above, this metaphor was first used by Paul in 1 Corinthians 10,17, «Because there is one bread, we who are many are one body, for we all partake of the one bread», and also in 1 Corinthians 12,27, «Now you are the body of Christ and individually members of it».

With one exception, therefore, σῶμα consistently means physical body in the literal sense throughout the letter. We must now decide whether Paul uses the word literally or figuratively in Romans 8,10.11 and 13. Since there is no illusion to «the body of Christ» understood metaphorically as the Christian community or the Church, it would seem that the word σῶμα in the present subunit could only have the literal meaning. Let us now study how the context and the unfolding of Paul's argumentation clearly support this conclusion.

Paul's last use of this crucial word was in Romans 7,24; bemoaning his captivity to the law of sin in his members, he appeals to be delivered «from this body of death», «ἐκ τοῦ σώματος τοῦ θανάτου τούτου». In chapter eight, however, Paul boldly declares, «For the law of the Spirit of life in Christ Jesus has set me free from the law of sin and death» (Rom 8,2). Thus the body that was once a prisoner to sin and death now comes under the sway of the Spirit. The tangible, material part of a human being has now become the temple of the Holy Spirit, as we noted above in our exegesis of Romans 8,9[37].

---

[37] «In the absence of good evidence to the contrary, we should probably assume that Paul retains his Pharisaical notion concerning the nature of the resurrection as a raising of the physical body, improved though it may be. And the repeated mentions in verses 9-11 of the dwelling of Christ and his Spirit within the believer favor our understanding the *sōma* as the physical abode of the Spirit who guides and energizes the believer's actions worked

This interpretation of σῶμα is also corroborated by what follows in the subunit. In his doctrine on the resurrection, Paul teaches that God will give life «to your mortal bodies» (Rom 8,11); in other words, the physical bodies of those Christians who have died will be raised just as Jesus' body was raised. Lastly, in Romans 8,13 «the deeds of the body» can only refer to the actual physical bodies through which we act in the world. Hence all three occurrences of σῶμα in the subunit present examples of the literal sense of the word.

We must now explain the use of the definite article before the singular noun. Paul writes «the body» as opposed to «your bodies» primarily for reasons of style. He already began the subunit in v. 9 with «You are not», while in the first clause of v. 10 he states «If Christ is in you». It would be redundant to continue with «your bodies are dead». He in fact reserves the possessive pronoun «your mortal bodies» for v. 11. It also seems that Paul uses τὸ σῶμα to correspond to τὸ πνεῦμα in the following clause. He is weighing each word in the sentence so as to balance the two clauses perfectly. For reasons of antithetical parallelism, therefore, Paul chooses the definite article to go along with the singular form of the noun. This concise term now fits beautifully with «the Spirit» that will follow.

Lastly we must account for the shift from σάρξ to σῶμα to σάρξ again, since the terms are not interchangeable for Paul. We have already seen how in Romans 8,2-8, to be «in the flesh» is contrasted to being «in the Spirit»; the flesh refers to that force which is allied with the passing powers of this world, namely sin and death. The distinction between flesh and Spirit is repeated in Romans 8,9. In vv. 10 and 11, however, where he is concerned with eternal life and the resurrection of the dead, Paul now uses σῶμα. The σῶμα will be raised up to everlasting life, not the σάρξ. As he is about to say in the following verse, at the resurrection God will give life to mortal bodies (Rom 8,11) and not to mortal flesh.

This distinction is supported by other Pauline texts that treat the resurrection of the dead. In Part One of this book, we noted that in his discussion of the resurrection body in 1 Corinthians 15,35-50, Paul refers to the change that will occur at the resurrection of the dead: «It is sown a physical body (σῶμα ψυχικόν), it is raised a spiritual body (σῶμα πνευματικόν)». (1Cor 15,44). The σάρξ, however, will not be changed in this way, since «flesh and blood cannot inherit the kingdom of God» (1Cor 15,50). The body has been created

---

out through the instrument of the body» (R. GUNDRY, Sōma, 38).

for eternal life and will be made spiritual at the resurrection of the dead. The
flesh belongs to this passing world and hence will not enter into the world to
come.

In Romans 8,12-13 Paul switches back again to σάρξ. He does this in order
to emphasize the point that life according to the flesh inevitably leads to death.
Paul exhorts the Romans who are still very much alive in this world to put to
death the «deeds of the body». In other words, even though they have received
the Spirit, they could still opt to live according to the flesh. The immediate
cause of anyone's deeds is his body, yet the ultimate cause is the sphere which
rules over him, namely, the flesh or the Spirit.

If someone lives merely in the sphere of the flesh, any rebellion against its
power is in vain. But this is not the situation of the Christian who has received
the Spirit. «By the Spirit» a Christian can resolve to reject the realm of the flesh
and instead use his body as an instrument of righteousness in the realm of the
Spirit. The Spirit empowers him to do the good, to engage in upright moral
behavior in the world. σῶμα is repeated here since it is the body that is the
instrument of all human action. Formerly subject to sin and death, it is the body
that one day will experience eternal life in the realm of God's Spirit.

– νεκρόν. The Greek word νεκρός appears frequently in the New Testament,
with sixteen occurrences found in Romans. It can be used either as an
adjective or a noun, although the latter usage is far more common[38]. In this
verse it serves as an adjective in agreement with τὸ σῶμα which precedes it.
As an adjective it means «dead», «no longer alive»; it may describe human
beings or things in both the literal and figurative senses. In Romans νεκρός is
used as an adjective three times, in 6,11; 7,8 and 8,10. As a noun, νεκρός
refers to «the dead» as opposed to the living. The plural noun form appears
about eighty-six times in the New Testament and thirteen times in Romans.
Two examples of the noun occur in the next verse where Paul teaches that
Jesus Christ was raised «from the dead», ἐκ νεκρῶν. In these two instances
the noun is used literally: Jesus knew death because he had actually died. Now
that he is raised, he no longer belongs to the dead[39].

---

[38] Cf. R. BULTMANN, «νεκρός, νεκρόω, νέκρωσις», in *ThWNT*; R. DABELSTEIN,
«νεκρός, νεκρόω, νέκρωσις», in *EWNT*.

[39] For other references to Jesus' resurrection from the dead, cf. Rom 1,4; 4,24; 6,4.9;
7,4; and 10,7.9. For the dead in general, cf. Rom 4,17; 11,15; and 14,9.

Since νεκρός occurs as an adjective in Romans 8,10, it is worth our while to study the other two adjectival uses in Romans. In all three occurrences of the word, νεκρός is used by the Apostle in the figurative sense. Since Paul also uses the verb νεκρόω as well as the noun νέκρωσις, we will study them as well.

Paul ends his passage on baptism with an exhortation to the Roman Christians: «So you also must consider yourselves dead to sin and alive to God in Christ Jesus» (Rom 6,11). They are obviously very much alive, but the Apostle urges them to act as if they were dead to this sinful world. This is clearly a figurative use of the adjective, one which Paul soon repeats in Romans 7,8 when he states that «Apart from the law sin lies dead». Since it is clear that only living things can die, Paul uses a metaphor in this verse to make a theological point. He is saying that sin is powerless and ineffective over human beings who live without the law. Because sin is dead, human beings are free to find new life with God.

After having exhausted the adjectival occurrences of νεκρός in Romans, we must now examine its cognates before returning to Romans 8,10. In Romans 4,19 we read «He [Abraham] did not weaken in faith when he considered that his own body had died (νενεκρωμένον), because he was about a hundred years old and the deadness (τὴν νέκρωσιν) of Sarah's womb». Paul uses these terms in the literal sense: the verb νενεκρόω and the noun νέκρωσις describe the pathological death of living tissue, whether plant, animal, or human. Hence, «had died» is used literally by Paul to describe Abraham's impotence and «deadness» to describe Sarah's barrenness. Since neither one is physically able to give new life, Paul considers them as good as dead. This hopeless situation comes to an end when God fulfills his promise by granting them a child in their old age. The Apostle seems to be saying that whenever God is involved with human beings, death is never the last word.

We are now left with the occurrence of νεκρός in Romans 8,10. Before we make any further remarks on the meaning of the adjective in this verse, however, it is necessary to examine the prepositional phrase that follows. So let us now examine διὰ ἁμαρτίαν and then we will be in a position to consider other possible interpretations of the clause understood as a whole.

– διὰ ἁμαρτίαν. The noun ἡ ἁμαρτία is the most often used word for sin in the New Testament, appearing a total of one hundred and seventy-three times. There are forty-eight occurrences in Romans, of which forty-two are in chapters five to eight. It clearly represents a very significant term for Paul as he develops his theology of righteousness in this part of the letter[40]. What then does he understand by it?

The word first occurs in Romans 3,9, «for we have already charged that all, both Jews and Greeks, are under the power of sin». Certainly one of the major themes the Apostle develops in Romans 1,18–3,31 is the universality of sin which has affected all humanity. Paul personifies sin; it is an earthly lord or ruler that dominates human beings and holds them in slavery. He develops this personification of sin throughout Romans 5–8 and contrasts it to his proclamation of God's righteousness through faith in Jesus Christ. We have seen on several occasions the antithetical nature of Paul's thought and argumentation; this four-chapter unit in the letter provides many fine examples of his propensity to compare and contrast differing themes and topics.

In Romans 5,12-21, the Apostle compares sin to grace, the trespass of Adam to the obedience of Christ. In this passage, ἁμαρτία and παράπτωμα are synonyms, but each term expresses its own unique nuance. ἁμαρτία represents the generic noun for sin as hostility to God; sin came into the world through one man (Rom 5,12) and brought death as its wages (Rom 6,23). παράπτωμα means a trespass of a rule or a law; it occurs in Romans 5,15-20 in reference to Adam's one act of disobedience to God's commandment. With the exception of two occurrences in Romans 11,11-12, παράπτωμα no longer occurs in Romans. Paul instead prefers the more generic term ἁμαρτία to make his point that sin reigned from Adam to Christ. For the Apostle, therefore, there is a clear connection between Adam's trespass, individual sin and the power of death. Everyone is subject to death because everyone in fact has sinned.

In chapter six Paul turns to his baptismal catechism in order to clarify his teaching on sin and grace. By dying with Christ in the sacrament, the Christian is liberated from sin: «For he who has died is freed from sin» (Rom 6,7). This liberation in turn leads to a new life, «So you also must consider yourselves dead to sin and alive to God in Christ Jesus» (Rom 6,11). Romans 6,16-23 goes on to develop the notion that in order to enter into the sphere of «righteousness for sanctification» (Rom 6,19) one must first be freed from the slavery to sin. «For the wages of sin is death, but the free gift of God is eternal life in Christ Jesus our Lord» (Rom 6,23).

---

[40] Cf. W. GRUNDMANN, «ἁμαρτία», in ThWNT; P. FIEDLER, «ἁμαρτία», in EWNT.

In chapter seven, the Apostle next explains how a Christian is liberated from the law. Sin exercises a demonic control over human beings since it brings death through what is good and holy. «It was sin, working death in me through what is good, in order that sin might be shown to be sin and through the commandment might become sinful beyond measure» (Rom 7,13). Having been sold under sin (Rom 7,14), human beings are now totally controlled by it (Rom 7,17.20). «The law of sin» (Rom 7,23) dwells in the members of the human body, acting as a poison which kills all who drink it. Given this agonizing desperation, it is no wonder why Paul cries out, «Wretched man that I am! Who will deliver me from this body of death?» (Rom 7,24).

There is no hope for humanity except for the salvation won by Christ and conferred on us through the Holy Spirit. Before turning to his exposition on life in the Spirit, Paul summarizes in Romans 8,1-4 what he has already taught since chapter five. He states that we have now been set free from the «law of sin and death» (Rom 8,2) and then goes on to explain that «God sent his Son in the likeness of sinful flesh (ἐν ὁμοιώματι σαρκὸς ἁματίας) and for sin condemned sin in the flesh» (Rom 8,3). It is the law that manifests the condition of sin and reveals its true nature, for the mind of the flesh is death (Rom 8,6) and those who live according to the flesh are at enmity with God (Rom 8,7). In short, it is impossible for any sinner to be in a right relationship with God.

In our study of the word σάρξ, we have already seen that to live «according to the flesh» means to act out of self-concern and self-interest. For Paul, to live according to the flesh, to live in a way that is hostile to God — this is the true meaning of sin. Its opposite, life «according to the Spirit» means to abandon egotism and self-centeredness for the sake of the realm of God's Spirit[41]. Although the entire subunit is meant to demonstrate the antithetical contrast between sin and righteousness, Paul condenses his thought most brilliantly in Romans 8,10, «the body is dead because of sin, the Spirit is life because of righteousness». διά with the accusative illustrates the causal use of the preposition[42]. In English it may be translated «because of», or «on account of». To counter the negative effects of sin, therefore, a superior power must be introduced to oppose sin's malevolent influence. The Apostle will consider this divine force, i.e. the Spirit, in the clause that immediately follows.

---

[41] See C.F.D. MOULE, «"Justification" in its Relation to the Condition κατὰ πνεῦμα (Rom 8,1-11)», 184-185.

[42] Cf. ZERWICK § 112; BDR § 222; HS § 226a, § 259g.

One final point still remains to be made with regard to Paul's understanding of sin. We have seen that through the use of antithetical parallelism, Paul contrasts ἁμαρτία to δικαιοσύνη in Romans 8,10. Sin, as we have proved, refers to the condition of hostility to God, which is simply another way of speaking about unrighteousness. The Apostle contrasts sin, the cause of unrighteousness and our enmity with God, to justification or righteousness, the cause of our fellowship with God. This is not the first time in the letter that Paul has done so. In Romans 5,10 he writes, «For if while we were enemies we were reconciled to God by the death of his Son, much more, now that we are reconciled, shall we be saved by his life». In short, while sin leads to death, righteousness leads to life.

– Now that we have examined the various words of this clause in detail, we have to reconsider the fact that Paul does not explicitly state a verb. In our opening remarks on Romans 8,10, we noted how the context allows us to supply a conjugated form of εἰμί in the verbless clauses: εἰ δὲ Χριστὸς [ἔστιν] ἐν ὑμῖν, τὸ μὲν σῶμα [ἔστιν] νεκρὸν διὰ ἁμαρτίαν, τὸ δὲ πνεῦμα [ἔστιν] ζωὴ διὰ δικαιοσύνην. Although this is a fine first approach to the text, should we limit our possibilities only to the present tense? It would seem apparent that if Paul did not specifically express the verb ἔστιν he did so for a reason. Therefore it would be wise to consider all the options with regard to the verb's tense. If we focus on the clause that we are presently studying, the past, present and future forms of εἰμί are all legitimate possibilities: τὸ μὲν σῶμα [ἦν, ἔστιν, ἔσται] νεκρὸν διὰ ἁμαρτίαν. Our interpretation will be much richer if we explore all three of these verb forms.

We start with the past tense: «the body was dead because of sin». There are several biblical references that use a form of the adjective νεκρός with εἰμί in the past. In fact, three passages clearly use the adjective in the literal sense. For example, in the LXX the Levite's concubine who was murdered by the Benjaminites is described as dead (a detail missing in the MT): καὶ εἶπεν πρὸς αὐτήν Ἀνάστα καὶ ἀπέλθωμεν· καὶ οὐκ ἀπεκρίθη, ὅτι ἦν νεκρά. καὶ ἔλαβεν αὐτὴν ἐπὶ τὸν ὄνον καὶ ἐπορεύθη εἰς τὸν τόπον αὐτοῦ (Jg 19,28). The second example of the literal use of the adjective also comes from the Old Testament. In refering to the Assyrians killed by the angel of the Lord we read: «And that night the angel of the Lord went forth and slew a hundred and eighty-five thousand in the camp of the Assyrians; and when men arose early in the morning, behold, these were all dead bodies (πάντες σώματα νεκρά)» (2Kg 19,35). Note that the LXX does not use the verb to be and that νεκρά is used to describe σώματα just as in Romans 8,10. The third example of the literal use of the adjective is found this time in the New Testament where Christ is described in this way: «And to the angel of the Church in Smyrna write: "The words of the first and the last, who died (ἐγένετο νεκρός) and came to life"» (Rev 2,8).

So just as with the two previous occurrences of νεκρός in Romans, we must now decide if Paul is speaking literally or figuratively when he writes «dead» in Romans 8,10. Throughout his letter, Paul addresses Christians who reside in Rome and who are obviously very much alive. Since the Apostle has just told them «If Christ is in you», then he cannot mean they were once dead in the literal sense. Therefore νεκρόν can only be used figuratively in the clause «although the body [was] dead because of sin». This is in fact how the adjective is used elsewhere in the New Testament. For example, in the story of the Prodigal Son, Luke describes the young man as once dead but now alive again: «"for this my son was dead and is alive again (ὁ υἱός μου νεκρὸς ἦν καὶ ἀνέζησεν); he was lost and is found." And they began to make merry» (Lk 15,24) and «It was fitting to make merry and be glad, for this your brother was dead (ὁ ἀδελφός σου οὗτος νεκρὸς ἦν καὶ ἔζησεν) and is alive; he was lost and is found» (Lk 15,32). Trespasses can also cause human beings to be considered metaphorically dead, as these passages suggest. «And you, who were dead (ὑμᾶς νεκροὺς ὄντας) in trespasses and the uncircumcision of your flesh, God made alive together with him, having forgiven us all our trespasses» (Col 2,13). «Even when we were dead through our trespasses, he [God] made us alive together with Christ (by grace you have been saved)» (Eph 2,5). In short, then, if we interpret «the body was dead because of sin», then Paul would be refering to that period when the Romans were still estranged from God. Before becoming Christians, they were still under the rule of the flesh and hence, like the Prodigal Son, they were not yet in a right relationship with God. In this sense, then, «the body was dead because of sin» describes their pre-Christian existence.

The second possibility is the present tense: «the body [is] dead because of sin». Just as we did above, we must first decide if the adjective is being used literally or figurativelly. And again, other biblical references can help us come to a better understanding of the text. For example, in a very famous story from the Old Testament, Solomon wisely determines who is the real mother of a new-born child. The LXX reads this way. καὶ εἶπεν ἡ γυνὴ ἡ ἑτέρα Οὐχί, ἀλλὰ ὁ υἱός μου ὁ ζῶν, ὁ δὲ υἱός σου ὁ τεθνηκώς. καὶ ἐλάλησαν ἐνώπιον τοῦ βασιλέως (3Kg 3,22). It is interesting to note, however, that the

word νεκρός appears in some witnesses, namely in the text of Origen: ὁ υἱός
σου ἔστιν ὁ νεκρός, υἱὸς δὲ ἐμὸς ὁ ζῶν; ἡ δὲ ἀλλὴ καὶ αὐτὴ ἔλεγεν
οὐχι. The adjective is obviously used literally here, as it is in the following
reference from the letter of James where the body is called dead. «For as the
body apart from the spirit is dead (τὸ σῶμα χωρὶς πνεύματος νεκρόν
ἐστιν), so faith apart from works is dead» (Jas 2,26). Conversely, the adjective
is used figuratively in another reference from the letter of James. «So faith by
itself, if it has no works, is dead (νεκρά ἐστιν)» (Jas 2,17).

   With this in mind, we are now ready to return to Romans 8,10, «If Christ is
in you, the body [is] dead because of sin». Clearly νεκρόν could not be used
literally here since Paul is addressing people who are still very much alive;
hence the adjective could only be used in the figurative sense. So what then
does Paul mean by this? νεκρόν conveys the sense of dull, torpid and lifeless.
Given humanity's sinful condition, the human body is presently incapable of
reflecting God's eternal glory; due to the flesh's temporary yet compelling
sphere of power, the body is not capable of radiating God's refulgent glory.
Since the source of eternal life is located in God alone, the believer has to
receive Christ's risen life through the mediation of the Spirit if he is to partake
in this eschatological reality which comes from God. The body in its present
situation cannot do this on its own; it must be redeemed, it must receive the
gift of the Spirit. In Romans 8,10, therefore, Paul asserts that «the body is
dead» because in this life the human body is unable to enjoy fully the eternal
life which comes from God[43].

   Lastly we consider the future tense: «the body [will be] dead because of sin».
There is of course no difficulty in interpreting this literally, since it is everyone's common experience that the body will indeed die. The following verse
supports this interpretation, since Paul will go on to speak of «your mortal
bodies». The physical life of the human body ceases and the mortal remains
break down and decompose. This anthropological reality obviously remains
true even for Christians. The important point, however, is that for the Apostle,
this process of death and dying finds its origin in sin: «Therefore as sin came

---

[43] Many exegetes have interpreted this crux in light of the sacramental meaning of the
adjective in Rom 6,11. Since baptism is not Paul's concern in Rom 8, this approach does
not seem helpful. It is better to perceive an allusion back to Abraham and Sarah's sterility.
For a discussion of the conversion–initiation position, see E. KÄSEMANN, *Commentary on
Romans*, 224. For a discussion of Paul's notion of baptism and death in ch. six, see J.D.G.
DUNN, «Salvation Proclaimed», 259-264 and F.A. MORGAN, «Romans 6,5a», 267-302.

into the world through one human being and death through sin and so death spread to all human beings because all sinned» (Rom 5,12).

To sum up, then, a closer consideration of the three possible verb tenses offers us a far richer appreciation of the clause. Paul purposely did not supply a conjugated verb and as a result the text conveys several significant nuances. First, «although the body *was* dead because of sin» (since it was under the sphere of the flesh), it can now become an instrument of upright Christian living in the world: «Do not yield your members to sin as instruments of wickedness, but yield yourselves to God as people who have been brought from death to life and your members to God as instruments of righteousness» (Rom 6,13). In the past the body was dead *because of* sin, but now, thanks to the Christ-event, the body is dead *to* sin: «So you also must consider yourselves dead to sin and alive to God in Christ Jesus» (Rom 6,11). Thanks to the Christ-event, Christians are able to live in the Spirit and praise and serve God in their bodies. Second, «although the body *is* dead because of sin» (since the natural body does not yet enjoy eternal life and thus is presently incapable of radiating God's splendor), at the general resurrection it will be transformed into the spiritual body so as to be able to reflect God's glory and majesty: «Lo! I tell you a mystery. We shall not all sleep, but we shall all be changed, in a moment, in the twinkling of an eye, at the last trumpet. For the trumpet will sound and the dead will be raised imperishable and we shall be changed» (1Cor 15,51-52). And third, «although the body *will be* dead because of sin» after this earthly life, it will rise on the last day because the Spirit is guarantee of eternal life: «he who raised Christ Jesus from the dead will give life to your mortal bodies also through his Spirit who dwells in you» (8,11). Thus «although the body was/is/will be dead because of sin» offers an ample variety of connotations and so we may assume that this wealth of meaning is precisely what the Apostle wanted his addressees to consider and reflect on.

– τὸ πνεῦμα ζωή. In our earlier discussion on πνεῦμα, we saw how the subunit (and indeed the entire chapter) is dominated by Paul's teaching on the Holy Spirit. In addition to the context (cf. «Spirit of God», «Spirit of Christ» in Rom 8,9; «Spirit of the one who raised Jesus from the dead», «his Spirit who dwells in you» in Rom 8,11), there is also a solid syntactical reason for insisting that Paul is in fact referring back to the «Spirit of life» mentioned in Romans 8,2.   In Romans 8,10 πνεῦμα is immediately followed by ζωή. Given that in the previous clause Paul used a noun followed by an adjective (σῶμα νεκρόν), why did he choose to upset the parallelism by using two nouns in the nominative case one after the other? For that matter, he could have just as easily repeated the expression from v. 2, «τοῦ πνεύματος τῆς ζωῆς», by putting the second noun in the genitive. Why then did the Apostle use this noun which means «life, existence», and not the adjective ζωός, which means «alive, living»?

Since the adjective refers to living things, ζωός would be a reference to a creature who has received life from God. Thus the adjective would have a purely passive meaning. But instead, Paul employs the noun and he does so in order to make a very important point. ζωή means life and hence it implies the giving of life. The noun conveys an active meaning; it is personified here to denote the very source of life, God. Hence πνεῦμα in this verse refers to the Holy Spirit understood as the giver of life[44].

This juxtaposition of two nouns is not unknown in the Pauline corpus. In 1 Corinthians 1,30 Paul describes Christ Jesus by using four consecutive nouns: ὃς ἐγενήθη σοφία ἡμῖν ἀπὸ θεοῦ, δικαιοσύνη τε καὶ ἁγιασμὸς καὶ ἀπολύτρωσις. «who became for us wisdom from God, as well as righteousness, sanctification and redemption». He does so in order to stress the point that Christ is indeed the source of all our wisdom, righteousness, sanctification and redemption. It is this active implication that is important, the fact that Christ is the origin of these rich blessings for us. Paul uses this technique again in Romans 8,10 by juxtaposing the nouns «Spirit» and «life» in order to make precisely the same point.

The Apostle had already contrasted the Spirit to the flesh in an earlier letter. In Galatians 5,16-26 he demonstrates how the two are opposed to one another. After an extensive list of vices which constitute the works of the flesh, Paul then goes on to list the Spirit's blessings: ὁ δὲ καρπὸς τοῦ πνεύματός ἐστιν ἀγάπη χαρὰ εἰρήνη, μακροθυμία χρηστότης ἀγαθωσύνη, πίστις πραΰτης ἐγκράτεια· «But the fruit of the Spirit is love, joy, peace, patience, kindness, goodness, faithfulness, gentleness, self-control» (Gal 5,22-23). Note that the subject, «fruit», is in the nominative; «the Spirit» is a subjective genitive; the verb «to be» is conjugated in the present indicative; and the predicate nominatives follow in the list of virtues.

This very simple, straightforward sentence from Galatians helps to shed some light on the difficult syntax we find in Romans 8,10. In a subjective

---

[44] Cf. P.J. ACHTEMEIER, *Romans*, 135; C.K. BARRETT, *The Epistle to the Romans*, 149-150; W.C. COETZER, «The Holy Spirit», 181; C.E.B. CRANFIELD, *The Epistle to the Romans*, 372; J.D.G. DUNN, *Romans 1-8*, 414; and E. KÄSEMANN, *Romans*, 214.

genitive, such as «the fruit of the Spirit», the genitive is the subject from which the fruit springs. The Spirit is therefore the source from which these virtues flow. He is the font which nourishes Christian life, for as Paul goes on to explain, «If we live by the Spirit, let us also walk by the Spirit» (Gal 5,25). Similarly in Romans 8,10, when Paul declares that «the Spirit is life» he means that the Holy Spirit is in fact the origin of life, both present and future. In his role as sanctifier, he supplies the foundation of ethical Christian conduct in this age and in his role as divinizer, he is the divine agent through whom eschatological life abounds for the age to come.

We have now examined the difficult syntactical problem posed by the first two nouns of the clause, as well as explained in greater detail why πνεῦμα in Romans 8,10 must refer to the Holy Spirit. With this work accomplished, we are now in a good position to investigate the word ζωή in further detail[45].

This noun has fourteen occurrences in Romans, of which four are found in chapter eight. For Paul, ζωή may mean physical, natural life, or it may also have a metaphorical sense. The only occurrence of the literal use of the word is found in Romans 8,38, where the Apostle refers to death and life as realities of the present, passing world. In the thirteen other instances in the letter, however, the term is used metaphorically to express an essential soteriological category. Life in this sense means eschatological life. It is another way of expressing the novel condition of those who share in the effects of the Christ-event. Paul speaks of «life» (Rom 5,17.18; 7,10; 8,6), «eternal life» (Rom 2,7; 5,21; 6,22.23), «his (Christ's) life» (Rom 5,10), the «newness of life» (Rom 6,4), the «Spirit of life» (Rom 8,2) and «life from the dead» (Rom 11,15). Clearly ζωή in all these passages is understood as spiritual life. Paul is developing his notion of the eschatological life; for him, it represents a new kind existence which harbors significant overtones for both the present and the future reality of the Christian.

We must now decide if in Romans 8,10 ζωή is used in a literal or figurative sense. Only the context can help us decide. We noted that in the previous clause the term νεκρόν is used figuratively if we provide the present tense: «although the body is dead because of sin». Through the use of antithetical parallelism, Paul is comparing this adjective to ζωή. This comparison could lead us to believe that the latter word is also used in the figurative sense. Moreover, given that ζωή follows the word «Spirit», it is reasonable to

---

[45] Cf. R. BULTMANN, «ζωή», in *ThWNT*; L. SCHOTTROFF, «ζωή», in *EWNT*.

conclude that we are dealing with spiritual life here. For both these reasons, therefore, we conclude that ζωή is used metaphorically by Paul in Romans 8,10.

This conclusion can be sustained even more decisively if we examine the unfolding of Paul's argumentation in greater detail. The former age characterized by sin, death and the law now gives way to the new age of the Spirit. That is what Romans 8,1-13 is all about. Up until now Paul has been preparing the ground for this chapter. In Romans 5,5 he stated how the Spirit has been poured into our hearts; now he develops the ramifications of that divine indwelling. The law of the Spirit of life has freed us from what once held us in bondage: the law, sin and death (Rom 8,2). The life of the flesh leads to death (Rom 8,6) and is hostile to God (Rom 8,7). «But the mind of the Spirit is life and peace» (Rom 8,6). The Spirit not only dwells in our mind but also in our body: God will give life to our mortal bodies through his indwelling Spirit (Rom 8,11). Therefore, in chapter eight Paul makes a major development in his argument. The Spirit is not just somewhere «out-there» calling us to a new and better life. Instead, he is ever present to us, dwelling within us, working out our salvation in the fullness of our being. ζωή is both present life, allowing us to live in freedom as children of God and future life, allowing us to share in the glory of Christ's resurrection.

«The Spirit is life because of righteousness» (Rom 8,10) is indeed the best translation of this clause. This spiritual life as described by Paul is lived out in the body yet transcends earthly limitations; it is at once somatic and eternal. It is given as a gift by God, not earned by human deeds or achievement. It is the experience of being in the Kingdom of God which is «righteousness and peace and joy in the Holy Spirit» (Rom 14,17). The power of the Holy Spirit transforms all creation as we await in hope the glory that is to be revealed (Rom 8,18).

– διὰ δικαιοσύνην. «Righteousness» is the last noun in Romans 8,10; it serves to round out the final clause of that verse by expanding the Apostle's understanding of πνεῦμα and ζωή. Since Paul's notion of righteousness dominates Romans, it would be impossible for us to do justice to this significant theological concept in just a few short lines. Nevertheless, a brief examination of the word's occurrence and usage in the letter will shed light on its meaning in v. 10[46]. We shall then be in a better position to exegete the clause understood as a whole and indeed, the entire subunit.

δικαιοσύνηoccurs fifty-seven times in the Pauline letters and thirty-three times in Romans. The term refers both to divine righteousness (God is righteous in all his ways and has the power to create, judge and redeem his people) and to human righteousness (human beings, through the gift of grace, now have the power to live righteous lives). As before in our exegesis, we are now faced with a choice between two options. In Romans 8,10, is Paul referring to the righteousness of God or to the righteousness of human beings? A close examination of the context will help us decide which.

We must understand the noun in light of its position in the clause, as well as its position in the verse as a whole. Paul writes «τό δέ πνεῦμα ζωή διά δικαιοσύνην». The word «righteousness» is an object of the preposition διά; as in the previous clause, it also provides an example of the causal use[47]. «Because of righteousness» immediately follows the Holy «Spirit» and «life», and hence it should be interpreted along with them. We have already seen in our previous discussion that these first two nouns are rich in eschatological-soteriological meaning. So too with δικαιοσύνη. In this clause Paul is speaking about the things of God. Through the use of antithetical parallelism, he contrasts God's Spirit, God's life and God's righteousness to that which is human in the previous clause. Therefore the Apostle is opposing divine righteousness to human sinfulness[48].

This is not the first place in the letter where Paul has contrasted righteousness to sin. The antithesis is also found in Romans 6,13-20. This exhortation is especially revelatory: «Do not yield your members to sin as instruments of wickedness, but yield yourselves to God as those who have been brought from death to life and your members to God as instruments of righteousness» (Rom

---

[46] Cf. G. SCHRENK, «δικαιοσύνη», in *ThWNT*; K. KERTELGE, «δικαιοσύνη», in *EWNT*.

[47] Cf. ZERWICK § 112; BDR § 222; HS § 226a, § 259g.

[48] «*Dia* avec l'accusatif (v. 10) n'exprime pas le but, mais la cause: (à cause de la justice). L'existence chrétienne dont Paul a rappelé le fondement (v. 3 et 4) et les modalités d'exercice ouvre à la vie grâce à la justice salvifique de Dieu. Dieu lui-même, par la puissance de l'esprit, accomplit la justice exigée par la loi. Le croyant n'est pas livré à ses seules forces, mais un autre, sans rien lui enlever de sa responsabilité, lui donne la possibilité de réaliser ce que la loi demandait. La *dikaiosynè* rappelle que cette vie est don, manifesté dans la mort et résurrection du Christ» (J.P. LÉMONON, «Le Saint Esprit dans le corpus paulinien», *DBS*, XI, 250-251).

6,13). The members of the body can serve either sin or God; they can be either instruments of human wickedness or instruments of divine righteousness. The choices one makes will either lead to death or life.

The Apostle rephrases his teaching in a far more concise way in Romans 8,10, «the body [was, is, will be] dead because of sin». Due to sin's influence on the body («dead» because it is unable to achieve eternal life), human beings are incapable of reflecting God's glory. But now, through the Christ-event («If Christ is in you» Rom 8,10), new eschatological life is offered because God has freely saved his people: «the Spirit is life because of righteousness» (Rom 8,10). Once they are redeemed and saved in Christ, then human beings have the freedom to cooperate with grace by either yielding their members to sin or to God. This is precisely the choice that Paul states in Romans 8,13, «If you live according to the flesh you will die, but if by the Spirit you put to death the deeds of the body you will live».

In short, in Romans 8,10 Paul speaks of the Spirit, life and righteousness in order to describe God's gratuitous and undeserved movement towards sinful humanity. God has inaugurated a new period in human history: a new day has dawned, the new final era has begun. Christians are drawn into this divine activity, called in the Spirit to eternal life and invited to join in the Father's loving and righteous reign. Thanks to God's untold graciousness, believers receive the Holy Spirit, share in Christ's divine life and become righteous in their dealings with God and with one another.

Moreover, by using δικαιοσύνη in Romans 8,10, Paul is echoing back to the main *propositio* of the letter: «For in it [the gospel] the righteousness of God is revealed through faith for faith; as it is written, "He who through faith is righteous shall live"» (Rom 1,17) as well as to the main *propositio* of chapters five through eight «so that, as sin reigned in death, grace also might rein through righteousness to eternal life through Jesus Christ our Lord» (Rom 5,21).

By means of the gospel, God as creator and redeemer manifests his gracious power. In his love for humanity, God has freely decided to bring human beings into a right relationship with himself. This grace is now revealed through Christ's death and resurrection and made manifest through the power of the Holy Spirit. Because God is righteous, he forgives sins and acquits sinners in a just judgment[49]. The redeemed now live in a new age since they find

---

[49] See J.A. FITZMYER, *Romans*, 834.

themselves in a new relationship with God, with one another and with all of creation. Former broken relationships are healed and restored by God thanks to his infinite love. What was once impossible for humanity because of sin is now possible for God because of his abundant righteousness.

3. Rom 8,11

Continuing the method of exegesis we have used with the preceding two verses, we will now study Romans 8,11. Here is the text.

εἰ δὲ τὸ πνεῦμα τοῦ ἐγείραντος τὸν Ἰησοῦν ἐκ νεκρῶν οἰκεῖ ἐν ὑμῖν, ὁ ἐγείρας Χριστὸν ἐκ νεκρῶν ζῳοποιήσει καὶ τὰ θνητὰ σώματα ὑμῶν διὰ τοῦ ἐνοικοῦντος αὐτοῦ πνεύματος ἐν ὑμῖν.

«If the Spirit of the one who raised Jesus from the dead dwells in you, the one who raised Christ Jesus from the dead will give life to your mortal bodies also through his Spirit who dwells in you».

–εἰ δὲ τὸ πνεῦμα τοῦ ἐγείραντος τὸν Ἰησοῦν ἐκ νεκρῶν οἰκεῖ ἐν ὑμῖν. This is the protasis of the fourth conditional sentence in the subunit. In our discussion of Romans 8,9 we examined the predicate «(he) dwells in you» which Paul repeats here. What really draws our attention in this verse, however, is the subject. The πνεῦμα θεοῦ of Romans 8,9 is now described as τὸ πνεῦμα τοῦ ἐγείραντος τὸν Ἰησοῦν ἐκ νεκρῶν in 8,11. By means of this repetition, Paul emphasizes the indwelling of the Spirit and manages to enclose 8,10 in a very effective way. Thus, «the Spirit of God dwells in you», «Christ is in you», and «the Spirit of the one who raised Jesus from the dead dwells in you» are all synonymous expressions. What is fascinating about the last one, however, is the link between the indwelling of the Spirit and the resurrection of Jesus. This is a very important point for the Apostle, since he will repeat this connection once more later in the verse.

Leaving aside Jesus and the Spirit for just one moment, we must now pay some attention to Paul's portrayal of God. We note that the Apostle describes God in Romans 8,11 as «the one who raised Jesus from the dead». This epithet is repeated in the apodosis, with only a slight variation of case and direct object: ὁ ἐγείρας Χριστὸν ἐκ νεκρῶν. These synonymous epithets, parallel to one another, serve to balance the sentence in a beautiful way. The change from «Jesus» to «Christ» is yet further proof that the names are equivalent for Paul (even if «Christ» is in fact a title). In his usual way, Paul attributes the resurrection of Christ to God the Father. Elsewhere in Romans he speaks of «us who believe in him that raised from the dead Jesus our Lord», (Rom 4,24) and «if you confess with your lips that Jesus is Lord and believe in your heart that God raised him from the dead, you will be saved» (Rom 10,9)[50]. This saving deed is an extension of his omnipotent power as creator, since it is God «who gives life to the dead and calls into existence the things that do not exist» (Rom 4,17).

The verb ἐγείρω appears ten times in Romans[51]. Used transitively, the basic meaning of the word is «to wake from sleep», «incite» and «raise»; used intransitively, it means «awaken», stand up», «rise»[52]. Of the ten occurrences in this letter, only once does Paul use the verb to mean «wake from sleep»[53]. In the other nine references, ἐγείρω is used transitively to refer to Jesus' resurrection. The fact that Paul repeats the verb twice in this verse underscores his insistence on the resurrection. It is important to note that the participles ἐγείραντος (in the protasis) and ἐγείρας (in the apodosis) are both in the aorist tense, showing us that Paul considers Jesus' resurrection to be a completed event in the past[54]. This detail is significant because the participle acts as a foil to the main verb in the apodosis, i.e. ζῳοποιήσει, which is of course conjugated in the future. The prepositional phrase «from the dead» serves to stress the point that Jesus Christ truly was saved from death. The Apostle attributes this extraordinary eschatological event to God the Father since as creator and redeemer he is Lord over life and death.

---

[50] Elsewhere in his genuine letters the Apostle also attributes the resurrection of Jesus to the Father. Cf. «and to wait for his Son from heaven, whom he raised from the dead, Jesus who delivers us from the wrath to come» (1Th 1,10); «And God raised the Lord and will also raise us up by his power» (1Cor 6,14); «we testified of God that he raised Christ, whom he did not raise if it is true that the dead are not raised» (1Cor 15,15); and «knowing that he who raised the Lord Jesus will raise us also with Jesus and bring us with you into his presence» (2Cor 4,14).

[51] Cf. Rom 4,24.25; 6,4.9; 7,4; 8,11(2x).34; 10,9; and 13,11.

[52] Cf. A. OEPKE, «ἐγείρω», in ThWNT; J. KREMER, «ἐγείρω», in EWNT.

[53] See Rom 13,11.

[54] «In Rom 8,11, when Paul says ὁ ἐγείρας Χριστὸν ἐκ νεκρῶν (the one who raised Christ from the dead), he views the resurrection of Christ as a complete event. When Paul uses the imperfect in 2Cor 1,9 (τῷ θεῷ τῷ ἐγείροντι τοὺς νεκρούς [the God who is in progress raising the dead]), he views the process as one that is in progress. And in 2Tim 2,8 ('Ἰησοῦν Χριστὸν ἐγηγερμένον ἐκ νεκρῶν [Jesus Christ raised from the dead]), the author emphasizes the state of Christ's risenness (cf. Metzger, «Grammars», 481)» (S.E. PORTER, Verbal Aspect in the Greek of the New Testament, 92).

– ὁ ἐγείρας Χριστὸν ἐκ νεκρῶν ζῳοποιήσει. The chief verb of the apodosis is ζῳοποιήσει, the future indicative form of the verb ζῳοποιέω which means «to make alive», «to give life»[55]. As we saw in our study of the word in 1 Corinthians 15,45, this verb is used only in the soteriological sense in the New Testament. It appears twice in Romans, both times in connection with the resurrection.

Paul uses this verb in Romans 4,17 when he speaks of God «who gives life (τοῦ ζῳοποιοῦντος) to the dead and calls into existence the things that do not exist». It is important to note that this verse represents a very significant theological statement. For Paul, God the Father is creator: first, he creates the things of this world from nothing, granting his creatures biological life; second, he recreates those who have died by granting them eschatological life. This verse, with its reference to both *creatio ex nihilo* and the resurrection of the dead, alludes to the glorification of creation, a theme which infuses the whole of chapter eight.

In Romans 8,11, the subject of ζῳοποιήσει is also understood to be God the Father. We remarked above that «the one who raised Christ from the dead» is clearly an illusion to God the Father. Thus in Romans, Paul attributes to the Father this role as giver of eschatological life which believers will acquire in Christ. The verb's future tense indicates that Paul is refering to a future event, namely, the final resurrection of the dead. Even though the Father is presented as subject of this act, the Spirit is nevertheless intimately associated with this divine giving. The Father will impart this new life «through the Spirit who dwells in you», as the rest of the verse goes on to specify.

These findings are thoroughly consistent with Paul's understanding of the Father and the Spirit as presented in 1 and 2 Corinthians. In 1 Corinthians 15,22 Paul makes an obvious reference to the general resurrection, «For as in Adam all die, so also in Christ shall all be made alive». This is an example of the theological passive; Paul is teaching that God will make all alive in Christ. In our exegesis of 1 Corinthians 15 in Part One, we noted that the Father represents for Paul the supreme giver of all life, whether biological or eschatological. The Apostle makes this point later in the chapter when he states that «God gives it a body as he has chosen» (1Cor 15,38). In addition, the essential role of the Spirit in this divine activity is also made clear when he states «the last Adam became a life-giving Spirit» (1Cor 15,45). Paul intends

---

[55] Cf. R. BULTMANN, «ζῳοποιέω», in *ThWNT*; L. SCHOTTROFF, «ζῳοποιέω», in *EWNT*.

this as a pneumatalogical statement, not a christological one, as our exegesis has already shown. Lastly, if there were still any doubts about the Spirit's role as the agent of this eschatological action, we need only reconsider one final reference, this time from 2 Corinthians. There Paul states quite explicitly, «for the written code kills, but the Spirit gives life» (2Cor 3,6). In this verse, the Spirit is clearly presented as the subject of the verb, as the doer of the action.

From this study of the verb we may draw the following conclusions. Paul attributes the giving of eschatologcal life to the Father and to the Spirit; never does he use Jesus Christ as subject of this verb. Why is this so? Perhaps it is because Jesus himself was raised from the dead, as the first half of Romans 8,11 makes quite explicit. Jesus, as a human being, received the fullness of this new eschatological life at his resurrection. The Father and the Spirit gave it to him in his humility as servant. Similarly, all those who believe in Jesus Christ will also receive the fullness of this eschatological life at their resurrection. The Father will make alive again all those who are in Christ through the Holy Spirit. Thus the full trinitarian dimension of this divine act becomes clear. Christ is declared Son of God at his resurrection when he receives his risen life from the Father through the Spirit; all those in Christ also share in this divine gift and so they too will receive their risen life in the same way. For believers, however, the grace is transmitted in Christ; it is christologically given to them, all the while remaining theological in origin and pneumatological in agency. In short, both for Christ as well as for all Christians, the Apostle understands the resurrection of the dead as a thoroughly trinitarian event.

– καὶ τὰ θνητὰ σώματα ὑμῶν. As the predicate object of the verb ζωοποιήσει, «your mortal bodies also» personalizes for the Romans the Apostle's claim about the general resurrection of the dead. This wondrous eschatological event will include them as well. That is the point of the καί which may be translated as «also» or «as well». In other words, just as God raised Jesus from the dead, so too he will raise «your mortal bodies». The word σῶμα appears here for the second time in the subunit; although here the noun is individualized for the Roman Church, it serves to connect Romans 8,11 to 8,10.

Paul describes their bodies as θνητά, an adjective which means «mortal»[56]. It occurs only six times in the New Testament, all of them found in the Pauline

---

[56] Cf. R. BULTMANN, «θνητός», in *ThWNT*; W. BIEDER, «θνητός», in *EWNT*.

corpus[57]. In the other reference in Romans, Paul states «Let not sin therefore reign in your mortal bodies, to make you obey their passions» (Rom 6,12). The body is that part of the human being most defenseless against sin and its accompanying effects, death and decay. The Apostle is of course referring to the natural body here, the one that is presently alive and dynamic yet will also decay in the grave after death. Paul wants to insist on the fact that God's power will in fact transform the «mortal flesh» (2Cor 4,11) and the «mortal body» (Rom 8,11) when Christ comes again.

It must be kept in mind that Paul makes this statement after having reminded the Romans that the Spirit dwells in them. Life according to the Spirit is now possible because the Spirit lives in their mortal bodies, filling that which is perishable with his divine power. Not merely is the human mind affected, as in Romans 8,5-8, but now through the gift of the Spirit even the human body is infused with the divine presence. Since God's eternal Spirit now resides in mortal human beings, death will not have the last word over God's beloved children.

– διὰ τοῦ ἐνοικοῦντος αὐτοῦ πνεύματος ἐν ὑμῖν. Before we undertake the exegesis of this prepositional phrase, we must first deal with a difficult textual problem. Since there are two strongly attested readings, textual critics are divided over the correct reading of this text[58]. The genitive reading is to be preferred not only on textual grounds, but also because it makes better sense in the context. It may be translated as «through his Spirit» or «by the agency of his Spirit»[59].

This is the only passage in all of the Pauline corpus where the Apostle gives the Holy Spirit an explicit role in the resurrection of the dead. For that reason, Romans 8,11 presents us with indispensable data for our discussion of the Spirit's agency in the resurrection. Let us first study the verb in this prepositional phrase and then examine some parallel texts in Paul's genuine letters.

---

[57] Cf. Rom 6,12; 8,11 and 2Cor 4,11, where it is used as a modifying adjective; and 1Cor 15,53.54 and 2Cor 5,4 where it stands alone in the neuter singular.

[58] The two variants arise from the use of different cases: the first group of witnesses shows διά followed by the genitive, the second has it followed by the accusative. Metzger and his committee chose διὰ τοῦ ἐνοικοῦντος αὐτοῦ πνεύματος ἐν ὑμῖν. «on the basis of text-types, including the Alexandrian (ℵ A C 81), Palestinian (syr^pal Cyril-Jerusalem) and Western (it^61? Hippolytus)» (METZGER, 517).

[59] This is the position held by most commentators. Cf. Barrett, Best, Black, Bruce, Cranfield, Dunn, Fitzmyer, Heil, Käsemann and Ziesler.

The verb ἐνοικέω means «to dwell within», «to live in/among»[60]. It occurs only twice in the genuine letters of Paul, both here and in 2 Corinthians 6,16, as well as three times elsewhere in the New Testament (cf. Col 3,16; 2Tim 1,5.14). Human beings are never the subject of this verb, unlike the LXX where it is often used to describe human dwelling or habitation. The subject may be «the Spirit» (Rom 8,11; 2Tim 1,14), Christ's word (Col 3,16), God (2Cor 6,16), or faith (2Tim 1,5). The object of the verb may be either a human being or the Church.

Paul uses the present participle of the verb in Romans 8,11. ἐνοικοῦντος does not express time but only aspect and for this reason the present participle is called atemporal[61]. It does not refer to actual present time, but rather expresses the timeless quality of the action being performed. Thus ἐνοικοῦντος beautifully expresses the unchanging nature of the Holy Spirit's indwelling and serves to highlight the eschatological setting of the passage. A comparison with another important text will help us understand what Paul means by this. «What agreement has the temple of God with idols? For we are the temple of the living God; as God said, "I will live in them and move among them and I will be their God and they shall be my people"» (2Cor 6,16). As with the Corinthians, so too with the Romans: the Spirit dwells within Christians as in a temple[62].

The Spirit sanctifies Christians by his very presence in them. He dwells in them and by so doing makes them holy. This understanding of the Holy Spirit's activity is essential for the Apostle[63]. In his very first reference to the Spirit in

---

[60] Cf. O. MICHEL, «οἰκέω», in ThWNT; R. DABELSTEIN, «ἐνοικέω», in EWNT.

[61] Cf. ZERWICK § 371-372; BDR § 339; HS § 227-228.

[62] «Whereas in 7,17 Paul admitted that sin dwelled in unregenerate human beings, now he affirms that the Spirit of God itself dwells in them. This indwelling Spirit is thus the driving force and the source of new vitality for Christian life. The life-giving Spirit has an OT background in Ezek 37,14. In v 9 Paul spoke of the Christian being "in the Spirit," now of the Spirit as "dwelling in" the Christian; again he is searching for ways to describe the ineffable union of the Christian with Christ and his vivifying Spirit» (J.A. FITZMYER, Romans, 491).

[63] «The Spirit is not the possession of some elite group within the church. It is another word for God's life-giving power present through Jesus to all that belong to him, active already in their lives in spite of the mortality that still belongs to the body, working toward righteousness and undergirding the promise that the Son's identification with them will issue ultimately in their sharing in his resurrection (cf. 6,5.8). The Spirit is not only a mind-set; nor is it merely the external power by which God raised Jesus from the dead. It is also the power of the risen Jesus to take men and women into his power and reshape life to

Romans Paul called him πνεῦμα ἁγιωσύνης, «the Spirit of holiness, consecration» (Rom 1,4). As we noted on several occasions in Part One, Paul had already developed his notion of the Spirit as sanctifying agent in his letter to the Corinthians: «you were washed, you were sanctified, you were justified in the name of the Lord Jesus Christ and in the Spirit of our God» (1Cor 6,11)[64]. Thus in Romans 8,11 Paul takes his argument one step further by explicitly describing the Spirit as both the agent of sanctification and the agent of the resurrection of the dead.

The new eschatological age is marked by the Spirit's fellowship; already present in the mind and the body of believers, he now abides in their whole being. His possession of them now complete, he will be able to direct their lives in an entirely new way. With this, the third reference in the subunit to the Spirit's living in a person (the fourth mention of divine indwelling if we take into account «Christ in you» from Romans 8,10), Paul seeks to underscore the connection between divine indwelling and the resurrection. Note also that Paul writes «through his Spirit», i.e. Christ's Spirit, in an effort to describe the Spirit in even greater detail[65]. By doing so the Apostle highlights the fact that the Spirit is indeed the agent of the resurrection and as such he is thus intimately associated with the risen Christ. Until the day when Christ comes again, the Spirit of Christ (who is in fact the Spirit of God) makes his home on earth by dwelling within those who believe in and witness to the Lord Jesus.

4. Rom 8,12

We are now ready to examine the fourth verse of the subunit. Here is the text of Romans 8,12.

> Ἄρα οὖν, ἀδελφοί, ὀφειλέται ἐσμέν, οὐ τῇ σαρκὶ τοῦ κατὰ σάρκα ζῆν·
> «So then, brothers, we are debtors, not to the flesh, to live according to the flesh»

A declarative statement, Romans 8,12 is the only sentence in the subunit that is not conditional. Not only is the verse different in this regard, but its

---

make it well pleasing to God — thus doing what the law could not do and reversing the power of sin. That is why Paul could call the gospel "the power of God for salvation to all who rely on him, the Jew first and also the Greek" (1,16)» (P.W. MEYER, «Romans», 1152).

[64] See also a similar conviction in 2Th 2,13, «God chose you from the beginning to be saved, through sanctification by the Spirit and belief in the truth».

[65] The pronoun is reflexive. Cf. ZERWICK § 210-211; BDR § 283; HS § 139g-i.

brevity gives the impression that it is unfinished. The sentence may be divided into two parts. The first half, Ἄρα οὖν, ἀδελφοί, ὀφειλέται ἐσμέν, serves as a conclusion to the doctrinal section that has come before; the second half, οὐ τῇ σαρκὶ τοῦ κατὰ σάρκα ζῆν, presents the introduction to the hortatory part that will follow. As a whole, therefore, the verse acts as a hinge that connects Paul's apostolic teaching to his fraternal parenesis.

As regards the second half, the parallelism that has marked the text until now is left unexpressed. Paul makes a negative statement, οὐ τῇ σαρκὶ τοῦ κατὰ σάρκα ζῆν and stops there, the rest of his thought remaining unexpressed. The Apostle no doubt expects the reader to provide the positive statement for himself, something like ἀλλὰ ὀφειλέται ἐσμέν τῷ πνεύματι τοῦ κατὰ πνεῦμα ζῆν[66].

– Ἄρα οὖν, ἀδελφοί. At the start of the verse, the particle ἄρα is immediately followed by the adverb οὖν. Earlier occurrences of the two may also be found in Romans 5,18; 7,3.25; in these references, as well as in Romans 8,12, both words act together as a conjunction[67]. By means of Ἄρα οὖν, Paul makes a forceful conclusion based on what has come before.

ἀδελφός is the first noun in this verse; the Apostle often uses it to refer to a fellow Christian. The word has this meaning here in Romans 8,12, as well as in Romans 1,13; 7,1.4; 8,29; 10,1;.11,25; 12,1; 15,14.30; and 16,17. A fellow Christian is one who is conformed to the image of God's Son, «in order that he [Christ] may be the first-born among many brothers» (Rom 8,29). Since Christ and Christians have God as their Father, they are all spiritually brothers in the same mystical family[68].

– ὀφειλέται ἐσμέν, οὐ τῇ σαρκὶ. By writing «we are debtors», Paul makes a point to include himself in his teaching, just as he had done earlier in the chapter when he said «in order that the just requirement of the law might be fulfilled in us, who walk not according to the flesh but according to the Spirit» (Rom 8,4). He counts himself among those who are called to live an ethical life according to the Spirit. It is interesting to note that in Romans 8,12 Paul returns to his antithetical mode of argumentation which marked the subunit before v. 11.

---

[66] See CRANFIELD, *Romans*, 394.
[67] Cf. BDR § 451,2; HS § 252,4.
[68] See J. BEUTLER, «ἀδελφός», in *EWNT*.

The noun ὀφειλέτης, Greek for «debtor», occurs seven times in the New Testament[69]. The Apostle uses it a total of four times, once in Galatians 5,3 and three times in Romans. ὀφειλέτης acts as a predicate nominative with the verb εἰμί in all four cases and has the sense of «being obligated».

This meaning of the noun appears clearly in Galatians 5,3 when Paul says, «I testify again to every man who receives circumcision that he is obligated (ὀφειλέτης ἐστὶν) to keep the whole law». In Romans 1,14, Paul uses ὀφειλέτης with the dative of the person to whom he is obligated: «I am a debtor (ὀφειλέτης εἰμί) both to Greeks and to barbarians, both to the wise and to the foolish». In other words, Paul has an obligation to the Gentiles, given his divine commission to preach the gospel to them. The noun is used in the figurative sense in Romans 15,27, «they were pleased to do it and indeed they are obligated to them (ὀφειλέται εἰσὶν αὐτῶν), for if the Gentiles have come to share in their spiritual blessings, they ought also to be of service to them in material blessings». Note how the genitive refers to the Jerusalem Church; since the mother Church had shared its spiritual wealth with the Churches in Macedonia and Achaia, Paul insists that the Gentiles are now obligated to make a financial collection to the Jews.

With this information, we are now in a position to understand Romans 8,12. ὀφειλέται ἐσμέν is immediately followed by οὐ τῇ σαρκὶ. What Paul means here is that they are no longer obligated to the flesh; they are not in debt to it since the Holy Spirit lives in them. What he implies of course is that they are obligated to the Spirit. Since Christ is in them (Rom 8,10), they ought to live according to the Spirit (Rom 8,4) and in this way please God (Rom 8,8).

– τοῦ κατὰ σάρκα ζῆν Before exegeting the meaning of this verbal phrase, we must first pay some attention to its form and then study how Paul uses the verb ζῶ elsewhere.

τοῦ ζῆν may be explained in two ways. It is either an example of a consecutive infinitive with the article τοῦ, or it is epexegetic[70]. There is a previous occurrence of a consecutive infinitive in Romans and curiously enough, this verse also begins with Ἄρα οὖν: «But if her husband dies she is free from that law and if she marries another man she is not an adulteress (τοῦ μὴ ἀποθάνῃ μοιχαλίδα)» (Rom 7,3).

---

[69] Cf. F. HAUCK, «ὀφειλέτης», in ThWNT; M. WOLTER, «ὀφειλέτης», in EWNT.
[70] Cf. ZERWICK § 383-386; BDR § 400; HS § 225.

As we saw in the exegesis on 1 Corinthians 15,45, the verb ζῶ, «to live», occurs one hundred and forty times in the New Testament[71]. There are twenty-three occurrences in Romans. In chapter eight it appears once in v. 12 and twice in v. 13. Before determining how the verb is used in this subunit, however, we must first examine how it is used elsewhere in Romans.

When used literally, ζῶ can refer to living one's natural, physical life (as opposed to dying a natural death). There are twelve occurrences of the verb used in this way in the letter. Paul is speaking of the physical life and death of the woman's husband in chapter seven: «Are you unaware [...] that the law is binding over one as long as one lives? Thus a married woman is bound by law to her husband as long as he lives [...] Accordingly, she will be called an adulteress if she lives with another man while her husband is alive» (Rom 7,1-3). The verb also has the literal sense later in the verse: «I was once alive apart from the law, but when the commandment came, sin revived and I died» (Rom 7,9). Paul also uses ζῶ literally when speaking of the spiritual worship of the Romans. In the past, worshipers offered dead animals to God, but they are to offer their living bodies instead: «I appeal to you therefore, brothers, by the mercies of God, to present your bodies as a living sacrifice, holy and acceptable to God, which is your spiritual worship» (Rom 12,1). Lastly, when exhorting the Romans to live upright Christian lives, he again speaks of the physical life of this world: «None of us lives to himself and none of us dies to himself. If we live, we live to the Lord and if we die, we die to the Lord; so then, whether we live or whether we die, we are the Lord's. For to this end Christ died and lived again, that he might be Lord both of the dead and of the living» (Rom 14,7-9).

In our study of the noun, however, we saw how life and death are essential soteriological terms for Paul. Obviously then, ζῶ can also be used figuratively. Used in this way, ζῶ refers to living or not living the new eschatological life offered by the Spirit. This in fact represents Paul's chief interest with the word.

Paul uses ζῶ in a pejorative sense to describe living for oneself, living in sin and alienation from God as determined by the present world: «How can we who have died to sin still live in it?» (Rom 6,2). The inevitable outcome of such a mindset is death understood as estrangement from God (Rom 8,6).

The opposite example of metaphorical usage is when Paul uses ζῶ in a positive sense. When employed in this way, the verb means sharing in the

---

[71] Cf. R. BULTMANN, «ζῶ», in *ThWNT*; L. SCHOTTROFF, «ζῶ», in *EWNT*.

eschatological life given by God. It describes the life of the righteous: «"He who through faith is righteous shall live"» (Rom 1,17) and «Moses writes that the man who practices the righteousness which is based on the law shall live by it» (Rom 10,5). It characterizes Christ's life and the believer's life in Christ: «the life he [Christ] lives he lives to God. So you also must consider yourselves dead to sin and alive to God in Christ Jesus [...] but yield yourselves to God as men who have been brought from the dead to life» (Rom 6,10-13). ζῶ can also portray God's eternal life: «And in the very place where it was said to them, "You are not my people," they will be called "sons of the living God"» (Rom 9,26).

Now that we have a better understanding of Paul's earlier uses of the verb, we are in a good position to make a judgment on the verb's meaning in the present subunit. Both in Romans 8,12 and in the first occurrence of ζῶ in 8,13, it is clear that the verb is used metaphorically to refer to the life marked by sin and death. It means living in the realm of those powers which are opposed to God. As we saw in our previous discussion, to live «according to the flesh» means to orientate one's life merely on the earthly level[72]. The phrase here is synonymous to «in the flesh» from Romans 8,9; by using it again, Paul refers back to the beginning of the subunit.

What does all of this mean for the moral life of a Christian? In order to enter into the new life offered by God, one must refuse to live in and walk according to the flesh. Such ethical living is not accomplished once and for all; on the contrary, Paul implies here that it requires an ongoing conscious decision. Since the σάρξ is hostile to God, to live «according to the flesh» means to live in a way which is opposed to the divine will. The phrase echoes the formula τὰ τῆς σαρκὸς φρονεῖν of Romans 8,5, thus providing another link in the chain that connects 8,9-13 to 8,1-8.

5. Rom 8,13

Here is the fifth and final verse of the subunit.

εἰ γὰρ κατὰ σάρκα ζῆτε μέλλετε ἀποθνήσκειν, εἰ δὲ πνεύματι τὰς πράξεις τοῦ σώματος θανατοῦτε ζήσεσθε.

«For if you live according to the flesh you are going to die, but if by the Spirit you put to death the deeds of the body you will live».

---

[72] Cf. E. SCHWEIZER, «σάρξ», in *ThWNT*; A. SAND, «σάρξ», in *EWNT*.

– εἰ γὰρ κατὰ σάρκα ζῆτε. This is the protasis of the fifth conditional sentence of the subunit. Paul takes the κατὰ σάρκα ζῆν of Romans 8,12 and places it in an If-clause. As we saw in the exegesis of the previous verse, the verb refers to living in the service of sin: κατὰ σάρκα ζῆτε has nothing at all to do with life in Christ. This protasis (expressed positively) also sends the reader back to the apodosis of Romans 8,9 (expressed negatively) where Paul had affirmed ὑμεῖς δὲ οὐκ ἐστὲ ἐν σαρκί. The shift from negative to positive accentuates the antithetical argument of the whole subunit. More importantly still, the repetition of the two clauses forms an inclusion which serves to unite the subunit. This presents further evidence proving that it is better to study these six conditional sentences together as one passage.

In addition, it should be noted that the verb ζῆτε is conjugated in the second person plural, as is the case for the other verbs in Romans 8,13 (cf. μέλλετε, θανατοῦτε, ζήσεσθε). Although unexpressed, the pronoun ὑμεῖς is understood in all four cases. This personal pronoun was last used at the start of Romans 8,9, thus the repetition of the second person plural helps to reinforce the inclusion. By using «you» in the plural, Paul abandons the first person plural of the previous verse in favor of direct address aimed at the Roman congregation. He does this for the sake of ethical exhortation. Thus the apodosis serves as a fraternal warning to his fellow Christians. «If you live according to the flesh» describes conduct contrary to the gospel of Jesus Christ and action which is also opposed to God's Spirit. Such behavior can only entail deleterious results for anyone who chooses to walk this morally dangerous path. Paul next goes on to develop these detrimental effects in the conclusion of the sentence.

– μέλλετε ἀποθνήσκειν. The apodosis of the sentence clearly spells out the consequences of such self-destructive behavior: death. μέλλετε plus the infinitive represents an example of the periphrastic future[73]. It implies the near future, that the consequences of the action to be performed are in fact imminent and impending. Paul is in effect giving his brothers some very sobering advice: If you act in a way which is hostile to God, then death awaits you in the not too distant future. μέλλω appears five times in Romans and in each occurrence the Apostle uses it to express what is to happen presently. In the past, Abraham's faith was reckoned to him as righteousness; so too very soon «It is going to be (μέλλει) reckoned to us who believe in him that raised from the

---

[73] Cf. BDR § 356,3; HS § 202k, § 203c.

dead Jesus our Lord» (Rom 4,24). In other words, God will not delay in his favorable judgment towards those who believe in his Son. Paul calls Christ «the one who was to come (μέλλοντος)» (Rom 5,14) and refers to the eschatological glory of the new age as «the glory that is to be revealed (τὴν μέλλουσαν δόξαν) to us» (Rom 8,18). Lastly, the Apostle assures his readers that neither «things present, nor things to come (μέλλοντα)» (Rom 8,38) will separate us from God's love in Christ Jesus. In all these instances, Paul envisions events that are to occur very soon. These references reveal that for him, the not yet dimension of the new age will soon be quickly fulfilled.

The verb ἀποθνῄσκω has forty occurrences in the genuine Pauline letters, twenty-three of which are found in Romans. As with the verb «to live», the verb «to die» is employed by Paul in the literal and figurative senses. Before deciding how Paul uses the word in Romans 8,13, we must first examine the other occurrences in the letter.

ἀποθνῄσκω can mean «to expire», to pass from this physical life; Paul uses the verb in this literal sense seventeen times. When referring to Christ's death on the cross, Paul uses ἀποθνῄσκω literally: «While we were still weak, at the right time Christ died for the ungodly. Indeed, one will hardly die for a righteous person, though perhaps for a good person one will dare even to die. But God shows his love for us in that while we were yet sinners Christ died for us» (Rom 5,6-8). Other examples of ἀποθνῄσκω used in reference to Jesus' physical death may be found in Romans 6,9. 10 (twice); 8,34; 14,9. 15.

ἀποθνῄσκειν also refers to the physical cessation of life when Paul demonstrates the effects of universal death on humanity: «But the free gift is not like the trespass. For if many died through one man's trespass, much more have the grace of God and the free gift in the grace of that one man Jesus Christ abounded for many» (Rom 5,15). The verb is also used literally when Paul explains that a widow is not bound to the law: «if her husband dies she is discharged from the law concerning the husband [...] if her husband dies she is free from that law and if she marries another man she is not an adulteress» (Rom 7,2-3).

The last four examples of the literal meaning occur in the hortatory section of the letter. When exhorting the Romans not to pass judgment on their neighbor, the Apostle speaks in a general way about any one's death: «None of us lives to himself and none of us dies to himself. If we live, we live to the Lord and if we die, we die to the Lord; so then, whether we live or whether we die, we are the Lord's» (Rom 14,7-8).

ἀποθνήσκωcan also be used figuratively, however. Given the soteriological categories of life and death, the figurative sense is far more significant for the Apostle. When Paul explains how a Christian shares in Christ's salvific death, he employs the verb in the sacramental sense: «How can we who died to sin still live in it?» (Rom 6,2) and «For he who has died is freed from sin. But if we have died with Christ, we believe that we shall also live with him» (Rom 6,7-8). Paul also uses ἀποθνήσκω in a figurative sense to describe a Christian's freedom from the law: «But now we are discharged from the law, having died to that which held us captive, so that we serve in the newness of the Spirit and not under the old written code» (Rom 7,6). Lastly, the verb retains its figurative sense when Paul speaks of his own death due to the presence of sin dwelling in him: «then I died and the commandment which promised life proved to be death to me» (Rom 7,10). Paul is of course still physically alive, but he is dead in as much as he is held captive by sin and the commandments of the law.

We may now return to the use of ἀποθνήσκειν in Romans 8,13. Is it used literally or figuratively? Given the eschatological background to the passage and the fact that Paul has just referred to life in the flesh, ἀποθνήσκειν could only have the figurative sense here. Life lived in hostility to God leads to death, namely, estrangement from God. Everyone, even those who have received the Spirit, will one day experience his physical death. But for those who refuse to give witness to the Spirit's presence in their lives, the future holds no promise of God's company.

– εἰ δὲ πνεύματι τὰς πράξεις τοῦ σώματος θανατοῦτε. This represents the protasis of the subunit's sixth and final conditional sentence. By placing the noun πνεύματι at the start of the clause, Paul emphasizes yet again the Spirit's action: it is «by the Spirit» that Christians are able to live ethical lives which are pleasing to God. Only «by the Spirit» will believers be able to share in the blessings of the new age inaugurated by Christ's death and resurrection. πνεύματι is an example of the dative of cause[74]. πνεύματι functions in the clause as a modifier of the verb θανατοῦτε. This noun was last used in the dative in the first clause of Romans 8,9 and so yet again the Apostle is sending the reader back to the start of the subunit. In 8,10 Paul had said «the Spirit is life». Now in 8,13, however, it is «by the Spirit» that one kills the deeds of the body. Why this paradoxical change? The Apostle is clearly making a rhetorical

---

[74] Cf. ZERWICK § 58; BDR § 195f; HS § 177.

choice of terms that creates a wonderful play on words. The Spirit gives life and yet also puts to death those actions which are contrary to God's will. That the source of life is able to kill something creates an striking contradiction for the Romans to ponder.

The next task at hand is an examination of θανατοῦτε. The verb is conjugated in the present indicative, thus stressing the continuous, ongoing nature of the action to be done. θανατόω, means «to kill», «to put to death», and it has eleven occurrences in the New Testament[75]. Paul uses it four times in his letters. The verb is used in the literal sense once when the Apostle describes the mortal dangers he has faced: «as dying and behold we live; as punished and yet not killed» (2Cor 6,9). The other three occurrences are used figuratively. In Romans 8,36, when Paul quotes the LXX of Psalm 43,23, he is alluding to perseverance in the face of evil: «For your sake we are being killed all the day long». θανατόω is used in the figurative sense earlier in the letter. Paul teaches his addressees that, in light of their baptism, «Likewise, my brothers, you have died (literally: been killed) to the law through the body of Christ» (Rom 7,4). Thus Paul understands their death sacramentally: their former self has now been killed thanks to their union with Christ. Lastly, when we consider the verb in Romans 8,13, it too is also used in the figurative sense. «εἰ[...] θανατοῦτε» could either be translated as «If you put to death» or «If you kill». What Paul means is that the Romans must mortify or cease doing τὰς πράξεις τοῦ σώματος.

The object of the verb is τὰς πράξεις τοῦ σώματος. What does Paul mean by «the deeds of the body»? The noun πρᾶξις means «act», «action», «deed», «function», and it occurs only six times in the New Testament[76]. There are only two occurrence in Paul's genuine letters and both of them are in Romans. In the hortatory section of the letter, Paul says: «For as in one body we have many members and all the members do not have the same function (πρᾶξιν)» (Rom 12,4). In 8,13, however, τὰς πράξεις is better translated as «the deeds of the body». The σῶμα still refers to the physical body, as it does throughout the Pauline corpus, but we must decide if Paul is talking about the body that is influenced by the flesh or the body that is influenced by the Spirit.

First we have to note that τὰς πράξεις τοῦ σώματος is the object of the verb. With this in mind, we conclude that it takes its meaning from the verb.

---

[75] Cf. R. BULTMANN, «θανατόω», in *ThWNT*; W. BIEDER, «θανατόω», in *EWNT*.
[76] Cf. C. MAURER, «πρᾶξις», in *ThWNT*; G. SCHNEIDER, «πρᾶξις», in *EWNT*.

Notice closely the syntax of this verse: τοῦ σώματος immediately precedes θανατοῦτε. Obviously for Paul, the concept of body and the concept of death are being closely connected here. Where else in the letter did he juxtapose these two words before? The answer can be found at the end of chapter seven when Paul cried out, «Wretched man that I am! Who will deliver me from this body of death (ἐκ τοῦ σώματος τοῦ θανάτου τούτου;)?» (Rom 7,24). Is this «body of death» under the influence of the flesh or the Spirit? Given the context, the obvious answer is the flesh and that is also what Paul understands by «body» here in Romans 8,13. «The deeds of the body» of death refer to those actions that are still influenced by the powers of the world which lead to death and are at enmity with God. Since every living human being is still influenced by sin in this world, Paul exhorts the Romans to kill the evil deeds that are committed by the body under the influence of the flesh[77]. But how then is this to be achieved? Ethical action in the new eschatological age can only be done «by the Spirit». Only «by the Spirit» (Rom 8,13) then can the Christian follow Christ as he lives out his call of discipleship in a still hostile and evil world.

– ζήσεσθε. The apodosis of the final conditional sentence is composed of one word: ζήσεσθε. This verb is used figuratively to refer to the final resurrection of the dead and to express the fullness of eschatological living. With it, the subunit comes to an end with a strong emphasis on the theme of eternal life, the end result of life in the Spirit. God, who is infinitely righteousness, now makes us righteous through the Spirit who dwells in us (Rom 8,11). In this chapter on the indwelling Spirit, Paul brings to completion the task he had set for himself at the beginning of Romans: Ὁ δὲ δίκαιος ἐκ πίστεως ζήσεται «the one who is righteous will live by faith» (Rom 1,17).

---

[77] «Thus, "put to death the deeds of the body" means "put to death the deeds worked out through the body under the influence of the flesh". For the body as the instrument, or outward organ, of sin, we may note Rom 6,13.19; II Cor 5,10; and for the body as the place where sin materially manifests itself, Rom 7,5.23 (cf. I Cor 6,20). "Body" then retains its usual sense and no shift in its meaning occurs between verses 10-11 and verses 12-13. Moreover, the parallel between "the body is dead" and "put to death the deeds of the body" breaks down in that it is the *deeds* of the body, not the body itself, which are to be put to death. The reason for the difference is that the Holy Spirit dwells within the body and will raise it at the resurrection. Hence, only its deeds done under the influence of the "flesh" become the object of mortification» (R.H. GUNDRY, *Sōma*, 39).

– A few comments on Romans 8,13 considered as a whole are now in order. The two conditional sentences which make up the verse are fine examples of antithetical parallelism. They represent the two moral paths which every human being may choose to follow: one leads to life, the other to death. Paul shows his strict attachment to his Jewish heritage in this clear allusion to the teaching of the Torah.

> See, I have set before you this day life and good, death and evil. If you obey the commandments of the Lord your God which I command you this day, by loving the Lord your God, by walking in his ways and by keeping his commandments and his statutes and his ordinances, then you shall live (וְחָיִיתָ ζήσεσθε)[78] and multiply and the Lord your God will bless you in the land which you are entering to take possession of it (Deut. 30,15-16).

The Jewish image of walking in God's ways means to conduct oneself in a way that is morally pleasing to God. The one who walks in God's ways obeys God's will. In Romans 8,4 Paul had already used this metaphor when he said, «in us, who walk not according to the flesh but according to the Spirit (μὴ κατὰ σάρκα περιπατοῦσιν ἀλλὰ κατὰ πνεῦμα)». We have already seen how the flesh/Spirit antithesis dominates Romans 8,5-9. The fact that it reemerges in 8,13 is rather telling. For a Christian, the presence of the Spirit by itself is not sufficient to guarantee correct ethical behavior. The Apostle recognizes that the flesh still manages to influence the believer in this life by drawing him away from God and into its own negative sphere of influence. For this reason, the believer must consciously cooperate with the Spirit and act «by the Spirit» (πνεύματι in Rom 8,13 is an example of the instrumental dative), in order to do what is morally pleasing to God.

The Apostle of course was not the first to formulate such an antithetical argument. The Qumran sect had earlier drawn a sharp distinction between the sons of light and the sons of darkness. Their Community Rule in fact speaks of the conflict between the spirit of light and the spirit of darkness[79]. The

---

[78] Note that the verb is conjugated in the second person singular in Hebrew and in the second person plural in Greek.

[79] The famous passage of the two spirits may be found in 1QS 3.13-23. The language of this part of the Community Rule resembles that of Paul's in Romans 8,1-13.

1QS 3.18-21: «He has created man to govern the world and has appointed for him two spirits in which to walk until the time of his visitation: the spirits of truth and falsehood. Those born of truth spring from a fountain of light, but those born of falsehood spring from

Qumran community realized full well that in the present life both opposing spirits influence the believer who seeks righteousness. Thus for this ascetical group in the Judean desert, only a stricter application of the law could insure proper ethical conduct in this life and eternal life in the next. Only by walking according to the Mosaic law could the righteous Jew at Qumran hope to find the way to everlasting salvation.

Paul, however, clearly viewed the experience of the Spirit in quite a different way. For him, there are not two spirits, but only one: the Holy Spirit. It is the Spirit alone who allows Christians to live according to God's will and walk in ways that are pleasing to him. The Apostle was firmly convinced that Christians had been liberated from the law and its constraints through faith in Jesus Christ. For him, the Holy Spirit represents the power by which Christians could live a morally upright life in the present and be assured of eternal life in the future. The hymn to God's love at the end of Romans 8 demonstrates that

---

a source of darkness. All the children of righteousness are ruled by the Prince of Light and walk in the ways of light, but all the children of falsehood are ruled by the Angel of Darkness and walk in the ways of darkness».

1QS 4.6-18: «And as for the visitation of all who walk in this spirit, it shall be healing, great peace in a long life and fruitfulness, together with every everlasting blessing and eternal joy in life without end, a crown of glory and a garment of majesty in unending light.

But the ways of the spirit of falsehood are these: greed and slackness in the search for righteousness, wickedness and lies, haughtiness and pride, falseness and deceit, cruelty and abundant evil, ill-temper and much folly and brazen insolence, abominable deeds (committed) in a spirit of lust and ways of lewdness in the service of uncleanness, a blaspheming tongue, blindness of eye and dullness of ear, stiffness of neck and heaviness of heart, so that man walks in all the ways of darkness and guile.

And the visitation of all who walk in this spirit shall be a multitude of plagues by the hand of all the destroying angels, everlasting damnation by the avenging wrath of the fury of God, eternal torment and endless disgrace together with shameful extinction in the fire of the dark regions. The times of all their generations shall be spent in sorrowful mourning and in bitter misery and in calamities of darkness until they are destroyed without remnant or survivor.

The nature of all the children of the men is ruled by these (two spirits) and during their life all the hosts of men have a portion of their divisions and walk in (both) their ways. And the whole reward for their deeds shall be, for everlasting ages, according to whether each man's portion in their two divisions is great or small. For God has established the spirits in equal measure until the final age and has set everlasting hatred between their divisions. Truth abhors the works of falsehood and falsehood hates all the ways of truth. And their struggle is fierce in all their arguments for they do not walk together» (G. VERMES, *The Dead Sea Scrolls*, 64-66).

all the hostile forces of this age have been vanquished by Christ's sacrificial death and glorious resurrection. Hence the flesh/Spirit antithesis belongs only to the present, passing age. In the future, at the time when eschatological glory «is to be revealed to us» (Rom 8,18), Christians will enjoy «the glorious liberty of the children of God» (Rom 8,21). The Spirit of sonship, already present in the hearts of all believers, represents God's pledge that this final victory is already assured.

6. The Rhetoric of the Subunit

Throughout the exegesis of this unit, time and again we found examples of Paul's antithetical style of argumentation. His Greek prose highlights the difference between the Spirit and the flesh, life and death, as well as the already and the not yet. If at times this contrast is clearly marked by the conjunction ἀλλά, as in Romans 8,9 («You are not in the flesh *but* in the Spirit»), at others it is more compact, more condensed. That is the case for example in Romans 8,10, where Paul places μὲν-δε clauses together in order to achieve the same effect. As we have seen, the subunit ends with two conflicting possibilities in Romans 8,13, if one leads a sinful life according to the flesh, then one will die alienated from God; if, however, one leads an upright life according to the Spirit, one will live eternally with God. The Christian remains free to choose which road he will walk on his way through this life.

In this subunit the Apostle not only contrasts words and images, but he also compares clauses and sentences. As we saw above in our study of 1 Corinthians 15, this stylistic phenomenon is called parallelism[80]. Grammarians in fact recognize that there are in fact three different kinds of parallelism: antithetical, synonymous and mixed. We may add a fourth to the list if we keep in mind that in Romans 8,12 the parallelism remains unfinished. Let us now take a closer look at this data, proceeding verse by verse.

Romans 8,9 is a concise example of mixed parallelism. It is antithetical in as much as the Apostle contrasts the flesh to the Spirit. It is synonynous, however, since he also insists that the God's Spirit is the same as the Christ's Spirit. In addition, the four clauses which compose the verse form a chiasm, another common stylistic phenomenon in Paul[81]. The form of the two sentences

---

[80] Cf. BDR § 485, § 489-490; HS § 294z-bb.
[81] Cf. BDR § 477; HS § 294cc.

presents an A-B-B´-A´ pattern in as much as the apodosis is represented in A and A´ and the protasis in B and B´.

Be paying close attention to the structure of conditional sentences, we also observed how the apodosis in Romans 8,10 is composed of two μὲν-δε clauses. Set so closely together in this way, these clauses provide an excellent example of antithetical parallelism. In a concise yet marvellous way, Paul compares the body to the Spirit, death to life and sin to righteousness. In short, with just twelve words, Paul manages to portray the seemingly boundless chasm which separates the human from the divine, a gulf which nevertheless has been definitivley bridged by God through the Spirit who dwells in the human body.

In contrast to vv. 9-10, the two clauses of Romans 8,11 offer a beautiful example of synonymous parallelism. The protasis speaks of «the Spirit of the one who raised Jesus from the dead», while the apodosis begins with «the one who raised Christ from the dead». The repitition serves to underscore the importance of the Father's initiative in the resurrection of the dead. Moreover, the Apostle begins by claiming the «the Spirit of [God] dwells in you», and concludes by insisting that the resurrection will occur «through his [Christ's] Spirit who dwells in you». The discord of the previous verses has been replaced by consonance and unity. The Spirit of God, who is indeed the Spirit of Christ, at last finds a secure home in the hearts of believers. The human and the divine are now at peace with one another. The harmony between God, Christ, the Spirit and believers in v.11 underscores Paul's insistence on God's ultimate victory over their common enemies, namely, sin and death.

Turning next to Romans 8,12, we already remarked in the close reading that this verse is incomplete. For this reason it can be considered an example of unfinished parallelism. Paul in fact returns to a rather negative tone when he writes, «not to the flesh, to live accrding to the flesh». The reader is left to complete the sentence on his own with a more positive conclusion, something like, «but to the Spirit, to live according to the Spirit». This was no doubt so clear to Paul that he found it utterly unnecessary to even state it. If he had, however, it would have represented an example of antithetical parallelism, thus serving as yet another contrast to the symmetry of v. 11.

Lastly, Romans 8,13 draws the subunit to a close with another example of antithetical parallelism. Each conditional sentence provides an opposing possibility. In the first, life according to the flesh leads to death, while in the second, life according to the Spirit leads to eternal life. Moreover, the Apostle ends this section with another chiasm, just as he had begun with one in

Romans 8,9. We recognize an A-B-B′-A′ pattern in as much as the first and fourth clauses speak of life, while the second and third speak of death.

In conclusion, Paul is quite capable of expressing the many delicate nuances and intricate subtleties which distinguish his theological, christological, pneumatological and ethical teaching by means of his complex yet compact style. Through the use of parallelism and chiasm, the Apostle presents his impassioned message of Good News to his addressees in a way that does justice to the complex themes and principal ideas of his thought. His remarkable Greek prose beautifully conveys the salvific content of the apostolic message he preaches «to all God's beloved in Rome, who are called to be saints» (Rom 1,7).

CHAPTER VI

Theological Reflections on Rom 8,9-13

1. The Bondage of Sin and Death

In the close reading of Romans 8,10, we spent a great deal of time wrestling with the verbless clause «although the body [was, is, will be] dead because of sin». We concluded that Paul left the verb unexpressed on purpose in order to foster a variety of possible interpretations. By modifying the verb tense in this way, we are able to focus on the effects of sin and death in the past, present, as well as the future and thereby come to appreciate better the adjective «dead» in its figurative as well as literal senses. In light of these findings, this brief essay seeks to develop Paul's understanding of the bondage of sin and death. In particular, we shall investigate the metaphorical sense of the clause «the body is dead because of sin» in light of some recent discoveries from the growing field of wellness and recovery. Before we turn to these rather contemporary considerations, however, we must first examine Paul's argumentation in this critical section of the letter more closely. How does the wider context, especially when considered in light of the contrast between chapters seven and eight, help us to understand the important issues that are at stake here?

In Romans 7 and 8 Paul uses an ancient rhetorical device called «αὔξησις» or «amplificatio». It is a kind of argumentation marked by the gradual increase of proofs and figures of speech so as to exaggerate and overstate the author's point[1]. The striking contrast between the two chapters is summed up in 8,2,

---

[1] «Accrescimento delle prove o delle figure, mediante il quale si perviene ad una maggiore adesione al messaggio» (A. PITTA, *Disposizione e messaggio della lettera ai Galati*, 222).

«For the law of the Spirit of life in Christ Jesus has set me free from the law of sin and death». In this critical verse, Paul opposes the Spirit to sin in especially sharp terms. Yet again we note the Apostle's antithetical reasoning as he paints a striking contrast between the forces of life and death at work in human beings[2].

In chapter seven, Paul deals with the relation of the law to sin; although it is good and spiritual, the law cannot save. The Apostle insists especially on the destructive power of sin and death through the frequent recurrences of the words ἁμαρτία (fifteen times) and θάνατος (five times). The repetition of these two key terms amplifies the negative tone of the argument and serves to underscore the painful condition of bondage which leads Paul to cry out «Wretched man that I am! Who will deliver me from this body of death?» (Rom 7,24). Paul forcefully exaggerates his point so that his addressees could not possibly doubt the power of the destructive forces which once held them completely captive.

In chapter eight the Apostle develops the other side of the antithesis by focusing on the Spirit and the new life which he brings. Here Paul insists on the liberating agency of the πνεῦμα (twenty-one times) and how it represents ζωή (four times) for those who believe. The repetition of these two key terms amplifies the positive tone of the argument and serves to emphasize the joyful condition of «the glorious liberty of the children of God» (Rom 8,21). The Apostle underscores his point in a powerful way so that his addressees could embrace the Good News of their own liberation. To this end, chapter eight outlines a very moving description of the Christian's ongoing journey towards more profound eschatological freedom. Thanks to the Spirit's presence in his mind and body, the believer is now empowered to live the spiritual life in this world. Hoping for what he does not yet see, he longs for the fullest expression of life in the Spirit when on the last day «he who raised Christ Jesus from the dead will give life to your mortal bodies also through his Spirit who dwells in you» (Rom 8,11). Thus Paul's gospel reveals itself for what it is: the Good News of eternal life for those who believe.

In these two contrasting chapters, therefore, Paul has laid out the principal routes of two very different and opposing itineraries. Sin and death lead human beings to captivity, since the law is powerless to save them; in contrast, the

---

[2] In fact the contrast between death and life is characteristic of this entire section of the letter. Cf. Rom 5,10.17.21; 6,4.10-11.23; 7,10; 8,2.6.10 and 8,13.

Spirit of God leads Christians to salvation by guiding them out of their slavery towards a new, fuller life in freedom. In this way, the Apostle implies that bondage can only be recognized as such after an experience of spiritual liberation. Only after the fact can one look back and see just how far one has come in one's journey towards more genuine eschatological life. It is usually only later on, after a significant conversion event, that one can recognize enslavement for what it is and thereby realize the full extent of one's previous imprisonment to the powers of sin and death. «To set the mind on the flesh is death, but to set the mind on the Spirit is life and peace» (Rom 8,6). Thus for the Apostle, the Spirit empowers the Christian to walk his spiritual path in communion with other believers so as to grow in deeper, more authentic joy, peace and freedom. This genuine eschatological freedom will reach its completeness at the resurrection of the dead when Christ returns in glory.

Now that we have examined the wider context in this section of the letter, we are presently in a good position to reconsider Paul's assertion in Romans 8,10. As we noted in the exegesis of this verse, the Apostle is clearly dealing here with living Christians, his addressees in the Roman Church. Nevertheless, in spite of the fact that these believers are in Christ and Christ is in them, they still experience in a very real way the pernicious destruction caused by sin in their lives. It seems clear that Paul is alluding to sin's harmful effects in the clause «although the body is dead because of sin» So what then does the Apostle suggest when he speaks of the human body which, for all intents and purposes, experiences death while it is still very much alive? Although he did not use this expression, we may rephrase the question by asking: Who are these «living dead» for the Apostle, how are they different from the «truly alive», and what are the symptoms of their condition? In Paul's remarkable outline of the eschatological journey towards freedom in the Spirit, we can glimpse what many people today would describe as a spiritual journey out of the bondage of addiction. To help us better understand some of the important issues at stake, we shall now consider some contemporary insights into the phenomenon of addiction as well as the path to wholeness undertaken by many in recovery[3].

---

[3] Over the last few years, scores of books have been published in the area of addiction and recovery, a growing field for anyone interested in wellness and spiritual wholeness. Although it is not possible to give a detailed bibliography here, the following books have helped tremendously in the writing of these reflections. For the experience, strength and hope described by recovering addicts, cf. *Alcoholics Anonymous* and also A.A.'s *Twelve*

Although he did not name it as such, Paul was very familiar with the reality of addictions, his own and those of others. Many recovering addicts readily relate to his words in Romans: «For I do not do the good I want, but the evil I do not want is what I do. Now if I do what I do not want, it is no longer I that do it, but sin which dwells within me» (Rom 7,19-20). This represents an extraordinary description of an addict struggling with his own obsessive-compulsive behavior: he consistently gives in to the evil he does not want to do. Although a part of his will truly wishes not to perform the addiction, another part is incapable of preventing the self-destructive behavior. In other words, he is completely powerless to stop himself. As a result, he does it again and again, whatever the «it» may happen to be and most often with harmful, if not lethal, results. Therefore an addiction is by definition anything that a particular addict is powerless over. If he could stop the obsessive-compulsive pattern, then he would not be an addict at all[4].

Although there is still a great deal of debate over the causes of addiction, many therapists are pointing to unhealthy parenting and child abuse as one of the leading causes. The child who grows up in a dysfunctional home feels unloved and isolated. He feels socially awkward and experiences a general sense of dissatisfaction with himself and the world at large. He is disconnected with himself and his surroundings and comes to analyze, rationalize and judge others as a matter of habit. Since he is unable to generate his own self-esteem

---

Steps and Twelve Traditions, as well as the basic text of the Augustine Fellowship, *Sex and Love Addicts Anonymous*, for the connection between abusive parenting, codependency and addictions, cf. M. BEATTIE, *Codependent No More*, P. MELODY – A.W. MILLER – J.K. MILLER, *Facing Codependence*, ID., *Facing Love Addiction*, A. MILLER, *The Drama of the Gifted Child* and ID., *For Your Own Good*; for remarkable insights into healthy and dysfunctional families, cf. J. BRADSHAW, *Bradshaw on: The Family* and ID., *Healing the Shame that Binds You*; for moving portrayals of the spiritual dimension of recovery, cf. J.A. MARTIN, *Blessed are the Addicts*, G. MAY, *Addiction and Grace* and ID., *The Awakened Heart*; and lastly, for recent articles that examine the connection between addiction, recovery and the Bible, cf. D. MCLAIN MASSEY, «Addiction and Spirituality», 9-18 and W.E. OATES, «A Biblical Perspective on Addiction», 71-75.

[4] «Addiction exists wherever persons are internally compelled to give energy to things that are not their true desires. To define it directly, addiction is a *state* of compulsion, obsession, or preoccupation that enslaves a person's will and desire. Addiction sidetracks and eclipses the energy of our deepest, truest desire for love and goodness. We succumb because the energy of our desire becomes attached, nailed, to specific behaviors, objects, or people. *Attachment*, then, is the process that enslaves desire and creates the state of addiction» (G. MAY, *Addiction and Grace*, 14).

from the inside, the child or adolescent desperately longs for approval from outside. He desperately seeks esteem, reassurance and encouragement from others. Although he continues to grow physically, his emotional and spiritual sides have been severely stunted. Perfectionism, procrastination and paralysis represent some of the worst symptoms of nascent addiction in the life of the growing child and adolescent. Unable to cope with reality in a healthy way, the child learns to shut down all his feelings and, by doing so, withdraws into his own little world which at first seems far easier to control.

The consequence of all this confusion and dysfunction for the addict-to-be is a great deal of pain and uneasiness. His discomfort becomes so extreme over time that he will do anything to lessen the sting of his suffering and distress. He will go to any lengths in order to assuage his angst. When Paul wrote «The sting of death is sin» (1Cor 15,56), he brilliantly captured this existential anguish experienced by the suffering individual in a dysfunctional family, organization, or society. He uses the metaphor of a scorpion to express his point: death lurks in the shadows, ever ready to sting its unexpecting prey. He injects a toxic venom into his victim, a substance which drugs the body and eventually causes a slow, painful death. For the Apostle, this poisonous substance is sin and its effects are always lethal. The body will eventually die, but it first comes to experience a kind of semi-death under the sphere of the flesh. In great anguish Paul cries out, «Wretched human that I am! Who will deliver me from this body of death?» (Rom 7,24).

The addict-to-be brings his pain and loneliness with him as he ages, first into adolescence and then into young adulthood. Through the years, he desperately continues his search for the answers that will save him from his living hell, his own «body of death». Sooner or later, alone or with others, he comes to discover what he believes to be the real response to all his questions, the true solution to life's difficulties. He has at last found the drug(s) of his choice. But unbeknownst to the poor suffering person, what a cruel deception lies in wait for him instead! It is at this point in his life that the individual becomes a full-fledged addict[5]. For a while, his addiction(s) soothes the terrible existential dis-

---

[5] «Because virtually anything in life can become an object of attachment, it is especially important to remember that there is a big difference between having strong feelings about something and really being addicted to it. The difference is freedom. We care deeply about many things and abhor many others, but with most of these we remain free to choose the depth and extent of our investment. They do not become gods. Remember, then, that true addictions are compulsive habitual behaviors that eclipse our concern for God and

ease festering in him, yet bit by bit they gradually come to enslave him. Some addictions lessen pain, while others augment pleasure. Some addictions spring from substance abuse (e.g., alcohol and drugs) while others represent the distortion of healthy human behavior (e.g., compulsive overeating, or sex and love addiction). Some addictions are down right deadly, as any heroin addict could attest, while others, like biting one's finger nails, could even be considered basically harmless to most people. Some are socially acceptable, (e.g., people pleasing, workaholism, compulsive shopping), some have recently become legalized by society (e.g., adult pornography or gambling), some are still unmentionable in polite company (e.g. bulimia and anorexia nervosa), while others remain severely sanctioned by society (e.g., child pornography or the frequenting of prostitutes). Regardless of the kind of addiction, however, an insidious process is always at work in the individual concerned: he completely gives himself over to the obsessive-compulsive behavior, thereby losing his soul in the process. Nothing else in life matters to him now but the drink, the adult book store, the slot machine, or the love relationship[6].

The addiction gradually and inexorably comes to take over the entire life of the addict. Over time, slowly or quickly, the addict can no longer manage his own life, whether he admits it or not. He effectively has handed the control of his life over to the given substance or behavior. Obsession and compulsion inevitably become his cruel, heartless masters. He is now hooked and hooked good, so much so that his dependency to the drug(s) of choice completely dominates his present situation. Nothing else matters to him but doing or getting «it». To complicate matters even further, one of the sure hallmarks of addiction is denial. In a dysfunctional family or community, the alcoholic

---

compromise our freedom and that they must be characterized by tolerance, withdrawal symptoms, loss of willpower and distortion of attention» (G. MAY, *Addiction and Grace*, 37).

[6] According to May, there are two kinds of addictions: attraction and aversion addictions, depending if they draw us towards or away from any given person, thing, or behavior. After presenting a rather informative and straightforward list which gives numerous examples of both kinds of addictions, May then summarizes the data. «*No* addiction is good, *no* attachment is beneficial. To be sure, some are more destructive than others; alcoholism cannot be compared with chocolate addiction in degrees of destructiveness and fear of spiders in comparison to racial bigotry. But if we accept that there are differences in the degree of tragedy imposed upon us by our addictions, we must also recognize what they have in common: they impede human freedom and diminish the human spirit» (G. MAY, *Grace and Addiction*, 39).

always seems to be the last to acknowledge his disease. It is quite typical that the addict resolutely refuses to admit or do something about his pathetic condition, denying that he even has a problem.

How does the addict experience all of this chaos? Some addicts describe their addictive behavior as «acting out». Since the addict is in fact dead emotionally as well as spiritually, he «acts out» in order to give himself a fleeting sense of feeling alive. But inevitably when the drug wears off or when the high has passed, he returns to his previous deadened state, even worse off than he was before. And so the vicious circle continues, because since he will do anything to avoid his pain, he feels compelled to «act out» yet again. In this horrible way, the addiction feeds on itself, consuming the addict in the process. This is why all serious addictions, if remained untreated, become fatal. They inevitably lead to premature death for the addict unless his addiction is arrested.

It matters little for the victim what the given addiction, or pattern of dependency, happens to be. After a certain period of time, the addict finally experiences so much pain and desperation that he feels himself on the verge of going out of his mind. Recovering addicts often describe the prospect of losing their souls (yet all the while remaining trapped in their bodies) as even more frightening than the possibility of physical death. What is left is a kind of zombie-like existence: the addict's body is ruthlessly controlled by the addictive substance or behavior, while the addict's soul remains completely paralyzed, unable to animate the body spiritually from within. This is a horrendous kind of living death which eventually devours the individual concerned and all to often, the relatives and friends who love him.

The good news in all of this horror is that there is in fact hope for recovery. Help for the addict usually comes in one of two ways: either there is an «intervention» (namely, when the friends and loved ones of the addict confront him on his self-destructive behavior and thereby help him to get into recovery), or the addict «hits bottom» (namely, when the addict himself realizes that his life has become unmanageable and thereby gets into recovery on his own). Only once one of these has happened can the addict begin to live his life in a sound and healthy way.

In light of these significant insights into addiction, we are now in a good position to bring this information to our study of Paul's description of the bondage of sin and death. Do we have any proof that the Apostle knew about obsessive-compulsive behavior? Many of his letters certainly attest to an intense struggle with his own weaknesses and failings, as well as those of his fellow believers. Although we would look in vain for the word «addiction» in any of Paul's letters, nevertheless the Apostle certainly was able to describe the phenomenon as he witnessed it both in himself and in others. As we noted above, his own description of the war that rages between the law of his mind and the law of sin represents a brilliant portrayal of addictive reasoning and behavior (Rom 7,13-25).

Certainly one way of describing this law of sin is to understand it in light of the merciless rule of addiction. Addicts often describe the struggle raging in their minds as a kind of all out war. The battle inside them presupposes a divided will, a common symptom which therapists look for when diagnosing the presence of addiction. For example, one part of the alcoholic's will truly desires to remain sober, while another part truly desires to drink again. One part of the gambler's will really wants to stop gambling, while the other part cannot wait to throw the dice again, hoping that this time he will really strike it big. In the end the compulsion to drink or gamble always wins out, controlling yet again the alcoholic or gambler who still suffers. The addict becomes so attached to the bottle and the dice that he turns them into false gods and worships them. Everything else, everyone else, is cast aside and considered unworthy of his time, attention and consideration.

This in fact is a definition of idolatry, a practice common in the ancient world and one that was very familiar to Paul, thanks to his many travels around the Roman Empire. With regard to the sins of the Gentiles, the Apostle considered idolatry to be their gravest transgression against the laws of God and nature. «Claiming to be wise, they became fools and exchanged the glory of the immortal God for images resembling mortal man or birds or animals or reptiles» (Rom 1,22-23). Given the fact that the addict exchanges the glory of God for the high he gets from his particular drug or behavior, surely addiction can be considered as a particular example of idol worship. The addict replaces the true, living God, who alone is worthy of worship, for an endless supply of natural or man-made substitutes. Placing them on the altar of his disordered desires, he bows down and pays them tribute and homage at the cost of his life.

Exegetes have debated for centuries over the meaning of Paul's famous «thorn in the flesh» (2Cor 12,7). Although no one will ever really be certain, could it not be an allusion to a bothersome addiction that kept tormenting him? Gerald May is convinced that this is the case[7]. Sooner or later, addictions teach

---

[7] See G. MAY, *Grace and Addiction*, 20.

us that we are not self-sufficient and all powerful as we had once mistakenly believed. In their own painful and distressing way, addictions reveal the fact that no one can go it alone in this life; everyone needs to live in fellowship with others and most especially, with the one true God who is the unique source of serenity, courage and wisdom.

By working through their addictions, countless people over the centuries have been deeply moved by the sufficiency of God's grace. In particular, the first group of recovering alcoholics gathered together for the sake of their recovery from alcoholism in the 1930's. The now world-famous Twelve Steps were originally formulated by Bill W., one of the co-founders of Alcoholics Anonymous. It is only once the alcoholic has accepted his powerlessness over alcohol that he can take the first step toward recovery. This seemingly contradictory dynamic is essential for all who wish to stop engaging in compulsive behavior. For the still-suffering addict, the acceptance of his own powerlessness at first represents a great paradox. Has he not already been wallowing in his powerlessness all his life? Yet to those who grasp the concept and put it into practice, it summarizes the mystery of the Twelve Step program. For this reason «Let Go and Let God» represents a favorite A.A. slogan.

The recovering alcoholics of our age have come upon a spiritual truth already known to many holy men and women throughout the ages. Paul clearly seems to have grasped it as well. It is only when we accept our own weakness and powerlessness that we can truly make room for God in our lives. It is interesting to note that people in recovery often refer to God as «a Higher Power», i.e., a power that is both greater than themselves and greater than their addiction. For the Apostle and for all Christians, that divine power is of course Jesus Christ, the Son of God. It is Christ alone who is able to come to the aid of the still suffering addict and restore him to sanity. With the help of a grace that truly amazes him, the recovering addict comes to rejoice in the fact that God can truly heal his divided will and really stop him from drinking (or gambling or smoking, etc.).

Although Paul did not use the term addiction in naming this spiritual disease (as we saw above, «idolatry» as described in Romans 1 comes closest in meaning), nevertheless he did perceive that their was a spiritual cure for the condition. He firmly believed that God could save the suffering addict and deliver him from his torment. «No temptation has overtaken you that is not common to everyone. God is faithful and he will not let you be tempted beyond your strength, but with the temptation will also provide the way of escape, that you may be able to endure it» (1Cor 10,13). God alone saves the suffering addict from his addiction, providing him with a way out of his self-destructive behavior and into a saner, healthier, more spiritual life. The new-found source of life in the addict's relationship with God is his very powerlessness. That is the sublime paradox of recovery. After having struggled with much temptation, the recovering addict at last realizes that his own power has gotten him nowhere, but that God's omnipotent power can restore him to new life if he only lets him.

To sum up then, although Paul never uses the word «addiction», a word unknown in antiquity, his letters certainly attest to the presence of the phenomenon in himself, in his fellow Christians and in his society. He eloquently describes some of the symptoms of addiction, for example the divided will common to all addicts (Rom 7,13-25) as well as the obsessive activity that characterizes their behavior (2Cor 12,7-10). If he is not in recovery from this debilitating disease, the addict will remain cut-off from himself, estranged from others and truly alienated from God. For all intents and purposes, he is emotionally, psychically and spiritually dead, even though his heart still beats and his lungs still breathe. For this reason, metaphorically speaking, we can regard the addict like one already dead. And that is precisely our understanding of the figurative sense of Romans 8,10 as explained in the close reading earlier in this chapter. The clause «although the body is dead because of sin» succinctly captures the distressing reality of the addicted. Personal sin and social sin have combined to keep addicts in the chains of bondage. Without the proper help and the necessary tools for recovery, they remain the living dead in our midst.

Jesus Christ clearly understood one dimension of his saving mission in terms of ministry to the sick[8]. He had mercy on all who grappled with despair and hopelessness, but most especially on those who suffered from debilitating emotional and physical infirmities. All four evangelists describe him as a man of great empathy and compassion who possessed miraculous powers in restoring the sick to health. In their understanding of the healing process, to cure means to expel those evil spirits which overpower human beings. «That evening they brought to him many who were possessed with demons; and he cast out *the spirits* with a word and healed all who were sick» (Matt. 8,16).

---

[8] Jesus saw himself as a physician sent by God to heal the sick. Cf. Mk 2,17; Mt 9,12 and Lk 5,31.

Like the Lord Jesus before him, Paul also knew that a spiritual disease required nothing less than a spiritual cure. «If Christ is in you, although the body is dead because of sin, *the Spirit is life* because of righteousness» (Rom 8,10). Understood in light of these findings on addiction, these three clauses can be seen as a superbly balanced statement on the striking contrast between spiritual poverty and spiritual richness as attested in the addict. Paul contends that by means of a spiritual recovery, Christ is able to revive even the living dead through his Spirit who is life. Having shared in Jesus' passion and death in a very special way, recovering addicts provide moving testimony of the paschal mystery to all of us. Through their recovery, they strive, one day at a time, to bring their experience, strength and hope to others who still suffer and await the good news of their redemption.

2. The Spirit is Life

In our theological reflections on «The Life-Giving Spirit» in Chapter III, section 2, we noted that in 1 Corinthians 15,44b-49 Paul primarily develops his anthropological and pneumatological concerns with regard to the first and last Adam. In particular, we spent some time reflecting on the essential agency of the Spirit in the creation of the spiritual body. For the Apostle, it is the life-giving Spirit who divinizes human beings at the parousia by transforming them into the image of the last Adam. In a similar way, Romans 8,9-13 offers another significant opportunity to study and reflect on Paul's profound pneumatology. What does this remarkable subunit tell us about his theology of the Spirit?

It is clear that Paul's thoughts in Romans 8,9-13 are also focused on what today is called the economic Trinity, the triune God at work in the salvation of the world. The Apostle is primarily concerned with how the Spirit manifests himself by dwelling in those who believe in Christ. Yet in some way this dense and complicated subunit leaves us with far more questions than it answers. Does Paul portray the Spirit in these brief verses in a consistent way? What light does this text shed on the Spirit's relation to the Christians of Rome (and to us by extension), as well as to God and to Christ? And what does the Apostle mean by his rather cryptic clause, «the Spirit is life because of righteousness»? We begin this present inquiry by returning to our analysis of the text and by reviewing the data we amassed in the course of the word study on «Spirit».

In our close reading of the subunit, we observed the various ways in which Paul describes the πνεῦμα, referring to him as «the Spirit» (v. 9, v. 10), «the Spirit of God», «the Spirit of Christ» (v. 9), «the Spirit of the one who raised Jesus from the dead» (v. 11) and «his Spirit», i.e., Christ's Spirit (v. 11). If we study these terms more closely, we discover that in fact they fall into three different groups. The Apostle calls him 1) the Spirit, 2) God's Spirit (God understood here of course as God the Father) and 3) Christ's Spirit. It would seem then that Paul has taken the trouble to make three clear and distinct assertions about the Holy Spirit.

Given these three different ways of describing the Spirit, as well as the complex and mysterious content of Paul's teaching in these verses, how are we to account for this variety of formulations? We could conclude that Paul is very unclear in his understanding of how God, Christ and the Spirit relate to one another and thus, constrained to use obscure language, the Apostle betrays his own lack of clarity[9]. Or we could determine that Paul in some way is using synonymous existential terms to equate the Christian's experience of the risen Jesus to his experience of the Holy Spirit and that the Apostle does not really intend to make an ontological statement at all[10]. But is not another interpretation just as possible? Could we not conclude that the Apostle in fact has a very clear notion of the difference between Christ and the Spirit, how they both relate to God, to one another and to Christians and that because of this he is using these varied terms in order to do justice to the divine mystery he wishes to reveal?

---

[9] Fitzmyer speaks of «Paul's lack of clarity in his conception of the relation of the Spirit to the Son. Normally, he uses "Spirit" in the OT sense, without the later theological refinements (nature, substance and person). His lack of clarity should be respected; he provides only the starting point of later theological developments» (J.A. FITZMYER, «Pauline Theology», § 62).

[10] «The point for us is that *Paul equates the risen Jesus with the Spirit who makes alive*. He does not say that Jesus by his resurrection became a spiritual body (though this is implied in the context). He does not say that Jesus by his resurrection became a living spirit (though that would have made a better parallelism in v. 45.) He deliberately says that Jesus by his resurrection became that Spirit which believers experience as the source and power of their new life and new relationship with God. As from his resurrection Jesus may be known by men only as life-giving Spirit» (J.D.G. DUNN, *Jesus and the Spirit*, 322). For a more systematic presentation of his understanding of the relationship between Jesus and the Spirit, see ID., *Christology in the Making*, 141-149.

Our close reading of Romans 8,9-13 would justify this interpretation. We have seen on several occasions in our study of this remarkable subunit that Paul's rich theology finds its fullest expression in the juxtaposition of seemingly different terms and phrases[11]. This stylistic feature does not impoverish his thought; rather, it greatly enriches it. Thus it would seem more logical to infer from the data that Paul employs three different ways to describe the Spirit because the Spirit should be considered in three different ways. If this in fact is true, how then do we interpret Paul's teaching in this subunit?

First, the Apostle refers to him simply as «the Spirit» in order to confirm his unique and particular existence. There is indeed a divine Spirit who dwells in believers and acts in them and that this Spirit, although intimately related to God and Christ, is in fact different from them. Second, the Spirit is not just anyone's Spirit; by defining him as God's Spirit, Paul links the Spirit to his divine source and tells us from whom he receives his authority and power, namely, God himself. In this way Paul firmly grounds himself in the tradition of the Old Testament by perceiving the Spirit as God's dynamic power at work in creation. Thus for Paul, the Holy Spirit clearly has his origins in the depths of God. And third, Paul teaches that this unique Spirit who is God's Spirit is truly the same as «Christ's Spirit» — there are not two different spirits for the Christian since there is only one Spirit. In this way the Apostle provides another glimpse into how the Spirit comes to us. The Father does not impart the Spirit directly; rather, God pours forth his Spirit into the hearts of believers only through his Son, Jesus Christ. That is why the Spirit of God is now christologically known to us and fittingly called «Christ's Spirit».

In light of this overview of the subunit, we can return to Romans 8,10 and appreciate better what Paul reveals there. The Apostle is clearly teaching that it is this one Spirit, who at the same time is both the Spirit of God and the Spirit of Christ, who is «life because of righteousness». At this point in the

---

[11] This is also supported from our findings in the previous ch. where we noted how in 1Cor the Apostle refers to the πνεῦμα as «Spirit», «the Spirit», «the Spirit of God», «the Holy Spirit», and the «life-giving Spirit». For Paul, the πνεῦμα gives spiritual gifts to believers, knows and reveals the mind of God, sanctifies Christians by uniting them together in the Church, the body of Christ, guides and instructs all believers in prayer and divinizes believers by transforming their natural bodies into spiritual ones. Rather than bewilderment, this richness of terms expresses the Apostle's fertile understanding of the Holy Spirit and his agency in our salvation. In short, a close reading of both 1Cor and Rom shows that Paul is not at all confused about his theology of the Spirit nor of his understanding of the economic Trinity.

course of his argument in chapter eight, Paul is making a profound statement in this verse about who the Spirit is for us. We have already seen in the close reading how the noun ζωή implies the very giving of life: following immediately after πνεῦμα in the clause, it undoubtedly conveys an active meaning. We may conclude from this that the Apostle teaches that the Spirit is in fact the divine giver of life; indeed, he is the very source of new eschatological life for Christians. Since the Spirit is God's as well as Christ's, then it is also true that God and Christ give life to believers through him. The Spirit is their singular agent in the transformation of Christians. It is he who leads human beings from death to spiritual life; it is he who at the parousia will change their natural bodies so that their risen bodies will truly be characteristic of himself, thus becoming truly «spiritual» at the resurrection of the dead.

When Paul declares that «the Spirit is life», he is expressing the new and extraordinary condition of those who share in the effects of the Christ-event. This reality represents a new kind of human existence with significant overtones for both the present and the future life of Christians. By this clause the Apostle means that the Holy Spirit is both the divine giver of eschatological life to Christians, as well as the divine gift itself. The Spirit is life because he is the very gift given by God to all who believe in Christ. As Paul said earlier in the latter, «and hope does not disappoint us, because God's love has been poured into our hearts through the Holy Spirit which has been given to us» (Rom 5,5). In his role as sanctifier, the Spirit is life now since he empowers ethical Christian conduct in the world, thus allowing Christians to witness to their risen Lord. In his role as divinizer, the Spirit is life for the future since he is the divine agent through whom God creates the spiritual body, thus transforming believers into the image of their risen Lord. Therefore ζωή characterizes both the present life of Christians, since it describes the new way of living in freedom that is proper to God's children and their future life as well, since it suggests that believers will also share in the splendor of Christ's risen and glorified body.

If the Spirit is life for us, then it is indeed reasonable for us to ask why this is so. What is it about the Holy Spirit that enables him to be our eschatological life? It would seem that the only reasonable answer is that the Spirit is life for us because he is first of all the very life of God. It would take the Church centuries to articulate in a clear and coherent fashion the many implications of the New Testament's teaching on the Holy Spirit, especially with regard to his origin in the Godhead and his intimate relationship with the Son in the work of salvation. Although the precise historical details and ramifications of the ancient trinitarian controversies lie beyond the scope of these reflections[12], in time of course the Church would speak of «generation» with regard to the Son and «procession» with regard to the Spirit. Even today the exact implications of the Church's dogma on this mystery are still being studied and discussed by theologians[13]. Certainly Paul's invaluable contribution in Romans 8 offers the Church a precious deposit of revelation with regard to the nature and relations of the three Persons of the Trinity. Through a deeper and more profound study of this chapter, exegetes can continue to make an important contribution to dogmatic and fundamental theologians as we together reflect on the mystery of the triune God who freely chooses to share his life with us.

Therefore, for us who are Christians, the Spirit is our life because the Spirit is first and foremost God's own life. He is life for us since he dwells in our bodies by his transforming presence, yet all the while he never ceases to remain both of God and of Christ. As giver of God's gift, he offers us a singular kind of life which transcends all earthly limitations. As the gift given, it is he who actualizes eschatological life in us by becoming our very life. He has his divine origin in both the Father and the Son and yet in him we find our true means to our heavenly destination: it is he who leads us out of the finitude of our humanity into the boundless infinity of the Godhead[14]. Although the

---

[12] For a fine introduction to this important controversy in the ancient Church, along with an excellent translation of relevant texts on the matter (from the controversial letters of Arius to the magnificent teaching of Augustine in his magisterial work *On the Trinity*), see W.G. RUSCH, *The Trinitarian Controversy*.

[13] See a recent article which treats the whole question of the difference between the Son's generation and the Spirit's procession, also known as «spiration». In describing the diverse characteristics of the Spirit's spiration, Galot underscores in a special way the Spirit's origin in the intimate life of the Father and the Son. «Si nous voulons chercher dans la révélation la nature de la différence entre génération du Fils et spiration de l'Esprit, nous devons tenir compte de toutes les propriétés attribuées à l'Esprit Saint, et de la manière dont elles lui sont attribuées. Du fait que l'Esprit ne se définit pas seulement comme l'amour divin, mais également comme Esprit vivifiant, Esprit de vérité, Esprit de puissance, la spiration par laquelle il procède du Père et du Fils demande à être définie d'une manière correspondante, sans se réduire au seul amour. La spiration se caractérise par un souffle de vie qui fait surgir la personne de l'Esprit, qui la fait jaillir de la vie intime du Père et du Fils. Dans l'Esprit s'affirment la profondeur infinie et l'intégrale richesse de la vie divine» (J. GALOT, «L'Esprit Saint et la spiration», 253).

[14] «Of itself nature does not open up any way to man which can lead him into the inaccessible light of the depths of the Godhead, into the inner life of God himself, into his presence and before his countenance. God himself, therefore, had to come in order to lift

body is dead because of sin, it is the Spirit who deifies us by allowing us to share in the very life of God the Father and by transforming our natural bodies into the likeness of Christ's glorified body. Thus Paul is able to summarize his thought in the very next verse and articulate in trinitarian terms the transcendent hope that characterizes the present lives of Christians: God will raise our mortal bodies from the dead through Christ's Spirit who dwells in us (Rom 8,11).

In conclusion, Paul presents a consistent yet unfolding portrait of the Holy Spirit in Romans 8,9-13. Never confusing him with God or with Christ, the Apostle spells out the Spirit's unique role in God's plan for the salvation of humanity in these profoundly mysterious verses. By means of a deliberate choice of words, he articulates in a very penetrating way the Spirit's origin in God as well as his action in the world. Why then did the Apostle wait until chapter eight in order to develop his pneumatology? It would seem that he first had to describe the impact of sin and death in the lives of Christians (Rom 6) as well as the law's inability to save (Rom 7). Only after having done this is he free to portray the Holy Spirit's agency in salvation, a very significant theme already announced in Romans 5,5. By chapter eight, Paul is able to demonstrate that it is in fact the Spirit who creates the eschatological tension which all believers live in; indeed, it is thanks to the Spirit that Christians are already children of God, even if we do not yet enjoy the fullness of eschatological life in spiritual bodies. Nevertheless the Apostle is ever consistent in his doctrine: by saying that «the Spirit is life because of righteousness» (Rom 8,10), Paul explains in pneumatological terms what he has already expressed christologically. For if we compare the end of chapter three to these verses on the Spirit, we shall discover some fascinating parallels: «since all have sinned and fall short of the glory of God, they are justified by his grace as a gift, through the redemption which is in Christ Jesus» (Rom 3,23-24). God shows his righteousness in the cross of Christ Jesus and he freely communicates its redeeming effects to us who believe through the agency of the Holy Spirit. The

---

us out of the cycle of birth and death and in order to build a way for us by which we could be led out of the bondage of our humanity, confined as it is to the finitude of its own nature and of the world, into the life of God himself. And *this* God who comes into *this* world for *this* purpose we call the Holy Spirit. The Spirit of God in the Christian sense, the holy Pneuma, is present where the deliverance of man from the world and from sin and from finitude is achieved and where the way is opened for him to enter into the presence of God himself» (K. RAHNER, «The Church as the Subject of the Sending of the Spirit», 188).

infinitely righteous God freely justifies us by his saving grace; as grace, this free, unmerited gift is itself divine. In Christ Jesus, God himself gives his Self to us through the Spirit who is eternal life.

3. The Glorified Creation

For Paul, the Christ-event represents the fundamental turning point in the history of humanity. Because Jesus died for us and was raised from the dead, all creation has entered into the last phase of its existence. The new and final age has definitively dawned for humanity thanks to the gospel concerning God's Son (Rom 1,3). For this reason the Apostle interprets Jesus' resurrection in both universal and cosmic terms: universal, because what God has done to Jesus he will also do to all who have his Spirit (Rom 8,11); and cosmic, because what God is doing through the eschatological transformation of human beings will reach its completion in the radical transformation of all creation (Rom 8,21)[15]. In short, Paul's apocalyptic eschatology is a hymn to God's glorious victory over the creation which was formerly enslaved by sin and death. By the agency of the Holy Spirit, God reveals his saving love for us in Christ Jesus through the magnificent splendor and majesty of his glorified creation.

In Romans 8, Paul's eschatological and apocalyptic thought are thoroughly interconnected[16]. His understanding of history and the world is eschatological, in that he is interested in narrating to his addressees in Rome the story about the last things. His novel vision is also equally apocalyptic, in that in his capacity as apostle he consoles the Roman Christians with hope in «the glory that is to be revealed in us» (Rom 8,18). The Apostle's apocalyptic eschatology is in fact characterized by two kinds of dualism. First, Paul describes a temporal dualism: the old age is passing away and a new age is now being

---

[15] Since the time of Augustine, the meaning of κτίσις in Rom 8,19ff. has been much discussed by exegetes. It means the whole created world as distinct from humanity. For this interpretation, cf. C.E.B. CRANFIELD, *Romans*, 414 and J.A. FITZMYER, *Romans*, 506. In these vv. Paul is underscoring the link between the salvation of all humanity and that of the whole nonhuman world.

[16] This position is widely held by exegetes today. For helpful background information on apocalypticism, cf. A.Y. COLLINS, «Apocalypses and Apocalypticism (Early Christian)», 288-292; and P. D. HANSON, «Apocalypticism», 28-34. For a fine overview of the study of eschatology in the NT, cf. D.E. AUNE, «Eschatology (Early Christian)», in 594-609; and E. SCHÜSSLER FIORENZA, «Eschatology of the NT», 271-277.

born (Rom 8,22). The powers of this age are giving way to the omnipotent power of God who is coming in glory to rule his creation. Second, the Apostle also depicts a spatial dualism. All the passing things of this creation, all the heights and depths of this universe (Rom 8,38-39a) are now yielding to the glorious «revealing of the sons of God» (Rom 8,18). Thus through the use of dualism, the Apostle underscores his notion of discontinuity with regard to time and space: God truly desires to glorify this world so that it will be utterly changed and fitted for eternity.

This two-fold dualism does not of course represent a new element in the Apostle's thought. In Part One we studied how Paul's argumentation in 1 Corinthians 15 is in fact characterized by two antitheses: the contrast between the before and after (a temporal difference) as well as between the earthly and the heavenly (a spatial difference). Paul underscores these two dualisms in order to prove that an earthly body can indeed become a spiritual one at the resurrection of the dead. In addition, we also noted the great pains the Apostle takes to differentiate between the material composition of earthly and heavenly bodies. Paul is basically doing the same thing in Romans 8, but in this chapter he chooses instead to feature the Spirit's role in the process of transformation.

Just as in 1 Corinthians 15, the spatial dualism described in Romans 8 can also be understood in material terms. For what will «the glorious liberty of the children of God» (Rom 8,21) be if not the revelation of their spiritual bodies? Certainly Paul is describing a change that will occur at the parousia when the Lord's glory will be fully revealed in all its splendor to the entire cosmos. Although it is true that the term «spiritual body» is not found in Romans 8, nevertheless the Apostle is alluding to its reality by stating «we await for adoption as sons, the redemption of our bodies» (Rom 8,23). We Christians eagerly await for something extraordinary to occur in the future; we long for the final and ultimate transformation of our natural bodies into spiritual ones marked by imperishability and immortality (see 1Cor 15,53-54).

This interpretation of Romans 8 is supported by the occurrence of a very significant term found in these two chapters devoted to Paul's apocalyptic eschatology; the key word in both is «image». The redemption of the natural body is identical to being conformed to the likeness of Christ: «For those whom he foreknew he also predestined to be conformed to the image of his Son, in order that he might be the first-born among many brethren» (Rom 8,29). Is this not precisely what Paul had already articulated so clearly in his discourse on the two Adams in 1 Corinthians 15? In describing the two races of human beings, he teaches that «Just as we have borne the image of the man of dust, let us also bear the image of the man of heaven» (1Cor 15,49). In other words, the redemption of the human body mentioned in Romans 8 offers Paul another opportunity to advance his eschatological teaching on the resurrection of the dead. The Apostle passes over a detailed discussion of the existence of the spiritual body, choosing instead to emphasize the Spirit's role in the process of its creation. We Christians groan inwardly while waiting for the redemption of our bodies since we already «have the first fruits of the Spirit» (Rom 8,23). Thus something that was hinted at in passing in 1 Corinthians 15 now becomes quite explicit in these lines from Romans 8, for Paul, the Spirit's indwelling is indeed a prerequisite for the resurrection of Christians.

Moreover, in these dense verses from Romans, the Apostle also develops a new facet of his complex eschatology. In 1 Corinthians 15 he is concerned primarily with the fate of believers and how they, both the living and the dead, will be changed on the last day. In Romans 8, however, Paul notably broadens his horizons; no longer content to limit his discussion to the bodily resurrection of human beings, he also describes how all of creation is caught up in the vivifying movement of God's Spirit. What before was limited to the fate of Christians is now enlarged to include the fate of the whole cosmos[17]. «We know that the whole creation has been groaning in travail together until now» (Rom 8,22). Since the whole creation has suffered the harmful effects of humanity's fall, so too it will come to share in the effects of Christ's redemption. Thus the Lord Jesus, thanks to his saving death and resurrection, rescues all God's sons and daughters and through them, the redemptive benefits of grace and new eschatological life overflow into the whole creation through the presence of the Holy Spirit. Believers, now redeemed in Christ, in turn become one of the means through which the Spirit renews the face of the earth. We may conclude from this that for the Apostle, the Church also has a very important role to play in the divine plan for the salvation of the world.

In fact throughout Romans 8, Paul describes the gradual outward movement of the Spirit. First, he emphasizes in Romans 8,1-8 that the way of the Spirit leads to life, in contrast to the way of the flesh which leads to death. The

---

[17] Rom 8 depicts a very close connection between the redemption of humanity and that of the whole universe. «La rédemption de l'univers est affirmée par l'Apôtre comme un *corollaire de la rédemption du corps de l'homme*, et par conséquent se fonde sur la résurrection même du Christ» (S. LYONNET, «Rom 8,19-22 et la rédemption de l'univers», 248).

believer experiences in his mind the war between these two forces, the struggle between the powers of the old age and those of the new. Then in Romans 8,9-13, this eschatological battle rages to a climax in the physical body of the believer. Although at times sorely tempted by those malevolent forces which are hostile to God, the Christian is nevertheless called to stand firmly under the banner of his true captain, Jesus Christ, whose indwelling Spirit ensures ultimate victory over God's enemies. Although God has won the war for humanity through Christ's death and resurrection, the battle between the two sides continues until the end of the world. The process of salvation has indeed already begun, but it will reach its completion only at the parousia.

Thus, little by little, the Spirit expands his influence over the lives of Christians. The process which began in the mind (Rom 8,5-7) is next extended so as to include the whole body (Rom 8,9-13). At the parousia, God will have finished his saving work in us by transforming the natural body into the spiritual body through the agency of the Spirit. And not only that, but the whole creation will likewise be changed as well, thus sharing in the freedom of God's children (Rom 8,18-21). From the human mind, to the human body, to the whole of creation — in this way the Holy Spirit transforms the entire universe «according to the will of God» (Rom 8,27).

In this way Romans 8 beautifully expresses Paul's conception of the redemption of the world. The Apostle is fascinated with the interaction between the human and the divine and he goes to great lengths to describe how God has revealed himself to human beings and continues to work among them. He is very keen to explain to his addressees how the three divine Persons cooperate in the redemption and transformation of humanity. In this chapter he presents a brilliant and original vision of the extensive sweep of salvation history.

God accomplishes the transformation of the cosmos through the agency of the Holy Spirit. Thus in Romans 8, Paul is developing a spiritualization of the wisdom theology of creation which was quite familiar to him. «For he created all things that they might exist and the generative forces of the world are wholesome and there is no destructive poison in them; and the dominion of Hades is not on earth» (Wis 1,14). Although God in fact made all his creatures good, since the time of Adam's sin (see Gen 3,15-17) the material creation has also fallen subject to humanity's decay and corruption. Thus Paul understands the Spirit as the divine agent who transforms creation's degenerate condition by allowing it to share in «the glorious freedom of the children of God» (Rom 8,21). One will look in vain for the mention of Christ Jesus in Romans 8,18-23 since Paul is clearly emphasizing the Spirit's role in bringing about «the glory that is to be revealed to us» (Rom 8,18), that is, the glorification of the whole of creation at the parousia.

Moreover, since as Christians we are in the Spirit and conversely, since the Spirit dwells in us, in a very real way the Holy Spirit can be said to represent our first and true contact with the divine. The starting point for all Christian experience of God is thus with God, the Holy Spirit. In other words, we have a first-hand experience of God in as much as we experience the Holy Spirit who has been given to us by God. God freely takes the initiative by choosing to enter into a saving relationship with us by means of his Spirit.

This understanding of the Holy Spirit is indeed grounded in our exegesis of the subunit. As we remarked above in the close reading, Paul refers three times to the indwelling of the Spirit in Romans 8,9-13. Although on numerous occasions Paul explains that believers are in Christ or that Christ is in believers, never once does Paul say that Christ dwells in us or, for that matter, that God the Father dwells in us. For Paul, only the Spirit dwells in believers. We may conclude from these findings that this divine indwelling in Christians is restricted to the unique sphere of the Holy Spirit. As Christians we encounter both God and Christ only in as much as their Spirit dwells in us.

But the indwelling of the Holy Spirit must not be conceived of in static terms. The Spirit does not take up his abode in us in order to rest or repose. On the contrary, he also creates, redeems and sanctifies, sharing completely in the Father and the Son's work of redemption. The Spirit has an important mission to accomplish since he is intimately bound up with the salvation of humanity initiated by God and achieved by Jesus Christ.

How then our we to conceive of Paul's presentation of salvation history? In a first moment it must be imagined as a movement outward from God towards his creation. We saw that our experience of God begins with the Holy Spirit who dwells in us. As the divine presence in our lives, he has been given to us from the magnanimous giver of all that is good, God himself. But the Spirit does not come to us directly from God, but rather from God through our Lord and Redeemer, Jesus Christ. This christological detour is absolutely essential for Paul. That is what is meant when we speak of the Spirit as now christologically known to us. Hence the Father sends, the Son is sent and the Spirit continues their saving mission of redemption by his divine presence in creation. By means of his dwelling in us, the Spirit reminds us of his roots in the Father and the Son, thus helping us to look forward with hope and joy for Christ's return in glory and for the eternal reign of God the Father.

Then, in a second moment, Paul's conception of salvation history can be imagined as the movement of the Spirit-filled creation back to God. Once in the mind and bodies of Christians, the Spirit's mission is to lead believers and indeed all creation to the Father. But this road back to the Father must inevitably lead through Jesus Christ. The Spirit works in the Church and in creation so as to bring all things to Christ, the unique Savior who suffered, died and rose again for the salvation of all. Conceived of in this way, the history of the whole world flows inevitably into Christ's resurrection. The end of the world represents its own coming to be in perfection, for in Christ it will discover the fullness of its purpose and the goal of its being[18]. Hence this return movement from the Spirit, to Christ and finally to the Father represents the second and final stage of salvation history. The entire cosmos, now magnificently redeemed and glorified, is at last at peace and in harmony with God, its loving creator.

The Holy Spirit remains present and active among us, encouraging us to hope in Christ's triumphant return. The Son of God, already glorified and seated at the right hand of the Father, in fact continues his work of salvation through his Spirit. Although he is seated before the Father's throne, nevertheless Christ is truly present among us, working in our hearts and in the world by means of the Spirit. He continues to fight against his enemies until that time when he will be completely victorious. Pauline eschatology clearly points to the goal of salvation history: that «God may be everything to everyone» (1Cor 15,28). Hence the Spirit fulfills his mission by gathering everyone and everything together in Christ, who in turn completes his work as redeemer after having vanquished his last enemy, death. Once the battle is over, Christ in turn

---

[18] «The end of the world is, therefore, the perfection and the achievement of saving history which had already come into full operation and gained its decisive victory in Jesus Christ and in his resurrection. In this sense his coming takes place at this consummation in power and glory: his victory made manifest, the breaking through into experience and the becoming manifest for experience too, of the fact that the world as a whole flows into his Resurrection and into the transfiguration of his body. His Second Coming is not an event which is enacted in a localized manner on the stage of an *un*changed world which occupies a determined point in space in this world of our experience (how could everyone see it otherwise, for instance?); his Second Coming takes place at the moment of the perfecting of the world into the reality which he already possesses now, in such a way that he, the Godman, will be revealed to all reality and, within it, to everyone of its parts in its own way, as the innermost secret and centre of all the world and of all history» (K. RAHNER, «The Resurrection of the Body», 213).

subjects himself, along with all that is, to God the Father. All creation now returns from whence it came, to the hands of the one who had first formed it in wisdom and in love.

In conclusion, Romans 8 is a splendid text overflowing with energy and movement. There is nothing fixed or stationary in these extraordinary lines. With great vision and insight, Paul describes where the Spirit comes from and where he is going, painting in broad strokes the entire sweep of salvation history. From the Father, in Christ, through the Spirit, God's love is poured out by means of the triune God's loving act of creation; through the Spirit, in Christ, to the Father, all that has been redeemed is now brought home into the bosom of the Trinity. This magnificent saving act has indeed already begun in Christ's resurrection from the dead. In a special way, Romans 8,11 beautifully summarizes how the three Persons of the Trinity actively participate in the resurrection of Christians. Moreover, the Apostle is utterly consistent with his earlier instruction in 1 Corinthians 15 where he had developed his understanding of the two Adams: what God has already done for Christ by raising him from the dead, so too he will do for all who believe in his only begotten Son. Thus the glorified creation described in Romans 8 represents Paul's vision of a recreated humanity at home in a recreated world. Alive forever in their risen bodies, human beings will rejoice with Christ, the last Adam, «the first-born of many brothers» (Rom 8,29). However we may describe it, the glorified creation revealed here is indeed the place where human beings will dwell fully and completely with God forever. What then is this extraordinary dwelling place if not heaven? While waiting for the redemption of our bodies and the glorification of the universe, we fulfill our mission as Christians by proclaiming our steadfast faith in the Lord's resurrection and by yearning with great hope and patience for our own.

PART THREE

CONCLUSION

Chapter VII

The Holy Spirit,
God's Agent in the Resurrection

In the preceding chapters, we scrutinized and reflected on two very profound yet enigmatic passages, 1 Corinthians 15,44b-49 and Romans 8,9-13. We explored the distinctive terrain of these two difficult texts in light of the specific composition of the letter in question, striving all the while to survey the general topography of Paul's theology, christology and pneumatology as articulated elsewhere in his genuine letters. By means of this exegetico-theological study of these crucial literary units, we have indeed arrived at some rather significant insights into Paul's doctrine concerning the person of the Holy Spirit as well as the essential role which the Spirit plays in the resurrection of the dead. It is now time to summarize these findings and rearticulate them in light of the thesis which was first stated in the introduction: for the Apostle Paul, the Holy Spirit is in fact God's agent in the resurrection of the dead. In this conclusion, therefore, we must consider in greater detail just how this thesis statement applies to Christ Jesus, to Christians and indeed, to all human beings.

Before proceeding with this indispensable application, however, we must first compare and contrast the two subunits that have captured our attention over the course of this long investigation. How do 1 Corinthians 15,44b-49 and Romans 8,9-13 differ? How are they similar? And could a concise comparison of both of these passages attest to a significant and meaningful evolution in the Apostle's doctrine on the Holy Spirit? To this essential task we now turn.

1. 1 Corinthians 15,44b-49 and Romans 8,9-13 Compared

1.1 *Differences Between the Two Subunits*

Since Paul wrote ad hoc letters to his fellow Christians in Corinth and Rome, we have taken great pains to emphasize the specific nature of each of these literary and semantic subunits in light of its unique context, function and purpose. Thus, before developing the many similarities which associate them, we must first affirm and appreciate some of the many differences that exist between both of these biblical passages. Only in this way can we hope to do justice to the Apostle's specific teaching to the Corinthians as well as to the Romans.

In 1 Corinthians 15,44b-49, Paul is instructing the saints of a Church he founded about the extraordinary nature of the spiritual body. Just before, in his argument from reason in vv. 35-44a, the Apostle teaches that God has in fact created many different kinds of bodies in the cosmos and that he can even transform an earthly body into a heavenly one by raising it from the dead. However in vv. 44b-49, Paul focuses his attention specifically on the human body, both natural and spiritual, by developing a very persuasive argument from Scripture. Thanks to a brilliant midrash of Genesis 2,7, he explains how God, through the agency of his life-giving Spirit, creates the spiritual bodies of both the last Adam as well as of all those who will resemble him. Thus in these verses the Apostle is keen to make known to the Corinthians his anthropological and pneumatological concerns.

In Romans 8,9-13, the Apostle is addressing his fellow Christians in the capital of the Empire on the mysterious ramifications of life in the Spirit. They belong to a Church he has not yet visited and so he takes great pains to impart to them some spiritual gift so as to strengthen them in their faith (see Rom 1,11). By disclosing to them the mysterious union that exists between God, Christ and the Spirit, Paul reveals in Romans 8,9-13 that the Spirit is both of God and of Christ: he cannot speak of the Spirit without mentioning the other two divine persons as well. By insisting that the Spirit dwells in them, the Apostle teaches his addressees that God will raise them from dead through Christ's indwelling Spirit: he cannot speak of their future resurrection except in light of the uniqueness of the Christ-event. Thus in these extraordinary verses the Apostle underscores both his trinitarian and pneumatological concerns as they relate to the resurrection of both Christ Jesus and of Christians.

1.2 *Similarities Between the Two Subunits*

What then are the similarities which connect these two important texts? In both units, Paul successfully demonstrates to his addressees that eschatological life in the Spirit finds its complete fulfillment in the resurrection of the dead. More specifically, he proves that the resurrection is indeed necessary since it represents the ultimate fulfillment of God's redemptive plan for humanity. In Christ Jesus, God gloriously defeats sin and death and thereby grants eternal life to his children. If this were not the case, then God would be incapable of saving his creation from utter destruction and such a God would not really be God at all. Moreover, Paul insists that this extraordinary act of salvation will come about through the agency of God's life-giving Spirit. When considered in this way, the agency of the Spirit is also necessary if God's children are to enjoy the fullness of divine life in their spiritual bodies. Thus the resurrection is necessary for redemption from sin and death and the Holy Spirit is necessary for salvation onto eternal life: in both of these extraordinary subunits the Apostle emphasizes that these two effects of the Christ-event do in fact go hand in hand.

Given all of the above, it would indeed be arbitrary to draw a sharp distinction between the Holy Spirit's agency in the creation of the spiritual body in 1 Corinthians 15 and his agency in the giving of eschatological life to mortal bodies at the parousia in Romans 8. In both cases, the Apostle clearly teaches that God raises the dead to eternal life through the agency of the Spirit who is life. These are two different ways for Paul to express his singular teaching on the divinizing action of the Holy Spirit who already dwells in the hearts of believers. In fact, the Holy Spirit is the very life of God now made manifest in the world through the passion, death and resurrection of Christ.

Not only is the Apostle's pneumatology similar in both subunits, but so too is his christology. In 1 Corinthians 15,45, Paul specifically refers to Christ as the last Adam and then goes on to develop his argument on the spiritual body in light of Genesis 2,7. Although the Apostle does not use this title anywhere in Romans in reference to Jesus, nevertheless he implies it in the Adam-Christ comparison of chapter five[1]. He returns to this notion in chapter eight when,

---

[1] «Although Paul does not refer in Romans explicitly to Christ Jesus as "the last Adam" as he does in 1 Cor 15,45, he admits implicitly that Christ plays such a role when he refers to Adam as the "type of the one who is to come" (5,14). Thus, for Paul, Christ has become the Adam or head of a new humanity, the source of a "newness of life" (6,4). The age "from

in speaking of God's redemptive plan, he states «For those whom he foreknew he also predestined to be conformed to the image of his Son, in order that he might be the first-born among many brothers» (Rom 8,29). Surely the occurrence of the word εἰκών in this verse represents another link to Paul's christology as articulated in 1 Corinthians 15,49. In fact, this first Adam – last Adam comparison remains operative throughout Romans 8, for the Apostle is intent on demonstrating that what God has done to Christ through his Spirit he will also do to Christians. He takes great pains to link Christ Jesus' resurrection from the dead to the resurrection on the last day of all who believe in Christ. If in Romans 8,9-13 Paul highlights the presence and activity of the indwelling Spirit, he does so in order to feature his essential agency in the transformation of believers into the image and likeness of their singular Redeemer, Jesus Christ, when he comes again in glory.

1.3 *Development of Paul's Doctrine on the Holy Spirit*

In light of the differences and similarities which have just been articulated, are we at all justified in speaking of a development in Paul's doctrine on the Holy Spirit and on the Spirit's agency in the resurrection of the dead? In the short time between writing 1 Corinthians and Romans, did the Apostle's thoughts on these crucial questions evolve at all? We should admit right from the start that the differences listed above are partly due to the particular kind of argumentation developed in each subunit. Paul's distinctive concerns in 1 Corinthians 15 are somewhat different from his considerations in Romans 8. Nevertheless, it would seem that we can indeed make a credible argument in favor of a certain degree of evolution in Paul's teaching in light of the development of his own reflections on these mysteries, since Romans 8 does in fact present a significant deepening of the major ideas touched upon in 1 Corinthians 15. This is especially true with regard to three important points: the Apostle's understanding of the role of the Holy Spirit, the articulation of his doctrine on the Trinity with respect to the resurrection and the extent and scope of the general resurrection of the dead.

Adam to Moses" (5,14) has come to an end and the period of the law of Moses has also ended (10,4); and Christ Jesus has become the source of divine salvation and uprightness for all, Jew and Greek alike, in this newly begun life of the eschaton, or end time. His "obedience" stands in contrast to the "disobedience" of Adam (5,19), to Adam's "trespass" (5,14) and his "transgression" (5,15)» (J.A. FITZMYER, «The Christology of the Epistle to the Romans», 85).

We begin with the first point, namely, the role of the Holy Spirit as agent in the resurrection of the dead. In 1 Corinthians 15 Paul is keen to underscore the effects of the Spirit's action and for this reason the second half of the chapter is intended to describe the creation of the spiritual body. In 1 Corinthians 15,38 the Apostle explicitly attributes the creation of the body to God and his midrash on Genesis 2,7 serves to highlight his understanding of God's active role in creation. Nevertheless, as we saw above in the exegesis of 1 Corinthians 15,44b-49 in Part One, the Apostle calls the risen body «spiritual» because it comes to be thanks to the agency of the «life-giving Spirit». Although the term appears only once in this subunit, the Spirit makes his presence felt throughout these important verses on the first and last Adam. In Romans 8, however, the Apostle wants to accentuate the cause of this eschatological activity; the divine agent at work is none other than God's Spirit, the very Spirit of the risen Christ. It is for this reason that Paul repeats the word πνεῦμα twenty-one times. In short, 1 Corinthians 15,44b-49 emphasizes more the result of God's creative work, the formation of the spiritual body, while Romans 8,9-13 emphasizes the eschatological agent who glorifies creation, the Spirit himself. Thus there is a development in Paul's teaching in as much as in Romans 8,11 he clearly ascribes to the Holy Spirit this unique role in the resurrection of the dead. This explicit reference to the Spirit's agency reveals a very significant pneumatological doctrine, one which the Apostle had merely implied in his first letter to the Corinthians.

As regards the second point, namely, the articulation of Paul's trinitarian theology with regard to the resurrection, we can also recognize a certain evolution in Paul's reflections. When considered as a whole, 1 Corinthians 15 is primarily christological and anthropological in intent; Paul is keen to pass on the tradition he has received with respect to Christ's resurrection and he wants to stress the radical transformation that will occur to the bodies of believers at the parousia. Although the Father and the Spirit are mentioned in this chapter, Paul does not explicitly articulate his theology of the Trinity with regard to the resurrection of the dead. In Romans 8, however, we discover the Apostle's mature thought, for in these verses he demonstrates a well-developed trinitarian theology of the resurrection. Paul cannot speak of the Father without also mentioning the Son and the Spirit along with him. Thus the Spirit of God, who is in fact the Spirit of Christ, represents the very life of the Father and the Son. Given the profound intimacy of the Father and Son's relationship in the Godhead, we may interpret this as a basic christologization of Paul's theology: God and Christ are simply inseparable. Thanks to their infinite love for one another, their eternal life, the Holy Spirit, proceeds from them both. Thus the Spirit is now fully revealed as God's omnipotent power and saving agent at work in the resurrection of both Jesus and of all who believe in him, as Romans 8,11 states in a most explicit way.

Lastly, as concerns the third point, the extent of the final and general resurrection of the dead, we may discern another development in the Apostle's teaching on the question. In 1 Corinthians 15, Paul describes the Church's faith in the resurrection of Jesus and how the eternal life won in Christ will be communicated to all Christians through the creation of the spiritual body. As the repetition of the pronouns «we» and «us» in this passage clearly shows (whether stated or understood in the verb), Paul is writing to his fellow believers about their common fate as Christians: «But thanks be to God, who gives us the victory through our Lord Jesus Christ» (1Cor 15,57). This same point also holds true for Romans 8, where the Apostle is also clearly addressing his fellow Christians: «So then, brothers, we are debtors, not to the flesh, to live according to the flesh» (Rom 8,12). Nevertheless, given his teaching on the glorification of all creation which follows in vv. 18ff., Paul implies that even those who presently do not have Christ's Spirit will also share in the revelation of the sons and daughters of God[2]. Since all creation will be set free from its bondage to decay, how then could God overlook non-Christians and exclude them from the resurrection on the last day? If even the sub-human world is to be glorified at the end of time, then surely all human beings will also come to enjoy the eternal life offered by God through the Holy Spirit. Thus it is reasonable to conclude from these verses that the mortal bodies of those who in this life were not Christian will also be raised from the dead as well. In this way, Romans 8,18ff. implies the final and general resurrection of all human beings, a point which we shall return to below.

2. The Holy Spirit's Agency in the Resurrection of the Dead

2.1 The Holy Spirit's Agency in the Resurrection of Jesus

Jesus' resurrection from the dead must be understood first and foremost as a trinitarian event: God the Father raises Christ Jesus from the dead through the agency of the Holy Spirit. This point has been made clear thanks to our

---

[2] This point is developed below in 2.3, «The Holy Spirit's Agency in the Resurrection of all Human Beings».

exegesis and theological reflections on 1 Corinthians 15,44bff., where Paul teaches that God creates the spiritual body of the last Adam through the agency of his «life-giving Spirit», as well as Romans 8,11, where the Apostle explicitly refers to «the Spirit of the one who raised Jesus from the dead». How then can we come to a better understanding of Paul's doctrine of the Trinity's role in the resurrection of the Son of God?

If we analyze the Apostle's teaching with the help of the philosophical categories of causality, then God the Father could be understood as the efficient cause of Jesus' resurrection[3] while the Holy Spirit would then represent the instrumental one. The adjective instrumental, however, requires a nuanced explanation: in no way does Paul understand the Holy Spirit as a tool employed by the Father in order to achieve a certain end. It is essential to recall that we are in fact referring to a divine person and for this reason the term agency is to be preferred to that of instrumentality. Nevertheless, the crucial point to be grasped remains the same: according to Paul, Jesus remains entirely passive in his own resurrection, since he is raised by the Father through the agency of the Holy Spirit. Thus Jesus Christ's human condition as a man «descended from David according to the flesh» (Rom 1,3) reaches its nadir in his death on the cross and in his utter receptivity to the new eschatological life which the Father and the Spirit desire to share with him. Only once it is dead and in the tomb is his natural body ready to undergo the radical transformation which occurs at the moment of resurrection. When Christ is «designated Son of God in power according to the Spirit of holiness by his resurrection from the dead» (Rom 1,4), he then receives his spiritual body and so enters into his new, exalted mode of existence in the Blessed Trinity. Thus, in his mortal body, the Son of God rises to new, eternal life through the power of the Holy Spirit[4].

---

[3] «Paul also expresses his faith in Jesus' "resurrection from the dead" (1,4; cf. 6,5), thus affirming that he "was raised (from the dead)" (4,25; 6,9; 8,34) or that he was brought "up from the dead" (10,7). Moreover, he makes it clear that Jesus "was raised from the dead by the glory of the Father" (6,4) and that "he no longer dies" (6,9). Thus Paul ascribes the resurrection of Christ to the Father (4,24; 6,4; cf. 8,11), regarding the Father as the efficient cause of Christ's resurrection. Consequently, he speaks also of "his life" as the risen Lord (5,10; cf. 14,19): he is one who "lives to God" (6,10) and enjoys "eternal life" (6,23)» (J.A. FITZMYER, «The Christology of the Epistle to the Romans», 87).

[4] For his understanding of the trinitarian dimension of the Paschal mystery, especially with regard to the connection between Christ's resurrection from the dead and the power of the Holy Spirit, consider the Pope's exegesis of these important vv. from Rom «The

Therefore, at the moment of his resurrection from the dead, Christ's condition radically changes. It is only then that the last Adam, now completely filled with the Holy Spirit, is said to become «a life-giving Spirit» (1Cor 15,45). Only once he has experienced the power of the Spirit can the risen Lord transmit him to others[5]. Thus it is Christ who now has the Father's authority to dispense the Holy Spirit to all who believe in the Son of God. He completes his own redemptive mission by sending forth his Spirit into the Church and into the world, thereby revealing God's Spirit as his Spirit. Thanks to this gift of the Son of God, the Holy Spirit is now christologically known to us.

2.2 *The Holy Spirit's Agency in the Resurrection of Christians*

The resurrection of Christians from the dead also represents a trinitarian event: God the Father raises from the dead those who believe in Christ Jesus through the agency of the Holy Spirit who dwells in them. Paul had already made this point quite clear in 1 Corinthians 15,44bff, thanks to his teaching on the creation of the spiritual body and the two Adams. As we saw above in the exegesis, the central idea of the whole subunit is that what God has done to the last Adam through his life-giving Spirit, he will likewise do to all who believe in him. Christ is but the first example of a whole new race of human beings. Similarly, Paul will articulate this same doctrine on the resurrection of Christians in Romans 8,11, yet this time the Apostle makes his teaching quite explicit: the mortal bodies of Christians will be transformed on the last day

---

definitive expression of this mystery is had *on the day of the Resurrection*. On this day Jesus of Nazareth, "descended form David according to the flesh", as the Apostle Paul writes, is "designated Son of God in power according to the Spirit of holiness by his Resurrection from the dead". It can be said therefore that the messianic "rising up" of Christ in the Holy Spirit reaches its zenith in the Resurrection, in which he reveals himself also as the *Son of God*, "full of power". And this power, the sources of which gush forth in the inscrutable Trinitarian communion, is manifested, first of all, in the fact that the Risen Christ does two things: on the one hand he fulfills God's promise already expressed through the Prophet's words "A new heart I will give you and a new spirit I will put within you, ...my spirit"; and on the other hand he fulfills his own promise made to the Apostles with the words "If I go, I will send him to you". It is he: the Spirit of truth, the Paraclete sent by the Risen Christ to transform us into his own risen image» (JOHN PAUL II, *Dominum et vivificantem*, § 24).

[5] «Being "the first fruits of those fallen asleep" (1 Cor 15,20), the risen Christ is completely filled with and penetrated by the Holy Spirit, in such a way that he simply becomes a "life-giving Spirit", i.e., source and giver of the Spirit, having this latter at his disposal» (J.H.P. WONG, «The Holy Spirit in the Life of Jesus and of the Christian», 71).

«through the Spirit who dwells in you». Thus the present indwelling of the Spirit in Christians is the sure guarantee that God will raise them from the dead just as he once raised his Son Jesus Christ.

Therefore those who believe in Christ will be recreated in the image of the last Adam, being raised from the dead just as he was. Christians will have imperishable bodies created for eternity; their spiritual bodies will also resemble that of the risen Christ. In spite of these striking similarities, however, some important differences between the two must be clearly affirmed. Christ was raised by virtue of his divine nature as Son of God, but Christians will be raised from the dead as the result of God's grace. As Paul had explained earlier in Romans with regard to justification, believers «are justified by his grace as a gift, through the redemption which is in Christ Jesus» (Rom 3,24). Moreover, as the Son of God, Jesus' resurrection was unique in as much as he was raised on the third day (1Cor 15,4), while believers will be raised on the last day. Thus the resurrection of Christians at the parousia represents the ultimate glorification of the Church, now fully revealed as the Body of Christ.

2.3 *The Holy Spirit's Agency in the Resurrection of All Human Beings*

We noted above in the section on the development of Paul's doctrine of the Holy Spirit that the Apostle has clearly directed his teaching on the resurrection to his fellow Christians. 1 Corinthians 15,44b-49 and Romans 8,9-13 form part of two different letters, each one written for believers about believers. Nevertheless, do these passages allow us who are Christians to hope in the resurrection from the dead of those who are not? Given Paul's teaching on the glorification of creation in Romans 8,18ff., it would be quite reasonable for us to respond in the affirmative.

In Romans 8, Paul describes the gradual expansion of the Holy Spirit's presence in the lives of Christians and indeed, in all creation. He describes a glorified world where all creation will be set free from its bondage to decay, thereby sharing in the eschatological victory of the sons and daughters of God. As we remarked above, if even the sub-human world is to be glorified at the end of time, then surely all human beings will also come to enjoy the eternal life communicated by the Holy Spirit. Thus it is reasonable to conclude from these verses that the mortal bodies of those who in this life were not Christian will also be raised from the dead as well. In this way, Romans 8,18ff. implies the universal resurrection of all the dead.

Paul understands resurrection as an event which entails the total transformation of the human being. The Apostle teaches that the Father, through the agency of the Holy Spirit, transforms natural bodies into spiritual ones created in the image of Christ, his Son. This constitutive change in the material composition of the human body also represents a significant change in its status: when raised from the dead, the human being is ipso facto transferred from the earthly realm to the heavenly one. Since it is composed of eternal, glorious and indestructible matter, the spiritual body is created for heaven: it is a heavenly body. Since it is formed through the agency of the life-giving Spirit, it is characteristic of the Holy Spirit: it is a divinized creation. The Holy Spirit dwells perfectly in the spiritual body, radiating in it the consummate glory of the Father and the Son. For this reason, no where in his letters does the Apostle describe a resurrection to eternal damnation[6], for how could that which is formed for glory in heaven be condemned to abasement in hell?

God raises the dead to eternal life so as to share with them his immeasurable love; in Christ and through his Spirit, he successfully carries out his salvific will towards all his creatures. God is gloriously victorious over all his enemies and demonstrates his infinite power through the glorification of his creation. The final verses of Romans 8 confirm this hopeful interpretation in as much as they describe how nothing can separate us from God who justifies (v. 33) and from Christ who intercedes for us (v. 34). Thus the unfolding of this chapter (as well as that of the entire letter when considered as a whole) emphasizes the fulfillment of God's redemptive plan for humanity. Paul himself articulates this point very clearly in his teaching on Adam and Christ: «Therefore just as one man's trespass led to condemnation for all, so one man's act of righteousness leads to justification and life for all» (Rom 5,18). Given all of the above, we may affirm that it is indeed God's will that all human beings be saved and thereby come to share in his eternal life.

---

[6] It would seem that Paul is not familiar with the narrative of the final judgment as found in Mt 25. It is of course Matthew's version of the parousia that has been officially adopted by the Church in the Fourth Lateran Council's teaching on Christ's second coming and the general resurrection of the dead. «venturus in fine saeculi, iudicaturus vivos et mortuos, et redditurus singulis secundum opera sua, tam reprobis quam electis: qui omnes cum suis propriis resurgent corporibus, quae nunc gestant, ut recipiant secundum opera sua, sive bona fuerint sive mala, illi cum diabolo poenam perpetuam, et isti cum Christo gloriam sempiternam» (H. DENZINGER – A. SCHÖNMETZER, *Enchiridion Symbolorum*, 801).

In conclusion, Paul's splendid description of the creation of the spiritual body in 1 Corinthians 15 and the agency of the Spirit of life in Romans 8 lays the sure foundation for solid hope in the universal resurrection of all human beings from the dead. At this point it should be noted that most all of the second century Apologists as well as the apostolic Fathers conceived of hope in the resurrection of the dead in universal terms and so they clearly taught that all humanity will rise from the dead[7]. By raising the dead to eternal life through the agency of his life-giving Spirit, God the Father will triumphantly complete his magnificent work of creation by transforming all human beings into the glorious image of his only begotten Son, Jesus Christ.

3. Final Pneumatological Reflections

The Holy Spirit represents God's life-giving agent in the resurrection of the dead. In his letters to the saints at Corinth and Rome, Paul preaches the extraordinary Good News which lies at the very heart of the Easter message: God has raised Jesus Christ to eternal life, the first fruits of a great eschatological harvest and he pledges to do the same to all who will die in him. In a concise and yet very profound way, 1 Corinthians 15,44b-49 and Romans 8,9-13 propose a remarkable summary of the Apostle's pneumatology, especially with regard to the impenetrable mystery of the resurrection of the dead.

In the proclamation of the gospel, humanity finds hope to believe in its own eschatological transformation: given the last Adam's corporeal solidarity with every member of the human race, one day all men and women will come to share in the splendor of Christ's risen body. At the parousia, the natural body of every human being will be changed into a spiritual one thanks to the agency of the Holy Spirit. It is God's salvific will that the human body should become characteristic of the life-giving Spirit, since the spiritual body belongs to the Holy Spirit in as much as he dwells in it completely. This indwelling of the Spirit, already begun in baptism, reaches perfection at the resurrection on the last day when human beings will become fully spiritual. Completely filled with the Holy Spirit, we shall be perfected by God's omnipotent power and thus divinized for eternal splendor. This will come to pass because it has pleased

---

[7] For an excellent summary of the teaching of the apologists and early Church Fathers on the resurrection, see P. PERKINS, *Resurrection*, 331-390. For another superb survey of the patristic understanding of the resurrection of the body, see B.E. DALEY, «The Ripening of Salvation», 27-49.

God to pour forth his very life into creation; the Spirit is the eternal life of God and of Christ sent into the world to transform and glorify it.

The divinization of human beings is the reasonable result of the *admirabile commercium*. God creates, redeems and saves the world out of love, sharing his divine nature with us so that we may become what he is. In Christ Jesus, the Father brings his wondrous work to completion through the agency of the Holy Spirit. God remains God and creation remains creation, yet something of God enters into the identity of man and something of man enters into the identity of God. In Christ, humanity is fully integrated into the Trinity; in the Spirit, divinity is fully integrated into the spiritual bodies of human beings. Yet divinization is not pantheism, since both Creator and creation keep their unique identities in spite of the marvelous exchange which has taken place. «O the depth of the riches and wisdom and knowledge of God! How unsearchable are his judgments and how inscrutable his ways!» (Rom 11,33).

The Church has been given the sacred mission to preach this joyful and consoling message to people of every age by her Lord and Savior, Jesus Christ. In its instruction on the Holy Spirit, Vatican II teaches that it is in fact the Spirit of life that permits the Church to keep the freshness of youth by the power of the gospel[8]. Called to live out the spirit of the Council in the world today, we who stand at the threshold of Christianity's third millennium ought to take Paul's Good News to heart and witness the gospel to everyone in our age. A renewed commitment to proclaim the Christian faith in the resurrection of the dead is surely possible, for «hope does not disappoint us, because God's love has been poured into our hearts through the Holy Spirit which has been given to us» (Rom 5,5).

---

[8] See Vatican II, *Lumen Gentium*, § 4.

ABBREVIATIONS

– al.	*et alii*, and others
AnBib	Analecta Biblica
AncB	Anchor Bible
AncBD	*Anchor Bible Dictionary*, ed. D.N. Freedman, I-VI, New York 1992
ANRW	*Aufstieg und Niedergang der römischen Welt*
Anton.	*Antonianum*
AThR	*Anglican Theological Review*
Bauer	W. BAUER, *Griechisch-deutsches Wörterbuch*, Berlin 1988[6]
BDR	BLASS, F. – DEBRUNNER, A. – REHKOPF, F., *Grammatik des neutesta-mentlichen Griechisch*, Göttingen 1990[17]
BEThL	Bibliotheca ephemeridum theologicarum lovaniensium
BGBE	Beiträge zur Geschichte der biblischen Exegese
Bib.	*Biblica*
BNTC	Black's NT Commentaries
BST	The Bible Speaks Today
BZNW	Beihefte zur *Zeitschrift für die neutestamentliche Wissenschaft und die Kunde der älteren Kirche*
c.	*circa*, about
CBQ	*Catholic Biblical Quarterly*
cf.	*confer*, compare
ch./chs.	chapter/chapters
CNEB	Cambridge Biblical Commentary on the New English Bible
DBS	*Dictionnaire de la Bible, Supplément*, Paris 1928 –
ed.	editor/editors
EpC	Epworth Commentaries
ET	*Expository Times*
etc.	*et cetera*
EThL	*Ephemerides theologicae lovanienses*

EWNT	*Exegetisches Wörterbuch zum Neuen Testament*, ed. H. Balz – G. Schneider, I-III, Stuttgart 1980-1983
ff.	and the following ones
FRLANT	Forschungen zur Religion und Literatur des Alten und Neuen Testaments
Fs.	Festchrift
Gr.	*Gregorianum*
GSL.NT	Geistliche Schriftlesung, Erläuterungen zum Neuen Testament
GTJ	*Grace Theological Journal*
HBC	*Harper's Bible Commentary*, ed. J.L. Mays, San Francisco 1988
HBD	*Harper's Bible Dictionary*, ed. P.J. Achtemeier, San Francisco 1985
HCR	*Hastings Center Report*
Hermeneia	Hermeneia. A Critical and Historical Commentary on the Bible
HeTr	Helps For Translators
HS	HOFFMANN, E.G. – VON SIEBENTHAL, H., *Griechische Grammatik zum Neuen Testament*, Riehen 1990^2
HThR	*Harvard Theological Review*
ICC	International Critical Commentary
id.	*idem*, same
IDB	*The Interpreter's Dictionary of the Bible*, ed. G.A. Buttrick (Vol. I-IV) – K. Crim (Suppl. Vol.), Nashville 1962-1976
Interp.	Interpretation
intro.	introduction
JBL	*Journal of Biblical Literature*
JSNT.S	Journal for the Study of the New Testament. Supplement Series
JSPE.S	Journal for the Study of the Pseudepigrapha. Supplement Series
KEK	Kritish-exegetischer Kommentar über das Neue Testament
LCL	Loeb Classical Library
LThPM	Louvain Theological and Pastoral Monographs
LXX	Septuagint
METZGER	B. METZGER, *A Textual Commentary on the Greek NT*, Stuttgart 1971
MSSNTS	Monograph Series, Society for NT Studies
MT	Masoretic Text
NAB	New American Bible
NCBC	New Century Bible Commentary
NDT	*New Dictionary of Theology*, ed. J. Komonchak – M. Collins – D. Lane, Wilmington 1987
Neotest.	*Neotestamentica*

NIBC	New International Biblical Commentary
NIC	New International Commentary on the NT
NIV	New International Version
NJB	New Jerusalem Bible
NJBC	New Jerome Biblical Commentary
NRSV	New Revised Standard Version
NT	New Testament
NT	*Novum Testamentum*
NTMes	New Testament Message
NTS	New Testament Studies
OCD	*Oxford Classical Dictionary*, ed. N.G.L. Hammond – H.H. Scullard, Oxford 1970
OT	Old Testament
PC	Proclamation Commentaries
publ.	published
repr.	reprint
rev.	revised
RevSR	*Revue des Sciences Religieuses*
RExp	*Review and Expositor*
RSV	Revised Standard Version
SBL	Society of Biblical Literature
ScEs	*Science et Esprit*
SCM	Society of Christian Missions
SJTh	*Scottish Journal of Theology*
SPCK	Society for the Promotion of Christian Knowledge
suppl.	supplementary
ThWNT	*Theologisches Wörterbuch zum Neuen Testament*, ed. G. Kittel – G. Friedrich, I-IX.X/1-2, Stuttgart 1933-1979
TNTC	Tyndale NT Commentaries
TPINTC	Trinity Press International NT Commentaries
transl.	translator
UBS	United Bible Societies
v./vv.	verse/verses
vol.	volume
WBC	Word Biblical Commentary
WRSGÖ	Weltgespräch der Religionen Schriftenreihe zur Grossen Ökumene
ZERWICK	M. ZERWICK, *Biblical Greek*, Rome 1963
1QS	Dead Sea Scrolls, Community Rule
§	paragraph

SELECT BIBLIOGRAPHY

1. Primary Texts and General Reference Works

ACHTEMEIER, P.J., ed., *Harper's Bible Dictionary*, San Francisco 1985.

ALAND, K. – BLACK, M.– MARTINI, C.M. – METZGER, B.M.– WIKGREN, A., in cooperation with the Institute for New Testament Textual Research, Münster/Wetphalia, *The Greek New Testament*, New York – London – Edinburgh – Amsterdam – Stuttgart 1975[3].

BALZ, H. – SCHNEIDER, G., ed., *Exegetisches Wörterbuch zum Neuen Testament*, I-III, Stuttgart 1980-1983.

BAUER, W., *Griechisch-deutsches Wörterbuch zu den Schriften des Neuen Testaments und der frühchristlichen Literatur*, publ. K. Aland – B. Aland, Berlin – New York 1988[6].

La Bible d'Alexandrie. 1. La Genèse, transl., intro. and notes M. Harl, Paris 1986.

BLASS, F. – DEBRUNNER, A. *Grammatik des neutestamentlichen Griechisch*, rev. F. Rehkopf, Göttingen 1990[17].

Concordance to the Novum Testamentum Graece, Institute for New Testament Textual Research and the Computer Center of Münster University, Berlin 1987.

DENZINGER, H. – SCHÖNMETZER, A., ed., *Enchiridion Symbolorum*. Definitionum et Declarationum de Rebus Fidei et Morum, Barcelona 1967[34].

ELLIGER, K. – RUDOLPH, W., *Biblia Hebraica Stuttgartensia*. Editio Funditus Renovata, Stuttgart 1984.

HAMMOND, N. G. L. – SCULLARD, H.H., ed., *The Oxford Classical Dictionary*, Oxford 1970.

HOFFMANN, E.G. – VON SIEBENTHAL, H., *Griechische Grammatik zum Neuen Testament*, Riehen 1990.

JOHN PAUL II, *Dominum et vivificantem*, 18 May, 1986.

KITTEL, G. – FRIEDRICH, G., ed., *Theologisches Wörterbuch zum Neuen Testament*, I-IX.X/1-2, Stuttgart 1933-1979

MAYS, J.L., ed., *Harper's Bible Commentary*, San Francisco 1988.

METZGER, B.M., *A Textual Commentary on the Greek New Testament*, New York 1975.

MOULTON, J.H. – HOWARD, W.F, *A Grammar of New Testament Greek*, I, *Prolegomena*, II, *Accidence and Word-Formation*, *Semitisms*, III, *Syntax*, and IV, *Style*, by N. Turner, Edinburgh 1906-1976.

NESTLE, E. – ALAND, K., *Novum Testamentum Graece*, Stuttgart 1979[26].

RAHLFS, A., *Septuaginta.* Id est Vetus Testamentum graece iuxta LXX interpretes, I-II, Stuttgart 1971[2].

VATICAN II, *Dei Verbum.* Dogmatic Constitution on Divine Revelation, 18 November, 1965, in *Vatican Collection*, ed. A. Flannery, I, *Vatican Council II*. The Conciliar and Post Conciliar Documents, Collegeville 1984, 750-765.

———, *Lumen Gentium.* Dogmatic Constitution on the Church, 21 November, 1964, in *Vatican Collection*, ed. A. Flannery, I, *Vatican Council II*. The Conciliar and Post Conciliar Documents, Collegeville 1984, 350-426.

ZERWICK, M., *Biblical Greek.* Illustrated by Examples, transl. J. Smith, Rome 1983.

———, *A Grammatical Analysis of the Greek New Testament*, transl., rev., and adapted M. Grosvenor in collaboration with the author, Rome 1988[3].

2. Books and Articles

ACHTEMEIER, P.J., *Romans*, Interp., Louisville 1985.

AHERN, B.M., «The Risen Christ in the Light of Pauline Doctrine on the Risen Christian (1Cor 15:35-57)», in *Resurrexit. Actes du symposium international sur la résurection de Jésus (Rome 1970)*, ed. É. Dhanis, Città del Vaticano 1974, 423-439.

Alcoholics Anonymous: The Story of How Many Thousands of Men and Women Have Recovered from Alcoholism, New York 1976[3].

ALETTI, J.-N. – *al.*, *Résurrection du Christ et des chrétiens (1Co 15)*, ed. L. De Lorenzi, Série Monographique de «Benedictina», 8, Rome 1985.

———, «La Présence d'un modèle rhétorique en Romains. Son rôle et son importance», *Bib.* 71 (1990) 1-24.

———, *Comment Dieu est-il juste?* Clefs pour interpréter l'épître aux Romains, Paris 1991.

ALEXANDRE, M., *Le Commencement du livre Genèse I-V.* La version grecque de la Septante et sa réception, ed. P. Nautin, Christianisme Antique III, Paris 1988.

ALTERMATH, F., *Du corps psychique au corps spirituel.* Interprétation de 1Cor 15,35-49 par les auteurs chrétiens des quatre premiers siècles, ed. O. Cullmann, BGBE 18, Tübingen 1977.

AMMANN, A.N., *-ΙΚΟΣ Bei Platon.* Ableitung und Bedeutung mit Material-sammlung, Freiburg 1953.

ARISTOTLE, *De generatione animalium*, transl. A.L. Peck, LCL 366, Cambridge 1979.

———, *Historia animalium*, transl. A.L. Peck, LCL 437.438.439, I-III, Cambridge 1984.

———, *Metaphysica*, transl. H. Tredennick, LCL 271.287, I-II, Cambridge 1980.

———, *Meteorologica*, transl. H.D.P. Lee, LCL 397, Cambridge 1978.

———, *Scripta minora.* De plantis, transl. W.S. Hett, LCL 307, Cambridge 1980.

———, *De generatione et corruptione*, transl. E.S. Forster, LCL 400, Cambridge 1978.

———, *De·caelo*, transl. W.K.C. Guthrie, LCL 338, Cambridge 1971.

———, *De partibus animalium*, transl. A.L. Peck, LCL 323, Cambridge 1983.

———, *Parva naturalia.* De respiratione, transl. W.S. Hett, LCL 288, Cambridge 1986.

AUNE, D.E., «Eschatology (Early Christian)», in *AncBD*, II, 594-609.

BALZ, H., «εἰμί», in *EWNT*, I, 950-954.

———, «εἴπερ», in *EWNT*, I, 954-955.

———, «ἔπειτα», in *EWNT*, II, 50-51.

———, «οὕτω, οὕτως», in *EWNT*, II, 1343.

BALZ, H., «φορέω», in *EWNT*, III, 1043.

——, «χοϊκός», in *EWNT*, III, 1044.

BARRETT, C.K., *The Epistle to the Romans*, BNTC, London 1991[2].

——, *The First Epistle to the Corinthians*, BNTC, London 1992[2].

BARTH, K., *A Shorter Commentary on Romans*, London 1959.

BAUMGARTEN, J., «ἔσχατος», in *EWNT*, II, 153-159.

BEATTIE, M., *Codependent No More. How to Stop Controlling Others and Start Caring for Yourself*, New York 1987.

BECKER, J., *Paul. Apostle to the Gentiles*, transl. O.C. Dean, Louisville 1993.

BEKER, J.C., *Paul the Apostle. The Triumph of God in Life and Thought*, Edinburgh 1980.

BEST, E., *The Letter of Paul to the Romans*, CNEB, Cambridge 1967.

BETZ, H.D., «The Problem of Rhetoric and Theology According to the Apostle Paul», in *L'Apôtre Paul. Personnalité, style et conception du ministère*, ed. A. Vanhoye, BEThL 73, Leuven 1986.

——, «Paul», in *AncBD*, V, 186-201.

BEUTLER, J., «ἀδελφός», in *EWNT*, I, 67-72.

BIEDER, W., «θανατόω», in *EWNT*, II, 319-329.

——, «θνητός», in *EWNT*, II, 379-380.

BLACK, C.C., «Pauline Perspectives on Death in Romans 5-8», *JBL* 103 (1984) 413-433.

BLACK, M., *Romans*, NCBC, London 1984.

BOLL, F. – BEZOLD, C. – GUNDEL, W., *Sternglaube und Sterndeutung. Die Geschichte und Das Wesen der Astrologie*, Darmstadt 1966[5].

BONNEAU, N., «The Logic of Paul's Argument on the Resurrection Body in 1Cor 15:35-44a», *ScEs* 45 (1993) 79-91.

BOUSSET, W., «Der erste Brief an die Korinther», in *Die Schriften des Neuen Testaments*, ed. J. Weiss, II, *Die paulinischen Briefe und die Pastoralbriefe*, Göttingen 1917, 74-167.

——, *Kyrios Christos. Geschichte des Christusglaubens von den Anfängen des Christentums bis Irenaeus*, Göttingen 1921[2].

BOYER, J.L., «First Class Conditions. What Do They Mean?» *GTJ* 2, I (Spring 1981) 75-114.

BRADSHAW, J., *Bradshaw on. The Family*, Deerfield Beach 1988.

————, *Healing the Shame that Binds You*. Deerfield Beach 1988.

BRANDENBURGER, E., «Alter und neuer Mensch, erster und letzter Adam-Anthropos», in *Vom alten zum neuen Adam. Urzeitmythos und Heilsgeschichte*, ed. W. Strolz, WRSGÖ 13, Freiburg 1986, 182-223.

BRUCE, F.F., «Paul on Immortality», *SJTh* 24 (1971) 457-472.

————, *The Letter of Paul to the Romans*, TNTC 6, Grand Rapids 1985², repr. 1989.

BÜCHSEL, F., «γίνομαι», in *ThWNT*, I, 680-688.

BULTMANN, R., «ζάω, ζωή, ζῳοποιέω», in *ThWNT*, II, 833-877.

————, «θανατόω, θνητός», in *ThWNT*, III, 7-25.

————, «νεκρός», in *ThWNT*, IV, 896-899.

BYRNE, B., «Living out the Righteousness of God. The Contribution of Rom 6:1-8:13 to an Understanding of Paul's Ethical Presuppositions», *CBQ* 43, IV (1981) 557-581.

CHANTRAINE, P., *La Formation des noms en grec ancien*, Paris 1933.

————, *Études sur le vocabulaire grec*, Paris 1956.

CHRYSOLOGUS, St. P., *Selected Sermons and Letter to Eutyches*, transl. G. Ganss, Washington 1953.

CLAGETT, M., *Greek Science in Antiquity*, Princeton Junction 1955.

CLAVIER, H., «Brèves remarques sur la notion de σῶμα πνευματικόν», in *The Background of the New Testament and Its Eschatology*, ed. W.D. Davies – D. Daube, Cambridge 1956, 342-362.

COETZER, W.C., «The Holy Spirit and the Eschatological View in Romans 8», *Neotest.* 15 (1981) 180-198.

COLLINS, A.Y., «Apocalypses and Apocalypticism (Early Christianity)», in *AncBD*, I, 288-292.

CONZELMANN, H., *1 Corinthians*, transl. J.W. Leitch, Hermeneia, Philadelphia 1988.

CRAIG, W.L., *Assessing the New Testament Evidence for the Historicity of the Resurrection of Jesus*, Studies in Bible and Early Christianity 16, Lewiston 1989.

CRANFIELD, C.E.B., *The Epistle to the Romans*, ICC, I-II, Edinburgh 1987.

CROWE, M.J., *Theories of the World from Antiquity to the Copernican Revolution*, New York 1990.

DABELSTEIN, R., «ἐνοικέω», in *EWNT*, I, 1114-1115.

DALEY, B.E., «The Ripening of Salvation. Hope for Resurrection in the Early Church», *Communio* 17 (Spring, 1990) 27-49.

DAVIES, W.D., *Paul and Rabbinic Judaism. Some Rabbinic Elements in Pauline Theology*, London 1955².

——, *Jewish and Pauline Studies*, Philadelphia 1984.

DAWES, G.W., «"But if you can gain your freedom" (1 Corinthians 7:17-24)», *CBQ* 52 (1990) 681-697.

DE BOER, M.C., *The Defeat of Death. Apocalyptic Eschatology in 1 Corinthians 15 and Romans 5*, JSNT.S 22, Sheffield 1988.

DE LA POTTERIE, I., «Le Chrétien conduit par l'Esprit dans son cheminement eschatologique (Rom 8,14)», in *The Law of the Spirit in Rom 7 and 8*, ed. L. De Lorenzi, Serie Monografica di Benedictina 2, Rome 1976, 209-241.

DIETER, H., «θεός», in *EWNT*, II, 346-352.

DOBBIN, E.J., «Trinity», in *NDT*, 1046-1061.

DUNN, J.D.G., «I Corinthians 15:45 – Last Adam, life-giving spirit», in *Christ and the Spirit in the New Testament*, Fs. C.F.D. Moule, Cambridge 1973, 127-141.

——, *Jesus and the Spirit. A Study of the Religious and Charismatic Experience of Jesus and the First Christians as Reflected in the New Testament*, London 1975.

——, «Salvation Proclaimed: VI. Romans 6:1-11: Dead and Alive», *ET* 93 (1982): 259-264.

——, *Romans*, WBC 38A-38B, I-II, Dallas 1988.

——, *Christology in the Making. An Inquiry into the Origins of the Doctrine of the Incarnation*, London 1989².

DUPONT, J., *Gnosis*. La connaissance religieuse dans les épîtres de Saint Paul, Paris 1949.

EDWARDS, J.R., *Romans*. NIBC 6, Peabody 1992.

ELLIS, E.E., «Christ and Spirit in 1 Corinthians», in *Christ and the Spirit in the New Testament*, Fs. C.F.D. Moule, Cambridge 1973, 269-277.

————, *Pauline Theology*. Ministry and Society, Grand Rapids 1989.

————, «*Sōma* in First Corinthians», *Interp.* 44 (1990) 132-144.

FEE, G.D., *The First Epistle to the Corinthians*, NIC, Grand Rapids 1991.

FEUILLET, A., «Le corps du Seigneur ressuscité et la vie chrétienne, d'après les Épîtres pauliniennes», in *Resurrexit*. Actes du symposium international sur la résurrection de Jésus (Rome 1970), ed. É. Dhanis, Città del Vaticano 1974, 440-488.

FIEDLER, P., «ἁμαρτία», in *EWNT*, I, 157-165.

FITZMYER, J.A., «The Letter to the Romans», in *NJBC*, 830-868.

————, «Paul», in *NJBC*, 1329-1337.

————, «Pauline Theology», in *NJBC*, 1382-1416.

————, *According to Paul*. Studies in the Theology of the Apostle, New York 1993.

————, «The Christology of the Epistle to the Romans», in *The Future of Christology*, Fs. L.E. Keck, Minneapolis 1993, 81-90.

————, *Romans*, AncB 33, New York 1993.

FORTNA, R.T., «Romans 8:10 and Paul's Doctrine of the Spirit», *AThR* 41 (1959) 77-84.

FURNISH, V.P., *Theology and Ethics in Paul*, Nashville 1968.

————, *The Moral Teaching of Paul*. Selected Issues, Nashville 1985².

GALEN, *De naturalibus facultatibus*, transl. A.J. Brock, LCL 71, Cambridge 1979.

————, *De semine*, ed., transl. and commentary P. De Lacy, Corpus medicorum Graecorum V 3,1, Berlin 1992.

GALOT, J., «L'Esprit Saint et la spiration», *Gr.* 74 (1993) 241-259.

GASQUE, W.W., «Tarsus», in *AncBD*, VI, 333-334.

GILLMAN, J., «Transformation in 1 Cor 15,50-53», *EThL* 58 (1982) 309-333.

GROSHEIDE, F.W., *Commentary on the First Epistle to the Corinthians*, NIC, Grand Rapids 1980.

GRUNDMANN, W., «ἁμαρτία», in *ThWNT*, I, 267-320.

————, «Χρίω, Χριστός», in *ThWNT*, IX, 482-576.

GUETTEL COLE, S., «Temples and Sanctuaries. Greco-Roman Temples», in *AncBD*, VI, 380-382.

GUNDRY, R.H., *Sōma in Biblical Theology with Emphasis on Pauline Anthropology*, MSSNTS 29, 1976.

GUTHRIE, W.K.C., *A History of Greek Philosophy*, V, *The Later Plato and the Academy*, Cambridge 1978.

————, *A History of Greek Philosophy*, VI, *Aristotle. An Encounter*, Cambridge 1981.

HACKENBERG, W., «γίνομαι», in *EWNT*, I, 594-596.

————, «σπείρω», in *EWNT*, III, 628-629.

HAHN, F., «Χριστός», in *EWNT*, III, 1147-1165.

HANSE, H., «ἔχω», in *ThWNT*, II, 816-832.

HANSON, P.D., «Apocalypticism», in *IDB*, Suppl. Vol., 28-34.

HARDER, G., «φθείρω, φθορά, φθαρτός», in *ThWNT*, IX, 94-106.

HARRIS, M.J., *From Grave to Glory*. Resurrection in the New Testament, Grand Rapids 1990.

HAUCK, F., «ὀφειλέτης», in *ThWNT*, V, 559-565.

HEIL, J.P., *Paul's Letter to the Romans*, New York 1987.

HENGEL, M., *The Pre-Christian Paul*, transl. J. Bowden, London 1991.

HÉRING, J., *La première épitre de saint Paul aux Corinthiens*, Neuchâtel 1949.

HERMAN, Z.I., «Saggio esegetico sul "già e non ancora" soteriologico in Rm 8», *Anton.* 62 (1987) 26-84.

HIPPOCRATES, *De natura hominis*, transl. W.H.S. Jones, LCL 150, Cambridge 1979.

HOLLANDER, H.W. – HOLLEMAN, J., «The Relationship of Death, Sin, and Law in 1 Cor 15:56», *NT* 35 (1993) 270-291.

HOLTZ, T., «φθείρω, ἀφθαρσία, ἄφθαρτος, φθαρτός, φθορά», in *EWNT*, III, 1009-1013.

HORN, F.W., «Holy Spirit», transl. D.M. Elliott, in *AncBD*, III, 260-280.

HORSLEY, R.A., «Pneumatikos vs. Psychikos. Distinctions of Spiritual Status Among the Corinthians», *HThR* 69 (1976) 269-288.

IMBELLI, R.P., «Holy Spirit», in *NDT*, 474-489.

JEREMIAS, J. «ʼΑδάμ», in *ThWNT*, I, 141-143.

———, «ἄνθρωπος», in *ThWNT*, I, 365-367.

KÄSEMANN, E., *Commentary on Romans*, ed., transl. G.W. Bromiley, Grand Rapids 1990.

KECK, L.E., *Paul and His Letters*, PC, Philadelphia 1988².

KELLERMANN, U., «σπέρμα», in *EWNT*, III, 629-632.

KERTELGE, K., «δικαιοσύνη», in *EWNT*, I, 784-796.

KITTEL, G., «εἰκών», in *ThWNT*, II, 378-396.

———, «ἔσχατος», in *ThWNT*, II, 694-695.

KLEINKNECHT, H., «θεός», in *ThWNT*, III, 65-123.

KREMER, J., «ἐγείρω», in *EWNT*, I, 899-910.

———, «πνεῦμα», in *EWNT*, III, 279-291.

———, «πνευματικός», in *EWNT*, III, 291-293.

KRETZER, A., «γῆ», in *EWNT*, I, 592-593.

KRUPP, E.C., *Beyond the Blue Horizon. Myths and Legends of the Sun, Moon, Stars, and Planets*, New York 1991.

KUHLI, H., «εἰκών», in *EWNT*, I, 942-949.

LAMBRECHT, J., *The Wretched "I" and its Liberation. Paul in Romans 7 and 8*, LThPM, Louvain 1992.

LANGKAMMER, H., «πρῶτος», in *EWNT*, III, 454-457.

LEDGERWOOD, L.W., «What Does the Greek First Class Conditional Imply? Grecian Methodology and the Testimony of the Ancient Greek Grammarians», *GTJ* 12 (Spring 1991) 99-118.

LÉMONON, J.P. «Le Saint Esprit dans le corpus paulinien», in *DBS*, XI, 192-327.

LEVISON, J.R., *Portraits of Adam in Early Judaism.* From Sirach to 2 Baruch, ed. J.H. Charlesworth, JSPE.S 1, Sheffield 1988.

LITTLE, J.A., «Paul's Use of Analogy. A Structural Analysis of Romans 7:1-6», *CBQ* 46 (1984) 82-90.

LLOYD, G.E.R., *Greek Science after Aristotle*, New York 1973.

――――, *Magic, Reason, and Experience.* Studies in the Origins and Development of Greek Science, Cambridge, 1979.

――――, «Aristotle's Zoology and his Metaphysics: the Status Questionis», in *Methods and Problems in Greek Science*, Cambridge 1991.

LÜDEMANN, G., «εἰ», in *EWNT*, I, 931-933.

――――, «ἐκ», in *EWNT*, I, 977-980.

LYONNET, S., «Rom 8,19-22 et la rédemption de l'univers», in *Études sur l'Épître aux Romains*, AnBib 120, repr., Rome 1990.

MARTIN, J.A., *Blessed are the Addicts.* The Spiritual Side of Alcoholism, Addiction, and Recovery, New York 1990.

MASSEY, D.M., «Addiction and Spirituality», *RExp* 91 (Winter 1994) 9-18.

MAURER, C., «πρᾶξις», in *ThWNT*, VI, 641-645.

MAY, G., *Addiction and Grace.* Love and Spirituality in the Healing of Addictions, New York 1988.

――――, *The Awakened Heart.* Living Beyond Addiction, New York 1991.

MCDANNELL, C. – LANG, B., *Heaven.* A History, New York 1990.

MEEKS, W.A. *The First Urban Christians.* The Social World of the Apostle Paul, New Haven 1983.

MEILAENDER, G., «*Terra es animata.* On Having a Life», *HCR* 23, IV (1993) 25-32.

MELODY, P. – MILLER, A.W. – MILLER, J.K., *Facing Codependence.* What it is, Where it Comes From, and How it Sabotages our Life, San Francisco 1989.

――――, *Facing Love Addiction.* Giving Yourself the Power to Change the Way You Love – The Love Connection to Codependence, San Francisco 1992.

MERLEAU-PONTY, M., *La Phénoménologie de la perception*, Paris 1945.

MEYER, P.W., «Romans», in *HBC*, 1130-1167.

MICHAELIS, W., «πρῶτος», in *ThWNT*, VI, 866-883.

MICHEL, O., *Der Brief an die Römer*, KEK, Göttingen 1955[10].

———, «οἰκέω», in *ThWNT*, V, 122-161.

———, «ἐπουράνιος», in *EWNT*, II, 116-118.

MILLER, A., *The Drama of the Gifted Child*. The Search for the True Self, New York 1981.

———, *For Your Own Good*. Hidden Cruelty in Child-Rearing and the Roots of Violence, New York 1990[3].

MITCHELL, M.M., *Paul and the Rhetoric of Reconciliation*. An Exegetical Investigation of the Language and Composition of 1 Corinthians, Louisville 1991.

MORGAN, F.A., «Romans 6,5a. United to a Death Like Christ's», *EThL* 59 (1983) 267-302.

MORISSETTE, R., «l'Antithèse entre le "psychique" et le "pneumatique" en 1 Corinthiens, XV, 44 à 46», *RevSR* 46 (1972) 97-143.

———, «La condition de ressuscité. 1 Corinthiens 15,35-49: structure littéraire de la péricope», *Bib.* 53 (1972) 208-228.

MORRIS, L., *The Epistle to the Romans*, Grand Rapids 1988.

———, *The First Epistle of Paul to the Corinthians*, TNTC 7, Leicester 1989[2].

MOULE, C.F.D., «St. Paul and Dualism. the Pauline Conception of Resurrection», *NTS* 12 (1965-1966): 106-123.

———, «"Justification" in its Relation to the Condition κατὰ πνεῦμα (Rom 8, 1-11)», in *Battesimo e Giustizia in Rom 6 e 8*, Serie Monografica di Benedictina 2, ed. L. De Lorenzi, Rome 1974, 177-201.

MURPHY-O'CONNOR, J., *1 Corinthians*, NTMes, Wilmington 1979.

———, «The First Letter to the Corinthians», in *NJBC*, 798-815.

———, «Corinth», in *AncBD*, III, 1134-1139.

NEWMAN, B.M. – NIDA, E.A., *A Translator's Handbook on Paul's Letter to the Romans*, HeTr, New York 1973.

NUTTON, V., «Roman Medicine: Tradition, Confrontation, Assimilation», in *ANRW* II.37.1, ed. W. Haase – H. Temporini, Berlin 1993, 49-78.

OATES, W.E., «A Biblical Perspective on Addiction», *RExp* 91 (Winter 1994) 71-75.

OBERLINNER, L., «δεύτερος», in *EWNT*, I, 699-701.

O'COLLINS, G., *The Easter Jesus*, London 1980².

OEPKE, A., «ἐγείρω», in *ThWNT*, II, 332-337.

ORR, W.F. – WALTHER, J.A., *1 Corinthians*, AncB 34, New York 1981.

PEARSON, B.A., *The* Pneumatikos-Psychikos *Terminology in 1 Coronthians*. A Study in the Theology of the Corinthian Opponents of Paul and Its Relation to Gnosticism, SBL Dissertation Series 12, Missoula 1973.

PENNA, R., *Lo Spirito di Cristo*, Brescia 1976.

PERKINS, P., *Resurrection* New Testament Witness and Contemporary Reflection, London 1984.

———, «Ethics (NT)», in *AncBD*, II, 652-665.

PERRIN, N., *The New Testament*. An Introduction, New York 1974.

PITTA, A., *Disposizione e messaggio della lettera ai Galati*. Analisi retorico-letteraria, AnBib 131. Rome 1992.

PLATO, *Timaeus*, transl. R.G. Bury, LCL 9, London 1929.

PORTEOUS, A.J.D., «Empedocles», in *OCD*, 382.

PORTER, S.E., *Verbal Aspect in the Greek of the New Testament, with Reference to Tense and Mood*, Studies in Biblical Greek 1, New York 1989.

PRIOR, D., *The Message of First Corinthians*. Life in the Local Church, BST, Leicester 1985.

RADL, W., «ἀλλά», in *EWNT*, I, 146-148.

———, «καθώς», in *EWNT*, II, 556-557.

———, «καί», in *EWNT*, II, 557-560.

RAHNER, K., «The Resurrection of the Body», in *Theological Investigations*, II, *Man in the Church*, transl. K.-H. Kruger, London 1963.

———, «The Church as the Subject of the Sending of the Spirit», in *Theological Investigations*, VII, *Further Theology of the Spiritual Life*, transl. D. Bourke, London 1971.

RAMSAY, W.M., *The Cities of St. Paul. Their Influence on His Life and Thought*, London 1907.

RIDDLE, J.M., «High Medicine and Low Medicine in the Roman Empire», in *ANRW* II.37.1, ed. W. Haase – H. Temporini, Berlin 1993, 102-120.

ROBERTSON, A. – PLUMMER, A., *The First Epistle of St. Paul to the Corinthians*, ICC, Edinburgh 1911; repr., Edinburgh 1986.

ROCHBERG-HALTON, F., «Astrology in the Ancient Near East», in *AncBD*, I, 504-507.

ROLLAND, P., «"Il est notre justice, notre vie, notre salut," L'ordonnance des thèmes majeurs de l'Épitre aux Romains», *Bib.* 56 (1975) 394-404.

———, «L'antithèse de Rom 5-8», *Bib.* 69 (1988) 396-400.

RUEF, J., *Paul's First Letter to Corinth*, London 1977².

RUSCH, W.G., transl. and ed., *The Trinitarian Controversy*, Sources of Early Christian Thought, Philadelphia 1980.

SAMBURSKY, S., *The Physical World of the Greeks*, transl. M. Dagut, London 1956-1960².

———, *Physics of the Stoics*, Princeton 1959.

———, *The Physical World of Late Antiquity*, Princeton 1962.

SAND, A., «ἄνθρωπος», in *EWNT*, I, 240-249.

———, «σάρξ», in *EWNT*, III, 549-557.

———, «ψυχή», in *EWNT*, III, 1197-1203.

———, «ψυχικός», in *EWNT*, III, 1197-1203.

SANDERS, E.P., *Paul*, Oxford 1991.

SARTON, G., *Ancient Science Through the Golden Age of Greece*, New York 1980.

SASSE, H., «γῆ», in *ThWNT*, I, 676-680.

SCARBOROUGH, J., «Roman Medicine to Galen», in *ANRW* II.37.1, ed. W. Haase – H. Temporini, Berlin 1993, 3-48.

SCHALLER, B., «Ἀδάμ», in *EWNT*, I, 65-67.

SCHEP, J.A., *The Nature of the Resurrection-Body*. A Study of the Biblical Data, Grand Rapids 1964.

SCHNEIDER, B., «The Corporate Meaning and Background of 1 Cor 15,45b — " Ὁ Eschatos Adam Eis Pneuma Zōiopoioun"», *CBQ* 29 (1967) 144-161.

SCHNEIDER, G., «πρᾶξις», in *EWNT*, III, 348-349.

SCHOENBORN, U., «οὐρανός, οὐράνιος», in *EWNT*, II, 1328-1338.

SCHOTTROFF, L., «ζῶ, ζωή», in *EWNT*, II, 261-271.

———, «ζῳοποιέω», in *EWNT*, II, 273-274.

SCHRAGE, W., «Ethics in the N.T», in *IDB*, Suppl. Vol., 281-289.

SCHRENK, G., «δικαιοσύνη», in *ThWNT*, II, 176-229.

SCHULZ, S., «σπέρμα, σπείρω», in *ThWNT*, VII, 537-547.

SCHÜSSLER FIORENZA, E., «Eschatology of the NT», in *IDB*, Suppl. Vol., 271-277.

SCHWEIZER, E., «πνεῦμα», in *ThWNT*, VI, 330-453.

———, «σάρξ», in *ThWNT*, VII, 98-151.

———, «σῶμα», in *ThWNT*, VII, 1024-1091.

———, «χοϊκός», in *ThWNT*, IX, 460-468.

———, «ψυχή, ψυχικός», in *ThWNT*, IX, 604-667.

———, «σῶμα», in *EWNT*, III, 770-779.

SCROGGS, R., *The Last Adam*. A Study in Pauline Anthropology, Philadelphia 1966.

SELLIN, G., *Der Streit um die Auferstehung der Toten*. Eine religionsgeschicht-liche und exegetische Untersuchung von 1 Korinther 15, ed. W. Schrage – R. Smend, FRLANT 138, Göttingen 1986.

Sex and Love Addicts Anonymous, Boston 1986.

SIDER, R.J., «The Pauline Conception of the Resurrection Body in 1 Corinthians xv. 35-54», *NTS* 21 (1975) 428-439.

TALBERT, C.H., *Reading Corinthians*. A Literary and Theological Commentary on 1 and 2 Corinthians, New York 1987.

TANNEHILL, R.C., *Dying and Rising with Christ*, BZNW 32, Berlin 1967.

TEANI, M., *Corporeità e risurrezione*. L'interpretazione di 1 Corinti 15,35-49 nel Novecento, Aloisiana 24, Roma 1994.

THEISSEN, G., *The Social Setting of Pauline Christianity*, ed., transl. and intro. J.H. Schütz, Philadelphia 1982.

THEOPHRASTUS, *De causis plantarum*, transl. B. Einarson – G.K.K. Link, LCL 471. 474.475, I-III, Cambridge 1976.

TOULMIN, S. – GOODFIELD, J., *The Architecture of Matter*, Chicago 1962.

TRAUB, H., «οὐρανός, οὐράνιος, ἐπουράνιος», in *ThWNT*, V, 496-543.

Twelve Steps and Twelve Traditions, New York 1981.

USAMI, K., «"How are the dead raised?" (1 Cor 15,35-58)», *Bib.* 57 (1976) 468-493.

VAN DER HORST, P.W., «Sarah's Seminal Emission: Hebrews 11:11 in the Light of Ancient Embryology», in *Greeks, Romans, and Christians*, ed. D.L. Balch – E. Ferguson – W.A. Meeks, Minneapolis 1990, 287-302.

VANNI, U., «Due città nella formazione di Paolo. Tarso e Gerusalemme», in *Atti del I Simposio di Tarso su S. Paolo Apostolo*. Turchia: la Chiesa e la sua storia, ed. L. Padovese, Roma 1993.

VERMES, G., *The Dead Sea Scrolls in English*, London 1988³.

WALTER, E., *Der erste Brief an die Korinther*, ed. W. Trilling – K.H. Schelke – H. Schürmann, GSL.NT 7, Düsseldorf 1969.

WATSON, N., *The First Epistle to the Corinthians*, EpC, London 1992.

WEISS, J., *Der erste Korintherbrief*, KEK, Göttingen 1910⁹.

WEISS, K., «φορέω», in *ThWNT*, IX, 57-89.

WOLTER, M., «ὀφειλέτης», in *EWNT*, II, 1344-1346.

WONG, J.H.P., «The Holy Spirit in the Life of Jesus and of the Christian», *Gr.* 73 (1992) 57-95.

YARBRO COLLINS, A., «Apocalypses and Apocalypticism (Early Christian)», in *AncBD*, I, 288-292.

ZIESLER, J., *Paul's Letter to the Romans*, TPINTC, London 1990.

INDEX OF AUTHORS

TABLE OF CONTENTS

PART TWO

ROMANS 8,9-13
THE INDWELLING SPIRIT AND BELIEVERS IN CHRIST

PART THREE

CONCLUSION

TESI GREGORIANA

Dal 1995, la collana «Tesi Gregoriana» mette a disposizione del pubblico alcune delle migliori tesi elaborate alla Pontificia Università Gregoriana. La composizione per la stampa è realizzata dagli stessi autori, secondo le norme tipografiche definite e controllate dell'Università.

Volumi pubblicati [Serie: Teologia]

1. NELLO FIGA, Antonio, *Teorema de la opción fundamental. Bases para su adecuada utilización en teología moral*, 1995, pp. 380.

2. BENTOGLIO, Gabriele, *Apertura e disponibilità. L'accoglienza nell'epistolario paolino*, 1995, pp. 376.

3. PISO, Alfeu, *Igreja e sacramentos. Renovação da Teologia Sacramentária na América Latina*, 1995, pp. 260.

4. PALAKEEL, Joseph, *The Use of Analogy in Theological Discourse. An Investigation in Ecumenical Perspective*, 1995, pp. 392.

5. KIZHAKKEPARAMPIL, Isaac, *The Invocation of the Holy Spirit as Constitutive of the Sacraments according to Cardinal Yves Congar*, 1995, pp. 200.

6. MROSO, Agapit J., *The Church in Africa and the New Evangelisation. A Theologico-Pastoral Study of the Orientations of John Paul II*, 1995, pp. 456.

7. NANGELIMALIL, Jacob, *The Relationship between the Eucharistic Liturgy, the Interior Life and the Social Witness of the Church according to Joseph Cardinal Parecattil*, 1996, pp. 224.

8. GIBBS, Philip, *The Word in the Third World. Divine Revelation in the Theology of Jen-Marc Éla, Aloysius Pieris and Gustavo Gutiérrez*, 1996, pp. 448.

9. DELL'ORO, Roberto, *Esperienza morale e persona. Per una reinterpretazione dell'etica fenomenologica di Dietrich von Hildebrand*, 1996, pp. 240.

10. BELLANDI, Andrea, *Fede cristiana come «stare e comprendere». La giustificazione dei fondamenti della fede in Joseph Ratzinger*, 1996, pp. 416.

11. BEDRIÑAN, Claudio, *La dimensión socio-política del mensaje teológico del Apocalipsis*, 1996, pp. 364.

12. GWYNNE, Paul, *Special Divine Action. Key Issues in the Contemporary Debate (1965-1995)*, 1996, pp. 376.

13. NIÑO, Francisco, *La Iglesia en la ciudad. El fenómeno de las grandes ciudades en América Latina, como problema teológico y como desafío pastoral*, 1996, pp. 492.

14. BRODEUR, Scott, *The Holy Spirit's Agency in the Resurrection of the Dead. An Exegetico-Theological Study of 1 Corinthians 15,44b-49 and Romans 8,9-13*, 1996, pp. 300. *Prima ristampa 2004*

35. LIMA CORRÊA, Maria de Lourdes, *Salvação entre juízo, conversão e graça. A perspectiva escatológica de Os 14,2-9*, 1998, pp. 360.

36. MEIATTINI, Giulio, *«Sentire cum Christo». La teologia dell'esperienza cristiana nell'opera di H.U. von Balthasar*, 1998, pp. 432.

37. KESSLER, Thomas W., *Peter as the First Witness of the Risen Lord. An Historical and Theological Investigation*, 1998, pp. 240.

38. BIORD CASTILLO Raúl, *La Resurrección de Cristo como Revelación. Análisis del tema en la teología fundamental a partir de la* Dei Verbum, 1998, pp. 308.

39. LÓPEZ, Javier, *La figura de la bestia entre historia y profecía. Investigación teológico-bíblica de Apocalipsis 13,1-8*, 1998, pp. 308.

40. SCARAFONI, Paolo, *Amore salvifico. Una lettura del mistero della salvezza. Uno studio comparativo di alcune soteriologie cattoliche postconciliari*, 1998, pp. 240.

41. BARRIOS PRIETO, Manuel Enrique, *Antropologia teologica. Temi principali di antropologia teologica usando un metodo di «correlazione» a partire dalle opere di John Macquarrie*, 1998, pp. 416.

42. LEWIS, Scott M., *«So That God May Be All in All». The Apocalyptic Message of 1 Corinthians 15,12-34*, 1998, pp. 252.

43. ROSSETTI, Carlo Lorenzo, *«Sei diventato Tempio di Dio». Il mistero del Tempio e dell'abitazione divina negli scritti di Origene*, 1998, pp. 232.

44. CERVERA BARRANCO, Pablo, *La incorporación en la Iglesia mediante el bautismo y la profesión de la fe según el Concilio Vaticano II*, 1998, pp. 372.

45. NETO, Laudelino, *Fé cristã e cultura latino-americana. Uma análise a partir das Conferências de Puebla e Santo Domingo*, 1998, pp. 340.

46. BRITO GUIMARÃES, Pedro, *Os sacramentos como atos eclesiais e proféticos. Um contributo ao conceito dogmático de sacramento à luz da exegese contemporânea*, 1998, pp. 448.

47. CALABRETTA, Rose B., *Baptism and Confirmation. The Vocation and Mission of the Laity in the Writings of Virgil Michel, O.S.B.*, 1998, pp. 320.

48. OTERO LÁZARO, Tomás, *Col 1,15-20 en el contexto de la carta*, 1999, pp.312.

49. KOWALCZYK, Dariusz, *La personalità in Dio. Dal metodo trascendentale di Karl Rahner verso un orientamento dialogico in Heinrich Ott*, 1999, pp. 484.

50. PRIOR, Joseph G., *The Historical-Critical Method in Catholic Exegesis*, 1999, pp. 352.

51. CAHILL, Brendan J, *The Renewal of Revelation Theology (1960-1962). The Development and Responses to the Fourth Chapter of the Preparatory Schema De deposito Fidei*, 1999, pp. 348.

52. TIEZZI, Ida, *Il rapporto tra la pneumatologia e l'ecclesiologia nella teologia italiana post-conciliare*, 1999, pp. 364.

53. HOLC, Paweł, *Un ampio consenso sulla dottrina della giustificazione. Studio sul dialogo teologico cattolico luterano*, 1999, pp. 452.

54. GAINO, Andrea, *Esistenza cristiana. Il pensiero teologico di J. Alfaro e la sua rilevanza morale*, 1999, pp. 344.

55. NERI, Francesco, *«Cur Verbum capax hominis». Le ragioni dell'incarnazione della seconda Persona della Trinità fra teologia scolastica e teologia contempo-*

56. MUÑOZ CÁRDABA, Luis-Miguel, *Principios eclesiológicos de la «Pastor Bonus»*, 1999, pp. 344.

57. IWE, John Chijioke, *Jesus in the Synagogue of Capernaum: the Pericope and Its Programmatic Character for the Gospel of Mark. An Exegetico-Theological Study of Mk 1:21-28*, 1999, pp. 364.

58. BARRIOCANAL GÓMEZ, José Luis, *La relectura de la tradición del éxodo en el libro de Amós*, 2000, pp. 332.

59. DE LOS SANTOS GARCÍA, Edmundo, *La novedad de la metáfora κεφαλή – σῶμα en la carta a los Efesios*, 2000, pp. 432.

60. RESTREPO SIERRA, Argiro, *La revelación según R. Latourelle*, 2000, pp. 442.

61. DI GIOVAMBATTISTA, Fulvio, *Il giorno dell'espiazione nella Lettera agli Ebrei*, 2000, pp. 232.

62. GIUSTOZZO, Massimo, *Il nesso tra il culto e la grazia eucaristica nella recente lettura teologica del pensiero agostiniano*, 2000, pp. 456.

63. PESARCHICK, Robert A., *The Trinitarian Foundation of Human Sexuality as Revealed by Christ according to Hans Urs von Balthasar. The Revelatory Significance of the Male Christ and the Male Ministerial Priesthood*, 2000, pp. 328.

64. SIMON, László T., *Identity and Identification. An Exegetical Study of 2Sam 21–24*, 2000. pp. 386.

65. TAKAYAMA, Sadami, *Shinran's Conversion in the Light of Paul's Conversion*, 2000, pp. 256.

66. JUAN MORADO, Guillermo, *«También nosotros creemos porque amamos». Tres concepciones del acto de fe: Newman, Blondel, Garrigou-Lagrange. Estudio comparativo desde la perspectiva teológico-fundamental*, 2000, pp. 444.

67. MAREČEK, Petr, *La preghiera di Gesù nel vangelo di Matteo. Uno studio esegetico-teologico*, 2000, pp. 246.

68. WODKA, Andrzej, *Una teologia biblica del dare nel contesto della colletta paolina (2Cor 8–9)*, 2000, pp. 356.

69. LANGELLA, Maria Rigel, *Salvezza come illuminazione. Uno studio comparato di S. Bulgakov, V. Lossky, P. Evdokimov*, 2000, pp. 292.

70. RUDELLI, Paolo, *Matrimonio come scelta di vita: opzione – vocazione – sacramento*, 2000, pp. 424.

71. GAŠPAR, Veronika, *Cristologia pneumatologica in alcuni autori cattolici postconciliari. Status quaestionis e prospettive*, 2000, pp. 440.

72. GJORGJEVSKI, Gjoko, *Enigma degli enigmi. Un contributo allo studio della composizione della raccolta salomonica (Pr 10,1–22,16)*, 2001, pp. 304.

73. LINGAD, Celestino G., Jr., *The Problems of Jewish Christians in the Johannine Community*, 2001, pp. 492.

74. MASALLES, Victor, *La profecía en la asamblea cristiana. Análisis retórico-literario de 1Cor 14,1-25*, 2001, pp. 416.

75. FIGUEIREDO, Anthony J., *The Magisterium-Theology Relationship. Contemporary Theological Conceptions in the Light of Universal Church Teaching since 1835 and the Pronouncements of the Bishops of the United States*, 2001, pp. 536.

76. PARDO IZAL, José Javier, *Pasión por un futuro imposible. Estudio literario-teológico de Jeremías 32*, 2001, pp. 412.

77. HANNA, Kamal Fahim Awad, *La passione di Cristo nell'Apocalisse*, 2001, pp. 480.

78. ALBANESI, Nicola, *«Cur Deus Homo»: la logica della redenzione. Studio sulla teoria della soddisfazione di S. Anselmo arcivescovo di Canterbury*, 2001, pp. 244.

79. ADE, Edouard, *Le temps de l'Eglise. Esquisse d'une théologie de l'histoire selon Hans Urs von Balthasar*, 2002, pp. 368.

80. MENÉNDEZ MARTÍNEZ, Valentín, *La misión de la Iglesia. Un estudio sobre el debate teológico y eclesial en América Latina (1955-1992), con atención al aporte de algunos teólogos de la Compañía de Jesús*, 2002, pp. 346.

81. COSTA, Paulo Cezar, *«Salvatoris Disciplina». Dionísio de Roma e a* Regula fidei *no debate teológico do terceiro século*, 2002, pp. 272.

82. PUTHUSSERY, Johnson, *Days of Man and God's Day. An Exegetico-Theological Study of* ἡμέρα *in the Book of Revelation*, 2002, pp. 302.

83. BARROS, Paulo César, *«Commendatur vobis in isto pane quomodo unitatem amare debeatis». A eclesiologia eucarística nos* Sermones ad populum *de Agostinho de Hipona e o movimento ecumênico*, 2002, pp. 344.

84. PALACHUVATTIL, Joy, *«He Saw». The Significance of Jesus' Seeing Denoted by the Verb* εἶδεν *in the Gospel of Mark*, 2002, pp. 312.

85. PISANO, Ombretta, *La radice e la stirpe di David. Salmi davidici nel libro dell'Apocalisse*, 2002, pp. 496.

86. KARIUKI, Njiru Paul, *Charisms and the Holy Spirit's Activity in the Body of Christ. An Exegetical-Theological Study of 1Cor 12,4-11 and Rom 12,6-8*, 2002, pp. 372.

87. CORRY, Donal, *«Ministerium Rationis Reddendae». An Approximation to Hilary of Poitiers' Understanding of Theology*, 2002, pp. 328.

88. PIKOR, Wojciech, *La comunicazione profetica alla luce di Ez 2–3*, 2002, pp. 322.

89. NWACHUKWU, Mary Sylvia Chinyere, *Creation–Covenant Scheme and Justification by Faith. A Canonical Study of the God-Human Drama in the Pentateuch and the Letter to the Romans*, 2002, 378 pp.

90. GAGLIARDI, Mauro, *La cristologia adamitica. Tentativo di recupero del suo significato originario*, 2002, pp. 624.

91. CHARAMSA, Krzysztof Olaf, *L'immutabilità di Dio. L'insegnamento di San Tommaso d'Aquino nei suoi sviluppi presso i commentatori scolastici*, 2002, pp. 520.

92. GLOBOKAR, Roman, *Verantwortung für alles, was lebt. Von Albert Schweitzer und Hans Jonas zu einer theologischen Ethik des Lebens*, 2002, pp. 608.

93. AJAYI, James Olaitan, *The HIV/AIDS Epidemic in Nigeria. Some Ethical Considerations*, 2003, pp. 212.

94. PARAMBI, Baby, *The Discipleship of the Women in the Gospel according to Matthew. An Exegetical Theological Study of Matt 27:51b-56, 57-61 and 28: 1-10*, 2003, pp. 276.

95. NIEMIRA, Artur, *Religiosità e moralità. Vita morale come realizzazione della fondazione cristica dell'uomo secondo B. Häring e D. Capone*, 2003, pp. 308.

96. PIZZUTO, Pietro, *La teologia della rivelazione di Jean Daniélou. Influsso su* Dei Verbum *e valore attuale*, 2003, pp. 630.

97. PAGLIARA, Cosimo, *La figura di Elia nel vangelo di Marco. Aspetti semantici e funzionali*, 2003, pp. 400.

98. O'BOYLE, Aidan, *Towards a Contemporary Wisdom Christology. Some Catholic Christologies in German, English and French 1965-1995*, 2003, pp. 448.

99. BYRNES, Michael J., *Conformation to the Death of Christ and the Hope of Resurrection: An Exegetico-Theological Study of 2 Corinthians 4,7-15 and Philippians 3,7-11*, 2003, p. 328.

100. RIGATO, Maria-Luisa, *Il Titolo della Croce di Gesù. Confronto tra i Vangeli e la Tavoletta-reliquia della Basilica Eleniana a Roma*, 2003, pp. 392.

101. LA GIOIA, Fabio, *La glorificazione di Gesù Cristo ad opera dei discepoli. Analisi biblico-teologica di Gv 17,10b nell'insieme dei capp. 13–17*, 2003, pp. 346.

102. LÓPEZ-TELLO GARCÍA, Eduardo, *Simbología y Lógica de la Redención: Ireneo de Lyón, Hans Küng y Hans Urs von Balthasar leídos con la ayuda de Paul Ricœur*, 2003, pp. 396.

103. MAZUR, Aleksander, *L'insegnamento di Giovanni Paolo II sulle altre religioni*, 2003, pp. 354.

104. SANECKI, Artur, *Approccio canonico: tra storia e teologia, alla ricerca di un nuovo paradigma post-critico. L'analisi della metodologia canonica di B.S. Childs dal punto di vista cattolico*, 2004, pp. 480.

105. STRZELCZYK, Grzegorz, *«Communicatio idiomatum», lo scambio delle proprietà. Storia, «status quaestionis» e prospettive*, 2004, pp. 324.

106. CHO Hyun-Chul, *An Ecological Vision of the World: Toward a Christian Ecological Theology of Our Age*, 2004, pp. 318.

107. VLKOVÁ, Gabriela Ivana, *Cambiare la luce in tenebre e le tenebre in luce. Uno studio tematico dell'alternarsi tra la luce e le tenebre nel libro di Isaia*, 2004, pp. 316.

108. GHIO, Giorgio, *La deliberazione vitale come origine ultima della certezza applicata a Dio. Indagine sugli elementi d'ignoranza presenti nella certezza*, 2004, pp. 258.

Finito di stampare
nel mese di Luglio 2004

presso la tipografia
"Giovanni Olivieri" di E. Montefoschi
00187 Roma • Via dell'Archetto, 10, 11, 12
Tel. 06 6792327 • E-mail: tip.olivieri@libero.it